Church — no spectator sport!

CHURCH—
NO SPECTATOR
SPORT!

**A theological and practical journey of
discovery in search of spiritual gifts**

by

Eric E. Wright

 EVANGELICAL PRESS

EVANGELICAL PRESS
12 Wooler Street, Darlington, Co. Durham, DL1 1RQ, England

British Library Cataloguing in Publication Data available

ISBN 0 85234 314 0

Printed and bound in Great Britain at the Bath Press, Avon.

Dedicated to the body of Christ and to those thousands of local
churches where believers joyfully worship the Lord and serve
one another, but particularly to
Long Branch Baptist Church, Toronto, who supported Mary
Helen and me as missionaries for eighteen years and then loved
us during nine years in the pastorate.

Acknowledgements

I would like to acknowledge the unflagging support of Mary Helen, my loving helpmate, along with the encouragement of Stephen and Catherine, Debbie and Brian, John and Shona, who all make up an unbelievably wonderful Christian family. I would like to acknowledge as well the very practical help with portions of the manuscript by a variety of friends, including Audrey Ogier, Ruth Richmond, Mildred Vaughan, Mavis Steeves, Janette Taylor and many others.

Contents

Introduction

Sport is big business. Whether ice hockey, soccer or tennis, professional sports attract enormous crowds. Spectators pack stadiums and arenas around the world to cheer on their favourites. Someone has humorously written to the effect that sport is largely a matter of tens of thousands of fans, desperately in need of exercise, watching small groups of athletes, desperately in need of rest — spectator sport!

Christians often approach church as if it were a spectator sport. Since we have our own set of heroes, churches that feature well-known preachers or personalities quickly fill with eager listeners. And listening is, after all, a spectator phenomenon. Don't get me wrong. I enjoy listening to God's gifted servants. Unfortunately, the opportunity to listen to good preaching is one positive aspect of a system with many problems. Consider for a moment the weekly worship service.

Early on Sunday morning lights come on in widely scattered homes. Soon the aroma of freshly brewed coffee wafts up the stairs. After a careful shave, Dad flicks fluff off his Sunday suit and picks a conservative tie. With breakfast laid out on the table, Mum shouts at Dad to wake up the kids while she takes her turn in front of the mirror. The youngsters straggle down the stairs and wolf down a hasty breakfast. Soon the revving of the family car shatters the Sunday stillness as Dad tries vainly to control his desire to blow the horn at his tardy brood. With the family finally on board, Dad speeds away to deposit his well-scrubbed cargo at the door of a local church or chapel, cathedral or rented hall.

The faithful greet each other at the church door with a cheery
'Good morning!' Before slipping into their well-worn pews, they
comment about the weather or last night's game. In North America
the more enthusiastic have already preceded the 'worship crowd' by
over an hour to participate in Sunday School or Bible classes.

The hour approaches. A deacon's frown freezes giggles from
squirming children. The rustle of notice-sheets and the murmur of
voices stills as the choir files in. Several dark-suited men take their
places on the platform. Radiating confidence and authority, one
strides to the pulpit. All eyes focus on the pastor as another Sunday
service begins.

Sports and sacred service — you may ask what they have in
common. Although church seldom attracts the crowds which clamour for tickets to a game, both are largely spectator phenomena,
dependent on hired professionals for their popularity. Commenting
on this phenomenon in *Revival*, Dr D. Martyn Lloyd-Jones writes,
'Now that, of course, is a complete denial of the New Testament
doctrine of the Church as the Body of Christ, where every single
member has responsibility, and has a function, and matters.'

Fortunately, all over the world, more and more emphasis is being
laid on personal participation. In sporting circles many people are
taking up jogging, skiing, tennis or hiking. In Christian circles many
are discovering spiritual gifts.

Down through history the participation of all God's people in
ministry has waxed and waned. The Protestant Reformation rediscovered, among other truths, the priesthood of all believers. Unfortunately, the legacy passed down to our generation has stressed
clergy more than laity. The biblical dynamic of the church as the
body of Christ with a host of interrelated parts, or as the temple of
God with its interlocking stones, has been dimly perceived. We
forget so quickly the lessons of history.

Too often, the pattern adopted has been more hierarchical and
passive than participatory. Professional clergy ministering to recep-
tive laity has become the accepted model of church ministry.
Churches almost universally practise one-man ministry — whether
that man be called pastor, minister or ruling elder. This denial of
universal priesthood has gouged a chasm between pastor and people
that many accept as normative. As a result Protestant churches have
developed a host of what Earl Radmacher has called 'petty, Protestant, parochial popes'.

I don't aim to deliver another diatribe against either the full-time pastorate or professionalism in ministry. Let me hasten to point out that I am a professionally trained pastor myself! I have no desire to discourage men from setting the highest standards of excellence in ministerial preparation. Nor is this an appeal for a moratorium on recruiting full-time pastors. Never! Rather I appeal for a return to the priesthood of all believers.

Every-member ministry is biblically normative. The ascending Lord never proposed that his church become a congregation of spectators! Paul writes in Ephesians 4 that when Christ ascended he gave gifts to men that all might participate in ministry. This book, then, concerns those gifts and their use in the local church.

You may sense a danger here. You may ask, 'Are not gifts part of the agenda of those modern movements which quickly derail us from our vision?' Genuine concern prompts such a question. The charismatic storm has certainly done more than rattle a few windows! This storm, however, rages within the circle of God's sovereign providence. And while this truant wind did knock out some traditional windows in its rather destructive course, could it be that God has used it as well to let in a breath of the fresh air of lay ministry? Instead of locking our doors and boarding up the windows even more securely, let us become open to ministry as the Lord intended.

Controversy does tend to distract us from ministry. A third wave of charismatic excitement threatens to swamp our carefully constructed bastions of orthodoxy. This wave provokes us to respond by climbing higher, building our fortresses more strongly and letting loose a barrage of theological rockets. There may be a time and place for that — theological confusion does stunt spiritual growth. But before we circle our defences and turn to face the imagined foe we need to evaluate our priorities. Is it a time for controversy or for mutual edification and growth?

After all, we are neither bound to walk in the ruts of tradition, nor constrained to ride the bumpy road of unfettered enthusiasm and novel experience. We have a third alternative: *'Sola Scriptura'* — the path delineated by Holy Scripture. 'Examine all things; hold fast to that which is true.'

Turning to Scripture, we find considerable emphasis on the practical outworkings of ministry. The storm of controversy surrounding the so-called 'charismatic gifts' obscures less controversial gifts such as faith and mercy. In the following chapters I will extract biblical principles about spiritual gifts, so we can understand them. I also want to show how crucial the non-spectacular gifts are in local church life, so we can use them.

The emphasis will be on the discovery, development and implementation of gifts rather than on theological controversy. Our shelves groan under the weight of books written about controversial gifts such as tongues. Less, however, has been published to help us develop speaking gifts, such as encouragement, or serving gifts, such as hospitality. For this reason I will largely confine my attention to a study of those gifts whose practical usefulness is widely accepted.

Doubtless, my readers deserve some explanation about what I believe concerning miracles, healing, tongues and interpretation. Let me state at the outset that biblical study and personal experience have led me to conclude that God raised up these sign gifts for a specific purpose for a specific historical period. In chapter 4 I give eleven reasons why I deduce that their relevance ceased with the close of the apostolic period. Doubtless, even these reasons will not answer all the questions. Nevertheless, the weight of evidence does cry out for a moratorium on controversy between different segments of the church and a revival of ministry within and between the churches.

Nothing prepares us to face questionable issues more than a strong local church in which the reality of mutual ministry creates a climate of warm devotion to Christ and to each other. Novel ideas and spectacular gifts will not help unhappy and hurting saints. Neither will barrage after barrage of polemic. Cold churches bereft of mutual ministry invite trouble.

We first need to strengthen the gifts that are clearly operative today, before we venture to explore or castigate the esoteric. Chuang Tzu wrote three hundred years before Christ, 'For all men strive to grasp what they do not know, while none strive to grasp what they already know; and all strive to discredit what they do not excel in, while none strive to discredit what they do excel in. This is why there is chaos.'

At times the panorama of modern Christendom does resemble chaos. Rather than seeking to discredit the views of others, my goal in this book is to call us to grasp more clearly what we agree on and develop more diligently what we may excel in. In this way, I trust, the body of Christ will prosper and God will be glorified.

Ever since I gave a halting testimony as a new believer, a concern for ministry has burned within me. My wife, Mary Helen, and I served as foreign missionaries assigned to Pakistan for over eighteen years. This experience gave us ample opportunity to explore these issues in a non-Western culture. Since then we have spent over twelve years in a Western context. As a pastor for nine of those years, I grappled with how to inspire all the saints to 'do the work of the ministry'. One of my earliest sermon series explored the subject of spiritual gifts. Now, as I visit various churches in an itinerant preaching ministry, my sense of the importance of this subject has only increased.

The controversy swirling around the subject of spiritual gifts must not be allowed to frighten us away from seeking our biblical heritage. Likewise, confusion about how to define the specific gifts must not become an excuse for us to be entertained spectators while others carry on the work of ministry. Ministry is your job and mine!

Part I:
Biblical parameters

1.
Spiritual gifts:
variety, sovereignty, unity

Like warm spring sunshine after a long winter, the discovery of the Scriptures' teaching on spiritual gifts quickens dormant potential. In a recent testimony meeting a lady stood up to describe how liberating it had been for her to learn that lay Christians, as well as Christian workers, possess gifts for ministry. Since that discovery several years ago her ministries of encouragement, hospitality and administration have flourished. Her children's stories in the morning worship service have greatly assisted in our children's outreach. But too often evangelical Christians, of a non-charismatic persuasion, avoid the subject for fear of excess.

In *The Gift of Honor*, John Trent describes an experience from his first day in seminary that illustrates our reticence to be candid about spiritual gifts. Howard Hendricks, his teacher, asked students to prepare for a test by getting out a three by five inch card. He said, 'Men and women, I'm about to give you a test. If you pass this test, I can almost guarantee you'll be successful in the ministry. If you fail this test, there's a great chance you'll wash out and won't make it.' He proceeded to ask them to write down on one side of the card their three greatest weaknesses.

John Trent quickly wrote down three weaknesses. No one in the class had a problem with this assignment. The next instruction, however, almost stumped them. Dr Hendricks asked them next to write down their three greatest strengths.

Instead of the ease with which they had written their weaknesses, students struggled to focus on three strengths. Dr Hendricks explained, 'In all my years of teaching, I've rarely met someone who can't quickly tell me his weaknesses. But if you don't know the strengths God has given you, that you can develop, you'll never be a success in the ministry.'[1]

Those involved in lay ministry struggle over the same problem. Despite frequent teaching on gifts during nine years as pastor of Long Branch Baptist Church, I continued to encounter a reluctance to acknowledge strengths. Although our deacons were repeatedly called upon to find other people with particular gifts to fill particular slots, they found it difficult to acknowledge their own gifts. The problem may stem from a misunderstanding about Christian humility. Whatever the cause, Scripture clearly calls us to serve Christ according to our known abilities and talents.

When we lay the record of the early church down beside the experience of most modern congregations, we find stark contrasts. The vibrant health of the early church mocks the sterility of many of our activities. While the primitive church was beset by problems that would make any modern pastor cringe, the dynamism of their corporate life swamped heresy, overcame misunderstanding and healed division. Nothing could contain the spread of the early church. Without doubt, one of the reasons for this vibrant growth was the powerful presence of the Spirit of God and the pervasive exercise of spiritual gifts. Genuine Christians long to see a recovery of the apostolic passion, gospel simplicity and spiritual effectiveness.

Some may consider the early church a relic appropriate for historical study, but no model for the church at the end of the twentieth century. Clearly, we cannot resurrect their exact pattern of ministry any more than we can resurrect the personalities that the Spirit used to make it such a dynamic force. Nevertheless, the Holy Spirit surely desires to reproduce in the church in our day the essential ingredients of apostolic church life. The involvement of all believers in ministries which correspond to their spiritual gifts is one of the most crucial of these neglected ingredients. There is scarcely a church that is not stunted in one way or another by a shortage of key ministries. This lack varies widely from church to church.

In one congregation there may be an abundance of preachers but a scarcity of leaders with administrative gifts. Few churches have a crowd out either for visitation or the prayer meeting. One church may have many visitors to their services but few members who open their homes in hospitality. Teachers may be abundant while those who follow up new Christians are few. Many may desire to be deacons, but few manifest wisdom and discernment. Vision and excellence in the preaching ministry may be hampered by lack of giving. Wherever we find the church there seems to be both a shortage of workers and an imbalance of ministries.

Flynn, in his book *Nineteen Gifts of the Spirit*, describes the problem in a church he knows. The superintendent of the Sunday School approached a soft-spoken chemist who had been a Christian for two years and asked him to help in the Sunday School. The chemist stated that he was not gifted in that area. Next, the superintendent approached a lawyer who had been a Christian for five years. The lawyer protested that he was not sure whether he did have teaching gifts. Meanwhile, down the street in another church, a mature believer ran in circles doing fourteen different jobs.[2]

Obviously, this unequal distribution of gifts cannot be traced to God's gift depot. Scripture, as we shall see, paints a clear picture of the bountiful manner in which Christ has provided gifts for the church. God is not miserly! No, the bottleneck must be somewhere else.

Ministry imbalance may be due to a variety of causes. Some who attend church regularly may volunteer for service but fail to qualify. Unconverted adherents who aspire to office and ministry are not spiritually gifted because they do not possess the Spirit. While their natural abilities may lend legitimacy to their aspirations for places of leadership, discerning church leaders wisely decline their offers. Building a spiritual body by using leaders who do not truly belong to Christ is impossible.

What of genuine believers? Have gifts been distributed to local churches unequally? Have gifted people fled their responsibilities in one assembly to join another, leaving the first suffering? Or are Christians confused about their places of ministry in the local church? Has ministry been relegated to an élite few? Is it a matter of laziness and lack of commitment on the part of the gifted? Have church structures stifled gift development? Or have gifts simply remained undiscovered and hence lain dormant and undeveloped? Are certain gifts exalted and others ignored? Have church leadership patterns fostered the development of gifts?

We want to look at these and other questions in the chapters ahead. Let's make a start by getting an overview of this subject from 1 Corinthians chapter 12. Before going on, take a few moments to read verses 1-14.

Have you read this controversial passage? Let us shelve for a moment the issue of tongues, miracles and healing to concentrate on some basic principles. We all know that the church in Corinth was a problem church prone to misunderstandings. To correct error, Paul stresses, in the first three verses of chapter 12, the importance of understanding spiritual gifts under the lordship of Christ. The Holy Spirit, he points out, will always lead us to acknowledge and submit practically to Christ as Lord. Hence, any consideration of gifts can only be carried out when we submit to the lordship of Jesus Christ.

Paul seeks to dispel confusion and restore balance by first emphasizing variety, secondly God's sovereignty and thirdly the unity of the church.

I. Variety

Verses 4-6 highlight the concept of variety. Variety is the spice of life precisely because God, the creator of life, loves variety. Flowers of every shape grace our gardens. Butterflies of every hue flit here and there. Birds of every kind make their nests in trees of every conceivable shape and use. Changing seasons and unpredictable weather spice our conversation. Diversity in the profile of noses, the colour of eyes, the texture of hair, as well as shape and stature, make any crowd a rich human mosaic.

Paul stresses the importance of variety in the church: 'There are varieties of gifts, but the same Spirit. And there are varieties of ministries, and the same Lord. And there are varieties of effects, but the same God who works all things in all persons' (1 Cor. 12:4-6, NASV).

Diversity has three facets. Verse 4 speaks of different kinds of gifts, verse 5 of various ministries and verse 6 of varying effects. These are not three groups of gifts but three ways of looking at the same thing. To quote Charles Hodge, 'He [Paul] is not, however, to be understood as here dividing these gifts into three classes, under the heads of gifts, ministrations, and operations; but as presenting them each and all under three different aspects.'[3]

We could set out these three different aspects of the gifting of God in chart form as follows:

English Translation	Greek Word	Special Emphasis	Example
Gifts	*charismata*	their source as from God	hospitality
Ministries	*diakoniai*	their sphere of responsibility	in the home
Effect	*energeiai*	the end result of their use	a deepening of love and understanding between host and guests

The first, and most common, word used for special endowments of grace is the word 'gift', which translates the Greek word *charisma*, singular, and the plural, *charismata*. *Charismata* has its root in *charis,* grace. In this sense they are gifts that owe their origin to grace as bestowed by the Holy Spirit, for example, hospitality, teaching and mercy.

The second word used to describe these endowments from God is the word 'ministries', which translates the Greek word *diakoniai*. The NIV translates this word as 'service'. The emphasis is not upon the gifted person but upon his sphere of ministry, that is, where the person exercises his gift. A gift could be exercised, for example, in one's home or in a congregation. Ministries are those areas of particular responsibility that God gives to a person as an arena for exercising a gift. A teacher might exercise his gift of teaching in a Sunday School class. Of course, he could also exercise it in his home through teaching his own family.

Ministries may sometimes be confused with church offices. Ministry, however, takes place not only in the church, but wherever Christians serve. Let me quote Alford in this regard: 'Appointed services in the church... These *diakoniai* must not be narrowed to ecclesiastical orders.'[4]

All believers can serve either in or out of the congregation. Perhaps this explains why the NIV translators chose 'service' rather than 'ministry', which is often used to describe full-time clergy.

Neither the diaconate nor the eldership is listed as a spiritual gift, precisely because they are not gifts but spheres of ministry. Deacons and elders are assigned areas of responsibility, where they are to exercise a variety of gifts. In the case of a pastor-teacher his pastoral gift may correspond closely with his sphere of ministry. Nevertheless, as we shall see later, this is not always the case. Grosheide states, 'The word *diakonia* does not exclusively denote the work of church officers; it may denote every service to the good of the church.'[5]

The third word, 'effects' ('working' NIV), emphasizes the end result of a gift's use. For example, the gift of hospitality moves its recipient to use his or her home to minister to others with the effect that bonds of love and understanding are forged between those invited. Or take the gift of evangelism. The effect of exercising the gift of evangelism in one's neighbourhood or at work would probably be the conviction and conversion of the lost.

To review what we have seen so far, the term 'gifts' emphasizes that these endowments originate in God's divine grace as their source. The word 'ministries' emphasizes the spheres of service in which these gifts are exercised, whether in terms of a formal church office or an informal area of ministry. Effects ('working' as the NIV has it) are the divinely produced results of the exercise of gifts.

Since this distinction is so important let me also quote Kling in this regard: 'The *"charismata"*, gifts, are qualifications or capabilities peculiar to Christianity... "eminent endowments of individuals in and by which the Spirit dwelling in them manifested Himself"... The *"diakoniai"*, ministries, are the manifold offices or functions in the church, (understood in their widest sense) in which these "gifts" were employed, and which indicate a division in the spheres of labour corresponding with these "gifts"... Finally the *"energamati"*, operations, are the various effects resulting from the exercise of the "gifts" in these particular "ministries".'[6]

Gifts, ministries and effects represent three aspects of the Holy Spirit's activity in and through the church. If we would understand the church as he has conceived it, we must understand and revel in these three facets of his varied artistry. First let us consider gifts.

1. Gifts

The term 'gifts' occupies first place in the passage, because gifts are basic to every ministry and its effect. Thirteen different gifts are mentioned in 1 Corinthians 12. To one is given the gift of faith, to one the word of knowledge, to another the gift of prophecy, to another the gift of teaching, and so on. Besides 1 Corinthians there are also key lists of gifts in Romans 12 and Ephesians 4. As the table below shows, the various lists exhibit both similarities and differences.

Romans 12:6-8	*1 Cor. 12:8-10,28-30*	*Ephesians 4:11*
Prophesying	Message of wisdom	Apostles
Serving	Message of knowledge	Prophets
Teaching	Faith	Evangelists
Encouraging	Healing	Pastors
Giving	Miraculous powers	Teachers
Leadership	Prophecy, prophets	
Mercy	Distinguishing spirits	
	Tongues	
	Interpretation	
	Apostles	
	Teachers	
	Helping	
	Administration	

A few gifts are not mentioned in these three key passages. Martyrdom appears to be a gift according to 1 Corinthians 13:3. Paul describes celibacy as a gift in 1 Corinthians 7:7. (Since neither martyrdom nor celibacy describe ministries but states of being, I do not count them as gifts.) 1 Peter 4:9 mentions hospitality. In all, Scripture lists at least twenty, and probably more, distinct gifts of the Spirit of God.

No one person has all the gifts, but no person is without a gift. Note the construction of the text: 'To each one the manifestation of the Spirit is given for the common good. To one there is given through the Spirit the message of wisdom, to another the message of knowledge...' (1 Cor. 12:7-8). Peter makes the same point: 'Each one should use whatever gift he has received' (1 Peter 4:10).

Each and every Christian receives a spiritual gift. And since variety predominates in the Spirit's bestowal of gifts, there is absolutely no basis for believing that there is any one gift that is universally possessed by all believers. Paul is emphatic on this point: 'Are all apostles?... Are all teachers?... Do all speak in tongues?' (1 Cor. 12:29-30). The obvious answer is 'No!'

New Testament variety ought to be duplicated in modern church life. There are no stereotypes. Paul was no carbon copy of Peter, nor Timothy of Paul. Stephen was distinct from Philip. Why, then, do we yearn for carbon copies of Whitefield or Spurgeon? Their zeal and commitment must be coveted, but surely the Spirit can be trusted to endow his church today with necessary gifts, without producing assembly-line similarity?

2. Ministries — areas of service

God gives to each of us a different sphere of ministry. Opportunities for service sometimes take the form of offices in the local church. In New Testament times there was the office of the apostle; Peter was an apostle. There was the office of the prophet; John the Baptist was a prophet. There was the office of the pastor-teacher exemplified by Timothy. Stephen was one who held the office of deacon. Then there was John, the elder, who wrote the Gospel that bears his name.

In some cases the gift, *charisma,* seems almost synonymous with the ministry, *diakoniai,* but we must not confuse offices with spiritual gifts. Confusion may occur when we consider the apostle, prophet or pastor-teacher because these terms represent both offices in the organization of the early church and spiritual endowments for ministry. As already noted, the office of deacon, like that of elder, however, is not a gift in the sense defined by the New Testament, but a sphere of responsibility. Then, too, deacons had various gifts. Philip had the gift of evangelism. Stephen, a deacon, exercised a prophetic preaching ministry. The Pastoral Epistles inform us that an elder should possess both the gift of administration and that of teaching. He may also have gifts of mercy or exhortation. Gifts are not synonymous with offices.

Then, too, the common offices in the church do not exhaust every sphere of ministry. All Christians possess gifts for ministry, but not all Christians have offices in the local church. Nevertheless, each one who has a gift has a divinely appointed place of service. This may as well be in the home, factory or neighbourhood as in the local assembly — although all should be tied into the church in some manner. Priscilla and Aquila probably did not have offices in the church but they had eminent gifts and divinely appointed spheres of ministry that even touched Paul! Dorcas certainly was gifted but held no office (Acts 9:36). The prophets who came to Antioch probably did not have organizational positions in the church at Jerusalem but did possess gifts that they exercised (Acts 11:27-28).

While gifts are not offices as such, yet every office-holder possesses gifts because everyone, whether or not he or she has an office, does have a sphere of ministry. Whether that place of ministry is formalized and recognized as an office in the church, such as elder, deacon, pastor, Sunday School teacher, steward, treasurer or whatever, does not matter. There are varieties of ministries that we must recognize and encourage by allowing freedom and scope for all believers to minister.

3. Effects

Paul continues his discussion of variety in verse 6. Various gifts exercised in different ministries produce a variety of effects. The effect of one ministry will be completely different from the results attendant on another's ministry.

Barnabas, the 'son of consolation', had the gift of encouragement. When he exercised his gift people were lifted up from discouragement. Peter, besides other gifts, had the gift of discernment. He read the condition of Simon's covetous heart and rebuked him boldly (Acts 8). Simon, the magician, was deeply convicted and the church escaped the influence of a hypocrite. Another of Peter's gifts resulted in the conversion of 3,000 on the Day of Pentecost (Acts 2).

There are many different kinds of effects. One believer may be used by God to encourage Christians to grow, while another is used to bring conviction of sin. The service of a third might lead to hungry people being satisfied, while a fourth might help to enlighten a puzzled mind.

Real understanding of the variety of gifts relieves us of the pressure to become like someone else. We don't have to reproduce like Dawson Trotman (founder of the Navigators), or preach like Spurgeon. All of us should be fruitful, but the fruit God harvests from our diverse ministries will vary according to our gifts.

Biblical descriptions of the church highlight the diversity inherent in its different members. Peter compared the church to a building made up of living stones. Each stone is distinct from the others. Stones have slightly differing shapes, textures, colours and different places in a building.

Paul writes of the church as a body (1 Cor. 12:12). It has hands. It has arms. It has eyes. It has a nose and ears. It has feet and all sorts of other different members. Each limb or organ is distinct from other parts of the body. When we voyage by microscope into the inner reaches of the body its diversity stuns us. God compares the church to this fearfully and wonderfully created focus of diversity. Forgive us, Father, for ever demanding sterile uniformity!

II. Sovereignty

Besides variety, the apostle also highlights God's sovereignty in the giving and use of gifts: 'There are different kinds of gifts, but the same Spirit. There are different kinds of service, but the same Lord. There are different kinds of working, but the same God works all of them in all men. Now to each one the manifestation of the Spirit is given for the common good... All these are the work of one and the same Spirit, and he gives them to each one, just as he determines' (1 Cor. 12:4-7,11). Differing gifts, areas of responsibility and effects are bestowed as the Lord wills.

1. Sovereignty over gifts

The Holy Spirit sovereignly distributes gifts according to his will. He knows each person and he knows each church. He distributes to each person as he sees fit for the good of the church. He doesn't lead us into a gift supermarket to pick and choose whatever we want. Gifts are just that: gifts, not choices. As previously noted, the word *'charisma'* derives its meaning from *charis*, 'grace'. The very word 'chosen' emphasizes that gifts owe their origin, not to personal skill or desire, but to the undeserved favour of God. The Spirit of God bestows gifts on the basis of his own grace and favour, not according to what we deserve or earn. 'We have different gifts, according to the grace given us. If a man's gift is prophesying, let him use it in proportion to his faith.'

The Holy Spirit retains absolute sovereignty over the kind of gifts he gives to any person, the number of gifts he gives to that person and whether those gifts are prominent or not. He retains sovereignty over how closely the spiritual gift he gives to you corresponds to the natural talents you have. He is sovereign over the spiritual effect of your gifts. There is no place for demanding certain gifts from God. Nor should we covet gifts possessed by others. God is the giver.

God was sovereign over my studies in forestry. I felt that I had some ability in that field and did fairly well in university. I enjoyed the courses and looked forward to a career in the great outdoors. But God had other plans. His bestowal of a spiritual gift upon me did not correspond too closely to that training in forestry, nor to the natural interests that I had been developing. Instead, I began to sense a gift for teaching, coupled with a missionary call to the Muslim world. Subsequently I went to the desert country of Pakistan that has few trees! God is sovereign in the bestowal of his gifts.

2. Sovereignty over offices and ministries

As in my case, the Holy Spirit exercises sovereignty in the choice of our sphere of ministry. How could it be otherwise? The Spirit glorifies Christ, who is Lord of the church, and King of the kingdom of God. As members of that body and citizens of that kingdom, let us happily submit to his will.

When it comes to the choice of a sphere of ministry, we need to remember that he bestows his gifts and his ministries either in the context of a local church, or to promote the future birth of a church. The image of the church as a body in 1 Corinthians 12 and Ephesians 4 presupposes an interdependent and corporate life on the part of all believers. He never gives us gifts for independent use or personal glory.

Although Jeremiah initially objected when God called him to a prophetic ministry among rebellious Israelites, he soon bowed to God's sovereign will, and went on to complete the work given to him to do. In a similar vein, God called Moses to lead Israel out of Egypt. Moses protested. But he soon learned that his protests were of no avail. God is sovereign in his appointments.

We need to acknowledge God's sovereign right to pick men and women of his own choice to fill particular slots in the local church.

When the apostles chose a replacement for Judas they said, 'Lord, you know everyone's heart. Show us which of these two you have chosen' (Acts 1:24). Matthias was chosen. In another case, God set aside Barnabas and Saul for missionary service, while the leaders of the church fasted (Acts 13). We must fast, if necessary, to ensure we find God's choice for a particular office.

Whether your sphere of ministry is in a factory, or school, in your neighbourhood, or among your relatives, that is his place for you. Accept it as from him. But don't exercise your ministry independently of the local church, for the Spirit gives gifts to edify the church.

3. Sovereignty over effects

We have already noted, from 1 Corinthians 12:6, that God has determined the degree of effect a given believer will achieve through the exercise of his or her gifts. To illustrate this point consider prophecy. Many Old Testament prophets, such as Jeremiah, lamented the lack of effect their preaching had on their audiences. The 400 years of prophetic silence which led up to the time of John the Baptist yielded meagre results. A cursory reading of biblical history leads us to conclude that God is sovereign over both the exercise of gifts and the results that follow.

Consider the ministry of Christ. During his lifetime, many people superficially accepted his teaching while others rejected him. As his message became progressively harder to accept, the crowds dispersed and even friends left him. Soon only twelve remained. Finally they too deserted him. One even betrayed him. By contrast Peter stood up to preach and 3,000 were converted. Does this mean that Peter was a better evangelist than Jesus? No, it means that God exercises sovereignty over the timing of fruitfulness in our ministries.

Samuel Zwemer laboured for years among Muslims in the Middle East with little effect. By contrast, without much human preparation, a tremendous revival broke out in post-war Indonesia. God brought hundreds of thousands of Muslims to Christ. A church sprang up overnight. What caused it? The sovereignty of God.

Merle and Gloria Inniger, missionary colleagues from Pakistan, gave a widow breakfast one morning. Twenty years passed by before the son of that widow came to the Innigers to say, 'Thank you.' Was this a fruitless ministry? No, God was sovereign over the timing of its results.

A knowledge of God's sovereignty should make us humble and give us peace. Teaching about spiritual gifts must not lead to pride or envy or discouragement — it should encourage us to persevere faithfully where we serve, knowing that the harvest is in the hands of God.

III. Unity

Lastly, let us note how gifts promote unity. In his high-priestly prayer in John 17 Jesus prayed, 'Father, make them one as we are one.' Jesus seeks to reproduce in the church the unity manifest between himself and the Father in the Godhead. Spiritual gifts, when properly exercised, will always tend towards biblical unity because of the following factors.

1. One source

Spiritual gifts come from the hand of God. Every gift is a gift of grace — undeserved, unmerited and sovereignly bestowed. All believers are sinners washed in the blood, partakers of the Spirit of God, recipients of regeneration and objects of grace.

Just as our new birth in Christ occurs through the ministry of the Spirit, so all the results of conversion can be traced back to God. When ministry proves fruitful, we know that the triune God, 'who gives ... to each one, just as he determines', has been at work.

2. One body

The mystical body of Christ manifests the unity that Christ has created between all its members. 'The body is a unit, though it is made up of many parts; and though all its parts are many, they form one body. So it is with Christ. For we were all baptized by one Spirit into one body — whether Jews or Greeks, slave or free — and we were all given the one Spirit to drink' (1 Cor. 12:12-14).

God combines our diversity of gifts and our distinctive individu-

ality into the marvellous unity that is the body of Christ. The image
of the body illustrates the vital connection we sustain with all other
believers. We should not wait for this unity to be demonstrated in
heaven, but take concrete steps to show our oneness practically in
the give and take of local church life. Like it or not, we are 'members
one of another'. Our mutual interdependence is just as important for
Christians today as it was for the Corinthians, who were so beset by
divisions.

Unfortunately, we frequently miss the opportunity to demonstrate oneness by acting as if we were independent rather than
mutually interdependent. Those with obvious gifts especially face
this temptation. Spiritual gifts, however, ought to enhance fellowship, not fragment it.

3. One aim

In 1 Corinthians 12:7 we read, 'Now to each one the manifestation
of the Spirit is given for the common good.' Verse 25 of the same
chapter proclaims, 'So that there should be no division in the body,
but that its parts should have equal concern for each other.'

God bestows gifts on people so that they might edify the body of
Christ. Edification necessarily means a growing oneness. Ephesians
4 highlights the contribution gifts make to edification: 'It was he
who gave some to be apostles, some to be prophets, some to be
evangelists, and some to be pastors and teachers, to prepare God's
people for works of service, so that the body of Christ may be built
up until we all reach unity in the faith and in the knowledge of the
Son of God and become mature, attaining to the whole measure of
the fulness of Christ' (Eph. 4:11-13).

When we use our gifts to serve one another, we draw closer to one
another. Genuine exercise of gifts seems necessarily to produce
oneness. How could it be otherwise? While we have different gifts
and different spheres of ministry, which result in different effects,
our goal is the same — to edify the church. Each should ask, 'How
can I use my gift to enhance the multicoloured mosaic that is the
body?'

Personal glory or prestige find no place in Spirit-led gift exercise.
The New Testament extols harmony and focuses upon the glory of
God. Paul reminds us that all 'are being built together to become a
dwelling in which God lives by his Spirit' (Eph. 2:22). We exercise

our gifts in our varied spheres to build a temple hallowed by God's presence. Our focus is on him even as our concern is for each other. Togetherness and mutual ministry promote the glory of Christ and the progress of his kingdom. Gifts promote unity.

Conclusion

A vision of the variety, sovereignty and unity of the gifts can keep us from getting stuck down some obscure or controversial blind alley. When we turn to this subject it is so easy to be sidetracked. We must keep to the interpretive high road where the biblical texts are clear. It is abundantly evident that there are varieties of gifts, varieties of ministries and varieties of effects over which God exercises sovereign control. It is also patently clear that gifts are bestowed not for personal pride but mutual edification and unity.

In Pakistan skilled craftsmen weave very beautiful oriental rugs. These rugs manifest a great variety of colours. There is also variety in the types of thread used. Wool threads predominate but they are woven into a hidden cotton warp and woof. The yarns and dyes of any one rug are the culmination of many different people exercising their individual talents in different parts of Pakistan. Shepherds up in the hill country care for their sheep until shearing time. Then the wool is transported, washed, graded, baled and sold. In a mill it is spun into yarn and dyed. In another part of the country a farmer grows the cotton that is harvested to become the main threads of the warp and woof. The cotton itself goes through many hands to reach the weaver.

An oriental rug is the result of a tremendous variety of input. All of this diversity of source and talent contributes to one masterpiece. As you look at the rug there is a unity of pattern and colour. It is one rug. But behind that unity there is the sovereignty of a craftsman in some little village. He sat down by his little loom and in his mind saw the pattern that would emerge. He sovereignly chose the various kinds of wool and the various colours of yarn to put them together into one unified pattern.

Like a weaver, God sovereignly takes diverse people, immerses them in varied ministries and weaves their different contributions together into the rich tapestry that is his church. Variety, sovereignty, unity — let us move on to explore the place of the Holy Spirit in this developing tapestry of gifts.

2.
The Holy Spirit:
awe and adequacy

The rich scenes painted on the ceiling of the Sistine Chapel in Rome made me catch my breath. The spectacle of biblical history captured on that lofty vault so entranced me that I didn't notice that the family had moved on. 'What kind of man must Michelangelo have been?' I mused.

Far more astonishing is the artistry of the Holy Spirit. From human personalities distorted and made ugly by depravity, he has crafted a living mosaic of rare beauty. He has baptized diverse individuals with a medley of abilities into the body of Christ. If we could but see his craftsmanship in the body of Christ as clearly as we can perceive Michelangelo's artistry, we would gasp in wonder and fall down in worship.

Gift discovery begins where we discover the glory of the Holy Spirit. Indeed, we are not ready for gift development until awe for his person captures our hearts. As we shall discover in the next chapter, this does not detract from, but rather enhances our appreciation of the person of Christ.

In Greek, spiritual gifts are called *pneumatika* as well as *charisma*. The use of *'pneumatika'*, which could be translated 'spirituals', implies that they owe their origin to the Holy Spirit. It reminds us to meditate on the Giver before we dissect the gifts themselves.

This is not easy. Although Paul writes that 'By one Spirit we were all baptized into one body...' (1 Cor. 12:13), nevertheless discussion of the Holy Spirit often generates confusion, division and even enmity. Evidently early Christians had the same problem. Why else would Paul urge the Ephesians to 'make every effort to keep the unity of the Spirit through the bond of peace. There is one body and one Spirit …'? (Eph. 4:3-4).

Contention and competition about the Holy Spirit, like thick fog, obscure the links forged between us by the blood of Christ. Claimed experiences of the 'fulness of the Holy Spirit', 'the baptism of the Holy Spirit', or 'signs of the Holy Spirit', rather than drawing true believers together, have served to accentuate differences. Without care, an emphasis on gifts could increase this confusion.

We need to maintain balance. If we focus too often on experiences or gifts, without being scripturally rooted, we run the danger of becoming self-centred instead of God-centred.

Scripture reveals the glory of the Holy Spirit — and he in turn points us to Christ. A true vision of Christ and his Spirit will suffuse our souls with a sense of reverential awe. Awe, in turn, will help us to maintain perspective. Without reverential awe emanating from a sense of the glory of God, in the person of the Spirit, the ministries we undertake may be sullied by our massive egos. Before proceeding to dissect the gifts, then, let us try to recapture our sense of reverence.

I. Reverential awe

When towering offices and close-packed houses, multiplying problems or wearing duties threaten to distort my sense of perspective, I love to head north in the car. As the asphalt ribbon unwinds, congestion and noise give way to fields and streams. A proper sense of perspective returns as the creative genius of Almighty God unfolds before my citified spirit. My wife, Mary Helen, and I have fond memories of a little cottage on a quiet lake. The lake mirrors the ever-changing artistry of God in sky and storm, leaf and ripple.

Similarly we, who serve Christ through the fruitful practice of his gifts, must keep the Holy Spirit in perspective through frequent perusal of his book. Without its spiritual ballast, imagined superiority may cause our inflated egos to float to giddy heights.

Temptations to pride dog the footsteps of any who set out to serve God. Spiritual pride, since it usurps the position of God, is the worst kind of conceit. Pride leads us to believe a lie instead of the truth. What lie? The lie of our own independence. What truth? That just as a child is dependent upon its mother, as apples on a tree are dependent upon the life of the tree, as our whole globe is dependent upon the life-giving rays of the sun, so every single believer is absolutely dependent upon the Holy Spirit, the channel of gifts and graces.

Genuine humility, the kind generated by a sense of reverence for the Spirit, enables us to maintain perspective. It helps us recognize our limitations as well as the divine resources available to us. Humility is one of the marks of Christian character, one of the fruits of the Spirit, a crucial facet of holiness. In the divine order of things, character and holiness always precede service and activity.

Reverential awe is an important facet of true biblical humility. Awe moves the humble person to maintain a proper respect for the Holy Spirit, while lack of reverence severely curtails our usefulness. Why? Christian ministry is not just the performance of certain duties, but the performance of these duties from the right perspective. Without reverence for God we cannot hope to do 'all to the glory of God'. Therefore, without reverence, we cannot truly serve God. Humility always moves us towards reverence. Without it, ministry becomes self-serving.

A plethora of conflicting teaching, encouraging us towards self-actualization, self-development or self-esteem, vies for our attention. As we shall shortly see, a biblically balanced perspective does lead to confidence. But pride, no less than a lack of confidence, is extremely hurtful. Too often people are tempted to seek a place of ministry in the church as a means of self-promotion. Opportunities for service may be viewed as stepping-stones to personal advancement.

How distinctly different is the teaching of our Lord, who said, 'Whoever wishes to be first among you shall be your slave' (Matt. 20:27, NASV). Jesus taught that the pathway to leadership led through the lowly fields of servanthood. If we maintain a sense of reverential awe we shall be more likely to walk humbly the paths of service.

Reverence for the Spirit ought not to be hard to discover. Just walk with hushed hallelujahs through Romans chapter 8. Here we find a gallery of sketches of the Spirit at work. We meet the Spirit who has set us free, who leads us, who helps us to get up when we stumble, who empowers us to put to death the clinging remnants of our depraved nature and who enables us to cry out to the Father,

'Abba — Daddy!' He is the Spirit who gives us our inheritance as children of God. He is the Spirit who groans with us in prayer and who keeps us secure in the love of God. He is at work in every humble believer. 'If anyone does not have the Spirit of Christ, he does not belong to Christ' (Rom. 8:9).

How can any inflated ego come to this passage without bowing in new-found humility? But the Spirit's glory is written in gold, not only in this chapter but throughout the New Testament. We are reborn only through the power of the Spirit (John 3:5). The Holy Spirit produces the fruit of godliness (Gal. 5:22-23). The Holy Spirit alone can make us conformed to the image of Christ (2 Cor. 3:18). Indeed, you and I are temples — tabernacles where the Spirit dwells (1 Cor. 3:16). Any sincere consideration of our dependence on the Spirit must generate humility.

How could we ever become proud? We came as hungry beggars to God. He clothed us in glorious dress, fed us with the bread of life and then pressed us into his service. As his humble servants we go out to share that bread, baked in the ovens of heaven, with other beggars like ourselves.

Unfortunately, our hearts are so deceitful and our memories so short! We must pray for a permanently clear view of the dynamic place of the Holy Spirit in all aspects of sanctification and service. Without such an overview, the reception of gifts may fan our self-esteem. Sadly, ministerial gifts, and real or imagined experiences of the Holy Spirit, often appear to inflate the recipient's ego. Too many develop a blithely superior attitude. The dismal record of fallen evangelists and pastors warns us about the danger of pride in ministry. Again and again we have seen men with eminent gifts come crashing down in disgrace. Instead of looking on them with condemnation, and a certain smug self-assurance, we need to take their falls as a warning.

Reverence and humility are the only tunics that we should wear in God's service. To usurp the honour and glory that is due to Almighty God through his Spirit by direct or hinted boasting would be but to clothe our inadequacies in vapour and expose our nakedness. Let awe, not ego, characterize our service as we develop our gifts. Let a clear sense of the rôle of the Spirit in bestowing and developing gifts keep us humbly dependent. But many Christians have a different problem.

II. Spiritual adequacy

Charismatic euphoria makes some Christians feel inferior. When they hear testimonies about the 'baptism of the Spirit', or 'speaking in tongues', they conclude that their own spiritual pilgrimage is somehow second-class. The proliferation of books on great experiences may have encouraged this tendency. Very few books detail the story of ordinary Christians helped by the Holy Spirit to persevere over long periods without dramatic experiences. This is not to defend complacency. Submission to the Spirit of God inevitably results in supernatural living. Nevertheless, the continual focus on the unusual experiences of others tends to discourage sensitive souls by making them feel inferior. They conclude that their experiences fail to measure up to those of others. Instead of seeking the Spirit, they may be led to seek an experience, thus denying the very adequacy of the Holy Spirit so widely proclaimed in Holy Scripture.

We must flee, not only pride, but feelings of inferiority. To put such feelings to rest, turn with me to Ephesians chapter 1, where we find Paul's description of the blessings of salvation. In verses 3-6 he soared into the stratosphere in describing the work of the Father. In verses 7-12 he has thrilled us with the work of the Son. The passage is so stretching that we may be emotionally drained by the time we reach verse 13, where we encounter the wonder of the Spirit.

Let us take time now to meditate carefully on the believer's adequacy for life and service as guaranteed by the Holy Spirit. Paul writes, 'You also were included in Christ when you heard the word of truth, the gospel of your salvation. Having believed, you were marked in him with a seal, the promised Holy Spirit, who is a deposit guaranteeing our inheritance until the redemption of those who are God's possession — to the praise of his glory' (Eph. 1:13-14).

Paul compares the Holy Spirit to a seal and to a deposit. Consider how these metaphors illuminate our adequacy for service.

The seal of the Holy Spirit

The Holy Spirit seals every one who believes in Christ. Verse 13 makes it clear that after hearing and believing the gospel of salvation, a person is sealed. Just as all are justified, so all are sealed.

Since this is controversial, but beyond the scope of this book, let me refer you to E. H. Andrews' book for a fuller treatment. He concludes, 'It is inconceivable that a man might be redeemed with the precious blood ... of Christ (1 Peter 1:18,19) without being sealed for that day of ultimate redemption of which Paul speaks in Ephesians.

'We conclude, therefore, that sealing is an integral part of the process of conversion, an inevitable consequence of the Spirit's regenerating work in the believer... This is wholly in accordance with our conclusion that, for the Corinthians as for all post-Pentecostal believers, the sealing of the Spirit was something that had accompanied their conversion to Christ. If Paul had thought of the sealing as an experience totally distinct from conversion, and one that any given believer may or may not have received at a particular time, he could not possibly have addressed a numerous readership, not all known to him personally, in these terms. Yet he states with confidence that the members of the church at Corinth had all received the sealing of the Spirit at some past juncture.'[1]

At Pentecost, Peter spoke about the same experience, sealing, but he used different terminology. While explaining the outpouring of the Spirit, he called on his hearers to 'Repent and be baptized, every one of you, in the name of Jesus Christ for the forgiveness of your sins. And you will receive the gift of the Holy Spirit. The promise is for you and your children and for all who are far off — for all whom the Lord our God will call' (Acts 2:38-39). The Spirit of God comes upon all whom the Father calls through the gospel. This reception of the Holy Spirit, as a gift, is indistinguishable from the sealing of the Spirit. The promise is to every called one, that is, to every converted person.

Romans 8:9 states that the Spirit is present in, indeed controls, everyone who belongs to Christ: 'You, however, are controlled not by the sinful nature but by the Spirit, if the Spirit of God lives in you. And if anyone does not have the Spirit of Christ, he does not belong to Christ.' Having or not having the Spirit — not speaking in tongues, or speaking a word of knowledge, or demonstrating any other gift — distinguishes believers from unbelievers. Every single person who is reborn by the Spirit is also, without exception, indwelt by the Spirit. Just so, every believer, without exception, is sealed by the Spirit at the time of his or her conversion.

The word 'seal' occurs about eighty times in the Authorized

Version. What is meant by this word? Ancient societies used seals
of various kinds. Some were baked clay cylinders with a hole
through the middle. Other seals were carved cylinders. In ancient
Middle Eastern usage a thong was often used to attach a seal to the
arm or to suspend one around the neck. The Scarab seals of Egypt
were semi-precious stones set in a ring and engraved with the
wearer's logo or signature. The use of signet rings developed from
this practice. When applied, seals would leave an impression in
damp clay. When used with dye, a seal would imprint an insignia on
papyrus or parchment. They fulfilled four distinct purposes.

Seals were a sign of secrecy

The contents of a packet or the entrance to a tomb could be sealed
shut to conceal the contents. God commanded Daniel to seal up the
last prophecy: 'Close up and seal the words of the scroll until the
time of the end... The words are closed up and sealed until the time
of the end' (Dan. 12:4,9).

The fifth chapter of Revelation tells us about the book sealed
with seven seals. Its contents had been kept secret (Rev. 5:1-5). In
ancient times seals ensured secrecy.

In this sense, only God knows the exact membership of the
church. 'Nevertheless, God's solid foundation stands firm, sealed
with this inscription: "The Lord knows those who are his," and,
"Everyone who confesses the name of the Lord must turn away from
wickedness"' (2 Tim. 2:19). This seal hides from general sight
God's secret, but sure, knowledge of his children.

We evaluate faith in professing believers by gauging the degree
to which they depart from iniquity. But we can easily make mistakes
of judgement. God alone knows infallibly because the identity of all
his children is sealed from our view. (Individually we know by the
witness of the Spirit whether or not we are personally sealed.)

Seals were a sign of ownership

Revelation chapter 7 mentions 144,000 'servants of our God' who
have a seal on their foreheads (Rev. 7:3-8). In this passage sealing
signifies ownership. As bond-servants, these 144,000 are God's
property, his special people.

In this sense, seals resemble brands. In the West, ranchers brand their cattle by burning into their hide the sign of the ranch. In similar fashion the seal of the Spirit has been burned into believers' hearts as an indelible and unchangeable sign of ownership. Believers are God's property for ever. 'The Lord knows those who are his' (2 Tim. 2:19). Believers have been purchased for the Father at the cost of the blood of Jesus Christ. Subsequently God has sent the Spirit into believers' hearts as a seal of his perpetual ownership.

Surely no believer who bears, as a sign of divine ownership, the royal seal of heaven should feel inferior.

Seals were a sign of authority

The Old Testament records how Queen Esther came trembling into the presence of her king. She brought a request. The king extended his sceptre to her as a sign of his acceptance. This gesture gave her leave to intercede for the doomed Jewish people. After hearing her request, King Ahasuerus offered to Mordecai and to Esther an even greater symbol of his authority. He gave them his signet ring: 'Now write another decree in the king's name on behalf of the Jews as seems best to you, and seal it with the king's signet ring — for no document written in the king's name and sealed with his ring can be revoked' (Esth. 8:8).

No documents could compare in authority with those sealed with king's signet ring. Using the king's seal, Mordecai and Esther were able to issue decrees, which not only saved the Jews, but punished their enemies. Whatever they sealed became irrevocable law. In this sense a seal signifies authority.

Remember, too, how Pharaoh promoted Joseph. As a sign of delegated authority Pharaoh gave him his signet ring. 'So Pharaoh said to Joseph, "I hereby put you in charge of the whole land of Egypt." Then Pharaoh took his signet ring from his finger and put it on Joseph's finger. He dressed him in robes of fine linen and put a gold chain around his neck' (Gen. 41:41-42). Pharaoh's ring was probably a scarab ring carved with the symbol of his authority. When Joseph wore Pharaoh's ring he wielded the authority of the king himself.

Do you sometimes feel insecure? Do you feel inferior to other Christians who profess more dramatic experiences or demonstrate more obvious gifts? Remember, if you are a true believer, you have been sealed by the Spirit of God as a sign that authority has been delegated to you. You have become, in this world, a bearer of the scarab ring of the King of Kings. You have authority to go out into this world as his ambassador. The indwelling Holy Spirit is your seal of authority. In a real sense no nation on earth has the right to bar the way of a bearer of this royal seal! You can stand in the midst of a godless world for truth, righteousness and justice. What an honour! What a high calling! What a mark of significance! But there is more.

Seals were a sign of protection and safety

The ancients sealed letters or containers to ensure safe delivery and protect from pilferage. The more valuable the thing to be transported, the more care went into its sealing.

Pakistanis still commonly seal packages to ensure safe delivery. I have often gone into the post office and watched a couple of postmen behind the counter sealing a mail sack. After tying the mail bag up tightly with cord, they made a tiny charcoal fire on a couple of bricks. Then they would take a bit of red sealing wax, melt it over the fire, and drip some on the cord. While it was still soft they would take the office seal and leave an impression in the wax, thus protecting the mailbag from pilferage.

The seal of the Spirit of God signifies that we shall be delivered safely to the heavenly portals. 'I give them eternal life, and they shall never perish; no one can snatch them out of my hand. My Father, who has given them to me, is greater than all; no one can snatch them out of my Father's hand' (John 10:28-29). Satan dare not break the seal of the Holy Spirit on a believer's heart. God sealed Job so that Satan could go so far but no further (Job 1:6-12). Believers are kept by 'the power that is at work within us' (Eph. 3:20).

We who have been sealed by the Holy Spirit as a sign of secrecy, ownership, authority and safety ought not to feel inferior or insecure. Our sealing provides heavenly assurance of our unique position. The indwelling Comforter is an earnest as well.

The Holy Spirit as a pledge

The Scriptures liken the Holy Spirit to a pledge as well as a seal. In biblical language, a pledge is 'a deposit guaranteeing our inheritance until the redemption of those who are God's possession' (Eph. 1:14). The New American Standard Version translates the key phrase, 'a pledge of our inheritance, with a view to the redemption of God's own possession'. God has given to every believer the person of the Holy Spirit, like a deposit, to assure him that God will complete all that pertains to his salvation.

Who are these privileged people who receive the Spirit as a pledge? In answer, Scripture compels us to reply, 'Everyone who truly believes.' Among Christians there are no spiritual 'haves' and 'have-nots'. The Holy Spirit dwells in each one, as a seal and pledge of God's eternal intentions.

What is meant by 'pledge'? As a word of commerce and law, pledge denotes that someone has deposited a sum of money on account to ensure compliance with a contract. It usually means that a purchaser has promised to buy something. In the imagery of this passage, God is the buyer and the sinner is the seller. The sinner, at the time of conversion, offers to God, as the purchaser, his bankrupt life — all he has and is. God purchases the sinner at a high price, the precious blood of Jesus Christ. This metaphor, like all figures of speech, has its limitations, but it demonstrates that God gives the sinner, at the time of his salvation, a number of assurances of his serious intent. What are these assurances?

The buyer has a serious intention to buy

The buyer puts down a deposit to assure the seller that he will return to buy the property in question. This money assures a seller of the buyer's commitment to pay the amount owing. It is not enough to say, for example, 'I'll buy this house.' The vendor's representative will ask us to prove our intention by giving him a down payment.

At conversion we become God's possession. God in turn gives us the Holy Spirit as an assurance that he is utterly serious about the completion of all that pertains to our salvation. This pledge guarantees that God not only justifies us, but will sanctify and glorify us. No wonder we read, 'Being confident of this, that he who began a good work in you will carry it on to completion until the day of Christ Jesus' (Phil. 1:6). Such a pledge, properly understood, can dispel any sense of inadequacy that arises from being called to serve the Lord. But that is not all it means.

A part payment has been given

A deposit is not the whole amount. It represents the first instalment. When God pours the Spirit of God into our hearts at conversion we experience the initial stages of his work in us. What a beginning! We are regenerated by the Spirit, identified with Jesus Christ, justified in God's sight and delivered from bondage to sin. We have peace with God and rejoice in being forgiven. All this is merely a down payment to be followed up by the Spirit's continuing work throughout our lives.

The resident Spirit carries on the process of our sanctification in order to conform us more and more to the likeness of Christ. 'Now the Lord is the Spirit, and where the Spirit of the Lord is, there is freedom. And we, who with unveiled faces all reflect the Lord's glory, are being transformed into his likeness with ever-increasing glory, which comes from the Lord, who is the Spirit' (2 Cor. 3:17-18). The Spirit continues actively to lead and direct the believer: 'Those who are led by the Spirit of God are sons of God' (Rom. 8:14). While he leads us into closer conformity to Christ, he produces within us spiritual fruit: 'But the fruit of the Spirit is love, joy, peace, patience, kindness, goodness, faithfulness, gentleness and self-control. Against such things there is no law' (Gal. 5:22-23).

Spiritual gifts themselves are part of God's ongoing payment of the coin of salvation. The indwelling Spirit, as both the source and enabler, becomes the guarantee of our adequacy in the service of Christ. As we face daunting tasks we can breathe a sigh of relief knowing that we have inexhaustible resources through the presence of the Spirit. So often we lose sight of his power and wallow in weakness and despair. No wonder Paul prays that we may recognize, not so much some external or future experiences of his power, as that power indwelling us now. 'I pray that out of his glorious riches he may strengthen you with power through his Spirit in your inner being... Now to him who is able to do immeasurably more than all we ask or imagine, according to his power that is at work within us' (Eph. 3:16,20). Such is the heritage of every believer!

The presence of the Holy Spirit within is a pledge of his continuing work and a sign of our adequacy because he 'is able to do immeasurably more than all we ask or imagine'. In another context Paul wrote, 'Not that we are adequate in ourselves ... but our adequacy is from God' (2 Cor. 3:5, NASV). A deposit, however, points also to the final payment.

The final payment will be given later

The redemptive work carried on by the Spirit will be brought to completion. In this sense, the indwelling Spirit is 'a pledge of our inheritance'. As Paul points out, 'If only for this life we have hope in Christ, we are to be pitied more than all men' (1 Cor. 15:19). Much more awaits us!

On a recent trip we drove south into an unbelievable sunset. The whole sky from east to west was a fresco of delicately changing light. It was as if we were driving ever closer to the glory of paradise. Life in the Spirit is a journey like that. Unbelievable glory awaits us! Death ushers believers into the radiance of Christ's living presence.

But all that is future. The indwelling Holy Spirit is God's present pledge that he will keep the covenant of salvation he has made with us. Under its terms God guarantees that we shall complete the journey, we shall be fully redeemed — made conformable unto Christ. We ought to rejoice humbly in the Spirit of God who has sealed us unto that day of glory and full redemption.

Since every Christian has the Spirit, we can say that every believer has the Giver as well as the gifts and power necessary for service. We must ask the Spirit to take away the sense of our own inadequacy and replace it with confidence in his person. Paul prays that 'the eyes of your heart may be enlightened in order that you may know the hope to which he has called you, the riches of his glorious inheritance in the saints, and his incomparably great power for us who believe. That power is like the working of his mighty strength, which he exerted in Christ when he raised him from the dead and seated him at his right hand in the heavenly realms' (Eph. 1:18-20). The Spirit-led adventure which we call the Christian life leads to a place where awe and profound joy meet in loving service. Instead of a frustrating rat race, the Spirit makes our life an unveiling of surprising possibilities and hidden potential. The discovery of our spiritual gifts accelerates this joyful pilgrimage.

According to Richard Bolles, this means discovering our 'mission in life'. Richard Bolles' self-help book on career counselling, *What Color Is Your Parachute?*, has sold four million copies and remained on best-seller lists for twenty years. In the appendix, Bolles, a committed Christian, integrates giftedness with devotion to God as follows:

> 1. Your first Mission here on Earth is … to seek to stand hour by hour in the conscious presence of God, the One from whom your Mission is derived…
> 2. Secondly, once you have been doing that in an earnest way, your second mission here on Earth is … to do what you can, moment by moment, day by day, step by step, to make this world a better place, following the leading and guidance of God's Spirit within you and around you.
> 3. Thirdly … to exercise that Talent which you particularly came to Earth to use — your greatest gift, which you most delight to use. [2]

When we discover and use our greatest gift or gifts we are 'surprised by joy', to use C. S. Lewis's evocative expression. Far from designing us for frustration, God's Spirit has designed us for fulfilment through ministries uniquely suited to our temperaments and talents. When we use the spiritual gifts that we discover in ways that extend God's kingdom, the Spirit produces within us a profound sense of delight and significance. We discover our mission in life. We find where we fit into God's grand design.

No wonder both pride and insecurity flee when we meditate upon the almighty potential of the resident Spirit, who is both a seal and an earnest! We bow in humble reverence even while we wonder at our adequacy for service.

Conclusion

Since the Holy Spirit dwells, as it were, in the holy of holies within us we are living temples of God. But the apostle introduces a word of caution: 'Do not grieve the Holy Spirit of God, with whom you were sealed for the day of redemption' (Eph. 4:30). We must not grieve him by what we say or do, nor by resisting the direction he gives. We must give him free rein to direct us and to develop within us whatever gifts he desires. We must not grieve this blessed person by becoming either puffed up over personal experiences and abilities, or grovelling because of imagined inferiority.

May the Holy Spirit develop within us an expectation of joyful service, a flowering of giftedness and a perspective that manifests a sense of awe and of adequacy. But there is another essential ingredient necessary if we would pursue gifted ministry. The Holy Spirit always directs our attention to Jesus Christ.

3.
The Son of God:
source and goal of gifts

After long ages of disinterest, the Holy Spirit and his gifts stand silhouetted in the spotlight. Such a focus, however, leaves sensitive souls with a feeling of gnawing emptiness. Some seek to fill this vacuum with new experiences, renewed enthusiasm or exciting meetings. Believers whose spiritual compasses are calibrated by Scripture soon realize that Christ is missing from centre-stage — a renewed emphasis on the Spirit can rob Christ of his rightful place. After all, he is the Lord of the gifts just as he is the Head of the church. Before we can pursue the subject of gifts we need to clarify the relationship Christ Jesus bears to the Holy Spirit.

I. The Son of God and the Spirit of God

The unique relationship the Spirit bears to the Son of God defines the parameters of the Spirit's ministry among us. The great confessions of faith reflect the equality of the persons while maintaining an order of relationship within the Godhead. The Westminster articles beautifully summarize this relationship: 'In the unity of the Godhead there be three persons, of one substance, power, and eternity: God the Father, God the Son, and God the Holy Ghost; the Father is of none, neither begotten, nor proceeding; the Son is eternally begotten of the Father; the Holy Ghost eternally proceeding from the Father and the Son.'[1]

The eternal procession of the Spirit — how he moves out from the Father and the Son — impacts on the place Christ should occupy in our service and devotion. In the Olivet Discourse, John repeatedly mentions that the promised Paraclete — the Holy Spirit — will come at the personal request of Christ. He is 'the Counsellor ... whom I [Christ] will send...' (see John 14:16,26; 15:26). Christ said, 'Unless I go away, the Counsellor will not come to you; but if I go, I will send him to you' (John 16:7). The Spirit proceeds, at the behest of the Son, to minister among us.

The Spirit brings glory to Christ

Further, we note that the Holy Spirit is to 'bring glory to [Christ] by taking from what is [Christ's] and making it known to you' (John 16:14). Christ sends the Spirit to illuminate his own teaching and to sensitize us to his own presence (John 14:17-18,20). He will exalt Christ by teaching you 'all things and will remind you of everything I have said to you' (John 14:26). The Holy Spirit 'will not speak on his own; he will speak only what he hears', by 'taking from what is mine [Christ's] and making it known to you' (John 16:13,14).

Even when the Spirit convicts men of sin, he directs them to focus on Christ. 'When he comes, he will convict the world of guilt in regard to sin and righteousness and judgement ... because I am going to the Father...' (John 16:8-10). When he convicts, the Holy Spirit draws attention to our Lord by producing a sense of guilt for sinning against Christ. He leads men and women to recognize that Jesus Christ alone offers escape from judgement and righteousness through justification.

As J. I. Packer points out in his book *Keep In Step With The Spirit*, Jesus taught that 'The Spirit would be self-effacing, directing all attention away from himself to Christ and drawing folk into the faith, hope, love, obedience, adoration, and dedication, which constitute communion with Christ. This, be it said, remains the criterion by which the authenticity of supposedly "spiritual" movements — the ecumenical movement, the charismatic movement, the liturgical movement, the small-group movement, the lay apostolate movement, the world missionary movement, and so on — and also of supposedly "spiritual" experiences, may be gauged.'[2]

The rest of the New Testament repeatedly highlights this Christ-illuminating ministry of the Spirit. He is the 'Spirit of Christ', the 'Spirit of him who raised Jesus from the dead' and he indwells believers to transform them into Christ's likeness (Rom. 8:9,11;

2 Cor. 3:18). Christ crucified and risen, not the Spirit, has become for us 'wisdom from God — that is, our righteousness, holiness and redemption...' so that we might 'boast in the Lord' (1 Cor. 1:31,32). There cannot be two central figures if we are to have New Covenant balance. 'For no one can lay any foundation other than the one already laid, which is Jesus Christ' (1 Cor. 3:11).

None of this detracts from the crucial role of the Holy Spirit. The Spirit breaks the shackles of both the law and our sinful natures in order to produce in us the 'fruit of the Spirit'. Nevertheless, the Holy Spirit spotlights Christ even as he carries on his own glorious work. Indeed, the Corinthian passage on gifts describes the Holy Spirit as the one who leads us to declare with our whole being that 'Jesus is Lord' (1 Cor. 12:3). The Spirit leads us to exclaim like Paul, 'May I never boast except in the cross of our Lord Jesus Christ' (Gal. 5:16,18,22,25; 6:14).

'For to me, to live is Christ' (Phil. 1:21). 'I consider everything a loss compared to the surpassing greatness of knowing Christ Jesus my Lord ... I want to know Christ ... I press on towards the goal' (Phil. 3;8,10,14). These are not statements of hyperbole on Paul's part! He expresses what he really believes. 'God placed all things under [Christ's] feet and appointed him to be head over everything for the church which is his body, the fulness of him who fills everything in every way' (Eph. 1:22). Paul had already revealed in chapter 1 God's cosmic purpose 'to bring all things in heaven and on earth together under one head, even Christ' (Eph. 1:10). Colossians further clarifies the Olympian place of Christ: 'All things were created by him [Christ] and for him. He is before all things, and in him all things hold together ... he is the beginning ... so that in everything he might have the supremacy ...' (Col. 1:16-18). The New Testament concludes with the trumpet sound of his supremacy resounding throughout the book of Revelation, the words of him who is 'the First and the Last' (Rev. 1:17; 2:8, etc.).

During a sabbatical on St Simons Island most days marched to their finale clothed in sunset colours. As evening approached, people would drive down to the shore and sit with their cars facing westward. Even those out walking on the beach kept turning their eyes towards the west to follow the subtle changes from crimson to mauve, from salmon to pink and burgundy. Today, as in New Testament days, the Holy Spirit directs our attention to the radiant glory of Christ.

The 'floodlight ministry' of the Spirit

Packer writes of 'the floodlight ministry' of the Holy Spirit illumi-
nating the marvel of Christ and his work of redemption like a
floodlight on a building. When we see floodlights we don't turn our
attention to the lights to try and make out their candle-power. We
focus on what they illuminate. Packer goes on to say, 'It is as if the
Spirit stands behind us, throwing light over our shoulder, on Jesus,
who stands facing us. The Spirit's message to us is never, "Look at
me…" but always, "Look at him, and see his glory" … The Spirit,
we might say, is the matchmaker, the celestial marriage broker,
whose role it is to bring us and Christ together and ensure that we
stay together.'[3]

Even in the fellowship we share with the triune God, the Holy
Spirit maintains a floodlight ministry. True, the New Testament
does speak of 'the fellowship of the Spirit' in several places (Phil.
2:1; 2 Cor. 13:14). But Greek scholar Kenneth Wuest points out that
even here the Holy Spirit works to deepen our companionship with
Christ. Bear with a lengthy but extremely perceptive quotation that
calls us back from the brink of false doctrine and erroneous experience: 'There is a danger of thinking that the phrase "fellowship of
the Spirit" means "companionship with the Spirit". Right here is
where some leave the path of sound doctrine and practice. They seek
the Holy Spirit and His fulness for His sake alone… Thus they lay
themselves open to the snares of Satan and the control of evil spirits.
There is no such thing in Scripture as the believer's fellowship or
companionship with the Spirit comparable to the believer's fellowship or companionship with the Lord Jesus. The Holy Spirit's
ministry is to glorify the Son, and in doing that He always calls the
believer's attention to the Lord Jesus, never to Himself. He keeps
Himself in the background. The Lord Jesus must always be central
in the life of the saint. He is the One with whom we have fellowship
in the commonly accepted usage of the word today. The Holy Spirit
makes this possible. Sir Robert Anderson's words are to the point
here: "In proportion therefore as mind and heart are fixed on Christ,
we may count on the Spirit's presence and power, but if we make the
Holy Ghost Himself the object of our aspiration and worship, some
false spirit may counterfeit the true and take us for a prey."

'The association which the correctly instructed saint has with the
Holy Spirit is in the form of a moment-by-moment conscious

dependence upon Him, a trust in Him for His guidance and strength, and a yielding to Him for His ministry of putting sin out of the life and keeping it out, and of radiating the beauty of the Lord Jesus through his every thought, word, and deed, this together with a co-operation with Him which takes the form of a mutual interest and active participation in the things of God.'[4]

Self-effacement undergirds the Holy Spirit's ministry of exalting Christ. Instead of drawing us into fellowship with himself he expedites fellowship with Christ. Of course, without the Holy Spirit we can experience neither fellowship with Jesus nor the ministry of spiritual gifts. Balance is crucial.

Nowhere is the floodlight ministry of the Holy Spirit more necessary than in the moonscape of charismatic and gift confusion. As we search the Scriptures for the gifts of the Spirit, let us pray for that selfsame Spirit to remind us frequently of the glory of Christ. The Spirit delights to do this because he, more than any, knows that spiritual gifts are gifts given by the ascended Son of God.

II. The Son of God and the source of gifts

The eloquence of Peter and the spectacle of fiery tongues that arrested the attention of bystanders at Pentecost continues to capture the imagination of believers. Many cry out for similar evidences of the poured-out Spirit today. Too often, however, they bypass Christ by failing to remember that the Spirit's descent was at the behest of the ascended Christ. Peter explained: 'Exalted to the right hand of God, he has received from the Father the promised Holy Spirit and has poured out what you now see and hear' (Acts 2:33).

The ascended Christ was and continues to be the source of the poured-out Spirit with all his fruits, graces and gifts. Even Pentecost, the most dramatic of the Spirit's appearances, focused on Christ, about whom Peter declared, 'God has made this Jesus, whom you have crucified, both Lord and Christ' (Acts 2:36). Think about it! The Holy Spirit himself directed Luke, the author of the book of Acts, to record that Pentecost, the most Spirit-anointed event in church history, was a Christ-centred event.

The New Testament consistently maintains this balance. Paul wrote that the measure of grace, in the form of gifts of the Spirit, which each of us receives is due to the decision of Christ: 'To each one of us grace has been given as Christ apportioned it' (Eph. 4:7). 'When he ascended on high ... and gave gifts to men,' the Son of God poured out undeserved tokens of his love in the form of spiritual gifts (Eph. 4:8). Believers receive their gift or gifts from the seated Christ. Christ is the gift-giver while the Holy Spirit is the gift-bearer.

This need not astonish us. The New Testament testifies that every facet of redemption is mediated to us 'in Christ' (see, for example, Rom. 8:1; 5:1-2; 3:24; 6:4-6).

Christ taught his disciples about the relationship he would always bear to them: 'I am the vine; you are the branches. If a man remains in me and I in him, he will bear much fruit; apart from me you can do nothing' (John 15:5). Fruitfully gifted ministry, no less than a fruitfully holy life, owes its success to the energy that flows from Christ the source.

Jesus is the 'light of the world', 'the bread of life' and the 'living water' — that is, the fount of all holy effects and all sustaining and refreshing ministries. Whenever we genuinely minister in his name by shining forth the true light, distributing the living bread, or giving the water of life, it will be through the Spirit as channel from the Son as source. What we do will only be 'acceptable to God through Jesus Christ' (1 Peter 2:5).

Christ is the Bridegroom and we are the bride. But I am sure you have been to weddings where a bridesmaid or other attendant stole the limelight! It would be just as ill-fitting for us to forget our heavenly Bridegroom and boast about our gifts, our ministries, or our successes. Like the bride in Song of Solomon, our fascination should be with him.

Michael Green, although not an author with whom I completely concur, is right when he laments, 'In contrast to a few years ago when one would rarely hear any teaching on the Holy Spirit, it seems that some people can speak of nothing else these days. There is a cult of the Holy Spirit, and often it has precious little to say about Jesus.' It 'tends to squeeze him out of the picture', by implying that 'allegiance to Jesus is only the lower reaches of the Christian life, the heights of which belong to the Holy Spirit'.[5]

As we continue to pursue the discovery of gifts our attention needs to remain focused upon Jesus Christ, because he is the source of gifts and graces and because we must render an ongoing account to him concerning the development and use of our gifts.

III. The Son of God and accountability for gifts

As Christians we must render an ongoing accountability to Christ who 'is the head of the body, the church ... so that in everything he might have the supremacy' (Col. 1:18). God's mysterious purpose includes not only the church, but is 'to bring all things in heaven and on earth together under one head, even Christ' (Eph. 1:10). This process of extending the pragmatic authority of Christ over everything corresponds in great measure to the growth of the church. Even now, Christ is seated at God's right hand, where 'God placed all things under his feet and appointed him to be head over everything for the church, which is his body...' (Eph. 1:20-23).

The authority of Christ over the universe, however, remains contested by dark forces outside the church, even while his lordship is openly acknowledged in the church. Outside the church men and women live their lives, more or less, in rebellion against God. But when sinners bow to Christ as Lord and join local groups of believers, they accept his acknowledged authority. Once they become part of the church, converted sinners acknowledge that everything, including the exercise of gifts, is subject to his authority.

Christ 'gave gifts to men ... so that the body of Christ may be built up until we all reach ... the fulness of Christ ... who is the Head' (Eph. 4:8,12-15). The exercise of gifts leads to the numerical and spiritual growth of the church. Body growth, in turn, is manifest when God's people become more Christ-like and more submissive to Christ as Head by conducting all ministry under his authority.

The metaphoric 'headship' of Christ symbolizes his position of absolute supremacy for,

'God exalted him to the highest place...
that at the name of Jesus every knee should bow...
and every tongue confess that Jesus Christ is Lord,
    to the glory of God the Father'

(Phil. 2:9-11).

In the church we become — or at least we should — the first to bow to his lordship. Gifts become endowments we use to serve him, by extending his kingdom — not our own. They should not be considered personal property. We shall ultimately have to give an account to him for their use.

The parables teach accountability

Many parables teach accountability for everything God has entrusted to us, including our spiritual gifts. How the parables of the virgins' oil, the talents, the pounds and the sheep and the goats all relate to the subject of spiritual gifts will be discussed in chapters 4 and 5. Suffice it to say, at this point, that these parables generally teach that God entrusts abilities and opportunities and brings needy people to our doorstep so that we can exercise stewardship. The master in the parables who has gone on a long journey, the ascended Christ, will return. During the interval before his return, his servants are to 'watch' by meeting spiritual needs and 'put this money to work ... until I come back'. Upon his return there is a time of accounting. 'For we must all appear before the judgement seat of Christ' (2 Cor. 5:10).

Building on the foundation

In 1 Corinthians 3 Paul reminds us that 'Each one should be careful how he builds.' Why? Because a day of accounting is approaching in which our 'work will be shown for what it is, because the Day will bring it to light. It will be revealed with fire, and the fire will test the quality of each man's work' (1 Cor. 3:10,13).

Many things test the hidden qualities of workmanship in buildings. Hurricanes and earthquakes call buildings into account. What a terrible accounting of shoddy builders there ought to have been in Soviet Armenia in the aftermath of the 1988 earthquake that left thousands dead in the rubble of their apartments! The same could be said of builders in the Miami area whose neglect of building code regulations greatly increased the destruction caused by Hurricane Andrew in 1992.

With people, as with buildings, real strength or weakness hides below the surface. On the great Day of Judgement our hidden motivation, whether to serve Christ sincerely as Lord or to promote ourselves, will be revealed. Knowing this, we should be careful that we exercise our spiritual gifts, not for our own aggrandizement, but for the Master's purpose. Of course, if we fail to develop what we have and, like the wicked servant, bury our gifts, that too will be judged.

Spiritual gifts are Christ-centred because they come from Christ as source and are exercised under a continuing accountability to Christ as Head of the church. But Christ is also our supreme model of ministry.

IV. The Son of God and the pattern of gift exercise

Like the Corinthians, we are often tempted to misuse our gifts to enhance our own image. What a contrast we find in the apostle Paul! Although one of the most gifted Christians of all time, Paul reminded the Corinthians of his determination to know 'nothing except Jesus Christ and him crucified' (1 Cor. 2:2). Rather than blow his own trumpet, the apostle chose to call himself 'a servant of Christ Jesus' (Rom.1:1). Fortunately, Paul derived his pattern of ministry from Christ, the suffering Servant.

The model of servanthood

Paul had no doubt heard how the mother of James and John had sought a high position for her sons in the promised kingdom. In the context of this blatant, albeit misguided, attempt to jockey for position in his future cabinet, Christ proceeded to lay down the parameters of Christian ministry: 'Jesus called them together and said, "You know that the rulers of the Gentiles lord it over them, and their high officials exercise authority over them. Not so with you. Instead, whoever wants to become great among you must be your servant"' (Matt. 20:25-26). Genuine Christian ministry clashes dramatically with worldly patterns of service, in which men and women compete for position, prestige and power.

Pictures of servanthood, drawn from the practice of slavery, stand as the enduring models of Christian service. Christ taught, 'Whosoever wants to be first must be your slave — just as the Son of Man did not come to be served, but to serve, and to give his life a ransom for many' (Matt. 20:27-28; Mark 10:45).

Two of the most remarkable Christians in my home church, both gone now, were church custodians. That is a lowly job: sweeping floors; cleaning toilets; washing windows. Both were remarkable for their cheerful approach to service. One welcomed visitors to the Sunday service with a cheerful word of encouragement. 'Isn't the Lord wonderful?' he would invariably say, with eyes that twinkled and a grip like steel.

The other caretaker also exuded Christian joy. He loved his job of cleaning the building. No task was too difficult for him to attempt. He always felt that his salary was more than he deserved! These two exemplify for me the spirit of servanthood. Alongside their example I hang in memory's gallery the picture of deacons who visit, Sunday School teachers who love noisy pupils and faithful pastors of small churches.

Jesus indelibly engraved the charter of servanthood on the memory of his disciples by taking up a towel and a basin and, to the disciples' astonishment, proceeding to wash their feet! Peter cried, 'Lord, are you going to wash my feet? ... No...' Jesus gently explained that this service was an evidence of identification with him. After completing his circuit of the disciples' dirty feet, he proceeded to explain what he had done: 'You call me "Teacher" and "Lord", and rightly so, for that is what I am. Now that I, your Lord and Teacher, have washed your feet, you also should wash one another's feet. I have set you an example that you should do as I have done for you' (John 13:3-15).

The towel and the basin are the enduring symbols of true ministry. When the Holy Spirit imparts gifts for service in the kingdom, he does not call believers to positions of power or influence, but to a life of humble service. Christ's model of servanthood applies just as much in the exercise of platform gifts, such as preaching or teaching, as it does in the ranks of those with serving gifts, such as mercy or helpfulness. Christ calls all believers to serve in the humble ranks of foot-washers anonymous.

Michael Green writes in a similar vein: 'Authentic Christian experience is stamped with the mark of the Servant. In the enthusiasm of the renewed emphasis on the Spirit these days he is sometimes presented as the pathway to power in the Christian life, the secret of success in personal living and service. There is truth in this, but it is only a half truth. The other side of the coin is ... the willingness to suffer which marked our Lord... This church at Corinth was infatuated with the theology of the Spirit whilst allergic to a theology of the Cross. They revelled in charismatic experiences of the Spirit... Paul comes down immediately like a ton of bricks on the attitude which regards the Spirit as a medium of religious experience or an embodiment of supernatural power, rather than as the vocation to and the equipment for the role of the Servant.'[6]

Serving involves suffering

The Holy Spirit would ever direct our attention to the basin and towel. Christian service is not misty-eyed, armchair piety or self-elevating duty, but the hard and unthankful work of serving. It involves suffering and sacrifice, because this is Jesus' way. Although he was

> '...in the very nature God...
> [He] made himself nothing,
>   taking the form of a servant...
> [He] humbled himself
>   and became obedient to death — even death on a cross!'
>   (Phil 2:6-8).

When we follow Christ we discover our path leads through valleys of sacrifice and suffering. 'For it has been granted to you on behalf of Christ not only to believe on him, but also to suffer for him...' (Phil. 1:29).

The study of spiritual gifts may legitimately proceed only when we plant our feet firmly under the shadow of the cross. Its shadow alone can keep us from an ego-fed cultivation of gifts as rungs on a ladder to success. While, as already noted, the discovery of our gifts produces a great sense of joy and fulfilment, it will also lead through some painful experiences. Let the cross serve to remind us that gifts are not steps on the way up to a higher position, but doorways to the servants' quarters and gateways into the arena of suffering.

Paul, as a 'bond-slave of Christ', understood this lesson well. As a gifted apostle, teacher, preacher, evangelist and shepherd he had no illusions about responsibility without suffering. He wrote, 'For it seems to me that God has put us apostles on display at the end of the procession, like men condemned to die in the arena. We have been made a spectacle ... fools for Christ ... weak ... dishonoured ... we go hungry and thirsty, we are in rags... We work hard with our own hands ... are cursed ... slandered ... we have become the scum of the earth' (1 Cor. 4:9-13).

What a contrast — the greatest ministers the world has ever seen viewed by worldly men as fools instead of occupying places of privilege and power! This theme recurs often in Paul's writings (see 2 Cor. 6:4-10; 11:16-33). Nor was Peter a stranger to this experience (1 Peter 4:13-16).

How foreign to Christ are the symbols of historic church leadership — the mitres, the crowns, the thrones and even, dare I say it, the elevated pulpits of our Protestant churches! And how strange twentieth-century preachers and bishops, with soaring cathedrals, TV empires or gorgeous vestments, seem in comparison with Jesus who took up the basin and towel of service! Oh yes, the symbol of the cross we find everywhere in modern churches, but it is usually forged of gold or idealized as part of the décor!

The way of love

What led Christ to take up a basin and wash feet? What made Paul such a willing slave? Surely the 'more excellent way' of love as described in a chapter sandwiched between two chapters about spiritual gifts (1 Cor. 13). Love is the bottom line of gift exercise. Without it ministry is only 'a resounding gong or a clanging cymbal' (1 Cor. 13:1).

Paul exhorts his readers to 'be imitators of God … and live a life of love, just as Christ loved us and gave himself up for us as a fragrant offering and sacrifice to God' (Eph. 5:1-2). Love for Christ and continued review of his pattern will sustain us in the ups and downs of service. John says, 'We love [him] because he first loved us' (1 John 4:19). It was this boomerang effect of the love of Christ that thrust Paul out in ministry. 'For Christ's love compels us,' he explained. He went on to write about the effect Christ's death for us ought to have on our lives: 'Those who live should no longer live for themselves but for him who died for them' (2 Cor. 5:14,15). Without the love of Christ constraining us, our ministries quickly deteriorate into a series of techniques and tasks lit dimly by the cold artificial light of our fallen egos.

Gifts are discovered, developed and exercised under the shadow of the cross. But what is the purpose of gifts?

V. The Son of God and the purpose of gifts

We read concerning God the Father that 'From him and through him and to him are all things. To him be the glory for ever!' (Rom. 11:36; see also Phil. 4:20). But while the glory of the Father will ultimately permeate the universe, there are many intermediate steps leading to that final goal. In the present age it is the Father's purpose to sum up all things in Christ, that through Christ all the universe might be reconciled to him (Eph. 1:10). As described in Colossians, 'God was pleased to have all his fulness dwell in [Christ] and through him to reconcile to himself all things, whether things on earth or things in heaven...' (Col. 1:19-20).

In achieving this objective, Christ consecrates the church as his agent. He has commissioned it to proclaim the gospel through which reconciliation of all things will be accomplished 'by making peace through his blood'. As Paul states, 'He is the head of the body, the church; he is the beginning and the firstborn from among the dead, so that in everything he might have the supremacy' (Col. 1:18).

Christ-centred church life

This demonstration of the supremacy of Christ is intrinsically linked up with the affairs of his body, the church. Christ rose from the dead and ascended to the Father's right hand, where 'God placed all things under his feet ... for the church' (Eph. 1:22). The spiritual progress of the church goes hand in glove with God's cosmic purpose in Christ. Whatever encourages the development and holiness of this body glorifies Christ and thus contributes to the ultimate glory of God.

No wonder every aspect of church life and witness must be Christ-centred. Showing us the way Paul writes, 'To me, to live is Christ' (Phil. 1:21). 'Whatever was to my profit I now consider loss for the sake of Christ ... compared to the surpassing greatness of knowing Christ Jesus my Lord ... that I may gain Christ ... I want to know Christ' (Phil. 3:7-10). Every Christian ought to echo Paul's earnest desire to know Christ. Christ, then, becomes the focus of all our life and ministry.

Becoming conformed to a Christ-centred pattern of life presupposes a commitment to Christ's purpose for the church. That purpose, among other things, involves the exercise of spiritual gifts. These gifts equip us to minister to one another in the body of Christ. Romans 12:5 informs us that 'In Christ we who are many form one body, and each member belongs to all the others.' With this point established, Paul proceeds to list the various gifts that we use to edify one another and thus promote the kingdom.

An amalgamation of various verses from Ephesians presents us with the same scenario. 'Christ ... gave gifts to men ... to prepare God's people for works of service, so that the body of Christ may be built up until we all reach unity in the faith and in the knowledge of the Son of God and become mature, attaining to the whole measure of the fulness of Christ ... we will in all things grow up into him who is the Head, that is, Christ. From him the whole body ... grows and builds itself up in love, as each part does its work' (Eph. 4:7,8,12-13,15-16).

Christ the source and the goal

Here in capsule form we find the essence of God's purpose for the church. Christ is the *source* of the gifts — they are from him — and Christ is the *goal* of the gifts, for we are to grow up into him. In the process of fulfilling these Christ-centred goals God in Christ is glorified and every believer in the church benefits.

In this light, the development and use of gifts constitute a crucial link that the Spirit uses to bring to fruition God's cosmic purpose. Failure to exercise spiritual gifts limits the development of believers in Christ-likeness! (2 Cor. 3:18). Stunted growth hinders the progress of the kingdom and delays the fulfilment of God's ultimate goal of summing up all things in Christ. Peter describes the exercise of gifts in these very terms: 'Each one should use whatever gift he has received to serve others ... so that in all things God may be praised through Jesus Christ. To him be the glory and the power for ever and ever. Amen' (1 Peter 4:10-11). Gifts exercised to bless one another result in God being exalted in Christ, thus fulfilling God's ultimate purpose.

What a stunning truth! Everything in the redemptive economy is intimately linked together as a chain of pearls that manifest the lustre of God their Creator. Christ is the string that binds together all the different aspects of our redemption, from initial conversion to ultimate glory. He is both source and goal. The Holy Spirit is totally aware of this linkage and promotes our knowledge of it. While the gifts are gifts of the Spirit, in that they are given through the Spirit, they are always given to exalt Christ. The Holy Spirit always moves gifted believers to become more Christ-like themselves and to use their gifts to the same end in others.

The Holy Spirit, himself, will always draw our attention to Christ as the source of our spiritual gifts, as the Master to whom we must give account for their use, as the model of their exercise and as the ultimate goal for which they are to be used.

Conclusion

With spiritual gifts possessing such a breathtaking present relevance and such eternal significance, it is no wonder that the devil seeks to spread confusion. He will try anything to keep Christians from focusing the floodlight of their Spirit-induced exercise of gifts on Jesus Christ, the Lord. He will use any means to keep Christians ignorant of their gifts or stunt their growth in the use of these gifts. He seeks to get them competing with each other instead of complementing each other. He wants us to dissipate our energies in arguments about gifts instead up taking up the basin and towel of ministry. He wants churches to muddle on with the majority of believers as spectators and a few eminent men trying to juggle all the ministry roles. He desires that we ever teeter between pride on the one hand and a sense of inadequacy on the other. He knows that if he fails, believers will unite to engage in mutual edification and widespread evangelism that will help the church to become a beacon banishing his darkness.

Several years ago I was fascinated by watching on television President Reagan yielding up the sinews of power to President-elect George Bush. As he and his wife left the White House to take up their private lives once more, Nancy Reagan seemed especially effusive in her affection for several faceless men who saw them off. Who were these men? Why were their faces not instantly recognizable after eight years of association with the Reagans? Their job had required them to remain in the shadows while President Reagan lived in the spotlight. They were the secret service men who had so faithfully and carefully watched over the lives of the first family. Nancy Reagan knew that her peace of mind and the safety of her husband had been in their hands. She deeply appreciated them.

Those who receive spiritual gifts from Christ need to exercise a similar shadow ministry. The spotlight is on Christ. Like those secret service men, believers should spend their energies serving him, not stealing the spotlight. The welfare of his body, the church, is at stake!

As we press on to explore the exact nature of each gift in the chapters that follow, we must carry with us a sense of destiny and perspective. Let us never forget that spiritual gifts have a central significance in God's unfolding purpose to glorify Jesus Christ. Amazingly, they also meet men and women at the point of their own need!

4.
Spiritual gifts and charismatic experience

Since I do not intend to cover the sign gifts, let me clarify, before I go any further, why I have chosen to exclude them from this study. It is not as though I have not considered their claims. Soon after our arrival in Pakistan, Mary Helen and I witnessed a 'charismatic revival'. The churches among whom our mission ministered gathered for a three-day spiritual convention of preaching and prayer. During the convention, in small groups of those predisposed to the 'Pentecostal' experience, 'tongues' broke out. Many raised their hands. Quite a few claimed, later, that they had received the fulness of the Spirit with speaking in tongues. Enthusiasts predicted that a great renewal of holiness would ensure. A goodly number professed faith in Christ.

Unfortunately expectations were dashed. The experience left the churches bruised and bleeding. In the place of greater holiness and humility it bred spiritual pride and division. Those who had professed faith showed little or no evidence of genuine conversion.

In the aftermath, some demanded that the unfettered speaking in tongues be allowed in worship. A number clamoured for healing meetings. When church leaders explained why they could not accept these requests, some of these new charismatics separated to start new groups. From that point on, the energies of the churches, instead of being directed into worship, teaching and evangelism, have often been dissipated by trying to stave off some new attack on their membership. Radical and even heretical groups have sprung up in most of the towns. Pentecostals and far-out groups from abroad jumped into the fray to further stir the pot. More and more aberrant groups confuse the Pakistani church scene with their claims. Instead of generating more evangelism among the vast Muslim majority, these groups have ignored Islam to concentrate their efforts on attracting sheep from other folds — often using monetary and material inducements just when missions have been trying so hard to develop indigenous support.

Even so, as missionaries in a tough Muslim land, we joined many others in praying for extra dynamism and effect to attend our efforts. We realized that aberrations can attend even genuine revival movements. Fairness dictated that we search the Scriptures for ourselves. When John Wimber and his friends postulated power evangelism, with its appeal for a renewal of gifts such as healing and miracles, many of us wondered whether this could be the edge we needed to reach Islam.[1] Vineyard Churches, affiliated with John Wimber, began to spread in North America and around the world. Missionaries pondered his ideas. Very few chose to go along with the whole Wimber scenario. Yet many did begin to feel that miraculous healing could be the missing secret of Muslim evangelism. Unfortunately, very little has been accomplished.

Neither power evangelism nor the charismatic movement have lived up to their claims. Instead, the search for ecstatic experiences and new power has distracted many from developing the ministries so sorely needed by the church. After a variety of experiences and years of study into the charismatic phenomenon I have concluded that the historic theological position is correct — signs and wonders have ceased. I believe that when God fulfilled the purpose for which he had created the charismatic gifts, he ceased to bestow them. Instead of something new, we need a revival of the preaching of the gospel of Jesus where power resides in the cross, not in phenomena. We need perseverance, prayer and faith. We need old-fashioned personal evangelism. We need church-planting. And we desperately need a renewal in every-member ministry.

What do we understand by the gifts of healing, miracles, tongues and the interpretation of tongues? These are the big guns of the Pentecostal and charismatic movement. In spite of their pivotal nature in the life of these groups, they are only mentioned in one of the passages dealing with gifts — 1 Corinthians chapters 12-14.

Miracles

Biblically, a miracle is an extraordinary work of God's power, in which God supersedes the natural laws of the universe to effect an action wholly supernatural. A miracle occurs when something happens that is inexplicable by natural law. God, of course, providentially works through the events of day-to-day life. Technically, however, neither providential circumstances nor answers to prayer qualify as miracles. Crossing the Red Sea on dry land, the collapse of the walls of Jericho, water from a rock, manna in the desert, fire from heaven on Elijah's altar, the feeding of the 5,000, the healing of a man born blind, the raising of the dead — these are miracles.

When I claim that the gift of miracles has ceased, I am not saying that God cannot work miracles. God works a miracle whenever he overrules the fallen will of a sinful person in regeneration. Rather, I claim that God does not now endue men with special power to effect miracles as he did to Moses, Elijah, Peter, Philip and Paul. The *gift of miracles* has ceased. With the exception of regeneration, miracles are now rare.

Healing

In Scripture, healing often exhibited miraculous characteristics. The miraculous nature of these occurrences sets them on a plane qualitatively distinct from that of healing as practised, even in charismatic circles, today. John MacArthur points out that six distinctives mark the healing of Jesus and the apostles.

1. Healing occurred by word or touch without theatrics, programmes or any specially prepared environment. Why don't modern healers frequent hospitals and needy regions of the Third World? (Matt. 8:2-3).

2. Healing occurred instantaneously (Matt. 8:13).

3. Healing was complete — total — without any period of recuperation (Luke 4:39).

4. Healing was indiscriminate, not limited by a schedule or screening process. Everybody could be healed (Luke 4:40).

5. Healing dealt with organic diseases and conditions — crippled legs, withered hands, blind eyes, palsy, leprosy — not functional diseases such as headaches, heart palpitation, lower back pain, etc.

6. They raised the dead. Healers today don't visit funeral parlours (Luke 7:11-16). [2]

God heals today in answer to prayer. Healing usually occurs through the acceleration of the body's natural healing agents. Medicine or the intervention of a doctor may be involved. James 5 does instruct us — if we feel constrained by faith — to call for the elders of the church to pray over us. God does not expect us to look around for a special person with the gift of healing. The biblical record would lead us to conclude that he does not condone healing meetings or healing campaigns. The *gift of healing* has ceased.

Tongues

The gift of tongues (and their interpretation) is mentioned only in the First Epistle to the Corinthians and the book of Acts. Two kinds of tongues make their appearance.

In the book of Acts — certainly at Pentecost — people spoke in *known* tongues. God used tongues at Pentecost to speak to the ethnically diverse crowd gathered in Jerusalem: 'Each one heard them speaking in his own language' (Acts 2:6).

The gift mentioned in 1 Corinthians, by contrast, appears to have been the ability to speak in *unknown* tongues. It represents a kind of ecstatic utterance for devotional purposes. 'For anyone who speaks in a tongue does not speak to men but to God. Indeed, no one understands him; he utters mysteries with his spirit' (1 Cor. 14:2). Since tongues were unintelligible to others in the church, Paul insisted that whenever someone spoke in tongues, 'Someone must interpret' (1 Cor. 14:27-28).

One similarity exists between these two kinds of tongues: both 'are a sign, not for believers but for unbelievers' (1Cor. 14:22).

Having sought quickly to clarify these four charismatic gifts, let me go on to give some of the reasons why I believe that they have ceased. We can approach this subject from two perspectives: that of sovereign history — the inspired record God has given of how he operates in history — and that of supernatural Christian experience — the main focus of God's supernatural activity in our world today. Treatment of this subject will have to be very limited.

I. Reasons from sovereign history

1. God's design to use natural means

We tend to focus on spectacular events in history. Supernatural interventions of God, in which he sets aside the laws of nature that he created, are actually very rare. For every fording of the Red Sea on dry land, millions of people got their feet wet. For every rock smitten in the wilderness to provide water miraculously, thousands of wells were dug by the sweat of human effort. For every time Jesus miraculously fed thousands, ordinary people cooked millions of meals with a pot and a fire.

God normally provides food through means he has ordained: the ploughing and planting of the farmer, the grinding of the wheat, the distribution of food through merchants, the baking of the bread. From creation God designed that we provide for ourselves using common, everyday means. If, like Israel in the wilderness, we yearn for the spectacular, we shall tend to adjust badly to ordinary life. Indeed, a longing for the miraculous devalues the glory of God's providence.

2. God's design in supernatural events

What was God's purpose in events such as the parting of the Red Sea, Jonah's stint in the belly of the fish, or the miracles of Jesus? Peter declares, 'Jesus of Nazareth was a man accredited by God to you by miracles, wonders and signs, which God did among you through him' (Acts 2:22). The rest of Scripture affirms this general principle. The author of Hebrews warns us about neglecting our salvation when God has gone to such extreme lengths to confirm its authenticity: 'God also testified to it by signs, wonders and various miracles, and gifts of the Holy Spirit distributed according to his will' (Heb. 2:4).

Obviously, miraculous events served to authenticate God's testimony about the identity of his Son and the wonder of our redemption. They also served to confirm revelation inspired through Moses, the prophets and the apostles. (Considerable space will be given to this matter in the chapters on the apostolic and prophetic gifts.) Once confirmation had occurred, miracles as a sign were no longer needed. The word 'sign' is used seventy times in the New Testament. Sixty of these refer to miracles (e.g., John 2:11). Hence a miracle is a sign that something is genuine. Paul calls tongues a sign. For this reason I label the charismatic gifts 'sign gifts'. (See Mark 16:20; John 5:36; 10:37-38; 20:30-31; Acts 2:33; Rom. 15:19 for further passages on this point.)

3. The danger of the spectacular

Charismatics claim that signs and wonders enhance church life and witness. If so, why did they not have a positive effect on Israel during their wilderness wanderings? Although they daily witnessed God's spectacular provision of their necessities, the Israelites lusted after the diet of Egypt. They kept arousing God to anger by grumbling and even demanding greater miracles. Paul warns about failing to learn from their history (see 1 Cor. 10).

Jesus too talked about the subtle dangers inherent in the miraculous. At first, his miracles advanced his popularity. Crowds thronged to hear him. At the beginning of his second year of ministry, he began to talk about the cross. The crowds dissipated quickly (see John 6:2,14-15,28-30,53,64,66). John comments that although he performed many 'miraculous signs in their presence, they still would not believe in him' (John 12: 37). Jesus warns us, 'An evil and adulterous generation craves for a sign; and yet no sign shall be given to it but the sign of Jonah the prophet [i.e. death and resurrection]' (Matt. 12:39, NASV). He knew that no necessary connection exists between seeing a wonder and becoming a believer, or even a better disciple. Our Lord speaks of a future generation in which 'False Christs and false prophets will appear and perform great signs and miracles to deceive even the elect — if that were possible' (Matt. 24:24). Could he be speaking of our day?

Only 1 Corinthians mentions the spectacular gifts. Moreover this epistle bristles with problems, including the abuse of gifts. Unfortunately, in our day as well, an emphasis on these gifts often precipitates the very problems that divided and stunted the Corinthian church.

Signs and wonders are dangerous. Far from encouraging faith, they arouse the baser instincts, create unrealistic expectations and derail real discipleship.

4. The decline of the abnormal

Signs and wonders occurred during three main periods: the Mosaic age, the prophetic era which followed Samuel and the time of Christ. Miracles did not occur in all epochs. 500 years passed without miracles before Moses arose to lead Israel. Following Joshua we look in vain for signs and wonders for a full 600 years until the rise of prophets such as Elijah. Miracles also ceased during the 400 silent years leading up to Jesus' birth.

Miracles occurred periodically, because they fulfilled a limited rôle in God's economy. God used them to authenticate crucial revelations of truth — not to satisfy some ongoing supernatural need in mankind. Even during the life of Christ we find miracles clustered around the time of his birth and during his first year of popular ministry. The last two years leading up to the cross showed a decline in their occurrence. In like manner we discover their decline as the book of Acts progresses. If we arrange the passages dealing with the gifts according to when they were written we find the same pattern. Paul wrote 1 Corinthians, with its mention of the sign gifts, around A.D. 55. Next comes Romans and then Ephesians, both with no mention of these gifts. Peter, who wrote his first epistle in about A.D. 66, ignores charismatic gifts. We find the same silence in early church history. We must conclude that the supernatural gifts occurred periodically in history and ceased after the New Testament became fully established.

5. The descent of the Spirit

As predicted by Joel, the descent of the Holy Spirit at Pentecost initiated a new era. This climactic event shut the door on the old covenant and opened a new era centred on the church. Signs and wonders drew attention to the crucial nature of this transition.

The birth of the church marked a fundamental realignment in God's programme. In the Old Testament, the Jewish people constituted God's covenant nation. Under the New Testament, God welcomes people from every tongue and tribe and nation into the church. Such a revolutionary change flew in the face of centuries of Jewish tradition. It aroused massive prejudice. In other periods of transition, such as that between the patriarchal era and the Mosaic epoch, God attested his new approach by signs and wonders. We are not surprised, then, when we find unusual events authenticating the birth of the church. God not only poured out the Spirit at Pentecost but on three other occasions: among the Samaritans (Acts 8:14-17), in the Roman family of Cornelius (Acts 10:44; 11:15-17) and upon Greeks in Ephesus (Acts 19:1-7). Tongues occurred on each of these occasions.

These three further Pentecosts mark particular steps God took to transform his mono-ethnic family into the multi-ethnic church. Their unusual nature served to convince reluctant Jewish Christians to accept a Gentile church. Far from promising a repetition of these spectacular phenomena, or encouraging us to tarry for the Spirit — to seek some kind of Pentecostal experience, Peter interpreted the event as a proof that the indwelling Spirit was now guaranteed to all repentant sinners at the time of their conversion (Acts 2:38-39; cf. Rom. 8:9). If we try to duplicate any of these Pentecostal experiences, we deny their historic importance and contradict Peter's interpretation.

6. The development of Scripture

God used signs and wonders to authenticate each significant addition to his developing corpus of truth. He did so at Sinai, among the prophets of Israel and in the case of the New Testament. The early church did not have a complete Bible as we have today. For several centuries the church endured intense persecution. They had to rely on scattered Gospels and epistles. Until that body of new revelation was incorporated into the canon of Scripture and became readily available to all, individual books were open to question. We can readily appreciate that God, in tune with the way he authenticated other revelations, arranged for signs and wonders to attest the character of those who wrote the New Testament books. As already mentioned, we see more miraculous activity early in the church's history and less as time passes. (Trace the occurrences of miracles in the book of Acts and note that only in the early epistles — James and 1 Corinthians — are charismatic gifts and healing mentioned.) Since we now have the complete revelation of God's will for human conduct (2 Tim. 3:16-17) attesting signs are no longer necessary.

II. Reasons from supernatural Christian experience

Signs and wonders, by their very nature, attract attention. Modern TV producers understand how an emphasis on the spectacular generates an ever-increasing pressure to raise the stakes. Viewers' appetites become jaded. Writers vie for ratings by throwing in more murders, more adultery and more stunts.

In the kingdom, we cannot afford to feed our carnal appetite for the spectacular nor be distracted from the real issues. An emphasis on tongues, healing and miracles tends to distract believers from the real focus of God's work in this age. At least five things become devalued in the process.

1. The wonder of conversion

The real sign of the Spirit at work in this age can be found wherever sinners respond to the gospel. The depravity, the darkness, the bondage and the deceitfulness of the human heart can only be overcome by the miraculous intervention of the Spirit. When the gospel is preached in apostolic power, sinners fall under conviction. The Holy Spirit arouses a longing for Christ which issues in repentance and faith. Sinners are reborn.

Enamoured by Christ's miracles, Nicodemus sought out the Master. Christ quickly turned his attention instead to his need to be born again. We must allow nothing to divert our attention from the wonder that we feel when we see someone like the Watergate conspirator Chuck Colson bowing to Christ. The conversion of head-hunters in Papua, the transformation of Quichua Indians in Ecuador, the salvation of Iranians, the regeneration of a materialistic

Wall Street broker — nothing can compare with these signs and wonders!

2. The witness of holiness

Even though they fulfilled a necessary role in redemptive history, the excitement that signs and wonders generated was extremely superficial. Disdaining their hollow plaudits, Jesus said to his followers, 'If anyone would come after me he must deny himself and take up his cross daily.' He demanded exacting discipleship demonstrated by the sign of spiritual fruitfulness. Warning against false prophets appearing in sheep's clothing, he called for holiness. The real confirming signs of genuine faith are manifested love, integrity, purity, good works and holiness.

3. The warfare of Christian living

An emphasis on external signs and wonders distracts us from preparing for spiritual warfare. We must focus on the real conflict that takes place in the minds and hearts of men and women. We are in a cosmic conflict, 'fighting against principalities and powers, the rulers of the darkness of this world'. If we keep emphasizing external manifestations of God's power, we may fail to develop the invisible weapons we need to succeed. To prepare for this conflict we must put on the armour of light.

In this age of instant rice and frozen dinners we look for short cuts to spiritual power by toying with the spectacular gifts. We long for power. It is no accident that John Wimber entitled his books *Power Evangelism* and *Power Healing*. Still, there are no short cuts to spiritual effectiveness through some mystical experience of power. Jesus' way is the way of the cross. There will be suffering. There will be trials. Those who persevere in holiness, in spite of sickness and weakness — these know real spiritual power

Too many blame their temperamental sins on the influence of demons. They fail to accept responsibility, confess their sins and apply the discipline necessary to overcome. They beat about for some instant road to sanctification. Sometimes they resort to calling for an exorcist. How sad to trivialize the very serious challenge of demon activity by seeing a demon under every bush! There is no substitute for the Spirit-empowered and disciplined exercise of the means of grace (see Eph 6:10-20; Rom. 5:3-5; Phil. 1:29-30).

4. The work of prayer

While we all realize the crucial importance of prayer, we tend to shrink from its discipline. Prayer is hard work. Answers may be long delayed. Again we look for short cuts. We seek external manifestations to bolster our invisible faith. Jesus, however, rebuked Doubting Thomas by commending those who believe even though they do not see.

Rather than giving our energies to the development of the very questionable charismatic gifts, why not give ourselves to developing the supernatural work of prayer? Jesus said, 'Truly, truly, I say to you, if you shall ask the Father for anything, he will give it to you in my name... Ask, and you will receive, that your joy may be full' (John 16:23,24, NASV). Of course, our requests must be consistent with the will of God and promote the glory of Christ in order to be answered. On our knees — that is where the real supernatural events of this kingdom era take place.

5. The way of normal means

God is the Creator and Sustainer of the world in which we live. As already noted, an over-emphasis on the supernatural devalues the God-ordained importance of normal means. God has providentially provided that work yield wages, wages be used to purchase food, health be the result of a balance of exercise and good food and, in the realm of the kingdom, conversions come about when people spend time witnessing. We may think longingly of the Garden of Eden when Adam and Eve could pick fruit right off the trees. With a view to the poor and destitute in our world, we may pray for God to provide miraculously for them as he did by the Sea of Galilee. But it is not going to happen. God expects us to use the means we have: to give sacrificially of our income and to organize practical relief efforts.

We may hope that our children grow up to be strong Christians in spite of our busyness and neglect, but God expects us to train them up daily in the things of God.

Perhaps we long for some spiritual crisis to usher us into the 'deeper life'. We may wistfully hope for a dream or vision that will suddenly illumine our minds to the deep things of God. God, however, expects us to apply diligent principles of Bible study and devotion.

We may think longingly of the Day of Pentecost when 3,000 responded to Peter's message. He probably didn't even have to prepare the sermon! Normally, however, to reach non-Christians, God uses Christians who have already established a friendly relationship with them over a period of time. Instead of encouraging us perpetually to seek some shortcut to sanctification and effectiveness, God purposes that we apply the normal means he has provided for us in every area of life.

Conclusion

An emphasis on the charismatic gifts is misplaced. Indeed, I believe they have ceased. I have sought to establish this conclusion from both sovereign history and supernatural Christian experience. What we need is a return to the cultivation of the normal gifts, the non-spectacular — but God-ordained — gifts of the Spirit. While conjecture and debate about signs and miracles may be fascinating — even necessary in its place — what we really need is a revival of ministry in all its variety.

God's people need the more immediate comfort to be found when the love of Christ is applied in the sixteen or so directions defined by the non-controversial gifts. The lonely need hospitality. Those who are hurting need mercy. The puzzled need wisdom. The lost need evangelism. The troubled need shepherding. The unorganized need leadership. And since God works in our world by his providence, our abilities and talents will bear some relationship to these divine endowments for ministry.

5.
Gifts and talents

Michelangelo pushed a block of granite down the street. 'A curious neighbour sitting lazily on the porch of his house called him and enquired why he laboured so over an old piece of stone. Michelangelo is reported to have answered, "Because there is an angel in that rock that wants to come out."'[1]

Elizabeth O'Connor compares the discovery of our spiritual gifts to sculpturing: 'We ask to know the will of God without guessing that his will is written into our very beings. We perceive that will when we discern our gifts... Every person has the task of releasing angels by shaping and transfiguring the raw materials that lie about... Whenever we struggle with what we are to do in life, we are struggling to uncover our talent or gift.'[2]

I believe she is substantially right. The Spirit takes the raw material we possess, our talents and skills, experiences and training, and sculpts our spiritual gift. But what connection can there be between talents and spiritual gifts?

The pastor of a typical evangelical church, to which we shall refer several times in the course of our study of the various gifts, teaches a class on spiritual gifts every Sunday. The class contains a cross-section of Christians. Musical talent comes naturally to Ann. Megan has little time for anything but her two toddlers and her home. Ron runs a successful small business. The teaching on spiritual gifts has, on the one hand, intrigued him and, on the other, puzzled him. He rejoices to learn about the variety of giftedness inspired by the Holy Spirit in the body of Christ. He is challenged to place his all on the altar of Christ-centred service. But he wonders what possible angel could be inside his block of granite trying to come out.

Ron served his apprenticeship as a tool and die-maker before working his way up to own a small company. In the process he took evening classes in administration and finance where he discovered a flair for business. He is a member of the voluntary fire brigade and loves to hunt and fish. Five years ago, when he was thirty-two, the honesty and witness of one of his die-makers led to his conversion. Since joining the church he has been a steward and helped with church finances. Now he is perplexed.

He mulls over the whole issue as he drives home with his family. 'What possible spiritual gift could a tool and die-maker have? Is there any connection between my experience in business, my courses in administration and finance and my love for the outdoors? What has my voluntary work with the fire brigade got to do with it?'

Some Christians contend that there is no connection between natural talents and spiritual gifts. Ronald Baxter, in a book with a profusion of valuable quotations on the subject, cites Harry Ironside: 'Natural brilliancy or ability is not to be confounded with divinely-bestowed gift.'[3] Baxter buttresses his own belief that there is little connection between our supernatural and our natural gifts by quotations from a number of scholars, including J. Dwight Pentecost.[4]

In all fairness, he balances his own belief by citing scholars with the opposite view. He quotes John Stott: 'Is it not *a priori* unlikely that God will give a spiritual gift of teaching to a believer who in pre-conversion days could not teach for taffy?'[5]

Baxter also quotes from Charles Ryrie who writes, 'To covet the better gifts is not a matter of sitting down and conjuring up enough faith to be able to receive them out of the blue. It is a matter of diligent self-preparation. For instance, if one covets the gift of teaching, he will undoubtedly have to spend many years developing that gift. The Holy Spirit is sovereign in the giving of gifts, but in the development of them He works through human beings with their desires, limitations, ambitions, and the like.'[6] He also quotes John Walvoord in similar vein.[7]

Some considerable difference of opinion exists concerning whether talents and abilities are in any way related to spiritual gifts. Some say there is no connection. Others see a little connection, while still others trace a very close connection. We need to settle this crucial question if we are to understand the relationship between our spiritual gifts and our natural abilities.

In large measure, the confusion can be cleared up by a study of stewardship in both Testaments. Many of our misunderstandings of doctrine and practice relate to our misunderstanding of the essential continuity between Old and New Testaments. This is especially true with regard to the relationship between the Old Testament teaching on the stewardship of human abilities and the New Testament teaching on spiritual gifts. To demonstrate this connection we begin at creation.

I. The stewardship of creation

In the beginning God created man and woman in his own image. This human likeness to God is admirably described in the *Westminster Confession:* 'He created man, male and female, with reasonable and immortal souls, endued with knowledge, righteousness, and true holiness, after His own image...'[8]

God created man in his own *moral* likeness. He also gave to man *personality* — the ability to think, feel and to make decisions. A third likeness is also inherent in the text: 'God said, "Let us make man in our image ... and let them rule over the fish of the sea and the birds of the air, over the livestock, over all the earth..."' (Gen. 1:26). Mankind, as God's representative, was to *exercise dominion over creation*. This latent ability to exercise rulership in a creative and developing way is part of what it is to be human. We read, 'God blessed them and said to them, "Be fruitful and increase in number; fill the earth and subdue it. Rule over ... every living creature"' (Gen. 1:28).

God made man and woman responsible for the creative management and order of the earth. This stewardship implies an ability to organize, to develop, to subdue and to administer the creation. Because of this created ability, 'The Lord God took the man and put him in the Garden of Eden to work it and take care of it' (Gen. 2:15). What did this care involve? Without benefit of agricultural training, God gave them agricultural responsibility. No doubt he knew that the creativity latent within them would blossom forth, enabling them to undertake whatever was necessary to nurture plant life properly. This innate creativity was part of the image of God in them.

God was so confident about Adam's ability to suit names to animal natures that he gave Adam responsibility for the key job of naming the animals: 'Whatever the man called each living creature, that was its name' (Gen. 2:19). This same ability was demonstrated when Adam named Eve:

'This is now bone of my bones
    and flesh of my flesh;
she shall be called "woman"
    for she was taken out of man'

(Gen. 2:23).

The effects of the Fall

Mankind, by creation, possesses certain latent creative and administrative abilities. You may say, 'The Fall destroyed all that.' I would agree that the Fall did distort and darken man's latent abilities. Nevertheless fallen men and women continued to develop skills. 'Lamech married two women, one named Adah and the other Zillah. Adah gave birth to Jabal; he was the father of those who live in tents and raise livestock. His brother's name was Jubal; he was the father of all who play the harp and flute. Zillah also had a son, Tubal-Cain, who forged all kinds of tools out of bronze and iron' (Gen. 4:19-22).

Adam's descendants developed in the three parallel areas of animal domestication, music and technology. While morality plummeted, creative ability ascended to the point where God had to judge the earth with a flood and confuse the people into different language groups. Mankind is a paradox, possessing both resident creative ability — due to God's creative image in man — and wickedness — due to the moral degeneration of God's holy image in man. The one owes its existence to the continuing common grace of God and the other to the depravity of man.

While the Fall affected every faculty of man, it did not totally extinguish God's image. God's image in man is the source of all that is good and attractive in man and his culture. 'Every good and perfect gift is from above, coming down from the Father of the heavenly lights, who does not change like shifting shadows' (James 1:17). These good gifts include the rain that he causes to fall on the just and the unjust, the growth of the crops, as well as beneficial aspects of culture such as government, family, music and technology. What is good in culture owes its origin to mankind's innate creativity, a gift of God. Thus, the Spirit of God, through the medium of common grace, both restrains the extent of evil and encourages the beneficial aspects of culture. This will continue until the Holy Spirit is taken away (2 Thess. 2:6-7).

We should never be puzzled by eminent gifts in unbelievers, nor surprised at skill in wicked men. We should expect such as part of our human heritage. We are all fearfully and wonderfully made under the superintendence of God who rules the universe.

The providence of God

In other periods, Christians believed deeply in the providence of God. Today, however, we seem to have largely turned over the world, with all its variety and beauty, and human culture, with all its art, music and technology, to the devil. This is not to say that the devil is not the 'god of this world', who abuses the gifts of God's common grace to dupe the inhabitants of this sphere into continued rebellion. We need to keep reminding ourselves that God is not a deistic absentee clock-maker but a presently ruling Sovereign.

Surely we do not have to experience insanity like King Nebuchadnezzar of Babylon before we acknowledge God's sovereign providence: 'At the end of that time, I, Nebuchadnezzar, raised my eyes towards heaven, and my sanity was restored. Then I praised the Most High; I honoured and glorified him who lives for ever.

'His dominion is an eternal dominion;
   his kingdom endures from generation to generation.
All the peoples of the earth
   are regarded as nothing.
He does as he pleases
   with the powers of heaven
   and the peoples of the earth.
No one can hold back his hand
   or say to him: What have you done?"'

(Dan. 4:34-35).

Passages such as this inspired the Westminster Assembly to write, 'God the great Creator of all things doth uphold, direct, dispose, and govern all creatures, actions and things, from the greatest even to the least, by His most wise and holy providence, according to His infallible foreknowledge, and the free and immutable counsel of His own will, to the praise of the glory of His wisdom, power, justice, goodness, and mercy.' [9]

Creation and providence, necessarily, forge a link between natural abilities and spiritual gifts. From creation we learn that God endowed mankind with creative ability when he stamped them with his image. In recorded history we catch repeated glimpses of the providence of God overruling evil and harnessing human potential to accomplish his purposes. If we fail to see this connection we do not profit from Nebuchadnezzar's harrowing experience. Unfortunately, in most circles, we act on the basis of the preposterous idea that God is not involved in the ebb and flow of human history. We carry on medieval superstitions by hallowing the sacred and disdaining the secular, as if God is only involved in sacred activities.

King Solomon entertained no such idea. In his eyes, all knowledge, whether of ethics or botany, flowed from God. 'He described plant life, from the cedar of Lebanon to the hyssop that grows out of walls. He also taught about animals and birds, reptiles and fish' (1 Kings 4:33; see also Col. 2:2-3).

Craftsmanship as a gift of God

Recognizing the sovereign hand of God behind human skill, Solomon was not embarrassed to ask the pagan King Hiram for craftsmen to work on the temple. He knew that the Sidonians possessed greater skills than the people of Israel. 'Send me, therefore, a man skilled to work in gold and silver, bronze and iron, and in purple, crimson and blue yarn, and experienced in the art of engraving, to work in Judah and Jerusalem with my skilled craftsmen... I know that your men are skilled in cutting timber there. My men shall work with yours' (2 Chron. 2:7-8).

The difference between the workmanship of pagan and devout men is not so much one of native human ability as the end for which the work is dedicated. Hiram's craftsmen used their skills for Baal and for Sidonian moguls of commerce, but when under contract to Solomon they dedicated their craftsmanship to Jehovah. Since they owed their skill to the instincts inherent in being created in God's image, God was not adverse to accepting their craftsmanship in his temple.

Earlier, during the Exodus, God had taken developing craftsmen and filled them with the Holy Spirit. Consecrated to God, their skills were used by God to construct the tabernacle: 'See I have chosen Bezalel ... and I have filled him with the Spirit of God, with skill, ability and knowledge in all kinds of crafts — to make artistic designs for work in gold, silver and bronze, to cut and set stones, to work in wood, and to engage in all kinds of craftsmanship. Moreover, I have appointed Oholiab ... to help him. Also I have given skill to all the craftsmen to make everything I have commanded you...' (Exod. 31:1-6). Were their skills miraculously imparted gifts given at that moment, or were they skills developed over a period of time, independent of the construction of the tabernacle? The text may appear to favour the sudden and miraculous. Such an interpretation, however, is not necessary, nor can it be substantiated from the rest of Scripture.

Were they filled with the Spirit and then became craftsmen? Or did they become craftsmen under the general superintendence of God's providence, only to be later specifically dedicated by the Spirit to this task? Let me quote Keil and Delitzsch, noted commentators, in this regard: 'Filling with the Spirit of God ... did not preclude either natural capacity or acquired skill, but rather presupposed them.'[10] Bezalel, like all craftsmen, owed his skill to God, who had providentially developed and supernaturally enhanced it.

In David's case, musical skill preceded spiritual anointing for service. Concerning other musicians in David's court, we read, 'Kenaniah the head Levite was in charge of the singing; that was his responsibility because he was skilful at it' (1 Chron. 15:22). Skill was developed before responsibility was given to lead in the worship of God.

Craftsmanship is a gift of God just as much before its use for a holy purpose as after it is consecrated to divine use. God has maintained, by his providence, a continuous supervision of human development from the time of creation down through all the centuries to our own day. In the process he restrained and overruled evil for his own glory. As a result, the skills and abilities a sinner lays at the feet of Christ at conversion are endowments he developed under common grace. In Christ they become dedicated to holy purposes.

Stewardship originates with creation and includes a responsibility for skills and their use. As fallen image-bearers people may dedicate their creative skills and administrative abilities to the

service of pagan deities or to fulfil their own desires. But God moves
some to consecrate their skills to his service. The Old Testament
pattern, in which natural skills were used in the building of tabernacle and temple, is reflected in the New Testament consecration of
gifts for the edification of the new temple, the body of Christ. Up to
this point, then, there is no discontinuity between natural ability
used in craftsmanship and ability dedicated to divine service.

II. Stewards of the kingdom

In the New Testament, Christ teaches stewardship in connection
with the kingdom of God. Let's focus most carefully on Matthew 25.
Note first the context. In the previous chapter Christ describes the
signs of the end of the age and of his return. He stresses the necessity
of servants watching for the return of the Master while they carry on
with their assigned tasks. Chapter 25 shifts to the very end of the age
and focuses upon how the returning Master will evaluate the
stewardship of his servants. Three parables — the ten virgins, the
talents and the sheep and the goats — illustrate this accounting
process. Among these, the parable of the talents is pivotal in
establishing a New Testament perspective on stewardship.

1. Stewards of talents (Matt. 25:14-30)

A rich man with considerable property and many servants goes on
a long journey. Before leaving he entrusts his possessions to their
care. The amounts entrusted to them vary because he gives to 'each
according to his ability' (v. 15). To one he gives five talents, to
another two and to another one. A talent, about $1,000 in silver
content, or up to twenty years' wages for an ordinary labourer,
represented a large responsibility.

After the owner leaves, his servants begin 'to put his money to
work' (v. 16) The servant with the five and the one with the two
talents both get busy and each increases his master's money by 100
per cent. A third servant is negligent and buries his talent. Considerable time elapses before the master returns to call his servants to
account.

The master commends equally the servant with the five talents
and the one with two. 'Well done, good and faithful servant!' he says

to each. The measure of their stewardship is not the amount of responsibility, which varies, or the amount of ability, which also varies, but the *degree of faithfulness* in the use of what God entrusts. Both are equally faithful. The wicked servant wastes the master's talent.

What does the parable mean? The man going on a journey is Christ. The period until he returns is the church age. Christ gives to each person a responsibility commensurate with his ability. We are responsible in his absence to use what he entrusts to further his business. This business is the kingdom and its extension. We are each responsible to use his deposit to build his church. The servants are professing Christians. According to this parable, faithfulness in using what the Master entrusts to us distinguishes true from professing Christians.

What do the talents represent? They must represent something, like ability, that varies from person to person. The talents mirror something that can be possessed by one who, while a professing Christian, is not truly regenerate.

Gifts of grace

Spiritual gifts could be substituted for talents in the parable. Peter links gifts of grace with faithfulness in ministry: 'Each one should use whatever gift he has received to serve others, faithfully administering God's grace in its various forms' (1 Peter 4:10). But, you may ask, how can an unregenerate person, even though a professing Christian, be entrusted with a gift of God's grace? In answer I would say, it is not saving grace, nor sanctifying grace, but common grace that is in view here. If gifts are, by providential preparation, related to pre-conversion abilities, then gifts could also be related to talents, if they are not identical.

1 Corinthians 12, in describing the distribution of gifts, paints a picture similar to this parable: 'He gives them [gifts] to each one, just as he determines' (1 Cor. 12:11) is reminiscent of the master going on a far journey who gives talents to each servant according to his own discernment of their varying abilities.

Paul also emphasizes, in Romans 12, the differences that exist between those who receive God's gifts. He exhorts us to evaluate that difference soberly: 'Do not think of yourself more highly than you ought, but rather think of yourself with sober judgement, in accordance with the measure of faith God has given you.' In other words, soberly evaluate the talent that the Master has entrusted to you. God will weigh our faithfulness in using what we do possess, not what we don't.

In the introduction to the passage on gifts in Ephesians 4, Paul talks of various portions of grace: 'But to each one of us grace has been given as Christ apportioned it' (v. 7). He cannot mean that God used different amounts of grace to redeem us. Surely, in that we are all equal. This varying amount of grace — in Romans 12 'faith' — corresponds both to the variety of gifts in the passages which deal with gifts and the variety of talents in the parable.

Are the talents in the parable gifts of grace? It would appear so. There is, however, the problem of reconciling the giving of one talent to a servant destined for eternal darkness who demonstrates the falsity of his profession by failing to use it. 'And throw that worthless servant outside, into darkness, where there will be weeping and gnashing of teeth' (Matt. 25:30). How can an unregenerate person have a gift of the Spirit? This would have to be the case if talent equals gift.

Accepting the continuity of teaching between the Testaments resolves the dilemma. In the context of the Old Testament, all men are stewards of the common grace of God entrusted to them through his image in them. They develop skills and abilities that they invariably misuse until dedicated by the Holy Spirit, as in the case of Bezalel, to God's holy purposes. Men and women of all cultures, irrespective of their relationship with God, share a common pool of basic abilities and skills.

If spiritual gifts were to be considered peculiar foci of all the skills and abilities we have as men and women then the continuity of stewardship would be maintained. The parable does link divine usefulness with 'natural ability'. In this sense spiritual gifts are the particular ways in which the Holy Spirit helps us develop a variety of natural abilities so they become focused on building the kingdom. This interpretation harmonizes abilities and gifts and provides a satisfying interpretation of the parable.

What other commentators say

You may consider my interpretation novel, even offbeat. I don't think it is. Consider how a number of respected commentators describe talents.

G. Campbell Morgan equates talents closely with both gifts of the Spirit and opportunities and responsibilities to do the Lord's work: 'Talents were given according to ability... It means this, He will never call a man to preach who has no natural ability for preaching. I am afraid we often do. He never does. Behind that wonderful little expression, "according as each man had ability", is a revelation of natural fitness, the ability of the personality as preparation for the reception of a supernatural gift, and that is always so. If a businessman has that ability, he will receive responsibility according to that ability, which is his natural ability, the natural baptized, empowered by the supernatural.'[11]

While describing the giving of gifts such as 'helps', Morgan states, 'But it is according to ability ... the natural creating fitness for the supernatural.'[12] Talents and spiritual gifts must be linked.

Since the relationship between spiritual gifts and natural talents is so important, let me quote at length from an older author, Matthew Poole. In common with others of his day, Poole had a high view of God's providence. He had no difficulty making the transition from abilities endowed by common grace to gifts bestowed by special grace. Commenting on the parable he says, 'By the goods, which the man is said to have delivered to his servants, are to be understood the gifts which God giveth to men... I see no reason to restrain these gifts to such as flow from Christ as Mediator, but rather choose to interpret it generally of all the gifts of God, whether of providence or of grace... The good things of Providence; under which notion also come all acquired habits, or endowments, such as learning, knowledge, moral habits, etc. which though acquired are yet gifts, because it is the same God who gives us power to get wealth ... who also gives men power to get knowledge, and upon study and meditation to comprehend the natures and causes of things and also to govern and bridle our appetites; or the gifts of more special providence, or distinguishing grace. I take all those powers given to men, by which they are enabled to do good, or to excel others, to come under the notion of the goods here mentioned, which God distributeth unequally according to his own good pleasure, and as seemeth best to his heavenly wisdom, for the government of the world, and the ordering of the affairs of his church.'[13]

Poole, with his high view of divine providence, projects a continuity of stewardship between what men receive naturally and what they receive supernaturally. Since God is sovereign over mankind in both states, whether fallen or redeemed, this is not hard to understand. God in his providence sovereignly bestows on men, lost and saved, whatever they have. Men and women owe all their good gifts to the grace of God at work either through the image of God within all men, or the Spirit of God within the redeemed.

To Poole, the talents in the parable include everything: 'God, in the day of judgement, will call all men to account for those gifts which he hath given them, how they have used the days of life, the measures of health, their knowledge, wit, memory, understanding, their wealth, estate, honours, dignities, relations, all their natural or acquired habits, all their enjoyments, etc.'[14]

I believe Morgan is right in noting that natural abilities pave the way for supernatural ministries. And Poole is correct in interpreting the teaching of the parable to mean that all men are stewards of whatever they have received. Poole's argument that both natural and acquired abilities are gifts owed to God is clearly scriptural. Indeed what he says is consistent with our point of relating, not equating, the creativity of God's image in man with spiritual gifts. Both saved and unsaved men have this image, so both saved and unsaved men and women have the potential abilities that underlie spiritual gifts. Please note that I am not claiming that spiritual gifts *are* natural abilities, but merely that in the providence of God they are related.

Lange,[15] Matthew Henry[16] and McQuilkin,[17] to name three other commentators, make the same link.

To summarize, the talents entrusted by the parting master in the parable illustrate a very broad concept. Commentators have interpreted them specifically as spiritual gifts or more generally, natural abilities. Many realize, though, that the concept includes opportunities to serve, knowledge, training, experience, indeed all endowments or potentialities for service. Surely, Poole, Henry, and others are right in interpreting the talents as the totality of all the capital God gives us to serve him with, whether received through the natural operating of providence, or bestowed by the supernatural work of redemption. There can be no absolute cleavage between spiritual gifts and natural abilities because God, by providence, is never divorced from the life of man. Another parable of stewardship, the parable of the ten virgins, demonstrates this connection.

2. Stewards of oil (Matt. 25:1-13)

The parable of the ten virgins teaches us to maintain our light by always keeping sufficient oil handy. Five virgins foolishly took no extra oil. When the bridegroom's coming was delayed their lamps began to go out. The five wise virgins took extra oil with them in their jars so they could maintain their light. Upon arrival, the bridegroom excluded five and invited five into the wedding banquet. The five excluded were off seeking oil.

The commendation of Christ, the Bridegroom, depends on our faithfulness as stewards of oil. The oil produces light. Without light there is no ministry and no preparation for the Lord's return. As Morgan and other commentators note, the oil symbolizes the Holy Spirit.[18]

All ten of the virgins shared many similarities. All had lamps, all were watching and expecting the coming of the bridegroom; but only five had sufficient oil. The radical difference between their acceptance by Christ is the oil and the light it produces — that is, the Holy Spirit and the effect he produces. The five foolish ones were without the Holy Spirit. They represent professing Christians without the energizing presence of the Holy Spirit. The Holy Spirit, as stressed in chapter 2, energizes us to use our spiritual gifts to shine forth in a dark world. Ministry and effect in the church are wholly contingent on an adequate supply of oil — on the Spirit.

May I press the point here by pointing out that, externally, the wise and foolish virgins were the same. Is it too much to say that, externally, Christians and non-Christians may be similar? The difference is not in what they bring to Christ, but in what they *receive*. Believers receive the Holy Spirit, who burns within them to produce the light of holy love. Both Christians and non-Christians bring a similar variety of experiences, training and abilities. The general ability of a non-Christian to teach or administer or to acquire knowledge or to communicate may be very similar to that of a Christian. Oil and its light make the difference. The Christian dedicates his lamp to the Holy Spirit who, according to his own sovereign will, causes natural skills and training to shine forth for the glory of Christ.

The oil, and the light it produces, surpasses in importance the containers. We must never lose a sense of absolute dependence upon the Holy Spirit to imbue the wicks of our skills with the light of divine effect. This highlights a danger. An emphasis on spiritual gifts can result in pride and carnality. We must remember that spiritual gifts are like empty lamps if they are not imbued with the oil of the Spirit.

The lamp and wick which both the saved and unsaved bring to the feet of the bridegroom are the same. The potentialities that God, by his common grace and divine providence, bestows on all men are similar in unsaved and saved alike. Abilities, talents, training and experiences constitute, together, the lamps that the Spirit fills with the oil of his gifted presence.

Conclusion

God, at conversion, takes us as we are and in the whole process of sanctification leads us to where we could not go. He finds us with warped and twisted remnants of his image in us. He saves us and begins a process of restoring his image in us that is complete when we become fully conformed to the image of his Son (2 Cor. 3:18). He finds us with a variety of imperfect abilities, skills, experiences, training, knowledge, potential, etc., which we are using for our own selfish ends. At conversion he revolutionizes our motivation, turning us in a new direction. All our capabilities, instead of being dangerous, become latent with spiritual potential for the kingdom. Selfish rebels become loving members of his body, the church, 'living stones ... built into a spiritual house to be a holy priesthood, offering spiritual sacrifices acceptable to God through Jesus Christ' (1 Peter 2:5).

The spiritual gifts that Christ gives, then, are not totally distinct from natural talents. Rather they are the way that the Holy Spirit gathers up all the natural potential we have through common grace and focuses it supernaturally. Outside of Christ we lived for ourselves. In Christ we receive spiritual gifts that redirect our natural abilities and skills into Christ-centred ministry.

We should note that gifts are not, in themselves, abilities. Rather, they constitute supernatural potentialities to channel our various abilities in edifying directions. That which distinguishes a spiritual gift of, say, communication from a natural ability to communicate is the supernatural effect it has in furthering God's work. This supernatural effect is as impossible of attainment without the Holy Spirit as it is for a lamp to give light without the oil. The lamps in the parable of the ten virgins illustrate our natural resources. The light that the oil produces illustrates for us the effect our particular gift has on the darkness of our world.

We must never confuse ability with gift, nor expect or strive for supernatural effect without the Holy Spirit. Packer writes, 'Ability to speak or act in a particular way — performing ability, as we may call it — is only a charisma if and as God uses it to edify... When, therefore, Christians are said to "have gifts" (Rom. 12:6), the meaning is not that they are in any respect outstandingly brilliant or efficient (they may be, they may not; it varies), but rather that God has observably used them to edification in specific ways already, and this warrants the expectation that he will do the same again. We need to draw a clear distinction between man's capacity to perform and God's prerogative to bless, for *it is God's use of our abilities rather than the abilities themselves that constitute charisma.* If no regular, identifiable spiritual benefit for others or ourselves results from what we do, we should not think of our capacity to do it as a spiritual gift. This principle was assumed in the original admissions procedure at C. H. Spurgeon's Pastors' College. Evidence was sought that candidates had already preached and taught to the blessing of others. In the absence of such evidence, the applicant, however able otherwise, was judged to lack gifts for the pastorate and was turned down.'[19]

Abilities then, are not themselves gifts. Gifts are rather how the Holy Spirit gathers up all our potentialities and baptizes them to produce edification in a particular direction. Gifts, like the barrel of a gun, focus the attention of the gifted believer in certain directions. Abilities, however, do provide raw material for the Spirit to use in preparing us for gifted ministry. This must be so, because the Spirit of the gifts is also the Spirit of common grace and providence.

Gifts are the sixteen or so foci of the Spirit, the specific directions of ministry that the Spirit gives to believers in the body. Some are gifted to focus on teaching the Word. Some concentrate on winning the lost. Others give themselves to encouragement. Still others gather all their abilities together to focus on organization and administration. Each of us has one or more areas of specialization into which the Holy Spirit gradually directs our attention.

In conclusion, a search for our gifts will lead us to make an

inventory of our natural abilities, talents, training, experience, etc.
In chapter 7 we shall consider how to go about taking such an
inventory.

Ron, the tool and die-maker mentioned at the beginning of the
chapter, is excited to learn that all his training and experiences can
contribute to the glory of God. The Lord will use his abilities and
training in administration and finance. The Spirit will somehow
focus his love of the outdoors and his experience in the voluntary fire
brigade into his spiritual gift. He wonders, 'What gift, like
Michelangelo's angel, is there in me that the Spirit will bring to
life?' That is hard to tell at the beginning of a search for ministry
focus. But what the Holy Spirit is doing with you and me, he has
done often before.

A certain man grew up in considerable poverty, which, in his day,
made formal education unattainable. He married early and struggled
to provide for his growing family. He made his living working for
a shoemaker while he indulged a deepening interest in both plants
and geography. At the same time he sought to minister in a small
country church. Another man in the same country grew up in a
family of comfortable means. His ability was early recognized and
schooling provided. He graduated from Cambridge with top marks
in mathematics. Upon conversion he chose a path of self-denial and
rejected marriage. Later he was ordained to the Anglican priesthood. Both of these men went as missionaries to India. God used
both in mighty ways. Paradoxically, the one from the poorer and less
educated background is more remembered. He was William Carey,
the nineteenth-century 'father of modern missions', while the
second was Henry Martyn, 'apostle to Islam'.

The reservoirs of natural endowments, training and experiences
that William Carey and Henry Martyn brought to the nineteenth
century were astoundingly diverse. Yet the focus on missionary
evangelism was similar — both filled an almost apostolic missionary role in the history of the church. Were they later-day apostles?
Well, for that discussion we shall have to wait until chapter 9. One
thing is certain, however: both took their stewardship as citizens in
the kingdom seriously, and both found their spiritual gifts impelling
them to respond to missionary needs. This response to need is
another mark of gifts, the very concern we shall consider next.

6.
Spiritual gifts and response to need

The search for our spiritual gifts, in the last chapter, led us into a past guarded by providence. Spiritual gifts, however, do not focus on the past, but on the present. Gifts equip us to meet the needs we see around us. The burdens and concerns different Christians feel differ according to their gifts. Consequently, if we can isolate these concerns we can illuminate the general area of a person's giftedness. In the same way that radar tracks aircraft, gifts track needs.

As I look around after a service, I am often amazed at how believers express their gifts by what they talk about and who they talk to. Doubtless, much conversation has no pressing agenda. People may talk about the weather, a new dress or last week's baseball game. But some believers have an agenda programmed into their subconscious by their spiritual gift. This built-in spiritual radar directs them to zero in on the needs people have. To show you what I mean let me describe what might happen after a typical service. The characters we shall meet in the chapters ahead might scatter after church as follows.

Ron beckons to the chairman of the deacons' board to join him in the corner. They discuss the agenda for a coming finance committee meeting. Megan lifts her head from prayer and heads straight for an anguished divorcee. Before long several young women, Christians with non-Christian husbands, join her to chat. Mike Sherwin, one of the deacons, moves around welcoming newcomers and then sits down beside a rather unkempt, out-of-work teenager. Meanwhile, Ann is in earnest conversation with the pianist about an appropriate solo for the following Sunday. Bob

Harris makes a lunch appointment with an unsaved man for whom
he has been praying for some time.

In the foyer, Harry has come up to the pastor with his open Bible
and is correcting his inadvertent mention of Joshua instead of Caleb.
Since Harry has corrected the pastor again, Mrs Ryan sidles up to
him with an encouraging report of comments she has overheard
about the blessing of his recent sermon series. At the far end of the
foyer three men gaze at the discoloured ceiling tiles and discuss how
to beautify the foyer. Near the library the young people surround
their leader to argue with some heat what music they should and
should not listen to. Up in the kitchen several women plan food for
the coming church outing. What people talk about, and whom they
talk to, often betrays their real concerns.

I. Needs bring gifts into focus

The body of Christ represents a complex of needs and opportunities
for service. One with the gift of administration sees the need of
organization. The antennae of an encourager vibrate in the presence
of discouragement and sadness. Practical needs in the church
building catch the attention of those with the gift of helps. The
evangelist focuses on the unsaved, while the shepherd steers disciples away from danger and binds up their hurts. Those with
different gifts focus on different needs. In a healthy body it must be
so.

The converse of spiritual concern is spiritual effectiveness. Since
different gifts focus on meeting different needs, their effects will
vary greatly. We should not expect an evangelist to have the same
impact as an encourager, for example. Spiritual gifts can be identified by the results they produce.

Paul warns us not to let 'any unwholesome talk come out of [our]
mouths, but only what is helpful for building others up according to
their needs, that it may benefit those who listen' (Eph. 4:29). While
unmet needs stunt growth, using our mouths to speak words that
meet real spiritual needs accelerates healthy growth. (We shall
study later the cluster of speaking gifts that must be brought to bear
here.) The next verse warns us, 'Do not grieve the Holy Spirit of
God' (Eph. 4:30). If we fail to speak edifying words we create a
vacuum of unmet needs. This vacuum hinders development and

contributes to the frustration that simmers beneath the surface of most disunity. Unmet needs are like distracting pains in our bodies. It is hard to be growing and spiritually alert when our body is wracked with pain! The spiritual body, the church, is no different.

Needs in the body of Christ

We don't normally think of the body of Christ as a complex of need-meeting relationships, but this is, in one sense, exactly what the church is. Paul's graphic picture of a body 'joined and held together by every supporting ligament' (Eph. 4:16) illustrates our inter-dependence upon each other in the church. The church, like the human body, grows as each part — that is, each organ, limb, nerve, gland and artery — does its work. The hand cannot function without the blood vessels supplying its need for oxygen and nourishment. The body at large cannot function without the hand picking up food and bringing it to the mouth. In the body there is an intricate interconnection of supply and demand, of needs and the provision of those needs, as each different part of the body fulfils its function. When the need of any part is not met, the body becomes unhealthy and disoriented.

To quote Paul in his First Epistle to the Corinthians, 'The body is a unit, though it is made up of many parts; and though all its parts are many, they form one body. So it is with Christ' (1 Cor. 12:12). He goes on, 'Now the body is not made up of one part but of many. If the foot should say, "Because I am not a hand, I do not belong to the body," it would not for that reason cease to be part of the body... The eye cannot say to the hand, "I don't need you!" And the head cannot say to the feet, "I don't need you!" On the contrary, those parts of the body that seem to be weaker are indispensable' (1 Cor. 12:14-15,21-22).

The body of Christ, and its manifestation on a local church level, is an interrelated network of needs. Every Christian is responsible to contribute to the meeting of the needs of the whole body by meeting the needs of individuals in that body. (This is not to ignore the needs of those in the world outside the church.) Paul says that Christians should have particular concern for each other. If one part suffers, every part suffers with that one part (1 Cor. 12:25-26). A need is an ache that becomes a festering sore if not attended to.

A variety of resources

We go to the grocer's because we need meat, fruit, vegetables and milk. We go to the clothes shop when we need clothing. We go to the garage because we need petrol or an oil change. We go to the shoe-repair shop if our shoes need repair. Since we continually live in a state of need, we keep seeking out the places where those needs can be met.

God has constituted the church as a one-stop shopping arcade where the Spirit meets our spiritual needs. In this place there are many different shops. Each has its own speciality. There is one which specializes in encouragement, one that deals in knowledge, another is known for discernment, another for mercy, and so on. Spiritual gifts are actually those specialities developed by the Spirit of God in individual believers in order to meet the variety of needs that exist in a local congregation.

Each of us, as a need-meeter, is a distribution centre. We are responsible to stock the spiritual resources our gift trains us to distribute. This shows how foolish it is to think we can hire a pastor or full-time worker to meet the needs of a local church. No single Christian is a complete department store! But how often we misunderstand New Testament ministry. Instead of using our gifts to meet the needs of other believers we expect a full-time worker — pastor or evangelist — to run a general merchandise department store by himself!

Too often we come to church with only one thing in mind instead of two. We look for our own needs to be met, but fail to do our bit to meet the needs of others. But church is neither a speciality shop run by the pastor nor a spectator sport to be watched from the sidelines. Christ underscores this concept in his parables.

II. Needs, concerns and the kingdom parables

The parables of the kingdom, in Matthew 25, paint a vivid picture. At this point, Matthew's Gospel prepares us for the end of the age and the return of Christ. The chapter begins with the parable of the ten virgins, in which oil illustrates the necessity of the Spirit of God. In the middle of the chapter, the parable of the talents directs our attention to the capital entrusted to the servants of the kingdom by the departing Christ. The chapter closes with the parable of the sheep and goats (Matt. 25:31-46). This latter parable describes the standards that the King will use at the final judgement.

The parable teaches us that at the end of time Christ will sit on a throne of judgement. He will separate people into two groups, as a shepherd might separate sheep from goats. He will gather the sheep on his right and the goats on his left. Those on his right, true believers, will go away into eternal life and those on his left, the unconverted, into everlasting punishment.

On what basis will the King make this division? He will evaluate how people respond to needy individuals who cross their paths. People who reach out to meet the needs of others attest by their action the reality of their conversion. Sheep are need-meeters! Christ will say, 'Come, you who are blessed by my Father; take your inheritance, the kingdom prepared for you since the creation of the world. For I was hungry and you gave me something to eat, I was thirsty and you gave me something to drink, I was a stranger and you invited me in, I needed clothes and you clothed me, I was sick and you looked after me, I was in prison and you came to visit me' (Matt. 25:34-36).

Christ commends need-meeters. They feed the hungry and give drink to the thirsty. They give the stranger a place to stay and clothe the destitute. They look after the sick and visit the prisoner. (Other passages present complementary teaching on the vanity of good works as a basis for salvation and show the emptiness of insincerity. Only genuine believers can serve Christ sincerely, because they alone have new hearts.)

In the judgement, those who are righteous — righteous in Christ — will be astonished when the Master mentions how they fed him when he was hungry. The righteous are not conscious of having ministered to Christ. They simply go about meeting needs. Verse 40 describes the King's reply to their puzzlement: 'I tell you the truth, whatever you did for one of the least of these brothers of mine, you did for me.'

The parable goes on to describe those who are cast out of Christ's presence into eternal punishment as those who fail to meet needs. The King will say, 'Whatever you did not do for one of the least of these, you did not do for me' (Matt. 25:45). The picture is clear: God divides people into two groups: goats, who have no ministry of meeting the needs of others, and sheep, who unconsciously go about ministering to needs.

The distinguishing mark of a citizen of the kingdom is a ministry of meeting needs. In other words, believers demonstrate their faith in Christ by works of unselfish compassion. Citizens of the kingdom are need-meeters.

Gifts and the response to need

The serving gifts closely correspond to the various ways in which sheep respond to needs. For example, the gift of giving leads a person to respond to those who are hungry, thirsty or destitute by providing them with food, drink or clothing. The gift of mercy leads a believer to respond to the one who is sick or in prison. One with the gift of hospitality invites a stranger home.

The needs mentioned by our Lord in this parable are some of the most obvious. This is not to say, however, that there is not a hierarchy of other needs. Scripture uncovers a vast array of spiritual needs as well. The ignorant need teaching. Those who are lost and bound for a Christless eternity need a compassionate ministry of witness and evangelism. The perplexed and puzzled need the ministry of discernment and wisdom. The confused and disorganized need the ministry of administration and leadership. Those with practical problems need the ministry of helps, and so on. Ministering to needs becomes the criterion used by the Master to evaluate the reality of our faith. Since God has integrally linked gifts with ministry, their exercise is a virtual necessity for every Christian.

We must view the exercise of gifts as the necessary consequence of Christian character. Since love is intrinsic to Christian character, every genuine Christian will manifest the Spirit's work within by undertaking ministries motivated by love. Love undergirds the gifts of the Spirit. Christian love is outward-looking. It produces within the growing Christian a concern for those with needs and an impulse to do something to meet those needs. To fail to respond to the needs we see around us, by exercising our ministry gifts, is to fail to love.

Church involvement then, should be viewed as the natural consequence of Christian character. When a balanced mutuality of ministry occurs, our needs are met along with those of others — and the whole church grows. But many Christians shrink from ministry.

III. Needs and ministries

Perhaps the word 'ministry' puzzles you. Consider its meaning. The Protestant Reformers rediscovered the priesthood of all believers in the sixteenth century. Unfortunately, since then the church has not made great strides in recovering the biblical concept of universal ministry. Without an understanding that all believers are called to ministry, spiritual gifts cannot be fully exercised. As long as this misconception reigns, full-time workers and lay persons will continue to view each other suspiciously across the clergy-laity gap.

In Peter's first epistle, the metaphor of a building replaces that of a body: 'You also, like living stones, are being built into a spiritual house to be a holy priesthood, offering spiritual sacrifices acceptable to God through Jesus Christ' (1 Peter 2:5).

Every believer is a priest of God responsible to offer spiritual sacrifices to God. A couple of verses further on we read, 'You are a chosen people, a royal priesthood, a holy nation, a people belonging to God, that you may declare the praises of him who called you out of darkness into his wonderful light' (1 Peter 2:9). All true Christians, as priests, are called to personally praise and glorify God and to help build a temple of praise.

Peter continues to explain the concept of ministry by saying, 'Each one should use whatever gift he has received to serve others, faithfully administering God's grace in its various forms' (1 Peter 4:10). Each Christian has a solemn responsibility to use his or her gifts to minister God's manifold grace to others in the body. In this way a spectrum of often informal ministries develops.

Ministry is never the sole responsibility of those whom we normally think of as the ministers of the local church — that is, the pastors and elders. Paul taught, 'It was he who gave some to be apostles, some to be prophets, some to be evangelists, and some to be pastors and teachers, to prepare God's people for works of service, so that the body of Christ may be built up ...' (Eph. 4:11-12). According to the apostolic pattern, pastors and teachers train God's people for works of service. Pastor-teachers are specialists dedicated to equipping members of that body with the skills they need in order to use their spiritual gifts. This role in no way minimizes the value or importance of the pastor-teacher, but rather clarifies and underscores its importance. To call this specialist a minister, however, distorts the meaning of the term in a biblical context.

The concept of ministry weaves its way throughout the whole fabric of revelation. Unfortunately, ministry too often speaks of the privileged position of the gospel minister, and conjures up images of clerical collars, black robes, pulpits and ministerial authority. We often visualize a man highly trained and set aside by ordination for ministry. We struggle with terms such as 'lay person' and 'full-time ministers' because the word 'ministry' has become historically equated with one ministry, namely the pastoral ministry. While the need for great preaching and great pastors has never been greater, nevertheless ministry must be demythologized and shared. Why? Scripture demands it. The logo in the Sunday bulletin of a church in southern California reflects a welcome balance. It reads, 'Home of 1200 Ministers.' It lists the pastoral staff as 'Equipping Ministers'.[1]

Discussion of ministry naturally leads us to a discussion of authority.

Ministry and power

Ministry is often confused with the image of someone who occupies a position of authority in a church hierarchy. In reality, however, a minister is a servant (slave) bound by an obligation to meet needs. A minister is simply someone who meets needs. Although he existed eternally as the all-powerful Son of God, Jesus chose to come among us as a servant. He went about meeting the needs of the blind, the dumb, the demon-possessed and the sick.

In chapter 3 we explored Jesus' concept of ministry. When the mother of James and John came seeking a high position for her sons, Jesus said, 'Whoever wants to become great among you must be your servant, and whoever wants to be first must be your slave — just as the Son of Man did not come to be served, but to serve, and to give his life as a ransom for many' (Matt. 20:26-28).

Just before his crucifixion, Jesus astounded his disciples by washing their feet. His words must have echoed in their hearts down through the years: 'Now that I, your Lord and Teacher, have washed your feet, you also should wash one another's feet. I have set you an example that you should do as I have done for you' (John 13:14-15).

Gifts, then, do not equip us to seek position or authority, but to take up the basin and wash dirty feet.

William Law, in *A Serious Call to a Devout and Holy Life*, emphasizes the need for servant-like humility in all we do by counselling us to '... condescend to all the weaknesses and infirmities of our fellow-creatures, cover their frailties, love their excellencies, encourage their virtues, relieve their wants, rejoice in their prosperities, compassionate in their distress, receive their friendship, overlook their unkindness, forgive their malice, be a servant of servants and condescend to do the lowest offices to the lowest of mankind.'[2]

The search for our spiritual gift will not lead us to seek a lofty position of authority but to walk through the valley of humble service. In that valley, according to the parable of the pounds, we all stand on an equal footing.

The parable of the pounds and equality in ministry

Where the parable of the talents assumes diversity of ability, the parable of the pounds (minas) teaches equality. Both parables deal with the activity of Jesus' servants in the interval between his departure and his return.

In the parable of the pounds there are two groups: the citizens and the servants. The citizens hate the absent king, while the servants accept his rule. To each of ten servants, the nobleman gives one mina before departing to receive a kingdom. This equality of stewardship signifies an equality of responsibility. As Peter states, we are all 'stewards of the manifold grace of God' (1 Peter 4:10, NASV). We each have an equal deposit of divine grace, equal spiritual resources and an equal inheritance of the Holy Spirit and his power (see Eph. 1:3,13-14,18-19; 3:2). All of us have the same amount of time, twenty-four hours a day. We all have equal responsibilities to be stewards of the resources entrusted to us. The only servant who is condemned is the lazy servant who, refusing to use his mina, hides it in the ground. The diligence of the servant who earns ten more minas is highly praised.

Both parables emphasize the equality of all believers. In the case of the talents, differing abilities bring equal rewards because of equal faithfulness. In the case of the pounds the sum originally entrusted to the servants is equal, while the reward varies, based not on position or gift but on diligence in the use of one's gift.

God has entrusted all believers with ministries. We must accept our call to serve and get busy meeting needs. The local church and its community provide each of us with a sphere of service.

IV. Needs and the local church

If we look beneath the surface in the average church we shall find a host of unmet needs that stunt the development of the body of Christ. There will be lonely people longing for someone to talk to, strangers who have no home to call their own, along with those who grieve. Others may be grappling with a sense of failure or deep depression, which renders them ineffectual in using their own gifts to edify others. Still others may be needing practical help of some kind. Some may be seeking to get by on a meagre budget. There may be missionaries home on furlough with unspoken monetary needs, or pastors struggling on stringent salaries. Many believers will be struggling with temptation and besetting sins. A few may entertain ideas that are unbiblical or even heretical. Many struggle with doubts, fears and worries. There are always those who are self-deceived without being truly converted. There may be new Christians who do not understand the faith and older Christians puzzled by suffering.

Why do so many unmet needs fester in the body of Christ? It could be that too many 'priests' are taking a holiday from ministry. It might be a lack of concern, a dearth of compassion. It might be the result of a failure to encourage lay ministry. Often the problem can be traced to the erroneous expectation held by members that a hired pastor is responsible for all these concerns. On the other hand, the cause could be due to the way we organize our churches — to our failure to delegate and mobilize the membership.

Positions or ministries?

Service in the local church is often parcelled out in packages labelled, for example, treasurer or deacon, Sunday School teacher or steward. The titles given or positions filled may, without care, divert our attention from their purpose — ministry. Pastor, for instance, means 'shepherd', a term that reminds us of the concern a shepherd has for the needs of his flock. The pastorate is more usually viewed as a position to be filled by a man with seminary training. Members usually expect him to fulfil a host of administrative and preaching functions that may range far afield from shepherding. The deacon, in New Testament terminology — a servant — denotes one who busily serves the church as a need-meeter. But today, in Baptist usage at least, deacon refers to a position of authority filled by voting at a regular church election. In similar vein, a trustee, chairperson of the ladies' missionary group, superintendent of the Sunday School, to name a few, focus more on positions to be filled than needs to be met. Before church elections, nomination committees frantically search for enough warm bodies to fill the empty positions.

The focus has shifted from the original intention — choosing people with gifts to meet crucial needs — to filling slots. No doubt suitability for office still deeply concerns most of those who are responsible for nominating people to fill those offices. Still the urgency to meet needs has largely been replaced by an urgency to fill a slate of officers and keep the organization functioning. Sometimes the original needs for which committees and organizations were established are forgotten. In this way, willingness to serve, more than ability to meet needs, tends to become the prized criterion of service. Commitment replaces giftedness. Organization gobbles up sensitivity to need. An impressive hierarchy of positions can even create artificial need, the need to fill a position, or to hold committee meetings, while the real needs remain unmet!

Since needs continue to fester, we keep starting up new activities and searching for new staff: an assistant pastor with responsibility for visitation, a hostess to run the catering, a discipleship co-ordinator, a prayer chairman, someone with responsibility for fellowship! Much of what we do is sincere and may even be helpful, but are we conscious of why we do what we do? Are we conscious of unmet needs? Don't misunderstand me. As you will see when we discuss the gift of administration, I believe deeply in the importance of organization.

Nevertheless, creating more activities and organizing more committees will not meet needs unless they somehow help us mobilize the whole body to participate in ministry. It would not harm us to dismantle some of our activities and reorganize them with the objective of meeting real needs. For example, does the ladies' missionary fellowship really meet to promote missions, or to fill the need ladies have for fellowship and outreach? If so, why not reflect that in the group's goals and shift missionary prayer to a revitalized prayer meeting? If door-to-door calling on a weekly visitation night proves ineffective, why not reorganize to promote friendship evangelism?

A need for flexibility

We need to keep asking ourselves why we exist as a church. What does Christ want us to do? What objectives give direction to our programmes? Clear goals will facilitate flexibility of programming keyed to changing needs. Unclear goals will cause us to render aimless devotion to static programmes. The resultant lack of clear direction will demotivate the membership.

All organizations tend to stray from their original mandates and fossilize. Churches are no exception. We desperately need to make some provision in our tight and frantically busy schedules to enable us to respond with flexibility to the ever-changing complex of human need. (Of course, this is not meant to indicate that the church has a mandate to meet all social needs. Worship, edification and evangelism must remain the basic emphases of the church.)

Nevertheless, churches patterning themselves on apostolic practice must, in some measure at least, imitate the great apostle and seek to 'become all things to all men, to reach some'. Flexibility should also become a hallmark of individual Christians. There is an important point to make here about spiritual gifts. With needs varying with the passage of time, the call for certain gifts will wax and wane. One glaring need may rivet our attention at one point, be met, and then give way to other needs.

For example, in a given church, God may use an emphasis on evangelism to call many sinners to Christ who then need discipling, hospitality and encouragement. As these converts mature in Christ they need training in how to teach, how to lead and how to evangelize. On another occasion a church may face financial stringency and need abundant exercise of faith and generosity. At that time someone with a latent gift of faith may come to the fore to encourage the group to trust God. Once the financial need fades other needs come into focus.

As time passes and a complex of different needs present themselves to us, the Holy Spirit may stir up different gifts in us — or different usages of the same gift. Some gifts may lie dormant until specific emergencies arise. Let me use a personal example of what I mean.

Some years ago Mary Helen and I went to Pakistan as missionaries. The critical need of established churches plunged me into a teaching ministry where that gift developed. When the senior field missionary went on furlough, conference chose me to act as field leader. It was a shock! Up to that time I had rather avoided administration. Necessity dropped it in my lap. Soon latent organizational and leadership qualities began to emerge. Extreme need hastened gift development.

As time passed I became involved in the genesis of theological education by extension in Pakistan. The desperate need of scattered Pakistani Christians for training necessitated heavy involvement again in teaching. I was compelled as well to begin writing home-study courses. This led me into a round of research and study that the Spirit used to enhance latent theological interest. As the years passed the extension work became well established and we returned to Canada.

Meanwhile in Canada our local church was without a pastor. While in Pakistan I had been involved continuously in various leadership roles with Pakistani Christians and missionaries. Nevertheless, it never dawned on me that I might have any pastoral gifts. Before long the deacon board of our home church asked me to become pastor. Accepting on a trial basis, I began to sense some latent shepherding gifts coming to the fore.

My story has been unusual, but I do believe that all of us can relate in some way or other to this pattern of gradual gift development through responding to various needs. Most of us have more than one spiritual gift. At different times, according to the needs around us, different gifts come to the fore. As time passes we often develop a mix of gifts with some one gift predominant. My predominant gift is teaching. Opportunity and need expedited its development over a period of time.

Perceived needs, and an inkling that I could help to meet them, moved me to participate in ministry. Soon after my conversion, a more mature Christian kept nudging me into situations where I had to do something: 'Eric, will you give your testimony?' 'Eric, join us Saturday to give out tracts.' 'Sunday School needs teachers. Why not take a junior class?' So it went on. This friend made sure that I had opportunities to develop.

Opening up opportunities for ministry

Leaders can create a climate that encourages ministry by providing opportunities for believers to serve. Failure to open up opportunities for ministry stifles gift development.

Sometimes we inadvertently develop efficient ways to keep

people out of ministry. I read recently about a city church with an efficient multiple staff of full-time workers. When the pastor did a survey he was astonished to discover that there were only 385 jobs to do in his whole congregation of several thousand. How pointless it was to preach about the priesthood of all believers without exposing unmet needs and offering opportunities for believers to become involved in meeting them!

If we limit Christian service too narrowly we really restrict the joy and excitement of ministry to an élite ministering class. If we do that we unconsciously discourage the goose of universal priesthood that lays the golden egg of joyful service. But you may object, 'We can't find people willing to help.' Ah, but how are volunteers recruited?

In a voluntary organization, like the church, we cannot compel anyone to serve the Lord. Motivation by inducing guilt does not work either. The usual route we take, finances permitting, is to hire professionals. Instead, why not try to get believers so excited about ministry that they happily volunteer? Impossible? It is tough — some will never volunteer — but it is not impossible.

Soon after completion of a series on spiritual gifts in our church, a woman came up to me to express her appreciation. She explained how she had grown up in a difficult family situation. Although she had attended church most of her life she had never sat under teaching about spiritual gifts. A sense of inadequacy and inferiority had dogged her footsteps. With a sparkle in her eye, she then shared how encouraging it was to realize that she had gifts and could minister.

Not too long after, her heightened sense of concern spotted a need I had! She offered to take over a task I was routinely performing. She has done it ever since — and done a much better job than I could.

Perhaps we have failed to communicate the excitement of being used by God to minister to the needs of others. Frederick Buechner writes, 'The place God calls you to is the place where your deep gladness and the world's deep hunger meet.'[3]

Did you notice how everything meshes together to produce joy? Needs target our gifts and the result is deep gladness through meeting human need!

Unfortunately much of the excitement and joy of service seems to be found outside the local church. Frank Tillapaugh, in his book

Unleashing The Church, describes the excitement of those in the parachurch movement. Disgruntled Christians, he points out, often gravitate to organizations like Campus Crusade or the Gideons. In these organizations things seem to happen. In reality, parachurch groups spring up because of perceived needs. The need of college young people, the need of the homeless or the need for Bible distribution touches the heart. Concerned believers may initiate a new ministry. Since most of these parachurch groups target specific needs they focus vision and breed excitement.

Tillapaugh goes on to comment that all too often our churches pursue traditional patterns without clear vision of their purpose. They become fortress churches, determined to maintain the status quo, focused on retreating from the world and defending present programmes. Such an atmosphere stifles ministry and discourages sincere concern. He suggests that we need to unleash the church from anything that restricts a clear view of our mission. Every church should look around for target groups — groups of people with similar needs. For example, there may be exhausted mothers with pre-school children, divorced women, unemployed, singles or the homeless. These groups represent real needs, which call us to respond in ministry. Knowing we are unable to do everything, a church should pray for committed people to come forward to target the most pressing needs. When several people do come forward with a vision for a target group and a plan to proceed, the church should get behind them. This process unleashes the church to meet ministry needs.[4]

Tillapaugh's concept of the church unleashed mirrors what I have been expressing about responding to needs. Every Christian should be encouraged to look around for lost and hurting people. When a believer identifies a concern, that believer should be encouraged to respond personally, if possible. Even in a fortress church individual Christians can respond to a host of needs, both within and without the church.

Look around you. What needs do you see? What needs do you long to see met? God may be awakening within you a dormant gift through the concerns that continue to exercise your soul. Where there is no vision the people not only perish, but believers are miserable! May God give you vision — vision of a lost and hurting world!

Conclusion

A study of spiritual gifts is a study in human needs, needs which cry out for ministry. The maturity of a church can in great measure be gauged by the degree to which hurts are healed and needs are met inside and outside the church. When all believers participate in this process by exercising their need-meeting gifts, edification and glory to Christ result! Christ designed his body, the church, to be a need-meeting depot as well as a centre of worship and praise.

Perhaps you are still not sure of your gifts. Don't despair, we continue in the next chapter to tabulate the various steps God can use to help us identify our spiritual gifts.

7.
Steps to gift discovery

Ann is puzzled about her particular gift. She feels deeply about the
need to promote a spirit of worship in her church. Yet she wonders
how her natural abilities fit into the gift mosaic. Ann is very musical.
The congregation listens with rapt attention whenever she sings a
solo, plays the piano during the collection, or accompanies others
with her violin. Although musical ministry gives her a real sense of
fulfilment, nevertheless she wonders where music fits into spiritual
gifts. Ann has taught Sunday School and done hospital visitation.
She loves gardening and crafts. In this chapter I want to suggest six
steps Ann, or any of us, can take to identify our spiritual gifts.

I. Why we need to discover our gifts

But first we need to address the question: 'Is the search for our gift
really valid?' Some Christians cast doubt on the whole process of
gift discovery.

Admittedly, the Bible nowhere gives a step-by-step procedure to
follow in finding our gifts. This should not surprise us. No sincere
Christian would question that the Bible teaches the deity of Christ
and the tri-unity of God. Yet these doctrines are not systematically
described in any one text but derived from collating widely scattered
passages. We must follow the same procedure to discover biblical
principles concerning gifts.

1. New Testament teaching on the use of gifts

The necessity of our search for gifts can be established from a number of perspectives. The Holy Spirit moved writers to list spiritual gifts in four places, indicating their importance. The lists also demonstrate that we can distinguish them one from the other. Without a procedure to distinguish them, the lists would serve to frustrate us. God does not arouse our interest, just to mock us.

Some might counter that the presence of miraculous gifts, such as tongues and healing in the Corinthian passage, proves that spiritual gifts had relevance during the apostolic era alone. They would argue that the cessation of these miraculous gifts, as attested by church history, throws doubt on the continuance of other gifts. As our study progresses, each gift will be examined individually to show the erroneous nature of this claim. Suppose we grant that 1 Corinthians contains gift material relevant only to the first century. We would still be left with three pivotal passages containing material crucial to believers throughout church history! (Personally, I do not grant such a cavalier approach to an inspired epistle!)

Who would be so bold as to remove Romans 12, or Ephesians 4, or 1 Peter 4 from the arena of modern church life? We cannot eliminate teaching on spiritual gifts from these chapters without creating a mishmash of disconnected material. God did not include material about spiritual gifts in the context of general teaching on church life to lead us down a blind alley.

Look at several passages. 'We have different gifts... If a man's gift is prophesying, let him use it in proportion to his faith' (Rom. 12:6). You can't use your gift if you don't know what it is! 'Now about spiritual gifts, brothers, I do not want you to be ignorant... But eagerly desire the greater gifts... Follow the way of love and eagerly desire spiritual gifts, especially the gift of prophecy' (1 Cor. 12:1,31; 14:1). (We shall consider the nature of prophecy in chapter 10.) Twice Paul exhorts the Corinthians to desire gifts. Now, to desire gifts without having any way of discovering them is to doom ourselves to frustration.

Paul wrote his epistles to dispel ignorance and frustration, not to add to them. In Ephesians 4 Paul writes that God designed the gifts of apostleship, prophecy, evangelism, shepherding and teaching to 'prepare God's people for works of service, so that the body of Christ may be built up' (Eph. 4:11-12). But without being able to identify their gifts, pastors and teachers will not know who they are. And without their ministrations believers will be unprepared for works of service — and the body will be stunted. With confusion about gifts as prevalent as it is today, it should not surprise us that stunted churches dot the landscape.

Peter urges, 'Each one should use whatever gift he has received to serve others' (1 Peter 4:10). But if we don't know what our gift is, how can we use it to serve others?

Paul instructs Timothy and Titus to discern character and note giftedness when they choose deacons and elders. Indeed Timothy himself is urged, 'Do not neglect your gift, which was given you through a prophetic message when the body of elders laid their hands on you' (1 Tim. 4:14). Obviously Paul, the elders and Timothy himself were all aware of the nature of Timothy's gift. The gift was bestowed (or identified and then consecrated) in the context of a prophetic message.

In the second epistle Paul reminds Timothy to 'fan into flame the gift of God, which is in you through the laying on of my hands' (2 Tim. 1:6). Timothy could not stir up what he did not know. It seems highly unlikely that these references to Timothy's gift, in epistles of such universal relevance, are meant to tantalize us with a reality that existed only in apostolic days! No! No! The New Testament widely assumes our ability to identify spiritual gifts.

Each of the main passages dealing with gifts weaves statements about spiritual gifts into the metaphor of the church as the body of Christ. 'In Christ we who are many form one body, and each member belongs to all the others. We have different gifts, according to the grace given us. If a man's gift is prophesying, let him use it...' (Rom. 12:5-6). 'There are different kinds of gifts... To each one the manifestation of the Spirit is given for the common good' (1 Cor. 12:4,7).

The Corinthian epistle interjects into teaching on the gifts a lengthy description of the interdependence of the various parts of the body (1 Cor. 12:12-31). Later in chapter 14 Paul highlights the value of prophesying above tongues. After pointing out that tongues were for private edification, he goes on to say, 'Try to excel in gifts that build up the church' (1 Cor. 14:4,12). That exactly describes my purpose in this book.

Normal church life is impossible without the exercise of gifts. In Ephesians Paul describes how the ascended Lord poured out gifts on the church 'so that the body of Christ may be built up' (Eph. 4:12). One cannot candidly read Ephesians 4 without noticing the crucial importance of the exercise of gifts in healthy church life. 'The whole body ... builds itself up in love, as each part does its work' (Eph. 4:16). The gifts of the Spirit energize the work that believers do to build up the body. What could be clearer than Peter's exhortation: 'Each one should use whatever gift he has received to serve others, faithfully administering God's grace in its various forms'? (1 Peter 4:10).

2. Ignorance about gifts

The cause of immaturity and declension in our churches can be traced to a number of factors, one of the most important of which is ignorance of the gifts. We all readily recognize gifts of preaching, pastoring and teaching but largely ignore the dozen or so other crucial gifts. The result is a spiritual body with some parts muscular and healthy while other limbs atrophy. Powerful preaching ministries may hide hurting congregations. Gifted evangelism may cover up inept organization. It is strange how we recognize so readily our garden's need for a balance of sun, soil, fertilizer, cultivation and water, but in church life we struggle on without bringing into play the whole spectrum of gifts designed by Christ for its development!

Stagnation and frustration result as many believers try to serve as square pegs in round holes. The discovery of our gifts liberates us from frustration. Howard Snyder writes, 'There is no teaching more practical than that about the gifts of the Spirit. The discovery of his spiritual gift often turns a frustrated, guilt-ridden Christian into a happy and effective disciple. In my own case the discovery of gifts has clarified the ministry to which God has called me and opened new vistas of service. When I identified and named my spiritual gifts, it seemed as if all the contradictory pieces of my life suddenly fell into place. I found the key to what God was doing in and through my life.'[1]

Too many Christians are either confused, mistaken or totally ignorant of their spiritual gifts. A parable illustrates the situation from the perspective of pupils in a rather unusual school.

> Once upon a time, the animals decided they should do something meaningful to meet the problems of the new

world. So they organized a school. They adopted an activity curriculum of running, climbing, swimming and flying. To make it easier to administer the curriculum, all the animals took all the subjects.

The duck was excellent in swimming; in fact, better than his instructor. But he made only passing grades in flying, and was very poor in running. Since he was slow in running, he had to drop swimming and stay after school to practise running. This caused his web feet to be badly worn, so that he was only average in swimming. But average was acceptable, so nobody worried about that — except the duck.

The rabbit started at the top of his class in running, but developed a nervous twitch in his leg muscles because of so much make-up work in swimming.

The squirrel was excellent in climbing, but he encountered constant frustration in flying class because his teacher made him start from the ground up instead of from the treetop down. He developed 'charlie horses' [i.e. cramp] from overexertion, and so only got a C in climbing and a D in running.

The eagle was a problem child and was severely disciplined for being a non-conformist. In climbing classes he beat all the others to the top of the tree, but insisted on using his own way to get there![2]

How discouraging to try to do what we are not gifted to do! And how wasteful of spiritual resources to pour every believer into one mould instead of encouraging a diversity of approaches to ministry!

After years in the pastorate, James Davey came to the conclusion, through the tender questioning of a friend, that he did not have a gift that he thought he ought to have for the pastorate. This discovery brought joy and liberty. 'Fifteen years of stumbling about came into focus, and with relief I admitted to myself that I did not have to have this gift to be a pastor.'[3]

Undue stress

Failure to discover one's gifts not only keeps many from ministry but contributes, in committed Christians such as James Davey, to undue stress. During thirty years of ministry I have met many committed Christians struggling to do what they are not gifted to do:

good personal workers struggling with administration; strong teachers trying to be evangelists; practical people, who long to be out cutting the grass or painting the windows, forced to sit out endless committee meetings. My own pilgrimage has included quite a few blind alleys.

I have often pondered how much of what we do is motivated by a desire to conform to the expectations of others. Understanding our own gifts can deliver us from false guilt and a vague sense of failure. Rick Wellock remarks, 'Paul's teaching about gifts is seen in connection with the command to avoid anxiety.'[4] God commands us to avoid anxiety — gift discovery dramatically aids in this regard. Serving where our gifts equip us to serve delivers us from the frustration of trying to do what we are not gifted to do. It eases anxiety engendered by failing to meet expectations.

Unfortunately too much teaching and preaching in evangelical circles lacerates instead of healing sensitive consciences. In response to an imbalanced approach to Philippians 4:13, 'I can do all things through Christ who strengthens me' (NKJV), the highly committed either collapse from overwork, fight guilt over not being able to produce, or struggle on in tasks for which they are not fitted. Preaching which motivates by inducing guilt fails to move the uncommitted, who turn off, even while it pummels the tender consciences of those already burdened down with duties. A biblical understanding of gifts alleviates anxiety, stress, frustration and false guilt.

The need to get involved

At this point another danger rears its ugly head! Some may be tempted to avoid doing anything until they are sure they have the gifts to do the task. This danger has led some Christian leaders to warn that pursuing gift discovery distracts us from obedience.

We must always balance narrowly focused ministry based on our gifts by a commitment to do whatever needs to be done. We must never passively wait for opportunity to knock. Gift discovery presupposes an active involvement in ministry on as broad a scale as possible. Too many are like the hundred-year-old books that Gail MacDonald found in a secondhand bookshop. As she turned the pages she discovered that she was the first one ever to read them.

How did she know? Here and there pages were still joined together at the edges where the publisher had failed to cut them properly. She had to split apart many of the pages to keep on reading.

Writing in her journal she said, 'Those books remind me of many people I know. So many neat things inside of us, untapped by disinterest, lying dormant — useless. Yet one of those biographies has marked my life. Too bad the original owner didn't know that there were special gifts in those books to challenge him and sold his unused books to the antique dealer.'[5]

If we fail to get busy in the service of Christ, we shall never discover the untapped resources the Spirit has entrusted to us. To gain an overview of this rich spiritual trove, consult Appendix I where a brief definition of each gift may be found.

II. Three groups of gifts

Gifts can be divided into speaking gifts, serving gifts and sign gifts. By speaking gifts, I mean those endowments of the Spirit whose main thrust revolves around the communication of biblical truth. Prophets were God's special preachers. On the other hand, God used the apostles to lay the foundation of the early church. Evangelism, shepherding, teaching, knowledge, wisdom and encouragement supplement these two basic gifts. Serving gifts endow believers with the spiritual ability to demonstrate Christian love in practical ways. Helpfulness and hospitality, giving and mercy, faith and discernment join the gift of administration in the area of servanthood.

The sign gifts, as mentioned already, constitute that group of spiritual manifestations given by God to attest his new covenant creation. After the early church had become well established, tongues, interpretation, healing and miracles ceased. Their subsequent exercise cannot be demonstrated to have occurred throughout church history. Normal church life does not depend upon their exercise.

Leaving controversy behind, we need to press on to create a climate conducive to the discovery and development of the normative gifts.

III. Creating a climate of gift discovery

1. Prayer

Since spiritual gifts are sovereignly bestowed gifts of grace, we must begin our search at the throne of grace. The Holy Spirit, agent of gift bestowment, would usher us through prayer into the presence of Christ, the Giver of the gifts. As we ponder our individual ministries in the body of Christ we face perplexity and mystery. We need wisdom.

So we pray earnestly for light. We need to pray over our local church situation, God's providence in our preparation, the burdens and concerns we feel, the dreams we have for the growth of God's kingdom and our current ministries.

Many have written books about spiritual gifts simply because, like church order, ambiguities exist. Various definitions of gifts overlap. Traditional views of local church ministry, as well as institutionalized approaches to service, further complicate our search. We need the mind of the Spirit to help us sort through a variety of texts and filter out a host of conflicting voices. No wonder we must bathe our search in prayer!

Personal peculiarities will make our discovery process very subjective. Our own mix of training, family nurture, hobbies, abilities, personality and experience provides a unique blend of ingredients that the Spirit will use in leading us into gifted ministry. No wonder a prayerful sensitivity to the Spirit undergirds true gift discovery.

Not only every individual, but every local church manifests a distinctly different set of needs at any one time. And every church is composed of a unique blend of individuals brought there by God. Can we possibly match our own providential preparation for ministry with local needs without a deeply spiritual dependence upon divine guidance? Clearly we must search prayerfully.

2. Local church involvement

Our Western culture worships individualism. Personal concerns about work, family, sports, holidays and care for a house may dominate our lives. If we lack an overriding sense of divine mission, church involvement may be pushed to the periphery of our lives. If that happens, the development of a sense of community will stagnate and its lack will harm our own personal gift development process.

Believers who shun wholehearted participation in church life stifle the growth of gifts. Spiritual gifts are not just things God bestows to make us feel more fulfilled. Spiritual gift development is inseparable from local church involvement.

While the Bible stresses community it does not deny individuality. 'To each one the manifestation of the Spirit is given,' but it is exercized in the context of community — 'for the common good' (1 Cor. 12:7). Throughout the passages dealing with gifts repeated reference is made to the body of Christ: 'The body is a unit, though it is made up of many parts... Now you are the body of Christ, and each one of you is a part of it. And in the church God has appointed ... gifts' (1 Cor. 12:12,27-28,31). To treat gifts as individual trophies is to deny their purpose. Gifts exist expressly to enable us to minister in the local church.

The search for gifts begins, then, in the context of our local church's life and ministry. While parachurch organizations may help to develop specialized gifts and Bible Colleges may aid us in honing and sharpening our gifts, without immersion in a local church, we tilt at windmills. One of the very reasons I spent the major portion of my missionary career in extension training in local churches, rather than in a residential Bible college, was because of a firm belief in the fundamental place of the local church in all Bible teaching and discipleship.

Be sure you are involved in a local church. Take part in its services. Support its programmes and prayer meetings. Help to keep the building clean and painted. Volunteer to make coffee and tidy up. Help in Sunday School and visitation. Get involved in follow-up of contacts and offer hospitality to new people.

Stephen and Philip developed in the context of local church ministry. Their giftedness flowered as they waited on tables! I cannot stress this point enough. Snyder writes, 'The urgent need today is that spiritual gifts be seen and understood in the context of ecclesiology, as in the New Testament... When spiritual gifts are misunderstood — through being over-individualized, denied, divorced from community or otherwise distorted — it is the church which suffers. The church truly becomes the church only when the biblical meaning of spiritual gifts is recovered. A church whose life and ministry is not built upon the exercise of spiritual gifts is, biblically, a contradiction in terms.'[6]

In reality the church cannot be the church as conceived by Christ without believers exercising their gifts. Nor can Christians be what they are to be in Christ without being immersed in body life. Of course, finding our place in the body involves bowing in submission to Christ.

3. Submission to the lordship of Christ

As already noted, Paul introduces the subject of gifts in Romans by an appeal to 'offer your bodies as living sacrifices'. Submission alone enables us to 'test and approve what God's will is', including his will concerning our sphere of service (Rom. 12:2).

As a necessary preliminary to gift discovery, we must reject the pattern of ego-enhancement that we see all around us. Instead we are to offer ourselves voluntarily as living sacrifices to God. Only then can we steer a pathway between pride on the one hand, and a sense of inferiority on the other. When we open our minds to the Spirit and submit our wills to Christ we become able to 'think of [ourselves] with sober judgement, in accordance with the measure of faith God has given [us]', which involves an accurate assessment of our gifts (Rom. 12:3).

Submission to Christ frees the log-jam of carnal debris that blocks the flow of ministry. We may resist bowing to Christ in the area of spiritual gifts for a variety of reasons. We might long for a place of public prominence, such as that which comes with exercising the gifts of preaching, shepherding, teaching or administration. But we may fear instead that God will call us to labour in some unknown place where no one will notice us. He may call us to hospital-visitation, and we wouldn't like that. Or it could be to work behind the scenes keeping the church building attractive. Christ is King. We can't choose the ministry we want. Bow in submission and leave the choice to him.

Conversely, we might hold back for fear of being thrust into the public spotlight. If we are of a timid or retiring nature, we may worry lest God calls us to stand in the public eye. I know that fear. I grew up painfully shy. Indeed, I probably subconsciously chose forestry as a profession because painful and embarrassing human relationships would be at a minimum. Then God converted me to Christ. I had to face the issue of submission to his will. Over a period of time the Spirit moved me to offer my life to the Lord for whatever he would choose. It was tough, until I yielded.

Uncommitted people avoid searching for their gift out of a desire to shun involvement. Elizabeth O'Connor writes, 'The identifying of gifts brings to the fore ... the issue of commitment. Somehow if I name my gift and it is confirmed, I cannot "hang loose" in the same way. I would much rather be committed to God in the abstract than be committed to him at the point of my gifts... Commitment at the point of my gifts means that I must give up being a straddler. Somewhere in the deeps of me I know this. Life will not be the smorgasbord I have made it, sampling and tasting here and there. My commitment will give me an identity.'[7]

Well said! If we enjoy 'hanging loose' while we profess submission to Christ in the abstract we live on the fence. Commitment calls us to involvement. We may value our weekends and evenings too much to search seriously for our gift. We may be afraid consecration will hamper our lifestyle. It could! But if we fail to submit to the Spirit and seek our gift we will be robbing the body of Christ of the ministry it needs. Without our commitment some members will suffer.

Not only so, but we ourselves will suffer from failing to develop our spiritual potential. God converted me as a very backward teenager. Social relationships brought pain. Slowly, very slowly, the Spirit liberated me from timidity. He led me into missionary service and later into the pastorate. I would never have chosen public ministry. But after nearly thirty years in the public spotlight I rejoice in the privilege of publicly proclaiming the Word of God. The Spirit has irresistibly led me out of the dark depths of insecurity and felt inferiority into the joy of taking part in the ongoing drama of the kingdom. Without submission to the Spirit, I would have remained a social pygmy blundering through life without any clear understanding of my own latent potentiality. Now I am able to look back over my life and celebrate the 'good, pleasing and perfect will' of God (Rom. 12:2). God is no man's debtor!

Desire for a place of prominence, or fear of a place of public ministry, no less than a desire to avoid involvement, causes different people to shun consecration for different reasons. Disobedience, too, dampens the enthusiasm of our search.

4. Obedience to the general commands of Christ

I assume, as you have been reading, that you have been evaluating how well you have done to create a climate conducive to gift discovery. You will be praying for wisdom and discernment. You will be a faithful member of a local church. You will be open to the Spirit's leading because you have presented your life as a living sacrifice to Christ. You want his will. But you are still puzzled. You may ask, 'But what can I actually do to begin to narrow the search?' I would answer: 'Be sure you are obeying the commands of Christ.'

Obedience to the general commands of Christ is one of the most basic of all prerequisites for gift discovery and development. The commands of Christ closely parallel the basic gifts. Charles Ryrie, reflecting a number of authors, writes, 'It is striking to notice that many of the commands to serve involve the same activities as are involved in exercising some of the gifts. For example, there is a spiritual gift of giving, but all Christians are to give. There is the gift of evangelism, but all are to witness.'[8]

Most gifts are endowments of the Spirit to specialize in service in an area where all Christians are commanded to be generally involved. Ryrie mentions giving and witness. Let us continue the comparison. Paul echoes Christ by commanding all of us to 'serve one another in love' (Gal. 5:13). We obey this command by trying to help other believers in any way we can. This general helpfulness corresponds to the special gift of helps.

All of us are commanded to 'encourage one another daily' (Heb. 3:13), while some of us are specifically gifted to specialize in encouragement. God commands every believer to rule his or her own spirit and every father to rule his own family, although not all believers have the gift of administration (Prov. 25:28; 1 Tim. 3:4-5, NASV).

Paul exhorts us: 'Let the word of Christ dwell in you richly as you teach and admonish one another with all wisdom' (Col. 3:16). Whether or not we have the gift of teaching, we are all commanded to teach and admonish in one sphere or another. Fathers and mothers are commanded to teach their children. Older women are commanded to teach younger women (Titus 2:4). While only some of us have the spiritual gift of teaching, all of us have some teaching responsibility. God has commanded it!

All of us are required to be merciful (Matt. 5:7). All must exercise discernment (1 Thess. 5:21). All of us are witnesses (Luke 24:48; 1 Peter 3:15). None can escape the universal command to be hospitable (Rom. 12:13). Even the unique gift of prophecy is to be sought by all! (see 1 Cor. 14:1-14). In similar vein all must have faith and give generously.

The importance of obedience should not surprise us. We show that we love others by obeying the commands of Christ that delineate the practical ramifications of love. Love and obedience are two sides of the same coin. The specific commands focus our love in specific directions. For example, 'Give and it shall be given unto you,' focuses our attention on those who need what we can give.

If we would discover our gifts, we should walk in conscious obedience to the commands of Christ. We should be generous, encouraging and believing. We should study the Bible and pray; we should witness and discipline our spirits. We should be helpful and merciful. If we compare gift discovery to going to school, obedience is on the curriculum for the beginners' class. Indeed, like arithmetic, obedience undergirds everything that follows.

As we become busy obeying the general commands of Christ facility in a certain area of ministry may develop. For example, as we express our concern for other believers by phone and letter, a ministry of encouragement may blossom. By loving others in this way, and so obeying Christ, we may discover that encouragement is our gift. Or, as we faithfully teach our children, a special capability to teach the Bible could develop into a gifted ability to teach Sunday School.

Fervent obedience promotes gift discovery because gift development parallels general growth in grace. Sanctification and ministry develop hand in hand. Disobedience, in turn, stifles gift discovery in the same way as it stunts growth in Christ. Obedience, of course, is an active, not a passive trait.

5. Active participation

Gail MacDonald, in her book *High Call, High Privilege,* describes the renovation of their New Hampshire retreat. Peace Ledge farm had lain unused for thirty years. When the MacDonalds began to clear away the weeds they discovered hidden under the undergrowth a well-laid out garden with worthwhile plants suppressed by weeds. They cleared out the weeds and watched the garden blossom. Today, people marvel at the beauty of the place. But its charm would have remained hidden if the MacDonalds had not laboured long and hard to clear up the mess.[9] Many believers have spiritual gifts of which they are unaware. Sluggish involvement in ministries may have obscured their presence.

Our spiritual gifts lie hidden for two completely different reasons. Either idleness or extreme busyness may serve to obscure their presence.

Being too busy

Consider first busyness as a bane to the discovery of gifts. Workaholics can't be still. Their busy lives leave them little time to reflect. Sometimes willingness to work, or an abundance of talents, or an inability to say no, makes people an easy target for those looking for volunteers. But being busy and exercising one's gifts are not necessarily synonymous. Busyness, in one sphere, may be a cover we use to avoid facing unpleasantness in another. Or activity might be the only thing we know that gives us a sense of fulfilment.

Ethel Marr, in an article with the suggestive title, 'Is There A Camel In The Tent?', describes an imaginary couple, Dick and Marcia. Moving to a new church, they kept their abilities under wraps for a year. Soon the secret leaked out and they became snowed under by a dozen responsibilities. The camel stuck its nose in their tent when they counselled at camp. Soon their inability to say no led to the whole 'sanctified talent camel' occupying the tent. Their life became filled with frenzied activity.

Ethel Marr discusses this common problem: 'Dick and Marcia never intended to overcommit themselves. But they loved the Lord, wanted to serve Him, and had listened to a lot of sermons on the parable of the talents.'[10] Being committed Christians contributed to their dilemma.

Ethel Marr goes on to trace the source of this problem to several myths about talents (and gifts). Among the myths she isolates are: 'God will give you strength to do anything'; 'If you don't do the job it won't get done, or at least done properly'; and 'If you have talents you should use them to the hilt.' Believing these myths leads sensitive souls to overcommit themselves. Willing souls end up doing most of the work in many a local church. This, in turn, keeps the slots filled and prevents a vacuum developing, which vacuum, far from being bad, could serve to draw more reticent souls into service. She concludes that 'If in reality there is no one to do a job, maybe it doesn't need to be done. At any rate I'm not responsible for the whole work of the Body of Christ, not even in my local church.'[11]

If we load up our lives with duties in a laudable effort to meet all the glaring needs we see, we shall fail to provide scope for others to develop their gifts — and we shall not give ourselves enough time to discover our own. Indeed, such a practice denies the body of Christ and promotes an erroneous sense that we are indispensable.

Frantic activity erodes both the quality of our ministry and the clarity of our direction. Ethel Marr continues, 'First is the myth that church activity is always service. If we are active in church work, we are "obviously" serving the Lord. And if we want to serve the Lord, we must "obviously" get ourselves involved up to the eyeballs in church work… The result is that many Christians resemble a child on a coin-operated horse at the supermarket. As long as the coin holds out they go like crazy, generating tremendous activity. But they don't get anywhere. When the coin runs out, they're still sitting where they started.' [12]

Overcommitment can hinder gift discovery and development by getting us too busy to be flexible enough to accept new opportunities for ministry that would help in our development. As a result we may be occupying a ministry space better suited to another believer. If so, we are blocking his or her development. Is there a camel in the tent? If there is, shoo him out by resigning a few positions to give you more time to develop excellence in one or two areas of giftedness.

Idleness

Of course, some are overly busy because others are under-committed. Far too many Christians fill pews but fail to take their place in body-ministry. Their passivity harms the church. In Romans 12 Paul closes the list of gifts by reminding us of the need for love and devotion and by urging us not to be 'lacking in zeal, but keep your spiritual fervour, serving the Lord' (Rom. 12:11). Paul rebukes Timothy for his timidity, his failure to stir up his gift, and for failing to fan the flames of his giftedness (1 Tim. 4:14; 2 Tim. 1:6).

Gifts are not like ornaments that we hang on a Christmas tree. God didn't give them to embellish our lives. They are not medals or awards that we pin on our coats. The Spirit bestows gifts for one purpose — active ministry. We will never discover our gifts until we become actively involved in service of some kind. Gifts develop by practice. If you or I are lethargic or cold in serving Christ, we will be proportionately ignorant of, and under-developed in, the use of our gifts.

Let us assume you are neither lethargic nor burnt out from busyness. Instead you are creating a climate conducive to gift search and development by giving attention to prayer, consecration, obedience and active participation in local church life and ministry. Next I want to suggest six steps you need to take.

IV. Six steps to gifts discovery

The six steps that follow describe six things we can do to evaluate our giftedness. They involve taking an inventory of the raw materials used by the Spirit in crafting our spiritual gifts. The Gift Evaluation Chart, found at the end of this chapter, summarizes the six steps. (An extra copy is included in the Appendix.) As we proceed in the succeeding pages to study each gift individually, I will refer you back to this chart again and again. By filling in the blank columns, gift by gift, you will embark on a journey of discovery that will enable you to get closer and closer to your own ministry treasure. The first column of that chart calls for an inventory of evidences of God's providence in your life.

1. Taking an inventory of providential preparation

In chapter 4 we considered the role of God's providence in our preparation for ministry. We concluded that God prepares us for service by leading us through a variety of experiences. An inventory of our natural abilities, our education and training, our ministry and work experiences, along with any skills we have acquired, will furnish us with a glimpse of the Spirit at work in endowing us with gifts.

Turn to the chart and note that column 1, 'Providential preparation', has two sections. Column 'A' provides space to list after each of the gifts any natural talents, skills, education, hobbies or training that might fit you for this area of ministry. Column 'B' provides space to list any present or past opportunities to serve in church or para-church organizations that might be related to this gift.

On a rough piece of paper jot down all the jobs, education, training, hobbies, interests or talents, etc., you have that could in any way be used by God to prepare you for service. First think of your life outside the church — in your home, neighbourhood and working world as well as your use of leisure time. You may want to note jobs you have had, courses you have taken or committees you have served on. You can list hobbies, special interests and voluntary work you have done outside the church.

When you have completed your rough list take up the chart and jot down opposite the appropriate gift anything even remotely related to any gift. You may want to refer to the short definitions of the gifts in Appendix I for help in relating your experiences to a corresponding gift. You don't have to write something opposite each gift. (Probably you have had no training in missions, for example.) This exercise is preliminary. Later on we shall explore each individual gift. Thinking through the various ways God has prepared you for a particular gift ministry by bringing opportunities or education, for example, across your path will make finding your gift easier. Feel free at any time to add to your columns or change what you wrote.

After filling in all you can on column '1A', proceed to jot down on another rough piece of paper any Christian work positions or ministries or tasks you have had. You might list stewarding or Sunday School teaching, being a deacon or in charge of the catering arrangements, sitting on the finance committee or caring for the church building. You may have worked outside of the church in a campus ministry, in evangelism or relief work. After you complete your list of Christian ministry experience, transfer each of these items to column 'B' opposite the gift they seem most to resemble.

For example, experience in Sunday School teaching might indicate giftedness in teaching. Being a deacon might indicate either abilities in administration or helpfulness. Counselling experience might indicate giftedness in exhortation. Work in finance could prepare for the gift of giving. Looking after the catering might show

giftedness in hospitality. Visitation or rescue mission experience
could reflect giftedness in evangelism. Committee work could be
noted opposite the gift of administration. Concern about the sick
might be a clue to the gift of mercy. Work on the maintenance of the
building probably demonstrates general helpfulness.

Do the best you can to match your past ministry experience with
the various gifts. Again, don't worry about being too accurate.
Adjustment can be made later. When you have filled in the first two
columns go on to consider the second step.

2. Taking an inventory of our sense of need

As noted in chapter 5, Christians are people who meet needs.
Spiritual gifts are those specialized endowments that enable different believers to meet different needs either inside or outside the
body.

Stop a moment and ponder the things that greatly exercise your
heart. As you look around in your community, in your local church
or further afield in the world, what glaring needs arouse your
concern? The Holy Spirit could very well be moving your heart
because of giftedness in that direction.

James A. Davey, in an article entitled, 'How to Discover Your
Spiritual Gifts,' encourages us to consider our local church and ask
ourselves questions such as the following: 'What is my greatest
concern for my church?' 'What do I think is very important in other
churches I visit?' 'What is lacking in the life of my church?'[13]

Mr Davey goes on to comment, 'Out of such heart-searching will
often come the conviction that some spiritual gift is not in evidence.
And if it is needed and not evident, perhaps it has been given but is
being repressed. When this kind of concern is vented in prayer it can
be the fulfilment of Paul's injunction to "earnestly desire spiritual
gifts". Understanding what you would wish in the way of spiritual
gifts is not a foolproof guide, but it is a valuable starting point.'[14]

Take up the chart again and fill in the third column, marked '2.
Sensed needs and burdens'. Don't fill in every space. Just make a
note opposite any gift about which you feel deeply. Note any gifts
you feel are lacking or weak in your church setting. As you
prayerfully ponder your own vineyard, what seem to be the greatest
needs that stare you in the face? Don't go on until you complete this

search for unmet needs. Unmet needs cry out for ministry. God might want to develop a gift in you to meet those needs!

3. Taking an inventory of effectiveness

Needs that are met indicate the presence of someone with spiritual gifts. For example, an unsaved person confessing faith in Christ probably indicates that the gift of evangelism has been in operation. A smoothly running committee points to someone exercising administrative gifts. Paul writes that gifts produce a variety of effects, of which the conversion of the lost and the organization of work are two. If we trace these effects we can in turn discover the gifts that produced them. Effects are nothing more than met needs. A trail of met needs will inevitably lead us to someone exercising his or her gifts.

To put it another way, people led by the Spirit to exercise their gifts inevitably produce spiritual fruit. Spiritual fruit comes in a great variety of shapes — from well-taught children, to grieving widows finding comfort, to a well-maintained building. When we discover effects such as these, we discover gifts in action.

Thinking back to the early days of my Christian experience, I realize that other Christians had quite an effect on me. My sceptical questions and ignorance about the Bible melted under the patient teaching of a man in a home Bible study. Down the street from my home a Christian neighbour graciously opened her home for this Bible study. Her son and daughter, also Christians, encouraged me during those roller-coaster years of floundering experience. A man with the gift of teaching, a woman with the gift of hospitality and two young people with the gift of encouragement indelibly shaped my early Christian experience. The effects they produced in my life demonstrated their spiritual gifts.

Think back over your own life. In what areas can you recognize some degree of spiritual effectiveness? Whom have you helped through witness, teaching, encouragement, mercy, giving, etc.? Maybe God used you to inspire your local church to trust God for some project. Perhaps God uses you to motivate others — one aspect of the leadership gift. Do others seek you out to talk over their problems? Are there practical things you do, such as repairing the church van, or cutting the grass, or delivering meals to shut-ins?

Where are you most effective in serving Christ? Where do you see fruit from your labours? While these are very subjective questions, nevertheless take your chart and fill any appropriate spaces under the third category. Most of the spaces will remain blank because you won't be fruitful in every area of giftedness. Look for the things you do that seem especially effective and appreciated by others. Don't go on until you have completed this assessment of spiritual effectiveness.

4. Taking an inventory of enjoyment or fulfilment

God did not create us for misery. When we glorify God we feel a deep sense of fulfilment and joy. True, the Christian life calls for sacrifice and a measure of suffering. Nevertheless, the suffering should not be the result of frustration traced to our inability to serve Christ well where he has placed us. Paul loved to preach. When we serve Christ in an area where we are fitted by giftedness, an enjoyment, a sense of fulfilment, makes the necessary trials of ministry seem bearable.

James Davey suggests that we should begin our search for gifts with 'our desires and aspirations'. We can ask ourselves, 'If I could be assured of success, what would I most like to contribute to my church fellowship?'[15]

What would you really love to do if you could? What are your internal desires? What longings burn within you? During those times of most intimate fellowship with God, what yearnings do you feel? God is not a 'cosmic kill-joy', going out of his way to make us miserable. As a rule, God prepares us to find a satisfying niche of ministry where we can use our gifts.

Davey points out, 'Regrettably, there is a kind of preaching that creates in the minds of many people the idea that God's will must always run counter to man's will, that surrender always calls for relinquishment of what we hold dearest. This may sometimes be so, but more often God leads us in paths and directions we would choose for ourselves... The internal desire signals the gift.'[16]

J. E. O'Day writes, 'Sit back and reflect on those things you really enjoy doing, activities that repeatedly bring satisfaction... There are in all of us patterns of desire, motivation and inclination that God has placed there.'[17]

Gail MacDonald quotes Findley Edge in *The Greening Of The Church* to say that, after looking within our hearts for a sense of fitness to a gift, we should 'seek out those moments when an awareness creeps up on us that we're often dreaming dreams about serving in a particular area. Are there moments when we find that our minds are a fountain of ideas and methods about how to engage in a certain project or service? When we find ourselves talking about certain ministries to others and we're not able to quench our own enthusiasm, we can learn something about our potential gifts.'[18]

Our particular gifts should produce a sense of excitement. If the gifts are undeveloped, the feeling may be more of a desire or longing. It may be a dream of what could be. When we discover our gift we will sense a fitness, like a comfortable shoe that seems made just for us. Of course, we minister in a broken and sinful world and any ministry will have its share of sacrifices; nevertheless God wants us to be joyful as well. Take a few moments now to fill in the next column. Go down the list of gifts and make a note opposite any that have given you a sense of fulfilment in the past or deeply draw your interest now. Don't go on until you have completed this fourth column.

5. Taking an inventory of others' counsel

Thus far our search has been largely a private affair. But exercises in gift discovery, like plans, 'fail for lack of counsel, but with many advisers they succeed'. Wise Christians always welcome the counsel of others. Pet ideas, imaginations and subjective feelings colour our choices. We run the risk of losing our way in a fog of subjectivity when we seek to discover and define our own gifts.

When we face important decisions that require subjective choices we would be wise to seek counsel. Actually, in healthy churches, pastors and deacons ought to be readily available for counsel. Most notably, pastor-teachers, in their role as equipping ministers, ought to be able to provide counsel and guidance. Don't be reticent to go to your pastor or to a church leader and talk over the whole matter of your gifts. Ask him what gifts he sees in you. Then too, your wife or husband, close friend or business associate can often give invaluable insight into your latent gifts.

Due to his natural timidity, Paul had to urge Timothy to stir up

his gift (1 Tim. 4:11-14). Elders in Timothy's church had had a hand
in discerning his gifts. Inexperience or timidity might be your
problem as well. Even if we possess considerable self-confidence,
we may seriously misjudge our own gifts. All of us need godly
counsel.

Gail MacDonald describes her experience: 'I guess I could say
that I owe the discovery and the development of my own gift of Bible
teaching to my husband. He claims that he saw it in me long before
I did. He lovingly pushed and chided me to say yes to teaching
opportunities. While I was terribly frightened in the early days of my
teaching experience, I soon grew to love what I was doing. Now I
feel at home teaching the Bible and am still surprised at the ministry
of the Holy Spirit in my life each time I am able to open the
Scriptures before a group of women. Gifts are like that.'[19]

Gail MacDonald's experience is quite common. Without friends
urging me to give my testimony I doubt that I would ever have
spoken publicly, let alone become a preacher. They must have
recognized something in me that I was blind to.

As you continue on your voyage of gift discovery ask friends to
help you chart a course. As you ponder what people have told you
in the past you might ask yourself questions like these: 'Have
spiritually mature people told me of certain abilities I possess? What
am I often asked to do in the way of spiritual ministry? Do others
express appreciation more often for one ministry I have than for
another? Are there certain things I am never asked to do?'[20]

Turn to the fifth column on the chart and mark any gifts you may
have that have been corroborated by the counsel or comments of
others. Don't be afraid to put down this book and go right out and
ask your wife or husband, or phone up a friend. Complete this
column on your chart before moving on.

6. Taking adequate time to discover your gifts

A potato matures in one season. Mighty oaks take a lifetime. Gift
development takes a lifetime too. Discovery also takes time. Gifts,
as we have seen, develop in a climate of prayer and submission,
obedience and love — aspects of Christian character. Eminent
giftedness in a young Christian is not unheard of. Charles Spurgeon
demonstrated powerful preaching gifts at an early age. But eminent

giftedness normally proves dangerous unless anchored in mature Christian character.

With a consistent Christian walk so important in those who minister in the Spirit, it is no wonder that considerable time elapses before most Christians come to a clear understanding of their gifts. Time produces, hopefully, the necessary humility and love so essential to the exercise of gifts. Don't be frustrated if you have not been able, as yet, to get a clear handle on your gift. Be patient. Persevere in your Christian walk. Clarity will increase as time progresses.

Time not only helps us to discover our gifts but also enables us to experience a broader range of Christian activities. Time exposes us to a variety of spiritual needs. We soon realize that no one gift is the panacea for all church ills. The whole array of gifts are crucial. Such exposure prepares us to work with others as a team. Indeed, as urgent needs present themselves, we find ourselves compelled by circumstances to adjust. Urgent needs call for immediate action. Whether we find ourselves gifted or not, we must respond. No wonder committed followers of Christ find themselves working in a variety of positions to meet a variety of needs. This gives exposure to different areas of need and helps us either develop some facility, or discover our ineptness in that area.

Billy Graham early became immersed in one ministry that called for a uniform gift-exercise throughout his life. Few of us have that experience. Most Christians develop competence in several areas. As needs vary, our ministries may vary. Gradually, however, we may become more specialized until we find our niche.

In my case, discovery and development have spanned several decades. As a new Christian I tried Sunday School teaching, tract distribution and personal witness. Sensing a call to missions, I enrolled in Bible College, where Christian service assignments thrust me into city ghettoes and onto an Indian reservation. Practical work experience in a church tested various other aspects of ministry and gave me an opportunity to preach once or twice. Missionary service involved evangelism, preaching, teaching and administration. Soon administration, teaching and writing came to the fore. After return to Canada a new area of ministry opened — the pastorate. Only in the last decade have I been clear about my cluster of gifts. Discovery and development have taken time.

But if we don't know what our gifts are until some time has

elapsed, how can we know where to minister? That is a good question. As already mentioned, obedience to the general commands of Christ lays out before us the path of service. Needs provoke a loving response. The commands of Christ inform us what that response should be. We should spend our time walking in obedience to these commands.

Suppose a poor family comes into the church. They have no home or job. The love of Christ ought to constrain us to help them find a job and a place to live. The love of Christ ought to move us to invite them home for meals.

Or suppose a widow falls ill and is admitted to the hospital. Love would motivate us to visit her. We discover our gifts by simply responding, as commanded by Christ, to the needs we see around us. Time will go by. Gradually it will become clearer to us that the Spirit has gifted us for effective ministry in a certain area. But if we don't obey Christ, we will never discover our gifts.

Conclusion

Turn to the final columns of the chart. Column 6 allows room for you to write down your present degree of obedience to the various commands that correspond, more or less, to the individual spiritual gifts. You might write in this column opposite the gift of evangelism, 'Weak,' indicating your need to be more active as a witness for Christ. In the column opposite teaching you might jot down, 'Teaching of children irregular,' to indicate that your family devotions need more effort. Fill in this column before moving on. Note that examples of general commands are printed in all but the first two columns. Missions and preaching do not lend themselves as well as other gifts to such an analysis.

A final column is left blank for you to write further notes as we go along. We are ready now to press on with a discussion of each of the gifts individually.

As we pursue our voyage of gift discovery, let us help others too to find their niches. Every pastor and every church must be in the business of fitting people into ministries that suit them. John, Marge, Bill and May abandoned a church that I read about, leaving the church splintered and marred. It took three years to repair the damage. Why? The pastor and board blamed the episode on spiritual problems, but in reality it was another case of square pegs in round holes.

John was an effective teacher but became immersed in committee meetings. Bill touched lives for Christ, but also ended up on the church executive board. May moved the congregation through her musical ministry but exhibited poor one-to-one skills. Enrolled in an evangelism class, she finally gave up. Marge quietly served behind the scenes in various roles where her gifts of helps and administration shone. But when assigned to teach junior high girls she floundered. All four experienced frustration and dropped out.[21]

Those in leadership positions in our churches need to make sure we don't duplicate this sad scenario. All of us can help by seeking to find and develop our gifts, as well as encouraging others to do the same. The first gift we shall consider in some depth is the gift of apostleship. Are there apostles today? Have missionaries inherited this gift? Let's find out.

Gift evaluation chart

| Gifts | 1. Providential preparation | | 2. Sensed needs and burdens | 3. Area of effectiveness | 4. Sense of fulfilment, enjoyment | 5. Counsel of others | 6. Degree of present obedience | Notes |
	A. Skills, hobbies, educ. exp.	B. ministry experience						
Speaking gifts								
Missions (Church-planting)								
Preaching								
Evangelism								'You are my witnesses'
Shepherding							'Bear one another's burdens'	
Knowledge							'Know the truth'	
Wisdom							'Walk in wisdom'	
Teaching							'Teaching them'	
Encourage-ment							'Encourage one another'	

Gift evaluation chart

Gifts / Serving gifts	1. Providential preparation		2. Sensed needs and burdens	3. Area of effectiveness	4. Sense of fulfilment, enjoyment	5. Counsel of others	6. Degree of present obedience	Notes
	A. Skills, exp., educ. hobbies, educ.	B ministry experience						
Helps							'Care for one another'	
Hospitality							'Be hospitable'	
Giving							'Give liberally'	
Mercy							'Be merciful'	
Faith							'… only believe'	
Discernment							'Test all things'	
Leadership (Administration)							'Rule your spirit'	

Part II:
The speaking gifts

8.
The speaking gifts: an introduction

Any study on gifts encounters a diversity of interpretations. Given the nature of the biblical data, this is to be expected. Each of the four lists of gifts differs from the others. Apostleship and shepherding describe both offices in the church and endowments for ministry. Other gifts, such as prophecy and teaching, wisdom and knowledge, overlap. Miracles and tongues disappear from sight as the apostolic age fades. We have a considerable complexity of data to harmonize!

Harmonizing teaching about gifts resembles sorting out data about church organization. The fragmentary nature of biblical teaching on the latter has led to, among others, Episcopal, Presbyterian, Baptist and Brethren interpretations. As with church order, so with gifts. We need to view those who have differing opinions with tolerance as long as all accept what is biblically clear. And there is much that is clear. But since equally conscientious interpreters differ, we must agree to tolerate some diversity.

Problems in defining gifts

Difficulty involved in interpretation has led some to avoid the subject of gifts altogether. Perhaps this explains why the biblical teaching on the priesthood of all believers did not survive the passage of centuries. God's call for believers to join together in body ministry did not even see much light during the Reformation. Skirting the subject, however, would be comparable to avoiding any

form of church organization just because we encounter difficulty in
defining the rôle of pastors, elders and deacons.

The problem of exactly defining gifts has led some to label
almost any ability a gift. These interpreters assume that the biblical
lists are suggestive, not comprehensive. For example, J. E. O'Day,
in a generally helpful little booklet, lists four reasons why we should
not confine our list to those gifts mentioned in the Bible. He writes,
'The Bible nowhere claims that the gifts listed by the apostles Paul
and Peter are the only ones.' However, the same argument could be
used against the canon of Scripture since the Bible neither lists the
books of the canon nor excludes others.

Secondly, he points out that there are considerable differences
between the lists. Some gifts occur in only one list and some in
several. 'If Paul knew that only a certain number of gifts existed,'
he says, 'he likely would have called attention to that fact and made
sure that all his lists agreed.' But why, then, does Paul not do that in
doctrinal areas? He mentions one facet of doctrine in one epistle and
another later.

Thirdly, O'Day notes that some spiritual gifts are similar to
universal Christian duties such as giving, faith and encouragement.
He interprets this similarity as an indication that any general
Christian responsibility, such as prayer or humility, might be
considered a gift in those who show special qualities in this area.
(We shall look at this idea as it comes up under our study of each
gift.)

Fourthly, he urges us not to limit ourselves to the biblical lists.
He reasons that there is too much difference of opinion on some of
the gifts. Puzzlement, however, does not free us to expand biblical
parameters; rather it challenges us to deeper study.

O'Day concludes, 'Don't be fooled into thinking that these are
the only gifts God has given his people! ... All these considerations
make it difficult to be dogmatic about what is and what is not a
spiritual gift. So don't be.'[1]

There we have an alternative opinion! While I don't agree with
O'Day, nevertheless his warning to avoid dogmatism about the
exact dimensions of each and every gift is good counsel. We need
to proceed with caution. The diversity of church situations and the
distinctiveness of each believer require us to avoid defining each
gift too narrowly.

O'Day, however, goes too far. Some fifteen gifts, in continuing use today, can be identified. They focus our attention on fifteen crucial facets of church ministry and direct us to give attention to specific needs that, in greater or larger degree, always exist in the church. If we fail to develop giftedness in these areas the corresponding needs they target will remain unmet and the church will suffer.

Variety in the ministry of the Spirit consists not just in the gifts themselves, but in the unique ways in which he leads individuals to minister. Our study in chapter 5 on the providence of God demonstrated that we bring diverse backgrounds and a variety of talents to the field of ministry. The fifteen gifts, however, are fifteen key areas of ministry that will manifest similarity wherever exercised. Every church will need the teaching and encouragement gifts, to name but two. If we totally open the field to any number of gifts we shall dilute this Spirit-inspired focus on specific needs that universally occur in the body. That is, if our sights range too far afield our ability to concentrate our ministries on actual needs will be diluted.

While I urge caution in defining too closely the gifts, nevertheless, I believe our journey in the pages ahead will be greatly helped by concentrating on fifteen gifts.

Two categories of gifts

Spiritual gifts can be divided into two groups: speaking gifts and serving gifts. In this distinction, too, there is a danger. While the speaking gifts are more foundational, the serving gifts are no less important. One group frees up the other for ministry. Deacons were chosen to care for widows in Acts 6, not because care of widows was any less important than the ministry of the Word and prayer, but to free apostles to use their gifts. James tells us that the essence of true religion is to 'look after orphans and widows in their distress' (James 1:27).

Some gifts become more prominent because they reside in those in positions of authority in the church. If we are not careful this fact may lead us unconsciously to stress prominent gifts. As a result, caste-like distinctions may develop.

Packer describes how Paul reflects an attitude totally at odds with ministry castes: 'From Paul's flitting to and fro between the two categories in Romans 12:6-8, where prophecy, teaching and exhorting, items one, three, and four in his list are gifts of speech and serving; giving, leading showing mercy, items two, five, six and seven are gifts of Samaritanship, we should learn that he saw no ultimate theological difference between them, however much they might differ as forms of human activity.'[2]

We must proceed with an attitude of respect for each of the gifts. True, Paul wrote, 'In the church God has appointed first of all apostles, second prophets, third teachers.' This text, however, occurs in the context of teaching on our equality in the body of Christ. An apostle is first among equals (1 Cor. 12:28). Equality and diversity of gifts mirror the same mix of equality and diversity between men and women that has been so misunderstood (Gal. 3:28). Pastors and preachers, far from being lordly potentates, are equal in the eyes of God with those exercising the gifts of helps or mercy.

The centrality of the Word

One more thing needs to be noted here. Speaking gifts relate to the pivotal ministry of the Word. Without the ministries of the Word we could not have a church. Note that I said 'ministries', in the plural, not 'ministry'. What are these ministries? In Protestantism we have given to preaching great prominence. Its importance must not be eroded. Nevertheless, we cannot ignore the fact that eight gifts deal with the communication of the Word.

This immediately highlights the variety of ministries acknowledged by apostolic practice. My own research in the book of Acts, which I record in *Tell The World*, led me to twenty different words used by the apostles for communication besides the traditional word 'preaching'. These words emphasize the broad spectrum of methods used by the apostles to communicate biblical truth. They are: 'to witness, testify, declare, speak, teach, proclaim, prove, reason, explain, persuade, give evidence, refute, demonstrate (prove or show), exhort, instruct, guide, bear the name of, carry on a ministry, a mission, and to admonish, encourage, strengthen.'[3] This breadth of method in communication highlights the need for each church to encourage a whole phalanx of ministries to buttress traditional preaching.

With these cautions in mind let us proceed to a study of the communication gifts. These eight gifts can be further divided into four groups. To use agricultural terminology, apostleship and prophecy are ploughing gifts, evangelism is a reaping gift, pastorship is a gathering gift, while teaching, knowledge, wisdom and exhortation are nurturing gifts. Consider first the gift of apostleship which God uses to plough virgin soil for the growth of his kingdom.

9.
The apostolic gift

The apostolic gift plunges us immediately into controversy. The Roman Catholic Church has historically claimed to be the only apostolic church by virtue of tracing a succession of prelates to Peter — a dubious claim indeed! Many Pentecostal churches allege they are apostolic by virtue of professing to demonstrate all the apostolic gifts, including miracles, healing and tongues. But neither Catholics nor Pentecostals, by and large, claim living apostles in their midst.

Some groups make just such a claim! H. R. Samadar of Calcutta, India, insists he is 'the Second Coming forerunner and the end-time apostle of Jesus Christ'. Further he states, 'In all the denominational churches including the Pentecostal churches there is no real Church of Christ,' because there is no apostle. He claims apostolic authority for his own church, 'All-One-In-Christ Church Fellowship'. Further, he believes that only those in it will be saved.[1]

Traditionally, Protestants have believed that the apostolic office ceased with the death of the twelve original apostles. In Protestant circles 'apostolic' means 'true to apostolic teaching'. Nevertheless, differences of opinion do exist. Walvoord, representing those who believe the gift completely ceased, states, 'The apostolic office died with the first generation of Christians, there being no provision for successors, nor have there been in the history of the church any who could stand with the apostles. The fact that apostles were chosen from those who were eyewitnesses of the resurrected Christ eliminates any possibility of later generations participating in the call to apostleship.'[2]

William McRae recognizes that men such as Barnabas, who are not among the twelve, are nevertheless called apostles in the Bible. But he writes, 'We believe that such persons were present only in the first century.'[3]

Other evangelicals believe that the gift continues, in some secondary sense, in the pioneer missionary. 'Officially, the apostolate ended with the apostles; unofficially the apostolic gift persists to our day as the missionary gift.'[4] Ray Stedman writes, 'The apostolic gift is still being given today, though in a secondary sense. It is part of the apostolic gift to start new churches. We call those who do this "pioneer missionaries" today.'[5]

The presence of these conflicting views on the gift of apostleship can be traced to two classes of biblical texts. Some texts point to an exclusive role for the Twelve, while others indicate a gift more generally found among believers at large. Let us look first at these exclusive texts.

I. Apostleship: a unique and temporary office

Christ instituted the office of apostleship in order to lay the foundation of the church. Paul writes that the body of Christ is 'built on the foundation of the apostles and prophets, with Jesus Christ himself as the chief cornerstone' (Eph. 2:20). The mystery of this unique group was first 'revealed by the Spirit to God's holy apostles and prophets'. The mystery concerned breaking down the wall of prejudice that divided Jews and Gentiles. Of these two streams of humanity Christ determined to 'create in himself one new man out of the two, thus making peace, and in this one body to reconcile both of them to God through the cross' (Eph. 2:15). This multi-ethnic church, constructed on the foundation laid by the apostles and prophets, will never be destroyed, for 'The gates of hell will not prevail against it' (Matt. 16:18, AV). Its creation finally brings to light the mystery 'which for ages past was kept hidden in God' (Eph. 3:9).

Once laid, a foundation does not need to be continually relaid. Clearly, the original apostles and prophets were unique men who filled an office that was foundational and thus temporary. God established the offices of apostle and prophet for a particular time. That time has come and gone.

Consider for a moment apostles as a group. Baxter quotes M. R. Vincent to show how specially qualified apostles were for their office: 'The distinguishing features of an apostle were: a commission directly from Christ, being a witness of the resurrection, special inspiration, supreme authority, accrediting by miracles, unlimited commission to preach and found ... churches.'[6]

Let's take a look at six apostolic distinctives.

1. A unique number, twelve

Jesus chose twelve apostles from among a host of disciples (Matt. 10:2-4; Mark 3:13-18; Luke 6:12-15). After his ascension the disciples, realizing the crucial need for twelve apostles, chose one to replace Judas, the betrayer (Acts 1:21-22). In an earlier discourse, Jesus had declared that the apostles were to 'sit on thrones, judging the twelve tribes of Israel' (Luke 22:30). The holy city 'had twelve foundations, and on them were the names of the twelve apostles of the Lamb' (Rev. 21:14). This evidence alone ought to prove sufficient to forever distinguish the original apostles.

2. A unique call from Christ

A personal call to office from Christ himself was a prerequisite to holding apostolic office. 'Jesus went out to a mountainside to pray, and spent the night praying to God. When morning came, he called his disciples to him and chose twelve of them, whom he also designated apostles' (Luke 6:12-13).

On the road to Damascus Jesus stopped Paul in his tracks and commissioned him as 'my chosen instrument to carry my name before the Gentiles and their kings and before the people of Israel' (Acts 9:6,15). Paul repeatedly affirmed that his apostleship was bestowed by Christ. His apostolic mandate did not originate as a personal choice or congregational call (Rom. 1:1; Gal. 1:1,11-12).

In Acts 1 we find Matthias being chosen to replace Judas. In Matthias' case Christ did not appear as he did in the case of Saul. Perhaps the group prematurely added Matthias 'to the eleven apostles' (Acts 1:26). However, since Paul himself refers to the other apostles as 'the Twelve', the point remains debatable (1 Cor. 15:5). Early church usage could have led him to use this terminology without necessarily denoting that Matthias' choice had the personal sanction of Christ. In that same context Paul describes his apostleship as that of a late-comer: 'Last of all he appeared to me also, as to one abnormally born. For I am the least of the apostles and do not even deserve to be called an apostle, because I persecuted the church of God' (1 Cor. 15:8-9).

Paul never denied his own apostleship. Indeed, he took pains to prove its genuine nature when he wrote to the Galatians and Corinthians. This suggests that doubt about his credentials existed in some quarters. This doubt may have been aroused by confusion due to the premature choice of Matthias by the pre-Pentecostal assembly. The early disciples did not wait for Christ to hand-pick a successor — Paul. Whatever the position of Paul relative to the Twelve, the necessity of a personal call from Christ, as a prerequisite, is never in doubt. And no other men in the New Testament record received a call to office as unique as Paul's Damascus Road experience.

3. A unique testimony to the risen Christ

Apostles were chosen from among those who could give eyewitness testimony to Jesus' person, teaching and resurrection. Jesus said, 'And you also must testify, for you have been with me from the beginning' (John 15:27). The early disciples understood the fundamental importance of objective witness. Hence Peter stood up and said, 'One of these must become a witness with us of his resurrection' (Acts 1:21-22). Apostles functioned as eyewitnesses of the resurrection of Christ.

Realizing the importance of eyewitness testimony, Paul affirms his apostleship by saying, 'Have I not seen Jesus our Lord?' and 'Last of all he appeared to me also' (1 Cor. 9:1;15:8).

In his first epistle, John underscores the intimate nature of the apostles' acquaintance with Christ: 'That which was from the beginning, which we have heard, which we have seen with our eyes, which we have looked at and our hands have touched — this we proclaim... The life appeared...' (1 John 1:1-2). The apostles had been so inextricably involved in Jesus' ministry, from his baptism in Jordan onward, that they could talk about Christ from first-hand experience.

In this sense no one can be an apostle who has not seen with his eyes the risen Christ. This, of course, blocks from apostolic office anyone during the last nineteen centuries. The office ceased when the original eyewitnesses died.

4. Unique authority from Christ

Christ bestowed on his apostles special authority: 'He called his twelve disciples to him and gave them authority to drive out evil spirits and to heal every [kind of] disease and sickness' (Matt. 10:1). The keys of the kingdom, given to Peter, symbolize his authority as an apostle (Matt. 16:19).

The position given to the gift of apostleship in the lists of gifts also reflects their priority: 'And in the church God has appointed first of all apostles...' (1 Cor. 12:28). It is to the apostles that a kingdom was given and thrones of authority were promised (Luke 22:29-30). But since their number is limited to twelve and the twelve died, there can be no succession of apostolic authority.

5. Unique inspiration

Apostles and prophets were the foundation of the church, mainly because they were uniquely inspired by the Spirit of God in all their teaching. Christ promised them the Spirit to 'teach you all things and ... remind you of everything I have said to you' (John 14:26; 16:13). Their teaching and writing was 'not in words taught us by human wisdom but in words taught by the Spirit' (1 Cor. 2:13; cf. Acts 15:28). They proclaimed and wrote God's revealed Word (Gal. 1:12; Eph. 3:5) To reject their instruction was to reject God (1 Thess. 4:8). What they wrote was, and is, Scripture — God's inerrant Word (2 Peter 3:16).

The early church viewed the apostolic office as so unique that they tested a book's authenticity by its apostolicity. Only books stamped as authentic by their apostolic accreditation were allowed to become part of the canon of the New Testament.

6. Unique authenticating signs

Special signs authenticated the office and teaching of apostles. 'The things that mark an apostle — signs, wonders and miracles — were done among you' (2 Cor. 12:12). Christ gave authority to the Twelve to enable them to 'drive out evil spirits and to heal every disease and sickness' (Matt. 10:1). Miraculous demonstrations set apostolic ministry apart from subsequent Christian ministry. 'Many wonders and miraculous signs were done by the apostles' (Acts 2:43; 5:12; 8:18).

As noted in chapter 4, many charismatics theorize that God uses signs and wonders today to authenticate the gospel. The vast majority of commentators down through history, however, have held that signs and miracles occurred in clusters during times of special inspiration for the purpose of authenticating revelation.

In summary, a wealth of textual evidence demonstrates that apostleship was a unique and temporary office. It was restricted to twelve men who were personally called by Christ to be eyewitnesses to his person and resurrection, chosen to wield unique authority and appointed to be the bearers of inspired revelation. Since no other foundation can be laid than Christ Jesus, so too, no other apostles but the Twelve may lay claim to apostolic office.

Nevertheless, further scriptural study presents us with a paradox. Some texts make mention of apostles other than the Twelve. Apostleship, it appears, was also reflected in a more general form than that demonstrated by the Twelve. Apparently, the gift must continue in some lesser role. Consistency demands that we harmonize these exclusive and general texts. Look at the evidence.

II. Apostleship: a general and continuing gift

1. Evidence of apostles other than the twelve

Acts 14 refers to Barnabas as an apostle, listing him ahead of Paul (Acts 14:4,14). In Galatians Paul writes of his early trip to Jerusalem, where 'I saw none of the other apostles — only James, the Lord's brother' (Gal. 1:19). This James is not the James mentioned as one of the Twelve. Paul describes both Silas and Timothy as apostles (compare 1 Thess. 1:1 with 2:6-7). Titus, who occupied a similar role, was very likely an apostle also. Romans concludes with a list of greetings in which we read that Andronicus and Junias are 'outstanding among the apostles' (Rom. 16:7). Since the word used here is plural, 'apostles', it seems likely to suppose that there were many others whose names are not recorded. Our count of the number of apostles now increases from twelve to over twenty! Such evidence requires us to broaden our definition of apostleship.

2. Mention of apostles in the lists of gifts

The lists of gifts found in both 1 Corinthians and Ephesians mention apostleship. One could argue that mention of apostles in the Epistle to the Corinthians would be natural since Paul wrote it relatively early in the apostolic era. But why mention apostles in as late an epistle as Ephesians? By this time the number of the apostles must have been seriously reduced by death.

Why would Paul mention apostles in an epistle dealing with the nature of the church? Why do so in a passage as crucial to church edification as chapter 4? Verse 12 records that the purpose for which Christ gave the gifts of apostles, prophets, evangelists, pastors and teachers was to 'prepare God's people for works of service so that the body of Christ may be built up'. Now if apostleship and prophecy had only temporary relevance, then it would necessarily follow that preparing people for works of service was completed in apostolic times. But did the work of equipping saints cease with the death of the apostles? Of course not. If the role of the last three, evangelists, pastors and teachers, continues, why not that of the first two? We can only solve this dilemma if we admit that, in some sense at least, the gifts of apostleship and prophecy continue.

What an enigma! We must harmonize these two apparently conflicting sets of biblical data. We should reason from what is clear. Clearly none of the more general apostles, such as Barnabas, shared the prerogatives of the Twelve. Barnabas was not numbered among the Twelve. He obviously could not have shared a place on the twelve thrones or in the twelve foundations of the New Jerusalem.

What, then, did these 'orphan apostles' share with their mighty namesakes? I would answer, 'church-planting'.

3. Apostles as church-planters

Besides laying the foundation of the church at large, apostles founded individual local churches. In this more general sense Paul describes his ministry in terms of laying a foundation: 'By the grace God has given me, I laid a foundation as an expert builder, and someone else is building on it' (1 Cor. 3:10). In this instance, Paul founded the Corinthian church. Others built upon the foundation laid by his missionary labours. Paul was a church-planter, founding churches all over the Mediterranean world.

In this sense, Barnabas too was an apostle. At first Barnabas was the eminent church-planter, but he was superseded by Paul. Silas, Timothy, Titus and others on the apostolic team must have carried on the same type of work.

Paul was not the only church-planter among the Twelve. Peter and John probably itinerated widely in order to supervise the growth of younger churches. They went to inspect the work of Philip in Samaria. Before they left Samaria they made sure that the infant church had experienced the presence of the Holy Spirit (Acts 8:14-25). Then 'Peter and John returned to Jerusalem, preaching the gospel in many Samaritan villages' (v. 25). In Acts 9 we read, 'As Peter travelled about the country, he went to visit the saints in Lydda' (Acts 9:32). Later in Joppa he received the dramatic missionary vision of the lowered sheet that signified that all peoples should be considered as 'clean' —candidates for salvation (Acts 10). After the vision and the visit by Cornelius' emissaries, Peter set forth, rather timidly at first, as a missionary apostle to Cæsarea. When he arrived at Cornelius' house, he crossed over the immense cultural chasm that separated Jews from Romans and founded a new cross-cultural church in his house (Acts 10:47-48).

God's love sent Christ to seek lost sheep. Christ in turn commissioned the Twelve, and those who follow, to 'preach the good news to all creation', and to 'make disciples of all nations' (Mark 16:15; Matt. 28:19). With this commission echoing within their hearts, the Twelve must have gone out seeking lost sheep. The vision of vast unreached multitudes outside their present areas of witness must have gripped them.

Paul epitomized this apostolic vision, in both the special and the more general sense, when he said, 'It has always been my ambition to preach the gospel where Christ was not known, so that I would not be building on someone else's foundation. Rather, as it is written: "Those who were not told about him will see, those who have not heard will understand"' (Rom. 15:20-21). The vision of reaching the unreached must have motivated all the apostles, Peter as well as Barnabas, Paul no less than Timothy — if they were true to Christ, as we believe they were.

The gift of apostleship seems to focus on pioneer evangelism and church-planting (Acts 20:13-38). The exclusive office of the apostles, as exemplified in the Twelve, ceased. But the gift illustrated by the apostles continues in the passion and ministry of pioneer missionaries.

4. Broader meaning and usage of the word 'apostle'

Is it only coincidence that the Greek word for apostle means 'one sent', while the word 'missionary', from the Latin, means essentially the same thing? Although derived from different languages, 'apostle' and 'missionary' have the same root meaning.

The *Didache,* written near the beginning of the second century, was penned after the death of the Twelve. It describes early church ministry. The *Didache* uses 'apostle' in two senses. It recognizes the unrivalled position of the original Twelve. But it mentions the presence at that time of itinerant apostles akin to present-day missionaries: 'Concerning apostles and prophets, so do ye according to the ordinance of the gospel. Let every apostle, when he cometh to you, be received as the Lord; but he shall not abide more than a single day, or if there be need, a second likewise; but if he abide three days, he is a false prophet (11:3).' [7]

Flynn quotes the *International Standard Bible Encyclopedia*: 'In the New Testament and in the other literature of the early church, the word "apostle" is used in a narrower and in a wider sense. The wider use of the word has descended to the present day, "apostles" or "holy apostles" is still the name for missionaries in some parts of the Greek church.' [8]

We have precedent, both in the New Testament and in early church history, for believing that there were two kinds of apostles: the Twelve, who founded the first churches, and general apostles, who were missionary church-planters. Early church historians wisely highlighted the exclusiveness of the Twelve by denoting them as 'apostles' while calling those who carried on a similar ministry 'missionaries'. We should never confuse missionaries with apostles. The original Twelve were absolutely unique in respect to their office and qualifications.

Some question whether the Twelve were missionaries in the broader sense. In Acts 15 we find Paul and Barnabas going up to Jerusalem to see the apostles and elders. Andrews comments, 'The Jerusalem apostles were not missionaries in the sense that Paul and Barnabas were, having never left their homeland.'[9] I find this distinction — leaving one's homeland — hard to accept for four reasons.

Firstly, God specifically called Peter to pioneer the church in the Jewish community (Gal. 2:7). While this occurred substantially in his homeland, it was pioneer work none the less.

Secondly, Paul likens his ministry to that of Peter: 'For God who was at work in the ministry of Peter as an apostle to the Jews, was also at work in my ministry as an apostle to the Gentiles' (Gal. 2:8). Clearly there is a correspondence between the two ministries. We are unwise to make distinctions between ministries on the basis of their distance from a missionary's home culture. Embarking on ships or making overland journeys didn't make Paul a missionary, any more than travelling around Palestine prevented Peter from being one!

Thirdly, as we have already noted, Peter did itinerate widely. Indeed, he travelled beyond Judea to visit Antioch (Gal. 2:11).

Fourthly, there is strong historical evidence that all the apostles travelled beyond Palestine. The presence in South India of the church of 'Thomas Christians' who trace their origin to the missionary journeys of Thomas has a continuing history going back many centuries.

I would argue, then, for a broader usage of the word apostle that approximates to our word 'missionary'. I would not be comfortable, however, to go as far as Calvin did. He wrote, 'According to the meaning and etymology of the word, all the ministers of the Church may be called apostles, because they are all sent by the Lord, and are His messengers.'[10]

Prudence would lead us to restrict our usage of the word 'apostle' to the Twelve while at the same time maintaining that the gift of apostleship, as pioneer church-planting, was bestowed by the Spirit on men other than the Twelve.

5. Missionaries and the more general apostolic gift

In essence the missionary gift is that endowment of the Spirit through which he bestows vision and ability on those sent out to do church-planting among the unreached. Consider six aspects of this definition.

Vision

Missionary vision superimposes the biblical mandate on the world as it is. Apostolic vision grew as events transpired. The apostles recognized the missionary nature of the covenant with Abraham: 'In you all the families of the earth shall be blessed' (Gen. 12:3, NASV). They knew Jesus' desire: 'I have other sheep that are not of this sheep pen' (John 10:16) and his marching orders: 'Make disciples of all nations' (Matt. 28:19). Peter's vision of the sheet let down from heaven had demonstrated that they ought to reach out to all peoples. The power of the Spirit, as manifest in four distinct cultural Pentecosts among Jews, Samaritans, Romans and Greeks, must have accelerated the growth of cross-cultural vision. While the vision of the early apostles was faltering and parochial at first, it gradually grew until it found mature expression in the apostolic bands led by Paul. How could it be otherwise? God is a missionary God.

Churches owe their origin and continuing spiritual health to the maintenance of this vision. True, churches exist for worship, edification and fellowship, but worship is not truly worship unless it celebrates God as he is — the great missionary God. Missionary vision must pulse through our churches as naturally as blood pumps through our veins. Yet it is seldom so. We exhibit profound concern about our buildings, our programmes and our budgets. Our vision is, largely, parochial and introverted. These things ought not to be so! Does any church have a continuing right to exist that is deaf to the missionary purpose of God?

Being sent out

The apostolic gift, as it continues in missionaries, involves being sent out by a local congregation. This sending is inherent in the very meaning of the word 'missionary'.

Barnabas fetched Paul to help him teach believers in the new church in Antioch. After a year of ministry there the church sent them with famine relief money to the saints in Jerusalem. Returning to Antioch, they continued serving on a local church level for some time. Later, while engaged in corporate worship with the leadership team, 'The Holy Spirit said, "Set apart for me Barnabas and Saul for the work to which I have called them." So after they had fasted and prayed, they placed their hands on them and sent them off. The two of them, sent on their way by the Holy Spirit, went to Seleucia' (Acts 13:2-4).

After their missionary journeys, Barnabas and Paul returned to the Antioch church to report on God's work. Missionaries who follow the apostolic pattern are set apart for ministry in a local church, are sent out from that church and return to that church to render accountability.

Missionaries in the apostolic mould are neither adventurers who love to travel, nor eccentric individualists who find local church life too confining. Missionaries need a profound sense of the centrality of the body of Christ. They are not mavericks who can never settle down, but rather visionaries who develop in a local church setting until church leaders recognize their potential missionary gifts.

The home church, however, cannot closely supervise missionaries in distant lands. Missionaries, like the apostles, must have flexibility on the field. Administering field work in any detail from a distant home church stifles the very genius of missions. But even while they maintain freedom for on-the-spot action, missionaries in the apostolic mould remain accountable to their sending church. Although William Carey's missionary vision was blatantly rejected by his denomination, nevertheless he patiently prepared himself for service and prayed until a small group arose to send him out. Missionaries are 'sent ones'.

Messengers

Missionaries, like apostles, go forth bearing a message. Thayer defines an apostle as 'a delegate, messenger, one sent forth with orders'.[11] Apostles were divinely commissioned to go forth proclaiming the gospel.

In Luke 9 Jesus called the twelve apostles to his side. He gave them power to drive out demons, to cure the sick and 'to preach the kingdom of God'. At his command, 'They set out and went from village to village, preaching the gospel and healing people everywhere' (Luke 9:1-6).

Paul explained the apostolic mandate to the Thessalonians: 'We speak as men approved by God to be entrusted with the gospel' (1 Thess. 2:4). The gospel is essentially the message of Christ — his incarnation, cross and resurrection. It includes an unveiling of mankind's need to believe and repent.

The early Christians were well known for their good works. We must remember, however, that these acts of mercy were the result of their acceptance of the gospel message and not the message itself. While the apostles healed, cast out demons and encouraged relief work, they never lost sight of their main task. They had been commissioned to bear witness to the risen Christ. A cursory reading of the New Testament confronts us with the obvious fact that communication of the gospel overshadowed all other apostolic ministries. They were messengers, not social workers.

'Mission' in the apostolic sense is essentially proclamation and not medical work, literacy work, relief ministry, education or technical training. While these latter ministries often cluster around missionary work, they are the peripheral fruits of mission work, never the central task itself. Failure to make this distinction has repeatedly led to de-emphasizing evangelism through the sincere but mistaken belief that alleviating physical needs should have precedence. (Obvious and emergency needs, of course, must be met. For a fuller discussion of this issue, see *Tell the World*.)

Missionary work in the apostolic mould will always emphasize evangelism (church-planting) because men's need for salvation is more desperate than any other need. Apostolic missionaries are essentially communicators.

Pioneers

The needs of the unevangelized grip the heart of the apostolic missionary. Paul declared, 'It has always been my ambition to preach the gospel where Christ was not known, so that I would not be building on someone else's foundation' (Rom. 15:20). Missionaries who follow in the steps of Paul preach in unchurched pioneer situations. Pastors and teachers minister where there is already a foundation laid, while those with the apostolic gift lay the foundations for new churches in unevangelized areas.

When God gave Peter the vision of the lowered sheet he said, in effect, 'Peter, stop being concerned only with the Jewish people while the Gentiles remain unreached' (see Acts 10). In essence, God gave Peter a pioneer vision. This vision of reaching out to the unreached always distinguishes apostolic missions. Missionaries who have caught this vision feel compelled to move out in witness into the unevangelized parts of the earth.

It has ever been so. During the last three centuries we have seen three great missionary thrusts into the dark places of earth, all fuelled by a burden for the unreached. First, Carey and his contemporaries pioneered work in the unevangelized coastlands of India, China and Africa. Secondly, Hudson Taylor and a gallery of 'faith missionaries' led the thrust into the vast unreached inland portions of these countries. This second era spawned the China Inland Mission, the Sudan Interior Mission, the Africa Inland Mission and a host of other groups. More recently, men such as Cameron Townsend recognized the presence all over the world of unevangelized tribes. Linguistic or cultural isolation had hidden them from view. Wycliffe Bible Translators, Gospel Recordings and New Tribes Mission, to name a few missions, were founded to reach these overlooked tribes and peoples.

Today the research of Ralph Winter at the US Center for World Mission, and those like him, has uncovered a new frontier. 17,000 unreached people groups must become the new target of pioneer evangelism. While most modern nations have churches, hundreds of distinct ethnic groups, peoples, have been overlooked in each nation. A people group cannot be reached without a team specifically aimed at them. This is today's task, planting churches among every one of these remaining 17,000 peoples. While there are approximately 7,000 reached peoples, over half the world remains beyond the reach of the gospel in an understandable form.

Church-planting

Church-planting, more than any other characteristic, distinguishes the apostolic gift. Paul wrote to the Corinthians to remind them that their very existence was evidence of his apostleship (1 Cor. 9:2;

2 Cor. 3:2; see also Rom. 15). In his parting speech to the Ephesian elders, Paul reviewed the various ministries that had engaged his attention among them. He essentially tabulated different facets of church-planting from evangelism to the nurture of converts and the appointment of leaders. Paul's church-planting success is written large in the pages of Scripture.

Missionary work is church-planting. Nothing else — not relief work, not hospitals, not schools, not Bible translation, not even radio evangelism, *per se* — must distract us from the main missionary task. These diverse activities have missionary validity only as they contribute to building the kingdom through establishing local churches. Local churches, in turn, become centres where compassion ought to be displayed in diverse ways.

Itineration

Both Peter and Paul were travellers. Missionaries who follow in their footsteps are not prone to settle down. They realize that church-planting involves development of leaders. Leaders fail to develop if more mature and gifted leaders keep gobbling up leadership responsibilities. God scattered the early Jewish church when they failed to understand this principle. As a result strong new leaders like Philip developed when they moved out from under the shadow cast by the Twelve.

Once a church was established Paul moved on. He writes in Romans 15 about going to Rome, then on to Spain. The pull of the unreached compels the apostolic missionary to avoid putting down deep roots in any one place. Paul realized that, while there was much yet to do in Greece and Asia Minor, the foundation had been laid there. He wrote to explain, 'So from Jerusalem all the way around to Illyricum, I have fully proclaimed the gospel of Christ... Now that there is no more place for me to work in these regions, and since I have been longing for many years to see you, I plan to do so when I go to Spain' (Rom. 15:19,23-24). Once a foundation is laid, missionaries should move on.

The amount of time necessary to lay a foundation varies from place to place. In the Muslim world this might mean staying for decades. Tribes may require fifteen years or so. Churches might spring up in a year or two among responsive peoples. But the time to move does come. One of the greatest tragedies of missions has been the construction of great mission stations in denial of this principle. Historically, long-term residence in Asia and Africa gave missionaries the time to construct beautiful missionary compounds and elaborate medical and educational institutions. This mission-station approach, however, usually led to paternalism and dependence. It stunted leadership development.

Conclusion

In summary, missionaries who inherit the apostolic gift possess vision, are sent out by local churches as messengers of the gospel and are commissioned to itinerate with a view to planting churches among unreached people.

While apostleship, as exemplified in the Twelve, was a unique and temporary office, it continues in a more general sense as the gift of pioneer missions. Such a synthesis of conflicting texts seems to be the only way to resolve this dilemma.

Historians have wisely reserved the title 'apostle' for those twelve unique men chosen by Christ to bear witness to his person and resurrection. Their calling, experience, witness, authority, inspiration and authenticating signs demonstrated their uniqueness. Apostles do not exist today. None succeeded the Twelve. The gift of apostleship, however, continues in those called to pioneer missionary work.

Before moving on to the next chapter, fill in the columns opposite the missionary gift in the gift chart. If you have had short-term missionary experience, courses on missions or feel a deep burden for missionary work, you will want to note this down.

10.
The prophetic gift

Whether seeking to read the entrails of animals or interpret the stars, mankind has always aspired to the prophetic gift. A yearning to slay fear of an unknown future has energized this search down through the centuries.

The quest for this mystical gift continues today — often dressed up in pseudo-scientific jargon. An article about the work of Dr Kary Mullis, a California molecular biologist, reports his assertion that 'Genes can "see" a child's future.' Dr Mullis predicts that in ten years we shall be able to read a child's whole future within a few hours of birth. He claims that the DNA in a single cell contains 'everything about the child'. According to Dr Mullis, all we wait for is the technology to read the future as already encoded in the DNA.[1]

Jean Dixon has been making predictions for years. She supposedly foretold the assassination of John F. Kennedy four years before he was elected president, the death by plane crash of Dag Hammerskjold, as well as the Communist takeover of China. But in a CBC radio show, the Great Randy (Mr James Randy) talked about the research of the *National Inquirer* into 364 of her prophecies. They found that only four had come true. The quality of these four was of the order of, for instance, that 'There will be a great medical breakthrough this year,' and 'There will be a scandal in Hollywood this year.'[2]

Some modern evangelicals seem to hunger after prophecy. A sincere young man in a congregation I was pastoring recently startled me by claiming that I was hindering the Spirit by forbidding prophecy. Quoting from 1 Thessalonians, 'Do not put out the Spirit's fire; do not treat prophecies with contempt,' he explained that by teaching that sign gifts had ceased I kept believers from giving 'a word of prophecy'. Fortunately discussion and prayer led this young man to moderate his evaluation. But the pressure to seek a fresh and 'authentic' word from God in the form of 'a word of prophecy' continues to increase.

Pentecostal and charismatic circles, particularly, face this challenge. J. I. Packer spent considerable time seeking to ascertain just what charismatics meant by prophecy. He concluded: 'By prophecy I mean the receiving and relaying of what purports to be a divine message. Prophecy is a regular feature of charismatic fellowship. The usual beliefs about it are (1) that it is a direct revelation from God of thoughts in his mind, which otherwise would not be known; (2) that it frequently includes specific directions by God, concerning his plans for the future; (3) that its proper verbal form is that of Old Testament oracles, in which the one who speaks is regularly God himself; and (4) that it was a sign gift in the apostolic church, which, with the other sign gifts, was in abeyance in the church from the mid-patristic era till the twentieth century. But all of this is doubtful.'[3]

Most of our charismatic friends believe that God continues to issue revelations. However, belief that God has continued to reveal himself in prophecy has been rarely held in church history. It has been confined mainly to the fringes of orthodox faith. The term Quakers use for continuing revelation is 'inner light'. George Fox, founder of Quakerism, taught that Christ continues to bring revelations directly to the hearts of his people.[4]

Throughout history consensus about prophecy and revelation has ruled the theology of main-line Christians. The vast majority agreed that the gift of prophecy is *not* an endowment through which God inspires new revelations. This unanimity has generally continued among traditional evangelicals and Reformed believers.

There consensus ceases and a variety of opinions proliferates. Does the gift of prophecy continue in any sense? Calvin believed that prophecy continues, not as ability to foretell the future, 'but the science of interpreting Scriptures, so that a prophet is an interpreter of the will of God'.[5]

C. H. Spurgeon, on the other hand, believed that the gift ceased. In his view prophets occupied a peculiar office. They served as a

'link between the glories of the Old and New Testament'.[6] J. I.
Packer believes that prophecy as revelation has ceased but that the
prophetic ministry continues in prophetic preaching.[7]

Modern confusion about prophetic revelations has even spread
to Reformed circles. Anthony Coppin writes about attendance at a
'Reformed and Renewed Pastor's Conference' in Hertfordshire,
England, in an article, 'Life in the Spirit'. He was obviously taken
aback by the charismatic practices and beliefs he saw there. He
reports that Bernard Thompson, one of the leaders of the conference,
describes prophecy as 'startling and a little frightening. We can,' he
tells us, 'claim inspiration but not inerrance for words of revelation
which Spirit-baptized believers bring!'[8]

This confusing new definition of inspiration and revelation
departs violently from the traditional view. Traditionally (upon
solid biblical grounds) revelation has been considered inerrant.
How could a product of the inspiration of the Holy Spirit be
otherwise? It is unthinkable to attribute error to a process that owes
its origin to the superintendence of the perfect God!

All around us fuzzy theological thought is blurring the definitions crystallized after centuries of painstaking biblical research.
Christians talk of 'words of knowledge', 'prophecies' and 'revelations'. They invest these communications with divine authority.
They charge those who refuse to acknowledge the authority of these
declarations with hindering the Spirit. Those who bring 'prophecies' assert that they have the same weight as Scripture because
God is their author. On the other hand, as we shall see later in this
chapter, the proponents of modern-day prophecies admit their
fallibility. But how can any believer attribute fallibility to a direct
word from God? Confusion over the implications of these claims
pervades the modern charismatic movement, particularly those in
the 'third wave'. (The 'third wave' is a term popularized by John
Wimber and the Vineyard movement. In their view, the first wave
was traditional Pentecostalism, the second, the charismatic movement and the third is a more moderate and generally evangelical
movement.)

We face, then, even greater diversity of opinion about the gift of
prophecy than about the gift of apostleship. Our approach to
prophecy will parallel our discussion about apostles. In both cases,
diverse texts need to be harmonized: texts that seem to deny the
continuation of the gift, on the one hand, and those which seem to
indicate the opposite. Let us look first at the more exclusive texts.

I. Prophet: a unique and temporary office

As mentioned in the previous chapter, the church is 'built on the foundation of the apostles and prophets, with Christ Jesus himself as the chief cornerstone' (Eph. 2:20). As the founding agents of the church, God chose to reveal to apostles and prophets truths that had been hidden from all ages (Eph. 3:5). There were only twelve founding apostles. Likewise, history has only seen a limited number of inspired prophets, every one of whom fulfilled three characteristics. Let us consider these three distinctives in turn.

1. The periodic nature of the prophetic office

Our study begins in the Old Testament. Some may assume that prophets were present during the whole Old Testament period. Such is not the case. Certainly, all Old Testament Scripture is prophetic in nature. Christ declared, 'All the Prophets and the Law prophesied until John [the Baptist],' indicating that even the Law was prophetic (Matt. 11:13). Further, Peter writes, 'No prophecy of Scripture … was ever made by an act of human will, but men moved by the Holy Spirit spoke from God' (2 Peter 1:21, NASV).

If we conclude, however, that prophets were always part of the Old Testament scene, we shall err. God revealed Old Testament Scripture at widely spaced intervals, not in a continuous process. 'In the past God spoke to our forefathers through the prophets at many times and in various ways' (Heb. 1:1). Periods of revelation were interspersed with long periods of prophetic silence.

Moses appears as the first major prophet of Old Testament history. When Moses descended the mount, he bore in his hands the law of God that had been inspired by the direct action of God. Of Moses, God's mouthpiece during the Exodus, we read, 'Since then, no prophet has risen in Israel like Moses, whom the Lord knew face to face' (Deut. 34:10).

The period of the judges follows the victory years of Joshua. During this era, prophets disappeared. Vision was rare (1 Sam. 3:1). Finally, Samuel arose to take up the prophetic mantle last worn by Moses. From the days of Samuel on through the kingdom period, as priests became increasingly corrupt, prophets became more common. God raised up the schools of the prophets to compensate for priestly failure. Elijah and Elisha prophesied during this period. Prophets of this era, however, did not add to the canonical literature that became Holy Scripture.

The golden period of prophetic greatness extended for about 400 years, from approximately 800 BC. to 400 BC. During this era prophets such as Isaiah, Jeremiah, Ezekiel and Daniel produced major works. Others, such as Amos, Hosea and Malachi, contributed powerful, but short, prophetic collections.

Malachi, the last of the Old Testament writing prophets, ushered in the 400 years of prophetic silence. This era extended until the coming of Christ. John the Baptizer broke that silence to introduce the Messiah.

The magnitude of Christ's ministry as Prophet, Priest and King eclipsed that of John. Jesus ushered in a new prophetic era. This period produced the New Testament canon, written, as he predicted, by the inspiration of the Holy Spirit under the supervision of the apostles. As already noted, the twelve apostles occupied a dual office. They were both apostles and prophets (Eph. 2:20). As apostles they founded churches while as prophets they completed the canon of Holy Scripture.

Besides the Twelve, other prophets appeared during the New Testament era. Agabus, one of a group of prophets who came down to Jerusalem from Antioch, predicted 'that a severe famine would spread over the entire ... world. (This happened during the reign of Claudius.)' (Acts 11:28). In Acts 21 Agabus predicted Paul's imprisonment (Acts 21:11). Besides Agabus, the text describes Philip's daughters as prophetesses (Acts 21:9). While these daughters had the gift of prophecy there is no indication, pro or con, whether they, like Agabus, had predictive powers.

This hasty overview establishes that before Christ came, God activated the prophetic office intermittently. He raised up prophets as the bearers of his revealed Word during periods of great need. Three main periods come to light: first, the time of the Exodus, which produced the books of the Law; second, the period of Israel's kingdom, during which the Writings were recorded; and third, the period of deterioration culminating in the destruction of Jerusalem, the Babylonian captivity and Israel's return, during which prophets wrote the books of history and prophecy.

Long periods of prophetic silence occurred. We find no evidence of prophecy previous to Moses, nor during the period of the judges.

Prophecy probably came sporadically during the kingdom period. Prophecy disappears during the 400-year period preceding Christ.

We must conclude that during Old Testament times prophecy appeared intermittently. What reasons can be given for its periodic occurrence?

2. The inspired function of the prophets

The word 'to prophesy' in Hebrew means 'to flow forth'. Andrews explains, 'These words convey the idea that in prophetic utterance the message of God was laid upon the heart of the prophet and flowed forth from his lips or from his pen.'[9]

Revelation

God appointed prophets to be his spokesmen, to bring to men a revelation of his will. Repeated phrases such as, 'The Lord said to Moses,' demonstrate that Moses served as God's mouthpiece. In Exodus we read that Moses conveyed to the people the very words of God: 'Moses assembled the whole Israelite community and said to them, "These are the things the Lord has commanded you to do"' (Exod. 35:1). In similar vein the book of Jeremiah, while it contains what Jeremiah wrote, really records what God told Jeremiah to write (see Jer. 1:1,2,4, etc.). To take one more out of thousands of examples, we read in Haggai, 'The word of the Lord came through the prophet Haggai' (Hag. 1:1).

Prophets spoke and wrote what God revealed to them. As a result their messages were God-breathed — inspired. 'For prophecy never had its origin in the will of man, but men spoke from God as they were carried along by the Holy Spirit' (2 Peter 1:21). In verse 20 Peter explains, 'No prophecy of Scripture came about by the prophet's own interpretation.' Hebrews reminds us that 'God spoke to our forefathers through the prophets' (Heb. 1:1).

From these contexts, we are forced to conclude that prophecy is synonymous with revelation. Revelation contains what God chose to reveal. It owes its origin to the will and movement of God.

In a similar way, New Testament prophets spoke and wrote as moved — inspired — by God. Paul reminds us in Ephesians that the mystery of Christ and the church, 'which was not made known unto men in other generations ... has now been revealed by the Spirit to God's holy apostles and prophets' (Eph. 3:5).

God specifically chose prophets (and apostles) to receive and transmit divine revelation. All believers could not have been chosen by God to receive revelation, or Paul would not stress his own uniqueness in this regard. Note how emphatically Paul links his prophetic and apostolic credentials with his reception of revelation: 'I want you to know, brothers, that the gospel I preached is not something that man made up. I did not receive it from any man, nor was I taught it; rather, I received it by revelation from Jesus Christ' (Gal. 1:11-12).

God inspired New Testament prophets, just as he had their Old Testament counterparts, to receive and transmit revelations from himself. He specifically arranged through the Holy Spirit that their teaching, preaching and writing be inspired. The completeness of the New Testament canon, coupled with the finality of its revelation, force us to conclude that the office of the New Testament prophet, like that of the Old Testament prophet, was temporary. It was necessary only as long as God continued to reveal the Scriptures (2 Tim. 3:16).

This whole matter of inspiration, revelation and the finality of Scripture is beyond the scope of a book of this nature. For further elucidation on this issue, consult one of the books written on the subject which I mention in the references.[10]

A unique process

The process whereby God inspired prophets and apostles is without parallel in common Christian experience. It has never been duplicated since their time. To claim otherwise is to undermine the authority and inspiration of Scripture — which any serious evangelical Christian will avoid at all costs.

In his classic work, *The Doctrine of Holy Spirit*, George Smeaton writes, 'The Holy Spirit supplied prophets and apostles, as chosen organs, with gifts which must be distinguished from ordinary grace, to give forth in human forms of speech a revelation which must be accepted as the Word of God in its whole contents, and as the authoritative guide for doctrine and duty.'[11]

Although traditional Pentecostals believe that the prophetic office continues in our day, they express alarm at many of the claims of modern prophets. In an attempt to focus on the uniqueness of biblical prophets, Raymond Carlson, General Superintendent of the Assemblies of God, writes, 'Prophecy by the New Testament apostles was different in authority from that of all other Christians in local churches. The writings of the New Testament are God's very words... No words spoken today can ever be on a par with the inerrant Scriptures.'[12]

Predicting the future

The prophet's ability to predict the future should also be considered. At the outset, we must realize that, on the whole, prophets were not predicters — foretellers — but rather forthtellers. Moses and John the Baptizer, two of the greatest prophets of all time, recorded little or no prediction. With minor exceptions, the entire content of Moses' prophetic ministry was either history, ethical statements (law) or exhortations for Israel to heed God's directives. He did warn them about the consequences of disobeying the law and he did predict that there would be another prophet raised up like him.

John, the Baptizer, prepared people for the coming of Christ by preaching of sin and calling for repentance. He did, of course, predict that the Messiah would appear among them.

The historical context

Prophets cannot be understood outside of their historical context. In the main, prophets were forthtellers, preachers appointed by God to herald his Word in a particular context. Consider Moses. God told him, 'Now go; I will help you speak and will teach you what to say' (Exod. 4:12). In obedience, Moses went to the people of Israel in their Egyptian bondage with a message from God. Likewise God commanded Isaiah to 'Go and tell this people...' The message God gave Isaiah dealt with people in a specific historic setting (Isa. 6:9-13). (This is not to deny that all Scripture is profitable for you and me in our diverse situations. The book of Psalms blesses people all over the world, as does Nehemiah — or any Old Testament book.)

The prophetic ministry of the apostles followed a similar pattern. Prediction was minimal. The major portion of their messages spoke to specific needs in concrete situations. The Gospels and epistles each appeal to different audiences. Even the most predictive of books, Revelation, brought a message from God to the seven churches of Asia in specific historical situations.

The content of the New Testament

Christ taught the apostles to expect a prophetic ministry. He described how the New Testament canon would be formed: 'The Holy Spirit ... will teach you all things and will remind you of everything I have said to you' (John 14:26). 'I have much more to say to you, more than you can now bear. But when he, the Spirit of truth, comes, he will guide you into all truth. He will not speak on his own; he will speak only what he hears and he will tell you what is to come' (John 16:12-13).

These passages in John mention three categories of content: first, an accurate reminder of what Jesus taught which became inscripturated as the four Gospels; second, a complete revelation of further truth which Jesus had withheld up to this time, due to their immaturity, and which they wrote down for us in the epistles; and third, a revelation of things to come, the predictive element, which we find mainly in the book of Revelation.

A study of the content of the New Testament shows that the vast majority is gospel, early church history, doctrine or teaching on Christian living. A few predictive elements, such as those found in Jesus' Olivet discourse, are included here and there. Even Revelation contains prophecy addressed as much to the specific situation in which God gave it as to future generations.

Prophecy in both Testaments consists of a maximum of forthtelling and a minimum of foretelling. To cry out for a return of the prophetic office out of a desire to listen to predictions is to demand something of the prophetic office that, even in its heyday, it rarely exhibited.

God's complete revelation

Scripture reveals that prophets, like apostles, were unique. Make no mistake, to claim that the office of the prophet continues in the church today is to claim a historical continuity that never existed. The claim is tantamount to asserting that God continues to deliver infallible revelation.

Such a claim is both inconsistent with Scripture and extremely dangerous. The canon of Holy Scripture is complete. Jesus predicted that the Spirit would lead the apostles into all truth. Did he, or did he not? Is the Bible complete or flawed? If he did what he predicted he would do, we have no further need of new revelations.

Paul wrote to Timothy that Scripture contains all the truth necessary for any Christian to be mature and complete in Christ (2 Tim. 3:15-17). Why this continual clamour for prophets to bring a 'revelation', a 'word from God', a 'prediction', when the Scriptures contain the adequate, all-encompassing and inerrant revelation of God's will for mankind? To demand the revival of the gift of prophecy, as manifest in biblical prophets, is to devalue the Scriptures and to encourage the manufacture of counterfeit miracles.

3. Testing prophetic validity

Around the world and down through history, people have claimed the ability to predict the future. With so much erroneous prophecy flying about, some method of distinguishing the true oracle of God from the false is essential. Superficially, many claim that miraculous signs attest the authenticity of their own ministry. We need to remember that the magic of the Egyptian magicians initially mimicked the signs Moses performed. In India Hindu, Sikh and Buddhist gurus echo Muslim 'holy men' in claiming power to effect miraculous cures. Some even demonstrate their power by walking on fire. But the Bible warns, 'Dear friends, do not believe every spirit, but test the spirits to see whether they are from God, because many false prophets have gone out into the world' (1 John 4:1).

The test of Scripture

If we would test a prophet we must first carefully compare his teaching with Scripture. John urges the readers of his first epistle to check whether a prophet's teaching enshrined or denied the reality of Jesus' incarnation and deity (1 John 4:2-3). Much earlier God had warned Moses not to be impressed by miraculous signs but to check the content: 'If a prophet ... appears among you and announces to you a miraculous sign or wonder, and if the sign or wonder ... takes place, and he says, "Let us follow other gods ... and let us worship them," you must not listen' (Deut. 13:1-3). Conformity to revealed truth takes precedence over startling manifestations of power.

Accuracy

Prophetic prediction must also be tested for accuracy. Since God can predict the future with 100% accuracy, any prophecy of his will come true. An accuracy rate of less than 100% necessarily shows that the bearer's prediction did not originate with God. 'If what a prophet proclaims in the name of the Lord does not take place or come true, that is a message the Lord has not spoken. That prophet has spoken presumptuously' (Deut. 18:22). A failed prophecy called for the perpetrator to be given the death penalty. All New Testament prophecy practised in the early church passed this litmus test (see Acts 11:27-28; 21:10-11). Perfect accuracy confirms a prophet's credentials.

How do those who claim that prophetic activity should and does take place today excuse inaccuracy? Michael G. Maudlin set out to investigate the excitement generated by reports of the predictions of 'The Kansas City Prophets' who operate in the 7000-member Kansas City (USA) Fellowship. He wrote, 'These men — pastor Mike Bickle, and prophets such as Bob Jones, John Paul Jackson, and Paul Cain — are creating a stir in charismatic circles. They claim that the prophetic gift should be restored in the church, that prophecy is a natural, biblical means for God to speak to his people, and that (here's the apocalyptic part) this increased prophetic activity is a sign of the emergence of the last-days' victorious church.'[13]

The Kansas City Fellowship has now joined the Vineyard group of churches under John Wimber, who is busy encouraging ordinary believers to seek the gift of prophecy.[14]

The stir created by Vineyard and KCF has moved traditional Pentecostals to issue cautionary statements. The Vineyard itself has delineated a series of checks and balances to test prophecy. 'All KCF and Vineyard leaders stress that the prophetic movement is immature and apt to make mistakes (except for, they stress, Paul Cain)... The church allows for a generous margin of error in prophetic words... Grudem, who teaches theology at Trinity Evangelical Divinity School and attends a Vineyard-affiliated church, argues that every prophet today will make mistakes.'[15]

Grudem claims that 'The Old Testament prophets who could not make mistakes without being declared false and put to death ... in the New Testament are not prophets but apostles... There is a discontinuity between the canonical revelation found in the Bible and the revelation received by modern-day prophets.' But as Robert Thomas, who teaches New Testament at California's Master's Seminary says, 'How can you have inspired utterance that has error?'[16]

The Vineyard magazine, *Equipping,* contains a series of articles introducing prophetic ministry. In article after article the magazine attests to the veracity of the revelations that God has given this man and that. In the same breath it warns that prophets make mistakes: 'Of course, prophets today do receive revelations from God. But in understanding and reporting what they receive, and in knowing what is from God and what is from their own minds or from a subtle suggestion of the Enemy, prophets do make mistakes... Every prophet today will make mistakes.'[17]

How can these men claim on the one hand to be the bearers of revelation when at the same time they admit to inaccuracy? The Bible is clear. We must refuse prophecy when it fails to be 100% accurate. This fundamental error occurs because so-called 'prophets' confuse their own interpretations with divine revelations. This, in turn, can be traced to a pervasive failure to distinguish illumination from revelation.

In illumination the Holy Spirit assists believers in interpreting the Scriptures. As sinners, albeit redeemed sinners, our minds are relatively darkened. We must depend upon the Spirit to grant us understanding of Scripture because 'These things are spiritually discerned.' As the Spirit helps us to understand and apply the Scriptures to our daily lives, our ability to interpret Scripture progressively increases. Our ability to interpret Scripture never will be absolutely perfect in this life. 'Now we see through a glass darkly, but then face to face.' The illumination of the Holy Spirit, then, unlike inspiration, is a relative grace because its pragmatic application depends so much on the exegetical skill and spiritual wisdom of the interpreter. While inspiration is inerrant, illumination, of necessity, is fallible.

Modern charismatics, I believe, mistakenly label their own interpretations as prophecy. Because of this confusion, they erroneously call for signs and wonders to confirm what they wrongly call prophecy.

The place of signs and wonders

As already noted in chapter 4, signs and wonders attested the veracity of prophetic revelation. Of Moses we read, 'Since then, no prophet has risen in Israel like Moses, whom the Lord knew face to face, who did all those miraculous signs and wonders the Lord sent him to do in Egypt' (Deut. 34:10-11). Peter, preaching on the Day of Pentecost, says that Jesus was 'a man accredited by God to you by miracles, wonders and signs' (Acts 2:22).

Scripture repeatedly reminds us of this principle. The crossing of the Red Sea and the gushing of water from a rock, among many other wonders, bore testimony to the authenticity of Moses' leadership. Likewise, an amazing cluster of marvels during the life of Christ and in the ministries of the apostles confirmed the authority of Christ and his apostles. The deaf heard, the lame walked, the dead were raised, snake-bite was neutralized and hearts were discerned. Some of the spiritual gifts themselves — notably tongues, healing and miracles — served to confirm revelation (Heb. 2:4).

No serious evangelical denies that God used signs, wonders and miracles to attest the ministries of the apostles and prophets. Indeed it is precisely the biblical clarity on this point that compels those who believe in continuing revelation to manufacture miracles to demonstrate the authenticity of their claim. God has tied revelation and wonders together. If signs and miracles cannot be demonstrated, new revelations cannot be claimed.

I have established the temporary nature of the prophetic office by recourse to three categories of biblical data. Firstly, prophets appeared at periodic intervals in history. Secondly, God called them to speak and write what he revealed to them. These revelations were rarely predictive. In the main they contained God's word for specific historical situations. Thirdly, prophecies were authenticated both by their perfect accuracy and by signs, wonders and miracles. The occurrence of these wonders coincided with the revelatory activity of the Spirit.

Since the Scriptures are complete the need for inspired prophets no longer exists. Should someone claim to be a prophet that claim must be examined in the light of the signs the said prophet professes to display and the accuracy of the revelation he claims to bring. Of course, both the scriptural and the historical record immediately cast doubt on such a claim.

Has this study fully exhausted the biblical data concerning prophets? Unfortunately, no, we still face some unexplained texts.

II. Prophecy: a general and continuing gift

Our discussions up to this point may give you to understand that I believe in the absolute cessation of prophecy. Not quite. I believe that, in one sense, the gift of prophecy continues in prophetic preaching. Four categories of evidence lead me to this conclusion.

1. Prophets as preachers

God chose Moses, Isaiah and John the Baptizer to communicate inspired revelation — but he also gifted them to preach the Word with power. Each brought God's Word to people in particular situations. The Greek word for 'prophecy' means simply to make public utterance or to speak out.

Moses spoke to Israelites groaning under Egyptian bondage. Isaiah preached to a nation in declension. Paul appealed to a Corinthian church in disarray due to scandals. The relevance of their messages to particular situations rendered their preaching memorable to their audiences.

They fulfilled two functions at the same time. God uniquely prepared them to bear his progressively revealed corpus of truth, the sum of which would become the Bible. Their messages touch our hearts today even though the original relevance of what they said fitted a particular historical context. They were both prophets and preachers.

Modern-day preachers who speak to the issues of the day follow the pattern laid down by biblical prophets. The New Testament contains considerable evidence that prophets functioned as preachers.

Note first the abundance of prophets present in the early churches. There were both inspired prophets responsible for the inscripturation of revelation and more ordinary prophets who carried on a ministry of preaching and teaching. The five men, including Barnabas and Saul, who gathered to worship God in Acts 13 are called 'prophets and teachers' (Acts 13:1). The text denotes either that there were at least two prophets, or that all five had both the gift of teaching and that of prophecy. I prefer this latter view.

The Jerusalem Council sent Judas and Silas to convey their instructions to the Gentiles. Concerning their stay in Antioch we read, 'Judas and Silas, who themselves were prophets, said much to encourage and strengthen the brothers' (Acts 15:32). Of Paul and Barnabas we read, 'But Paul and Barnabas remained in Antioch, where they and many others taught and preached the word of the Lord' (Acts 15:35).

We conclude that a prophetic ministry involves preaching and teaching. These references multiply the number of prophets far beyond those inspired few who gave us our canon.

Other references abound. At least one prophet attended Timothy's commissioning (1 Tim. 4:14). Several must have been present in Ephesus (Eph. 4).

1 Corinthians 14 contains an extended description of the gift and how it contrasts with tongues. 'Two or three prophets should speak, and the others should weigh carefully what is said' (v. 29). If we count both participating prophets and evaluating prophets there must have been between five and ten in Corinth. Paul indicates that a considerable number of men with the gift of prophecy took turns speaking to the Corinthian church: 'You can all prophesy in turn so that everyone may be instructed and encouraged' (v. 31). New Testament texts, then, specifically mention prophets in Jerusalem, Antioch, Corinth and Ephesus. One quickly gains the impression that prophets commonly ministered in the early churches.

We have already noted in the previous chapter that the inspired apostle-prophets who laid the foundation of the church (Eph. 2:20) were twelve in number. Besides these twelve, two or three other writers, companions of the apostles, such as Luke and Mark, wrote Bible books. These writers shared with the Twelve the gift of inspiration. But who were all the other prophets who form a group distinct from the inspired, 'foundation-laying prophets'? I believe they were Spirit-led preachers.

2. Exhortations to seek the gift of prophecy

If God had reserved the gift of prophecy exclusively for those he chose to lay the foundation of the church, we would not find a general exhortation to seek the gift. We read, however, 'Eagerly desire the greater gifts.' One of the greatest is prophecy. Paul specifically states, 'Desire spiritual gifts, especially the gift of prophecy... I would rather have you prophesy... Be eager to prophesy' (1 Cor. 12:31; 14:1,5,39).

These exhortations would be meaningless unless meant to encourage, not only the Corinthians, but believers today to seek the gift. To deny this is to empty the epistles of their relevance. You may ask, 'Then why not seek the gift of tongues?' As already noted, the gift of tongues fulfilled a different function. It served to authenticate revelation. Then, too, Paul assigned to tongues a very low priority (1 Cor. 12:28,31;14:1,19).

Each of the three main gift lists mentions the gift of prophecy. Only the gift of teaching is mentioned as consistently. The frequency with which it is mentioned, in epistles of both early and late origin, shows that its use is crucial. If we arbitrarily excise the role of prophecy from our corpus of teaching about the church, how can we confidently apply other apostolic directives? Such a procedure would call into question our whole system of interpretation.

Of particular note is the inclusion of prophecy in the list of the five key equipping gifts in Ephesians 4. Prophets join apostles, evangelists, pastors and teachers as men given to 'prepare God's people for works of service, so that the body of Christ may be built up' (v. 12). The mention of prophets and apostles in this passage makes no sense unless they have some continuing function. If three of the gifts — pastors, teachers and evangelists — continue, and the need for equipping the saints continues, then why are apostles and prophets included only to be withdrawn?

Ephesians occupies a foundational place in the New Testament. It contributes fundamental truths about the church. Paul teaches that Christ gave five gifts, including apostles and prophets, to equip the saints so that the church might function smoothly. It is absurd to suppose that the work of equipping the saints can carry on without the equipping gifts! There is no indication in Ephesians of their withdrawal. We can only conclude that God meant prophecy to continue as a gift.

3. Detailed descriptions of the prophetic gift

1 Corinthians chapters 12-14 give a detailed description of the gift of prophecy. In the course of pointing out the necessity of love in the

exercise of gifts Paul writes, 'If I have the gift of prophecy and can fathom all mysteries and all knowledge ... but have not love, I am nothing' (13:2). This text shows that prophecy deals with fathoming mysteries and knowledge.

The fourteenth chapter provides further light. Paul establishes the superiority of prophecy over tongues. In verses 3 and 4 we read, 'Everyone who prophesies speaks to men for their strengthening, encouragement and comfort... He who prophesies edifies the church.' Obviously, God designed the gift so it could be used to build up the church. How? Prophets edify by applying God's Word to people's specific needs. They strengthen those who are weak. They encourage the discouraged. They comfort the sorrowing. Non-inspired modern prophets mirror the ministry of the inspired prophets of old. God specifically gifts them to apply the Word to particular situations.

In the section from verse 22 on we read, 'Prophecy, however, is for believers.' In verse 32, prophecy is exercised so that 'everyone may be instructed and encouraged'. Of course prophecy also profoundly affects unbelievers, in a way tongues cannot. The unbeliever, hearing tongues-speaking, thinks 'that you are out your mind' (14:23). But when an unbeliever hears prophesying, 'He will be convinced by all that he is a sinner ... and the secrets of his heart will be laid bare. So he will fall down and worship God, exclaiming, "God is really among you!"' (14:24,25). While the gift of prophecy is mainly directed towards believers, God also uses it to bring unbelievers under deep conviction.

Definition of the gift

We can define prophecy, in its continuing form, as that spiritual ability to communicate biblical truth in powerful and relevant ways so that people sense a word from God directed to them in their situation. It is Spirit-filled preaching that may include instruction, encouragement, exhortation or comfort.

Two kinds of prophecy

Note the difference between inspired prophecy and edifying prophecy. Inspired prophecies have an unbidden, Spirit-produced element to them as if the Spirit overrides the will of the prophet. 'For prophecy never had its origin in the will of man, but men spoke from

God as they were carried along by the Holy Spirit' (2 Peter 1:21). References such as this one lead some to view prophecy as a form of ecstatic speech. The prophecy spoken of in 1 Corinthians, however, is far different.

Paul describes something orderly and controlled: 'The spirits of [the] prophets are subject to the control of [the] prophets' (1 Cor. 14:32). Prophecy, in this form, involves orderly presentations of truth which flow from the speaker's mind and will. This text seems to demonstrate a discontinuity between inspired prophecy and what, for want of a better term, I am calling 'edifying prophecy', which owes its origin (under the Spirit's general guidance) to the speaker's own personality and preparation.

Let me explain what I mean. I am not arguing that the personality and experience, the vocabulary and natural gifts of inspired prophets were in abeyance when they spoke or wrote God's inspired Word. With few exceptions, such as the Ten Commandments, I do not believe that inspiration was a process of mechanical dictation. Nevertheless, God kept supernaturally inspired prophets from error so that they could infallibly communicate his will to men and women. On the other hand, God uses the more general gift, edifying prophecy, to interpret the already infallibly recorded Word to people today.

Inspiration is evidence of the absolute superintendence by the Spirit, while illumination, as noted earlier, is evidence of the relative control by the Spirit.

A picture of two kinds of prophecy emerges: inspired prophecy that produced the inerrant canon of Holy Scripture (and occasionally included prediction) and prophecy as convicting and edifying preaching. Prophetic preaching draws its power from a broadly based acquaintance with Scripture and ongoing dependence on the Spirit. It includes the ability to size up situations and needs and bring a relevant message. Prophetic preaching leads to conviction, consolation, rebuke or encouragement. Prophecy, as a continuing gift, requires the *illumination* of the Spirit, but not the *inspiration* of the Spirit.

Prophecy and preaching

The gift of prophecy is preaching. Of course, all prophets were preachers. Moses, whose astounding sermons are recorded for us in Deuteronomy, was recognized as a great preacher. But while we can emulate Moses' preaching ability, we can never mimic his divinely granted ability — or that of any other inspired prophet — to bring an inerrant revelation from God.

Let me reiterate what I said earlier because it is precisely at this point that our charismatic friends blur the distinction between inspiration resulting in revelation and illumination resulting in good exegesis and preaching. In a vain attempt to resurrect a historic institution, that of the inspired prophets, they claim continuing revelations. Their practice, at first glance, might seem like an admirable attempt to call people to accept the authority of what God reveals, and re-create a sense of the supernatural in their midst. Unfortunately, this misguided practice has been used to lend divine credence to a plethora of non-biblical ideas and practices. When any Christian group claims divine authority for one of their pronouncements, they invite disaster. History is littered with the heretical wreckage produced by this propensity to baptize human practices with counterfeit divine unction.

No wonder traditional Pentecostals react with alarm to the claims of modern 'prophets'. The General Superintendent of the Assemblies of God writes, 'Arbitrary and absolute direction by a prophetic gift is not in accordance with New Testament teaching... A study of church history indicates that every group of people who have claimed to restore apostolic authority to the Church and its government have been arbitrary and demanding. Those who come under their leadership find themselves under bondage.'[18]

The problem arises from confusing those biblical prophets, such as Isaiah and Paul, who wrote the canon under the inspiration of the Holy Spirit, with a different class of prophets, such as Judas and Silas, who preached under the illumination of the Holy Spirit. The church has always distinguished between illumination and inspiration, between interpretation and revelation, between authoritative prophecy and powerful preaching. Failure to make these distinctions spawns a school of fishy ideas and outright errors.

As the New Testament unfolds we read less about prophecy and more about preaching. Paul exhorts Timothy to 'Preach the Word; be prepared in season and out of season; correct, rebuke and encourage — with great patience and careful instruction' (2 Tim. 4:2) — a kind of preaching indistinguishable from the prophecy described in 1 Corinthians 14! Both involve instruction based on a careful evaluation of people's needs. Being prepared 'in season and out of season' reflects the need for preaching to be relevant to specific times and situations. Titus was to prophesy by bringing Christ's 'word to light through ... preaching' (Titus 1:3). The gift of prophecy involves preaching Christ and him crucified in order to challenge people to submit to him. 'The testimony of Jesus is the spirit of prophecy' (Rev. 19:10).

This transition in terminology in the New Testament from the use of prophecy to preaching probably shows that God wanted to safeguard the unique position of those few prophets who were the bearers of inerrant revelation.

In the light of Paul's prohibition on women preachers, you may ask how the presence of female prophets squares with equating prophecy with preaching. 'Philip ... had four unmarried daughters who prophesied' (Acts 21:9). I would argue that these women were prophetesses in the special and unique sense. They did not preach but brought a predictive message which God authenticated by its accuracy. Indeed Luke mentions Philip's daughters in the context of a prophet, Agabus, who predicted Paul's imprisonment. These women brought predictions, and possibly revelations, during a transitional age, but they did not preach (Acts 21:10-11).

Is equating the ongoing gift of prophecy with preaching consistent with the history of biblical exposition? Yes.

4. Prophecy as viewed in church history

Flynn writes, 'The Early Church had many prophets, who usually employed their gift in their own local congregation. Some eminent prophets itinerated. The *Didache*, an early manual of church practice, commanded that wandering prophets be supported: "Every true prophet who shall settle among you is worthy of his support."'[19]

What an intriguing tradition! This stipulation of the *Didache* demonstrates that although the canon was complete, the early church believed in the continuity of a prophetic ministry. It presents these early prophets as resident preachers. Interestingly, this reference points out a fundamental difference between apostles and prophets. The *Didache* warned that apostles (since their ministry was pioneer church-planting) should not be supported over a long period. Prophets, however, could be supported as resident ministers because they laboured to edify already established churches.

Calvin gives his view: 'By prophesying I do not understand the gift of foretelling the future, but the science of interpreting Scriptures, so a prophet is an interpreter of the will of God.'[20] Interpretation of the will of God underlines a preacher's need to size up a situation and then bring relevant Scripture to bear on the central issues involved.

Berkhof, Criswell and many others could be quoted in this regard. J. I. Packer sums it up: 'Rather than supposing prophecy to be a long-gone first-century charisma now revived and therefore to be dressed up in verbal clothes that will set it apart from all other forms of Christian communication over the past eighteen or nineteen centuries, we should realize that it has actually been exhibited in every sermon or informal "message" that has had a heart-searching, "home-coming" application in its hearers, ever since the church began. Prophecy has been and remains a reality whenever and wherever Bible truth is genuinely preached — that is, spelled out and applied, whether from a pulpit or more informally. Preaching is teaching God's revealed truth with application.' [21]

Conclusion

Evidence compels us to distinguish between inspired prophets, who joined the apostles in laying the foundation of the church, and their uninspired progeny who carry on the preaching of the Word today. God raised up the former at intermittent periods of history to record inspired revelation. Mighty signs and wonders authenticated their ministries. The latter continue to come among us preaching the Word. Prophetic preachers are fallible. No miracles attest their instruction. But a fire burns within them to preach.

The kingdom needs preaching prophets today as never before! 'History tells of no significant church growth and expansion that has taken place without preaching ("significant", implying virility and staying power, is the key word there). What history points to, rather, is that all movements of revival, reformation, and missionary outreach seem to have had preaching (vigorous, though on occasion very informal) at their centre, instructing, energizing, sometimes purging and redirecting and often spearheading the whole movement. It would seem, then, that preaching is always necessary for a proper sense of mission to be evoked and sustained anywhere in the church.'[22]

The gift of prophecy, in its continuing form, is heart-searching, applicational preaching deeply rooted in biblical exposition. Do you have the gift of preaching? Paul encourages us to aspire to great gifts such as this one. If you find such a desire burning within, take steps to feed the flame by taking appropriate action.

Good preaching requires a mix of communication skill, broad biblical knowledge and facility in interpreting Scripture. More than almost any other spiritual gift, the development of the gift of preaching rests on the development of other gifts. For example, the preacher must possess, in generous measure, spiritual giftedness in the areas of knowledge, wisdom, encouragement, teaching and even shepherding and evangelism. The best way to evaluate one's potential for preaching is to evaluate one's giftedness in these other areas. If we find defects there, they need to be repaired before further attention is given to preaching. This will require careful evaluation of the chapters ahead. Often preaching grows out of the development of other gifts.

To become a good preacher, you first need to *study the Bible in depth*. This may take place either through rigorous personal discipline at home or by scheduling formal study of biblical subjects such as Bible survey, biblical theology, systematic theology, etc. Find evening classes in these subjects in your area, sign up for correspondence courses or enrol in a Bible School or seminary.

Secondly, you should *develop skill in analysing the Bible*. Courses on Bible study methods, hermeneutics and exegesis will help here.

Thirdly, *study people*. Relevant preaching is well illustrated out of the realities of daily life. Read newspapers. Develop a file of clippings and illustrations on relevant subjects. Be sociable. Seek to understand what makes people tick. Imagine what sort of a message you would give to speak to issues people live with, such as a cancer diagnosis, loss of job, rocky marriages, temptations, death, worry, etc.

Fourthly, *gain practice in communicating biblical truth*. You might begin by sharing your testimony, giving a short devotional talk in a home Bible study, or teaching Sunday School. The principles of teaching are closely allied to those of preaching. Indeed in the book of Acts, the two are often mentioned side by side.

Whenever you speak in public ask for feedback from your wife, a friend or a church leader. Determine to work on your shortcomings. Take courses on preaching, teaching, communication, etc. I have listed in the references the titles of some good books on preaching.[23]

If you are already preaching, check yourself against the characteristics below. According to Packer, biblical preaching has five qualities.

1. Preaching is presenting God's message to man, and is thus biblical in content.

2. Preaching has the purpose of informing, persuading and calling forth an appropriate response.

3. Preaching always has the perspective of being life-changing in its application.

4. Preaching is declaration of the Word with authority.

5. Preaching effects an encounter with God in his presence and power.[24]

Do you long to preach God's Word in life-changing power? Scarcely a greater desire can be imagined, as long as that which fuels the fire within is a desire to glorify God.

Evaluate your desires and experiences against the five characteristics of true preaching given above. Fill in the columns on the chart you studied in chapter 7.

11.
The gift of evangelism

Over thirty years ago I was taught, as a new convert, that every Christian should be a soul-winner, an evangelist. Witnessing joined prayer, Bible study and Christian fellowship as necessary duties to be kept in balance.

Before long my new friends were showing me their version of how to witness. One took me with him to hand out tracts and testify on Toronto's main street. Wanting to be a good disciple, I asked God to conquer my fear and shyness and help me become a soul-winner.

In the years that followed I heard hundreds of messages reinforcing the credo that 'Every Christian must be a soul-winner.' So high did evangelism come on my list of priorities that I went on into missions and served in Pakistan for sixteen years. I engaged in bazaar evangelism, village visitation, literature distribution and many other kinds of outreach.

Gradually, however, my missionary colleagues moved me into teaching and administrative roles. In spite of my being extremely busy, guilt produced by never being much of a soul-winner would surface from time to time. You see, although I was involved, and still am, in all kinds of evangelistic outreach, somehow I never became very effective in 'winning people to Christ'. Where did I fail? Or was I bearing an unnecessary load of false guilt?

Discovery of the biblical teaching on spiritual gifts moderated my sense of failure. The biography of a great evangelist like George Whitefield, or a sermon on soul-winning, can still arouse tinges of guilt. But more and more I conclude that these pangs of discomfort do not originate with the Spirit. For if every Christian is a soul-winner then every Christian has the gift of evangelism — which cannot possibly be true.

Jim Davey writes, 'Insisting that all ought to be winning souls (as opposed to witnessing) instead of recognizing that not all have gifts that especially fit them for such personal evangelism is to produce frustrated, defeated believers. And usually a person frustrated in this way will be thwarted in ever finding out what his true ministry in the body is.'[1]

Motivating God's people to do evangelism by inducing a sense of guilt has not worked. Campus Crusade has estimated that it takes, on average, the equivalent of one thousand laymen and six pastors working one year to see a person converted.[2]

Their estimate highlights a problem. Most churches rarely see people converted. Something must be wrong when a task so repeatedly emphasized by Christ in the Great Commission and so often talked about yields such meagre results. Are those with the gift of evangelism rare? Is the gift restricted to men like Billy Graham?

Bob Harris represents another dimension of the problem. Although Bob has the gift of evangelism, he longs for another ministry. Scarcely a week goes by without Bob having an unusual opening to share the gospel with neighbours, casual acquaintances or people at work. God honours his efforts by bringing people to faith. Unfortunately Bob has always wanted to be a deacon. Disappointment surfaces when he sees men of his age and experience serving as officers in his home church. He doesn't realize how wistfully others listen when he tells about the exciting opportunities he has to witness. Many Christians would love to have his evangelistic gifts.

As we study evangelism, we need to steer a middle course between the danger of producing guilt in those without the gift and providing an excuse for those who fear evangelism or choose to disobey Christ's command to be his witnesses. We need to encourage those, like Bob, who have the gift to use it rather than covet other ministries. Without many like Bob, the church will die.

The word 'evangelist' literally means 'a messenger of good', or 'a messenger of the good news'. In Greek, it is closely related to the word *evangel,* meaning 'gospel' or 'good news'. Five times, in various forms, Christ reiterated the command: 'Go into all the world and preach the good news to all creation' (Mark 16:15). Obedience to this Great Commission, as demonstrated by early Christians, is absolutely fundamental to church life. We read, 'Those who had been scattered' by the persecution following the death of Stephen 'preached the word wherever they went' (Acts 8:4). Yet, strangely enough, the word 'evangelist' occurs only three times in the New Testament.

Christ gave five classes of gifted men responsibility to 'prepare God's people for works of service' (Eph. 4:11) Among these five, only apostles and prophets surpass evangelists in fundamental importance.

A second reference to evangelists occurs in connection with Paul's epistle to his missionary envoy, Timothy. Paul urges Timothy, 'In the presence of God and of Christ Jesus ... in view of his appearing and his kingdom ... Preach the Word ... with great patience and careful instruction ... keep your head in all situations, endure hardship, do the work of an evangelist, discharge all the duties of your ministry' (2 Tim. 4:1,2,5).

Although evangelism was not Timothy's main gift, the faithful exercise of his ministry required him to do evangelistic work. That Paul felt it necessary to remind Timothy of this fact probably indicates that he dragged his feet at this point.

Both passages mentioned thus far indicate that this gift occupies an abiding place in the ongoing life of churches. The word crops up a third time in connection with Philip. Paul travelled towards Jerusalem at the end of his third missionary journey. We read that he 'reached Cæsarea and stayed at the house of Philip, the evangelist' (Acts 21:8). Philip is the only person in Scriptures specifically called an evangelist!

During subsequent church history, however, Christian scholars also called Matthew and the other Gospel writers 'evangelists'. This is due in part to the fact that they were the writers of the *evangel*. But the early church must have recognized in them evangelistic gifts as well.

We have, then, Philip who was an evangelist, Timothy who was to do the work of an evangelist, and the apostles who had evangelistic ministries.

When we search for the model evangelist, we naturally turn to Philip. A study of his life serves two purposes. First, Philip exemplifies the steps any Christian needs to take in the process of discovering and developing his or her gifts. Secondly, Philip illustrates the evangelistic gift itself. As we follow Philip's growth as a disciple we shall gradually unravel the dimensions of his gift.

There were four stages to Philip's development. We see him first as Philip, the believer.

I. Philip — the believer

Philip appears on the scene in Acts chapter 6. At that juncture, the apostles faced a potentially divisive situation concerning the distribution of help among widows. The congregation selected from their midst seven men with exemplary Christian lives to help them solve the problem. They chose Philip, along with Stephen and the other five, because it was evident that they were 'full of the Spirit and wisdom' (Acts 6:3).

Any study of spiritual gifts soon highlights the importance of the congregation. The Holy Spirit gives gifts to be exercised in the midst of congregational life for the express purpose of edifying the body of Christ. If, like Philip, we would discover and develop our gifts we must be active in the local church. We can find no precedent in the New Testament to support today's individualistic approach to ministry. Of course, when persecution broke up the congregation, believers were forced to act on their own. Philip subsequently fled to Samaria where he began to preach the gospel on his own. He had to — he was alone. Later the Spirit specifically directed Philip to leave Samaria and go alone to meet an Ethiopian enquirer.

Normally, the discovery of gifts occurs in the context of local church involvement. Be a member. Be involved. Be faithful to the services and ministries of the local church. Be at the prayer meeting and Bible Study. Philip was 'among' them before he ministered 'to them'!

What first distinguished Philip and the other six in the eyes of the congregation? Was it his abilities, talents, background, or culture? No! The congregation chose Philip, and the rest, because of their consistent Christian lives. They demonstrated two things that are essential in a maturing Christian: wisdom and the Holy Spirit. Early believers 'devoted themselves to the apostles' teaching' with the result that they became wise in the things of God (Acts 2:42).

Stephen's address to his persecutors in Acts 7 illustrates his wisdom. 'They could not stand up against his wisdom or the Spirit by whom he spoke' (Acts 6:10). Wisdom, absorbed as they listened to the apostles' teaching, prepared these seven men for ministry.

Besides wisdom, growing Christians, like Philip, have their hearts open to the Holy Spirit. All seven were 'full of the Spirit' (Acts 6:3). An openness to the Spirit's filling presupposes submission to God's revealed will. Obedience confirms that submission (Rom. 12:2). The Holy Spirit is given to those who obey the Word (Acts 5:32). Of course, submission to the Spirit involves the lifelong obedience resulting in a day-to-day filling (Eph. 5:18).

To be recognized as full of the Spirit, Philip and the others must have shown evidence of the Spirit's presence. The 'fruit of the Spirit' provides that verification (Gal. 5:22-23). Godly attitudes, holy character and righteous acts attest to the Spirit's activity in a life. The congregation at large must have seen these evidences in Philip in order to conclude that he was full of the Spirit.

Spiritual gifts develop as we grow in grace and as we manifest, in increasing measure, the fruits of the Spirit. The gifts and the fruits of the Spirit develop together. How could it be otherwise? The fruits of the Spirit reflect facets of love. Spiritual gifts are the concrete expressions of that love in various kinds of ministry.

When Christians like Philip grow, they come face to face with human need. By a natural process, then, Philip, the believer, became Philip, the servant.

II. Philip — the servant

Philip and the other six laboured far from centre-stage. Nevertheless, continuing harmony in the Jerusalem church depended to a great extent on their attention to a seemingly menial task. Thousands had joined the church. Many were poor. Some were widows, without any means of support. Provision for their needs taxed the resources of the fledgling congregation. In the process of providing for these women, some widows from a Greek background had been overlooked. Believers from that culture were upset. This tiny ripple of discontent could have spawned a tidal wave of disunity. Even more dangerous, the apostles could have been diverted from ministries of prayer and teaching. Failure to calm the rising storm could have shipwrecked the early church.

Needs, such as that of the Grecian widows, challenge believers to respond. This response produces a creative ferment that stimulates the development of spiritual gifts. In our discussion of the steps to take in order to discover our gifts, a sense of concern for need was identified as the second step. Love responds to perceived needs by seeking to find a way to meet those needs, whether they be those of the lonely or the lost.

Fortunately, believers in the first church tackled the problem head on by choosing seven men. Philip joined Stephen and the others in waiting on tables. He became a servant, charged with helping to distribute food.

Serving tables seems to be light years away from doing evangelism. What a humble task! Philip could have objected that this task wasted his potential. He could have protested that serving was demeaning. Instead, he embraced the challenge with enthusiasm. As a result, 'The word of God spread. The number of disciples in Jerusalem increased rapidly, and a large number of priests became obedient to the faith' (Acts 6:7). By meeting concrete needs in humble ways Philip and the others ensured the continuous growth of the church.

What if Philip and Stephen had refused the servant's towel? What if they had insisted on a conspicuous ministry? Fortunately, their submission to the Spirit had prepared them to be servants. Gift discovery begins with learning to serve humbly. It develops in the same way. Indeed whether we become famous preachers, or deacons, or administrators, or fill a less conspicuous position, we must always be willing to do whatever needs to be done, even if that means washing dishes, fixing the heating system, painting or visiting shut-ins.

We develop giftedness by responding enthusiastically to the material and spiritual needs we see around us. Woe betide the congregation that calls a preacher who has never learned servanthood by involving himself in practical work. Paul warns Timothy not to appoint anyone to a church office who has not first been tested — probably for this very reason (1 Tim. 3:10; 5:22). Spiritual fruitfulness often follows learning to be practically useful.

Too many Christians today have 'itchy feet' when it comes to church attendance. They get fidgety when they stay too long in one congregation. Faithfulness over the long haul, in believers such as Philip, creates an attitude conducive to gift development and church growth. With so many moving from church to church there is often a shortage of people to respond to local congregational needs. This lack hinders many churches from developing a broad range of ministries. And this, in its turn, feeds the dissatisfaction of those looking for an ideal church with a wide range of activities. Those who hop from one church to another could help to short-circuit this vicious circle if they would stay put!

Waiting on tables does not mean we cannot do other things as well. Stephen didn't only serve Greek widows. His powerful witness soon led to his martyrdom, which, in turn, spawned intense persecution that scattered the church. Philip fled Jerusalem as a refugee.

III. Philip — the refugee

After Stephen's martyrdom, Saul went about throwing Christians into prison. While the apostles stayed in Jerusalem to ride out the storm, believers fled to remote areas of Judea and Samaria. Philip was one of those unwilling refugees. But instead of being silenced, 'Those who had been scattered preached the word wherever they went. Philip went down to a city in Samaria and proclaimed the Christ there' (Acts 8:4-5).

Early believers boldly proclaimed their faith in Christ. Today we call this activity 'witnessing'. (Their proclamation wasn't preaching from a pulpit.) As already mentioned, there are twenty-three different words used in the book of Acts to denote the communication of the gospel.[3] The early church witnessed in all kinds of settings, using a variety of methods.

Those early disciples bore witness, not because they had discovered within themselves the gift of evangelism, but because Christ had commanded them: 'Go into all the world and preach [communicate] the good news' (Mark 16:15). 'You will ... be my witnesses ... to the ends of the earth' (Acts 1:8). 'Whoever acknowledges me before men, I will also acknowledge him before my Father in heaven. But whoever disowns me before men, I will disown him before my Father in heaven' (Matt. 10:32-33). Normal Christian living, in those early years, included obedient witness.

Pentecost initiated a pattern of every-member witness. 'All of them were filled with the Holy Spirit and began to speak in other tongues as the Spirit enabled them' (Acts 2:4). Too often, when we study this passage, the issue of tongue-speaking distracts us from noticing the purpose for which the tongues were given. 'Each one heard them speaking in his own language ... the wonders of God' (Acts 2:6,11). The whole congregation, through the miracle of Pentecost, bore witness to Christ. This Spirit-induced concern continued. When persecution broke out after the imprisonment of Peter and John, all the believers met to pray for boldness to witness (Acts 4:29).

Christians must either obey Christ and witness, or see their Christian walk deteriorate. A climate in which witnessing becomes the norm produces an atmosphere conducive to the discovery of the gift of evangelism.

Evangelism, like all gifts, develops through use. In a climate where witness was a way of life, Philip's gift of evangelism began to blossom. He was not alone. Obedience to this command became one of the three or four key objectives of the church. They sought to glorify God in worship, to teach all that Christ had revealed, to provide Christian fellowship and to evangelize the world. While they may have failed fully to comprehend Christ's strategy of reaching first Jerusalem, then Judea, Samaria and the ends of the earth, nevertheless they embraced witnessing as a way of life. The warmth of their fellowship led them to congregate in Jerusalem. It took persecution to thrust them out in broader witness. But while they may have been slow to grasp the missionary strategy of the Lord, they were quick to preach Christ wherever they went. Early Christian practice encouraged the growth of the gift of evangelism.

Philip learned well. No sooner had he arrived in Samaria than he began preaching Christ with powerful effect: 'They believed Philip as he preached the good news of the kingdom of God and the name of Jesus Christ, they were baptized, both men and women' (Acts 8:12). Philip, the refugee, developed quickly into Philip, the evangelist.

Unfortunately, the climate in our churches today is not so invigorating for potential evangelists. We strategize to send out missionaries to the ends of the earth, but often fail to 'gossip the gospel' to our friends and neighbours. Too often, we forget that evangelism is one of the main goals of the church.

Of course, we pay lip-service to evangelism. Billy Graham has held crusades all over the world. 'Evangelism in Depth' stirred Christians in Latin America to action a couple of decades ago. Many churches conduct seminars on personal evangelism using 'Evangelism Explosion' material. New evangelistic techniques and strategies continually flow from the drawing-board.

Campus Crusade, the Universities and Colleges Christian Fellowship, Nurses' Christian Fellowship, Every Home Crusade, Christian Business Men's Club and Youth For Christ, to name but a few, represent a host of parachurch groups that have sprung up to fill the evangelistic vacuum. Still, the results are disappointing.

Although Canada has its full complement of evangelistic organizations, the proportion of evangelicals dropped from 23% in 1930 to 6.3% in 1980. (Studies in 1993 show some increase.) According to the *World Christian Encyclopedia*, there are now fewer evangelicals *per capita* in Canada than in most parts of Africa. Canada represents just one glaring example of the failure of the Western church. Believers in the United Kingdom lament conditions there.

The example of the early church encourages us to promote a climate conducive to evangelism by emphasizing four things.

1. The place of evangelism in church life

Every church needs to keep evangelism on the front burner. Churches expend massive amounts of energy keeping various activities and committees functioning without ensuring that they clearly contribute to the church's goals. If they fail to contribute, however, their continuation is suspect.

While I was pastor at Long Branch Baptist Church, we defined our objectives in terms of three simple goals: to worship Christ, to edify believers and to evangelize the lost (thanks to suggestions from Lou Worrad, former pastor of Philpott Tabernacle, Hamilton, Canada). We sought to keep these objectives before the congregation at all times. Meetings and organizations were evaluated in terms of how they contributed to these three goals. One of these objectives focuses on evangelism.

Long Branch sits on a major road in an older part of a large city. Residents of the area betrayed an indifference to spiritual things. The small numerical growth in our membership concerned us.

Conversions were few. The price of housing in the community forced young couples to move further and further away. In their new locations, they invariably joined growing suburban churches.

We could have been tempted to rest on our oars. After all, city churches cannot have the same expectations as suburban churches. We might truthfully have pointed to the lack of committed Christians to staff a wholesome variety of teaching and worship ministries, let alone increase our outreach.

Maintaining the status quo, however, is not a biblical option. A church exists to evangelize. So we kept trying to reach out. We showed evangelistic films in the summer. We distributed a pre-evangelistic Christian newspaper in the community. We ministered to senior citizens in a retirement home. We operated a phone ministry. Concerned members began a club for unchurched young people and a drop-in-centre for youngsters on the streets. We repeatedly emphasized the need for all of us to be involved in friendship evangelism.

I am thankful to say that this climate of continued emphasis on evangelism seems to have developed evangelistic giftedness in some members. It also clarified the purpose of our building.

2. The role of church buildings in evangelism

Apostolic precedent leads us to conclude that evangelism takes place in the world at large. As a corollary, meetings organized for church buildings serve the saints.

Evangelism, at least pre-evangelism, takes place outside the church building. It occurs in our neighbourhoods, in the workplace and among our friends and relatives. In an earlier era unsaved people came to services held in church buildings and were converted there. That time is largely past.

Failure to realize that persuading unsaved people to attend meetings held in our church buildings is counter-productive dooms us to live in an evangelistic *Alice In Wonderland*. We do not live in the thirties and forties when such might have been the case. We waste energy trying to devise ways to entice sinners in, when we could be out gossiping the gospel like the early Christians.

Unfortunately, many still believe that evangelism is 'getting somebody to come to church'. This dangerous misunderstanding leads many to expect the preacher to do their evangelism for them by focusing his preaching on the unsaved. True, multitudes flocked to hear C. H. Spurgeon preach in a building in the nineteenth century. Even Spurgeon himself recognized the limitations of church buildings when he said, 'I rejoice that God allows us to preach in churches and chapels, but I do not pretend that we have any apostolical precedent for it, certainly none for confining our ministry to such places.'[4]

Richard Halverson, in his book *The Timelessness of Jesus Christ*, comments, 'The work of the church is outside the establishment. Outside the church. In the world. And it takes every member to do it! Nowhere in the Bible is the world exhorted to "come to church". But the church's mandate is clear: she must go to the world.'[5]

Church buildings do not limit evangelism in every setting. In the southern United States, for instance, church-going is still part of the culture. In that setting powerful gospel preaching in regular services can serve an evangelistic purpose. I am not denying that the children of believers need to be evangelized in Sunday School or church. Nor am I saying that God never converts people through preaching in a church meeting. No! But evangelism is usually initiated outside the church building.

Jesus evangelized by a well, under a tree, by the side of the road, or wherever he happened to be. The sovereign purpose behind the persecution that scattered the church from Jerusalem was precisely to get them to move out into Judea, Samaria and the world at large. Philip's gift didn't become obvious while he remained under the shadow of the apostles.

3. The context most conducive to evangelism

Evangelism occurs most naturally when Christians establish a network of relationships with their neighbours, friends, relatives and colleagues at work. Christ calls us to live lives of salt and light — lives that intrigue unbelievers. The natural relationships we form become the context which God uses to arouse interest in the gospel. This context is pregnant with opportunity for evangelism. When we turn to the Gospels we note that, almost without exception, Jesus called his apostles through a network of relationships. Peter and Andrew, like James and John, were brothers. Philip and Nathanael were friends. All but one came from Galilee. Most were neighbours in the town of Bethsaida. Some had been disciples of John, a cousin of Jesus. Mary and Elizabeth were related. The gospel subsequently spread to Simon's mother and other women who knew each other.

'Sterling Huston of the Billy Graham Evangelistic Association reports that "75 per cent of all who come forward at our crusades were brought by a friend or family member, and 80 to 90 per cent of the completely unchurched who make commitments came because someone they knew had done the sowing and watering."'[6]

Sowing and watering serve to prepare the way for harvest. A gifted evangelist seldom reaps a harvest of conversions unless a host of Christians have been sowing the seed among their friends and neighbours. Speaking of the harvest of souls in Corinth, Paul said, 'I planted the seed, Apollos watered it, but God made it grow. So neither he who plants nor he who waters is anything, but only God who makes things grow' (1 Cor. 3:6-7). 'One sows and another reaps' (John 4:37).

Recent terms such as 'friendship evangelism' or 'lifestyle evangelism' spotlight the rediscovery of the importance of relationships in evangelism. But the concept is apostolic. Christ called his disciples, largely, from the midst of a network of natural relationships. The same is true today. 'Win Arn and Charles Arn, of the Church Growth Institute, have asked over 14,000 lay people the question, "What or who was responsible for your coming to Christ and your church?" Less than 10 per cent credit a pastor, a visitation programme, or an evangelistic crusade. Between 75 per cent and 90 per cent say they owe their Christian faith to a friend or relative. This is the most natural process whereby someone becomes a disciple of Christ, they say. It is this process churches should strengthen and encourage.'[7]

Fortunately, there will always be exceptions. In India, merchants recycle paper by using it to wrap up purchases. A poor villager bought three cigarettes from the village shop. Taking them home, he unrolled the piece of paper in which they were wrapped and began to read. The story, torn from a gospel tract, stirred his heart. Through amazing circumstances he sought the crumpled address on the tract and found a pastor who led him to faith in Christ. God's Spirit is not bound to work in any one way! But that knowledge should not deter us from cultivating relationships with those around us.[8]

Joseph Aldrich pinpoints another problem that effectively short-circuits evangelism. He says, 'Unfortunately the average Christian has no non-Christian friends and tragically the non-Christian has no Christian friends.'⁹ We must keep this in mind when we plan church activities. For if we plunge believers into a round of church activities that leave no time to develop relationships with non-Christians, then we shall stifle witness. Somehow, we must encourage every Christian to take the time to develop a network of relationships with fellow workers, neighbours and relatives.

There in our neighbourhoods and workplaces we can show ourselves warm and friendly, interesting and helpful. Consistency and integrity of lifestyle should arouse the curiosity of unsaved friends. In post-apostolic times people commented, 'My, how these Christians love one another!'

Somehow we have to keep evangelism in the forefront of our thinking. Jesus instructed the apostles: 'The harvest is plentiful but the workers are few. Ask the Lord of the harvest, therefore, to send out workers into his harvest field' (Matt. 9:37-38; Luke 10:2). At Long Branch Baptist Church we sought to keep the matter before us by the expedient of a simple motto: 'Each one reach one.' The motto emphasized our individual responsibility for witnessing, without burdening us with a complicated programme.

In a climate where evangelism was natural, Philip grew as a witness. But what set him apart as an evangelist?

IV. Philip — the evangelist

On his way to Jerusalem, Paul stayed in Cæsarea at the 'house of Philip the evangelist' (Acts 21:8). Some time during the period between Saul's violent persecution of the church and the conclusion of his third missionary journey, Philip, the servant, had become known as Philip, the evangelist. Evangelism became the main focus of his life.

While Acts frequently alludes to witnessing Christians, Philip is the only witness specifically described in the Bible as an evangelist. He could not, however, have been unique.

Jesus predicted that his disciples would become 'fishers of men', that is, evangelists noted for their success in catching souls. Success in fishing for men presupposes effectiveness in drawing men to faith in Christ.

This harvest image, drawn from the sea, indicates that God bestows on some the ability to draw men to Christ. We can equate the gift of evangelism with success in soul-winning. The apostles certainly demonstrated this. The multitude converted at Pentecost, along with other examples of the kind, identifies Peter as a gifted evangelist. Paul's successful ministry points the same way. Early Christian writings outside the Bible contain other references to evangelists.

What distinguishes this gift from other gifts? Let us see what we can find from biblical and historical sources on this point.

1. Evangelists focus on the need of the lost for salvation

Acts 8 takes up Philip's story: 'Philip went down to a city in Samaria and proclaimed the Christ there' (Acts 8:5). As a Jew, Philip had been taught to avoid all contact with Samaritans. Some powerful force overcame this cultural prejudice. That force was, no doubt, his Spirit-produced compassion for the lost.

Compassion for unreached people ought to throb within each one of us. It must grip the heart of those with the gift of evangelism. A sensitivity towards certain needs, as discussed in earlier chapters, helps to isolate an area of giftedness. In those with the gift of evangelism, the desperate need of lost people for salvation engages their concern. Paul cries, 'Since then, we know what it is to fear the Lord, we try to persuade men' (2 Cor. 5:11). 'Christ's love compels us' (2 Cor. 5:14). Compassion for the lost inspires evangelistic inventiveness. 'I have become all things to all men so that by all possible means I might save some' (1 Cor. 9:22). As these verses show, Paul was an evangelist.

In the presence of lost Samaritans, Philip's compassion soon motivated him to overcome his prejudice in order to witness to them. Later, God's call to take the gospel to the lost Ethiopian provoked a similar response (Acts 8:26-27). Acts 8 concludes with Philip travelling throughout the region 'preaching the gospel in all the towns until he reached Cæsarea' (Acts 8:40). Every gift focuses on a particular area of need. The evangelist focuses on the lost.

2. Evangelists reap a harvest of conversions

Different gifts produce different effects. As Philip exercised his evangelistic gift, he found people listening with rapt attention (Acts 8:6). They did more than listen: 'They believed Philip as he preached the good news of the kingdom of God and the name of Jesus Christ' (Acts 8:12). The effects of Philip's evangelistic work were so dramatic that reports reached the apostles in Jerusalem, who sent Peter and John to check into the authenticity of his ministry. They found evidence of genuine repentance and faith. Philip's effectiveness demonstrated that he was an evangelist.

Evangelists reap a harvest of souls. In the words of Jesus, they fish for men. We must distinguish sowing the seed, which I equate with witnessing, from reaping a harvest. 'One sows and another reaps... I sent you to reap what you have not worked for. Others have done the hard work, and you have reaped the benefits of their labour ...' (John 4:37-38), 'so that the sower and the reaper may be glad together' (John 4:36).

Sowing and reaping, though distinct, are both essential for a harvest. The hard work of witness rests upon all of our shoulders. But we should not get discouraged if we don't see many people converted. Keep on witnessing. We may not be evangelists. We can trust God to send someone with the gift of evangelism to reap a harvest of our hard work.

Even evangelists, however, do not always reap. The book of Acts describes a harvest epoch that followed 400 years of spiritual famine. Although a pre-eminent evangelist himself, Jesus saw relatively few genuine conversions. The apostles reaped where Jesus had sown.

It is often thus. G. Smith, a Moravian missionary, laboured for years with only one known convert. After his death 13,000 repented.

3. Biblical evangelists both itinerated and followed up converts

Jesus took his fishermen-in-training with him from town to town. He also sent them out two by two. After Pentecost, Peter itinerated around Jerusalem before going much farther afield. Paul's evangelistic journeys occupy much of the book of Acts. Philip, the only one called an evangelist, certainly travelled a lot. 'Philip went down to a city in Samaria and proclaimed the Christ' (Acts 8:5). He travelled to intercept an Ethiopian official on the way to Gaza (Acts 8:26). After explaining Christ and baptizing the official, he continued on his way from town to town until he came to Cæsarea.

When Paul returned to Jerusalem, years later, Philip was still in Cæsarea. Did he settle down to serve one church? We don't know. Most probably he continued his work of itinerant evangelism using his home in Cæsarea as a base.

Since an evangelist's heart burns with love for the lost, he will often go from place to place seeking the unreached. Concerning evangelism in the post-apostolic age Eusebius writes, 'The disciples of that time ... starting out upon long journeys they performed the office of evangelists, being filled with the desire to preach Christ to those who had not yet heard the word of faith, and to deliver to them the divine Gospels. And when they had only laid the foundations of the faith in foreign places, they appointed others as pastors, and entrusted them with the nurture of those that had recently been brought in, while they themselves went on again to other countries and nations, with the grace and the co-operation of God.'[10]

Personally, I don't view itineration as an essential ingredient of evangelism. Multitudes of laymen who stay in one church show by their effectiveness in winning the lost that they possess evangelistic giftedness. I do believe, however, that genuine evangelists are open to follow the leading of the Spirit from place to place in search of the lost.

Itinerant evangelists, however, who fail to supervise the follow-up of converts and the planting of churches seem divergent from the biblical pattern. Biblical evangelists, such as Philip and Paul, led people to faith. They didn't stop there. They followed up these converts by prescribing a regimen of discipleship training. They made sure that converts were grounded and established in local churches. New Testament evangelists closely tied their ministry to church-planting. Philip planted churches in Samaria. Paul planted in many cities. The nurture of converts takes precedence over the urge to travel.

Alex Rattray Hay seeks to correct some misconceptions about evangelism, which restrict the gift too narrowly. He writes, 'There is no Scriptural ground for considering that the Evangelist's ministry was limited to the preaching of the way of salvation. The

New Testament Evangelist was, indeed, a preacher of Christ to the unsaved, but his ministry was not fulfilled until he had gathered the converts together as an assembly of the Body of Christ and delivered to them the whole counsel of God. He was the extension agent, the church-planter, the missionary responsible for establishing the Church in unevangelized regions and the counsellor of the churches established.'[11]

I see no necessary reason why those with evangelistic gifts cannot exercise their ministries either in one locality or in a variety of locations. While the itinerant evangelistic church-planter resembles Paul, a resident evangelist might reflect the pattern of Philip and Timothy.

Richard Baxter, a seventeenth-century English pastor, emulated Paul in evangelizing both in public and from house to house. He did so without extensive travels. The town of Kidderminster, where he laboured, contained about 2,000 people in some 800 homes. When he arrived the town was renowned for revelry and ignorance. Baxter set out to visit each home and instruct the families in the things of God. The Spirit crowned his efforts with remarkable success: 'When I came thither first there was about one family in a street that worshipped God and called on his name, and when I came away there were some streets where there was not past one family in the side of a street that did not do so; and that did not by professing serious godliness, give us hope of their sincerity.'[12]

Baxter exhibited evangelistic gifts in a local town setting over a period of some fifteen years. A narrow profile of what an evangelist is or does will not serve us well. Situations and needs, churches and evangelists vary greatly. God, we remember, loves variety!

Philip is our model evangelist. He exemplified concern for the lost, ability to communicate the gospel, effectiveness in winning the lost and openness to itinerate in outreach. These qualities, especially the third, characterize the gifted evangelist.

William Hendriksen advances the view that they were 'travelling missionaries, of lower rank than apostles and prophets' and wonders if 'Philip was a deacon-evangelist'.[13] Wisely, I believe, he goes on to urge that we should not multiply offices beyond ministers, elders and deacons. He implies that there ought to be considerable flexibility and diversity of expression in these offices. Since every believer, whether in a formal office or not, receives a different mix of gifts, this view seems sensible. At all costs we must avoid confining those with church responsibilities to a strait-jacket woven by tradition rather than Scripture. Church offices should inspire creative outreach, not dampen the exercise of gifts.

Conclusion

Diverse views exist about evangelists. The overwhelming majority of commentators, however, define evangelists as soul-winners who reap a harvest of lost men and women. We can define the gift as follows: the gift of evangelism is that Spirit-produced concern for lost men and women that moves the gifted person towards outreach wherever that may lead. This concern is combined with an ability to communicate the gospel so effectively that people respond in faith and repentance.

History illustrates the importance of evangelism. Calvin, although a noted preacher and theologian, became the human instrument in God's hands to transform Geneva and French-speaking Switzerland. Indeed he is called the 'evangelist of Europe' for his work in spreading the faith throughout Europe and into Great Britain. 'In less than 11 years, from 1555 to 1566, 121 evangelists, personally trained by Calvin, were dispatched into persecuted France from Geneva. In their first four years these pioneer Presbyterian evangelists founded 2,000 new French Calvinist congregations.'[14] Calvin, like Luther before him, was an evangelist.

George Whitefield demonstrated the evangelist's heart. As an ordained minister in the Church of England, he had been taught to restrict preaching to hallowed church buildings. But when he saw the plight of thousands of unreached coal miners, compassion compelled him to go out into the fields where they could be reached. Against all the conventions of the Church of England, he initiated field preaching and ushered in the great Evangelical Awakening. With a heart on fire for the lost, he galloped from one end of England to the other. He travelled to Scotland and Ireland. He took ship to America seven times where he eventually died. Wherever he went conviction fell and people flocked to Christ. John and Charles Wesley learned their field preaching from him and initiated Methodism that subsequently swept the countryside of England and spread through America in the saddlebags of itinerant preachers.

Evangelists helped to write the history of the church. We need a multitude more like them in our day. Obedient Christians can develop into evangelists under the tutelage of the Spirit. Witness remains a crucial part of that obedience, for all of us, whether or not we have the gift of evangelism.

Norman Geisler excused himself from witnessing by reminding himself that he didn't have the gift of evangelism. He says, 'I comforted myself ... that I had the gift of teaching other people the Word of God, a task different from evangelism because it involved Christians.' Concern about his lack of witnessing led him to pray for opportunities. A professing Christian student in the college where he taught came to him in distress asking about coming to Christ in genuine faith. He led her to Christ! He was thrilled and told himself, 'True, you don't have the gift of evangelism but you're supposed to do the work of an evangelist! True, you don't see many non-Christians during the day, but did you ever pray to have some come by?' God rebuked him, by reminding him that all of us are witnesses.[15]

With these thoughts in mind, take the chart you began in chapter 6 and fill in the spaces that relate to the gift of evangelism. As you move from column to column you may begin to realize, either that you show signs of possessing the gift, or that you need to be more obedient in witnessing for Christ.

After an evangelist has established new Christians in their faith they need the nurture of those with the gift of shepherding to which we now turn our attention.

12.
The office of the pastor

Ann and Megan slip into their accustomed seats in the Bible class. Last week's study on witnessing and evangelism led to considerable heart-searching. Over coffee, Ann is animated: 'I can't believe it! I prayed for an opportunity to witness and yesterday my neighbour enquired about our faith.'

'It's been a challenging week,' Megan replies, 'but at least this morning we can relax a little. The pastoral gift is for pastors!'

Megan shouldn't be so sure about that. Many women exhibit shepherding gifts without being in full-time service. But before we consider whether women can possess the shepherding gift or not, we need to clarify the issue of leadership. For I am not suggesting, as commonly proposed in some liberal churches, that women assume leadership over men.

In this chapter I want to look at traditional assumptions about leadership and ministry in order to clarify the shepherding gift. As it is, modern Christians generally assume, without discussion, that church leadership is the function of a man with pastoral gifts. Is this assumption accurate? Does such a practice help or hinder the development of spiritual gifts?

Without clarification, a host of men and women may reject outright any suggestion that they have been given a shepherding role in the local church. That would constitute a tragedy of global proportions.

For many years I did not even consider whether I had pastoral gifts. The perceived role of a pastor scared me away from checking whether I had the gift. After serving in Pakistan in teaching, writing and administrative roles for sixteen years Mary Helen and I returned to Canada. Our home church was without a pastor. I filled in here and there until I found myself taking regular services. Two years later, the church called me to be their pastor. The invitation came as a shock.

The challenge of the pastorate has enriched our lives. Four years into the experience, however, questions began to buzz around my mind like bees on a warm summer day: 'If pastoring is my gift why do I feel stress?' 'Why is our city church not growing numerically?' 'Shouldn't visitation and hospital calling be easier?' 'Will sermon preparation ever become more routine?' 'Why do board meetings drain me so?'

The mental bees continued to buzz. Eventually we sat down with several friends and asked them to be candid. 'I am wondering if my gifts are in areas other than the pastorate? What do you think?'

They replied, 'We really believe you have pastoral gifts. We recognize your love for teaching but thank God for your pastoral ministry in our midst.'

I later traced my confusion about the pastoral gift to unbiblical perceptions I had absorbed about the pastorate. My confusion is common.

Let me say at the outset that, given current views of the role and position of the pastorate, there will be few who will either desire or ask for this gift. Certainly Ann and Megan won't. What a terrible pity! We need a host of believers cultivating the shepherding gift if our churches are ever to become the caring communities that Christ mandated.

To pick our way through this minefield of assumptions and traditions, we need to unearth the biblical teaching on leadership. We need to clarify the offices of elder and deacon. We must discover how God intended spiritual gifts such as teaching, shepherding and administration to fit into the leadership equation.

As we go along, we shall need to relate the biblical data to the pragmatic situation, where, on the whole, pastors serve as church leaders. Although present patterns owe more to historical development than biblical exegesis, undue criticism is not warranted. Pastors have personally enriched most of us. We cannot deny that. (I hope not — I have been one for some time!) Nevertheless, we should not read back into the Scriptures what we see in local church life. We need to take the opposite tack.

While this detour seems to take us away from our subject, the study of spiritual gifts, we shall soon see the need for it. Without clarity here, we cannot synthesize New Testament teaching on the gift of shepherding, understand how it relates to the modern practice of pastoring or relate this gift to other gifts.

Then, too, it is a very practical detour. With the pressures of modern society, the call to care for hurting people is more urgent than it has ever been. Megan worships in a congregation of 150. Her pastor is able and compassionate. But, like most pastors, he is very busy. And unknown to him, Megan is sliding into deep depression. Megan desperately needs pastoral ministry. Where can she find it?

I. The office of pastor

From the very beginning of the early church, pastoral care has played a crucial role. Jesus instructed Peter to 'feed my sheep'. Not too many years later we find Peter in Joppa comforting a church in grief. James shepherded the burgeoning Jerusalem congregation. Paul handled church problems throughout the Mediterranean world. His letters exude the fragrance of pastoral concern.

While we could look in many directions, let's focus mainly on one New Testament church, the church of Ephesus. It could be the church across town. The pastorate occupied a key office in that church. But from Ephesians 4 we discern the following points.

1. One office — at least two gifts

Spiritual leadership requires the dual gifts of shepherding and teaching. Jesus, when he ascended, 'gave some to be apostles, some to be prophets, some to be evangelists, and some to be pastors and teachers' (Eph. 4:11). According to the Granville Sharp Rule of Greek grammar, when 'and' joins two items in a series without an intervening article, the two items are linked together. For example, the 'and' in 'our great God and Saviour, Jesus Christ' (Titus 2:13) indicates that God and Saviour are not two distinct beings, but one and the same. That is, Jesus Christ is both God and Saviour. When we apply this rule to 'pastors and teachers' in Ephesians 4, we come to understand that 'teachers' describes, or is connected with, the preceding noun, 'pastors'. We conclude that the office of church leader is to be occupied by a person or persons exhibiting both pastoral and teaching gifts. They are pastor-teachers.

Scholars as eminent as John Calvin have believed that the two gifts indicate two distinct offices. Charles Hodge objected to this unnatural interpretation on the grounds that it led to making 'teachers a distinct and permanent class of ... officers in the church. The Puritans in New England endeavoured to reduce the theory to practice and appointed doctors as distinct from preachers. But the attempt proved to be a failure. The two functions could not be kept separate... The absence of the article ... proves that the apostle intended to designate the same persons as at once pastors and teachers... Every pastor or bishop was required to be apt to teach.'[1]

Augustine, Jerome and most modern commentators concur.[2] The office of pastor requires multiple gifts, as we shall soon see — pastoral, teaching and administrative gifts. The responsibilities of the office are too varied to be fulfilled by one spiritual endowment. Indeed the variety of terms used for the office of church leader reflects the multi-faceted nature of the task.

2. One office — three terms

Office-holders are variously called 'pastors', 'elders' or 'overseers'. The first term, *poimen,* means 'shepherd' and is used only once for the pastoral office (Eph. 4:11). All other usages of this word in the New Testament refer to Christ. For example, Jesus is called 'the Shepherd and Overseer of your souls' (1 Peter 2:25). Several other texts describe the ministry of spiritual leaders in the church as 'keep[ing] watch over ... the flock' (Acts 20:28). The NIV translates this verbal phrase as a noun and so commands elders to 'be shepherds of God's flock that is under your care' (1 Peter 5:2). The Old Testament used the Hebrew equivalent of 'shepherd' more frequently than the New in describing spiritual leaders. The term was commonly used in Jewish synagogues.

The second term, *presbuteroi* — translated 'elders', reflects qualities of age or maturity. The New Testament uses this word most frequently. For example, we read that 'The elders who direct the affairs of the church well are worthy of double honour, especially those whose work is preaching and teaching' (1 Tim. 5:17).

'Appoint elders in every town' (Titus 1:5). On his way to Jerusalem, Paul called the Ephesian elders to his side so he could share his concerns about the future of the church (Acts 20). Reflecting the Ephesian pattern, a group of men called 'elders' led every early church.

The third term, *episkopoi,* has been translated 'bishops' and more recently 'overseers'. 'Bishop' is the direct English translation of the Greek, meaning one who watches over or looks out for. Due to the connotation now attached to 'bishop', more modern translations, such as the NIV, uniformly use the word 'overseer' which more accurately communicates to an English audience the meaning of the term. *Episcopoi* — overseers, exercised oversight in a local congregation. There are three main references: 'The overseer must ... know how to manage his own family ... take care of God's church...' (1 Tim. 3:1,5). 'An overseer is entrusted with God's work' (Titus 1:7); and Paul writes 'to all the saints in Christ Jesus at Philippi, together with the overseers and deacons' (Phil. 1:1). Overseers exercised oversight — management of the congregation — while occupying an office distinct from deacons.

Do we have three different leadership offices — pastors, elders and overseers? No, all three terms are used interchangeably for the same office. Consider the group of men Paul had called to his side from Ephesus. 'From Miletus, Paul sent to Ephesus for the elders of the church' (Acts 20:17). The veteran church-planter exhorts them to 'Keep watch over yourselves and all the flock of which the Holy Spirit has made you overseers. Be shepherds of the church of God, which he bought with his own blood' (Acts 20:28). In Paul's usage 'shepherd', 'overseer' and 'elder' are just three different terms for the same men. 'Overseer' and 'elder' are used synonymously in Titus 1:5 and 7.

Peter also used the terms interchangeably. 'To the elders among you, I appeal... Be shepherds of God's flock that is under your care, serving as overseers...' (1 Peter 5:1,2).

Lightfoot writes, 'It is a fact now generally recognized by theologians of all shades of opinion, that in the language of the New Testament the same officer is called indifferently "bishop" [overseer] or "elder" [or "presbyter"].'[3] To these two can be added the commonly used word 'pastor', meaning 'shepherd'.

While used for the same office, the three terms are not, however, synonymous. Each indicates a different facet of leadership. This we shall consider shortly. In the process of our studies thus far it has become increasingly clear that church leadership, in any one local church, was the responsibility of more than one man.

3. One office — multiple office-holders

A group of elders led each New Testament church. Paul directed Titus to appoint elders (plural) in every town (Titus 1:5). Philippians was written to 'saints ... overseers and deacons' (Phil. 1:1). Peter addresses 'the elders among you' (1 Peter 5:1). As already noted, Paul, on his way to Jerusalem, calls together a group of men, called elders, from the infant church in Ephesus (Acts 20).

Some might counter the overwhelming textual evidence pointing to a plurality of elders in each church by conjecturing that each town had more than one church. If so, they would argue, a plurality of elders in a particular town would not necessarily mean a plurality of elders in one church. Each church could have been presided over by one elder. No evidence, however, exists to support the idea that one church had only one elder. James, alluding to a need in the context of a single local church, suggests that those who are sick call 'the elders of the church' (James 5:14).

In his *Expository Dictionary of New Testament Words,* Vine, in defining the position of elders/bishops/overseers states that 'The Divine arrangement seen throughout the NT. was for a plurality of these to be appointed in each church...'[4]

Stedman adds, 'Elders or bishops were always limited to one locality, one church, in New Testament days. A man who was an elder or pastor in one church was not also an elder in another place... The ruling elders correspond most closely to the present concept of a pastor, but in the early church there was never a single pastor or elder but always several.'[5]

Unfortunately, the pattern of shared leadership did not continue long. Hay traces the deterioration. As early as the second century the elders in a congregation chose one of their number to preside and called him bishop.[6] Gradually the practice of elders earning their living outside of the pastorate died out, until by the fourth century there was strong pressure for elders to separate themselves from secular life. The impetus to establish an episcopate of several churches with a presiding bishop gained momentum. Depending

upon the qualities of the leaders, the change was good or bad.
Varieties of organization are not necessarily evil in themselves but
become good or bad depending on the men that run them. Nevertheless, this shift did open the way for the chasm that exists today
between clergy and laity. It hastened the collapse of the New
Testament practice of universal priesthood. This lost pattern of
shared leadership is a loss we can ill afford.

Christ wisely laid down a pattern of shared responsibility. He
chose twelve apostles to work together. He sent disciples out two by
two. A group of elders led each local church. Wherever our studies
on the pastoral gift may lead us, one conclusion is clear: biblical
precedent underlines the wisdom of shared leadership.

Sharing leadership minimizes three serious dangers the church
leader faces, whether he be called pastor, ruling elder, minister,
bishop or chairman of the board.

The risk of abuse of position

The first danger is abuse of position. Jesus taught, and demonstrated, that leaders must fight the drive for power and domination
that infests all the children of fallen Adam. Shared leadership helps
to moderate this dangerous temptation.

While I was working on this chapter, another terrible exposé of
pastoral immorality and abuse besmirched the reputation of the
body of Christ. A pastor in Texas was found to be drawing a salary
of $152,000 a year, was caught shoplifting and was accused of
multiple sexual affairs. In the video played on TV, he thundered
against his accusers crying, 'I am responsible to no board! I am
responsible to no church! I am called of God and responsible to him
alone.' What a travesty of biblical leadership!

A plurality of elders is wise precisely because, 'No one man is the
sole expression of the mind of the Spirit; no individual has authority
from God to direct the affairs of the church. A plurality of elders is
necessary as a safeguard to the all too human tendency to play God
over other people.'[7]

Unrealistic expectations

Shared leadership, secondly, protects us from the danger of unrealistic expectations. Church leadership, which is widely perceived as
fulfilled in the modern pastorate, requires the exercise of a variety

of gifts. These gifts include administration, preaching, teaching, evangelism, mercy, faith, exhortation and shepherding, to name a few. Yet all these gifts rarely, if ever, flower in any one man. Unfortunately, the perception of the pastor as a multi-talented strong leader who is a combination saint, preacher, counsellor, organizer, father, friend and all-round good fellow too often wins out over the reality — until some idolized pastor falls from his pedestal.

Pulpit committees scour the land in search of this ideal, a sort of Sir Galahad who will come on a white horse and single-handedly slay all the dragons laying siege to the church — without, of course, upsetting too many people. Do we dare forget that Christ alone can fulfil all these expectations? Others who try to climb this pastoral Mount Olympus are almost certain to come crashing down.

Elizabeth Davey, a pastor's wife, comments that too often we have created an imaginary world in which we call a pastor to play a rôle as if on a Shakespearean stage. She asks, 'Is the part we have assigned him even possible? ... Have both parties created an illusion that our minister is to be a super-human messiah ...?'[8]

Most believers do one or two things well while they are mediocre in other spheres. By projecting an illusory ideal we end up with men who put people to sleep while they try in vain to preach like Lloyd-Jones instead of admitting that they have other gifts. If we fail to adopt a pattern of multiple leadership, we doom congregations to solo-leaders who exhibit excellence in one area while performing dismally in other spheres.

Church leadership is too challenging for any one man. The great men held up as examples of the ideal pastor all had feet of clay in certain areas. Whitefield was an evangelist and preacher without peer, but his weakness in organization left a vacuum into which Wesley galloped with his Methodist wagon. A. W. Tozer, whose writings have stirred the consciences of several generations, simply didn't visit.

I am not belittling men of eminent gifts. The Bible is replete with heroes like Abraham, David and the apostle Paul. But few of us ever achieve their distinction. Snyder, in a chapter entitled, 'Must the Pastor be a Superstar?', describes this rarity: 'Meet Pastor Jones, Superstar. He can preach, counsel, evangelize, administrate, conciliate, communicate and sometimes even integrate. He can also raise the budget. He handles Sunday morning better than any quiz master on weekday TV... His church, of course counts itself fortunate. Alas, not many churches can boast such talent.'[9] Multiple leadership is the better way!

Overworked pastors and underdeveloped church members

Multiple leadership, thirdly, protects pastors from burn-out and laity from rust-out. Stedman, describing the historical development of a professional class of priests, states, 'When the ministry was thus left to the professionals there was nothing left for the people to do other than to come to church and listen... Soon Christianity became nothing but a spectator sport... This unbiblical distortion has placed pastors under an unbearable burden. They have proved completely unequal to the task of evangelizing the world, counselling the distressed and brokenhearted, ministering to the poor and needy ... relieving the oppressed and afflicted, expounding the Scriptures, and challenging the entrenched forces of evil in an increasingly darkened world. They were never meant to do it. To even attempt it is to end up frustrated, exhausted, and emotionally drained... This distortion has resulted in a sadly impoverished church.'[10]

Multiple leadership helps to avoid abuse of power, unrealistic expectations, over-worked pastors and under-developed laity, while enhancing body life and gift development. The diversity of responsibilities inherent in church leadership necessitates a sharing of that leadership. Let's look a little closer at those responsibilities.

II. The responsibilities of pastoral office

Paul asked four things of the elders he appointed. Let us consider the first three of these responsibilities in this chapter — equipping, teaching and overseeing. The fourth, shepherding, will be examined in chapter twelve.

1. Church leaders as equippers

Paul wrote that church leaders are gifted for the purpose of 'equipping the saints for the work of ministry' (Eph. 4:12, NKJV). Or, as the NIV has it, pastor-teachers were given to the body of Christ, 'to prepare God's people for works of service, so that the body of Christ may be built up' (Eph. 4:12). God calls all believers to mobilize for ministry. He gives to each ministry gifts. All need training in how to use their gifts. Without their mobilization and training local church growth cannot be achieved. Here lies the crucial role of the pastor-teacher.

God appoints the pastor-teacher and, as we have established, the elder or overseer to a specific ministry of development. Their function is not to do all the work of ministry, but to train other believers to fan out in varied ministry. By appointing church leaders to this function, the risen Lord provided a framework in which the whole body can move towards maturity demonstrated in 'the fulness of Christ', that is, Christlikeness (Eph. 4:12-16).

The word variously translated 'perfect', 'equip' or 'prepare' is borrowed from usage for nets needing mending. It captures the idea of rendering people fit or complete, so they become useful. Hendriksen gives the sense of the passage: 'Christ gave some men ... for the purpose of "perfecting" or providing the necessary equipment for all the saints for the work of ministering to each other so as to build up the body of Christ.'[11]

In real-life situations the entire flock is not engaged in spiritual labour. At least two reasons for this emerge. First, many are uncommitted and don't want to be involved in ministry. They avoid responsibility. No amount of teaching on spiritual gifts will make any difference until they submit to Christ.

Second, others either feel inadequate to minister, remain unaware of their gifts and responsibilities or are unequipped to serve. This latter group challenge pastor-teachers to get busy developing a programme of training for ministry. Training for ministry is the specialized function and main focus of the church leader.

The whole church structure needs to mirror this in-service training model. Sunday School and Bible classes, worship services, midweek Bible Studies, outreach ministries and committees — in short, everything should contribute to the equipping of disciples. The church ought to be the hothouse where budding ministers take root and grow.

The church leader who catches this vision will structure everything he does to develop ministering disciples. He cannot just spend his time leading worship, or teaching, or preaching or organizing. He must, as well, strive to raise up a host of disciples who depend on him less and less as they mature in faith and service.

Paul succeeded as a leader precisely because he left a Timothy and a Titus behind. The elders in Ephesus might have wept at his departure, but they could carry on without him. And that pastor will be successful who trains other shepherds, other teachers and other administrators who rival him in ability. This, to use Frank Tillapaugh's suggestive term, unleashes the church by tapping the potential inherent in God's people. Every church leader should be able to say, 'I have told the Lord that I will thank Him for whatever leadership He raises up in the church, even if it means they will someday replace me... When we began to build a staff I asked God for men and women who would excel me. God has honoured that request.'[12]

Let me illustrate from our experience in Pakistan. This principle, discipleship training, undergirds all missionary activity. Historically, missions failed where a paternalistic dependence on missionaries took root. Conversely, missions have been a resounding success where indigenous churches led by equipped church leaders continue to mushroom.

Paternalism was the greatest difficulty we faced in Pakistan. We had to fight continually against feeding our own carnal egos by allowing nationals to grow dependent on us as foreign missionaries. Pakistani pastors fought the same battle. It was almost impossible to encourage believers to develop their gifts because no pattern of equipping laymen had been developed. A century of dependence, the legacy of colonialism, blunted their vision of ministry and their understanding of the priesthood of all believers.

Few pastors there had a vision for training Timothys, because an élitist view of ministry permeated their understanding of the pastorate. In their mind, ministry meant doing all that needed to be done in the church themselves: leading services, preaching, visiting, conducting funerals, etc. This, of course, kept their position secure, because laymen were not raised up to challenge their authority. Pakistan may seem distant. But what we saw so starkly in Pakistan is unconsciously the pattern in much of the world. Pakistanis didn't invent; they inherited the pattern.

Missionaries, largely, see the danger of creating dependence. Why don't we recognize the same error in our own backyard? What is true in missionary church-planting is just as true in Western church development!

God has woven into the very fabric of the New Testament the master/disciple relationship. Being a disciple necessarily means being in training. Healthy churches cannot develop where this discipleship process is not encouraged. Christian leaders, of necessity, must be equippers.

Equipping requires demonstration. No wonder the apostle exhorted church leaders to exemplify the Christian life. Paul said, 'Join with others in following my example, brothers, and take note of those who live according to the pattern we gave you' (Phil. 3:17). He expected Timothy to be an example (1 Tim. 4:12). Peter encouraged elders/overseers/shepherds to 'serve, not lording it over those entrusted to you, but being examples to the flock' (1 Peter 5:2-3). The necessity of demonstrating the exercise of gifts is, by the way, another reason for multiple leadership in a local church. One man cannot be a model for all the gifts!

In a sense, all spiritual gifts are demonstrated gifts. How can we describe the gift of mercy, or giving, or helps, or administration without giving examples? God expects church leaders to exemplify what they seek to train others to do. The Holy Spirit gives gifts, but the responsibility to teach believers how to develop and use their gifts he delegates to others. The church leader, as equipper, is the catalyst here and, as such, he must be a teacher.

2. Church leaders as teachers

While teaching will be discussed in more detail in a following chapter, we need to note several issues related to teaching, in the context of our discussion of church leadership.

Teaching and prophecy are the only gifts mentioned in all three of the main gift passages. Paul puts teaching on a par with shepherding as an essential equipping gift. An elder must be 'able to teach' (1 Tim. 3:2). 'He must hold firmly to the trustworthy message as it has been taught, so that he can encourage others by sound doctrine and refute those who oppose it' (Titus 1:9).

Paul gave special honour to the teaching ministry of church leaders by indicating that this ministry deserved special honour and wages. 'The elders who direct the affairs of the church well are

worthy of double honour, especially those whose work is preaching
and teaching... The worker deserves his wages' (1 Tim. 5:17,18). In
the early church, where tent-making leadership was the norm, this
stress is unusual. It indicates that the teaching and preaching
ministries of church leaders are so important that those who give
more time to them ought to be supported financially. The almost
universal practice of hiring full-time paid pastors rests on such
support.

Paul reiterates the importance of teaching in his farewell to the
Ephesian elders: 'I have not hesitated to preach anything that would
be helpful to you but have taught you publicly and from house to
house' (Acts 20:20,21,24-27).

In the early church, the apostles gave elders the twin responsibilities of equipping the saints for ministry and teaching the Word. The
two are, of course, two sides of the same coin. Equipping is a crucial
facet of good teaching. Good teaching always involves application
to life and ministry. It is, however, helpful to separate equipping for
ministry from other aspects of teaching. Not all teaching has
ministry as its focus. Teaching may illuminate the glory of God and
lead us to worship. Teaching may be doctrinal. Teaching may
uncover our resources in Christ and lead us to find hope and joy.
Teaching may focus on character development. Teaching has always been central in evangelical church life.

Christ expects elders to be equippers and teachers. He also calls
them to administer church affairs.

3. Church leaders as overseers

In his parting message to the Ephesian elders, Paul exhorts them to
exercise not only their gifts of teaching and shepherding but also
their gifts of leadership. 'Keep watch over yourselves and all the
flock of which the Holy Spirit has made you overseers' (Acts 20:28).
Ability to manage scores high on the list of qualifications laid out for
elders: 'He must manage his own family well and see that his
children obey him with proper respect. (If anyone does not know
how to manage his own family, how can he take care of God's
church?)' (1 Tim 3:4-5; cf. Titus 1:6).

Elders directed church affairs in New Testament times. In
Jerusalem 'James and all the elders' led the church (Acts 21:18).

Apparently James was 'first among equals' (Acts 12:17; 15:13). The leadership, however, did not make decisions unilaterally. In the crisis over the care of widows, the apostles outlined the problem, suggested a possible solution and then said, 'Brothers, choose seven men from among you... This proposal pleased the whole group. They chose Stephen, a man full of faith and of the Holy Spirit; also Philip...' The entire assembly of believers took part in choosing the first deacons.

Some years later, Paul and Barnabas returned to 'the church and the apostles and elders, to whom they reported everything...' (Acts 15:4). A party of converted Pharisees opposed their neglect of the law. The church leaders, that is, the apostles and elders, got together to discuss the issue (Acts 15:6). Finally James, the recognized leader of the group, summarized their findings and made a recommendation that was accepted. Next they apprised the whole assembly of the situation. As a result, 'The apostles and elders, with the whole church, decided to choose some of their own men and send them to Antioch with Paul and Barnabas' (Acts 15:22). Throughout the record of the New Testament church a pattern of gifted and decisive leadership, sensitive to the needs and concerns of the congregations, emerges. New Testament leadership maintained authority without domination through careful recourse to consultation.

They honoured their leaders. Paul writes, 'Hold them in the highest regard ... because of their work' (1 Thess. 5:13). Hebrews commands, 'Remember your leaders, who spoke the word of God to you... Obey your leaders and submit to their authority. They keep watch over you as men who must give an account. Obey them so that their work will be a joy, not a burden' (Heb. 13:7,17). New Testament churches were not amorphous congregations of believers led by the Spirit without recourse to human leadership. Leaders, possessing delegated authority from Christ, the Head of the church, gave direction in the affairs of that church. Clearly, part of the responsibility of church leaders is to lead! Just what it means to lead will be discussed in the chapter on the gift of administration.

Dangers of abuse

Leadership, of course, is always open to abuse, whether focused on one man or resident in a committee. Plurality of leadership is a safer pattern, but even a group of leaders can be dictatorial. In Great

Britain grave concern is expressed about what is called 'heavy shepherding', a form of leadership manifest in assemblies where leaders enforce their imagined right to direct the affairs of all believers. Pastors who practise heavy shepherding issue directives to believers about whom they may associate with, what they should wear, whom they should marry and even where they should work.

Heavy shepherding is cultic. But what of our more middle of the road evangelical churches? Unfortunately, abuse is much more prevalent than we like to believe. Earl Radmacher, in a series of messages at a convention I attended, expressed sorrow that the Reformation had stopped short of reforming the Roman concept of hierarchical leadership. He warned the pastors present not to be 'petty, Protestant, parochial popes'! The tendency to 'lord it over others' pops up like mushrooms everywhere. It can be found in the rather innocent desire of laymen to elevate pastors, the tendency of seminaries to idealize the ministerial position and the desire of denominations to enforce overly stringent ordination requirements. I have noted indignation expressed in some pastors' meetings I have attended about the erosion of pastoral authority, the dangers of small groups and other perceived threats to the pastor's position. The symptoms are all around us. I believe the New Testament pattern of shared leadership provides a wise antidote to the multiple dangers of one-man leadership.

Of course, as already noted, multiple eldership itself is open to grave abuse of authority. Cantankerous men and women in positions of perpetual authority thwart the growth of too many churches. Recently, I have been appalled by coming across church after church stuck in the mud because a leadership faction refuses to share authority. 'This is our church,' they cry. 'We've been here forty years (or sixty)! We built it. We paid for it. We're not about to let some upstart mess around with our church.'

The divine right of kings is passé. But some church boards seem to believe in their divine right to hire and fire pastors. They seem to think they are called to keep them poor and humble while they refuse to rotate responsibilities. Myriads of churches have been stunted by one man, or a group of elders with long tenure, running the church as if it were their own private fiefdom. As a result many pastors pace up and down pondering how to lead their church ahead in the face of board resistance. Many give up and move on.

Such practices violate the spirit of the New Testament, where believers are urged to give double honour to those elders (pastors) 'whose work is preaching and teaching' (Tim. 5:17). Some independent churches view the pastor as a short-term hireling, tolerated as long as he does not cross the board! His vision for the church is thwarted at every turn by elders or deacons who view him as a temporary servant in their church.

Whenever a church calls a pastor, New Testament precedent requires that he share authority with other elders. He must also be allowed freedom, as James was, to lead. No pastor can do a proper job in a climate where responsibility is piled on while authority is grudgingly shared. There should be a clear understanding of the responsibility of the church to care for his monetary needs, support him in sickness or stress, provide for his retirement, deal with his transfer in a gracious and proper way and have recourse to a grievance process. Yes, as a reviewer of this manuscript forcefully informed me, not only pastors are tempted to abuse authority but elders and deacons as well!

Servant-leadership

Jesus warned his disciples about the subtle temptation to act like the Gentiles, who love to 'lord it over them, and their high officials exercise authority over them'. He taught them to resist the pattern of hierarchical leadership practised in the pagan world and opt instead to become servant-leaders (see chapter 3). In large measure the early church followed his pattern. They exposed aberrations, such as 'Diotrephes, who loves to be first' (3 John 9). Peter exhorted church leaders to avoid being domineering over those in their charge (1 Peter 5:3). Very early in his missionary endeavours, Paul turned over leadership, as in Ephesus, to a group of elders. He showed how to share leadership — and move on.

Servant-leadership does not mean the absence of authority. As Head of the church Christ exemplifies authority. He delegates responsibility to parents, to political leaders in the world at large and to church leaders. But Christian leadership must be qualitatively different from worldly leadership that relies on position, power and hierarchy. As Stedman points out, 'The world's view of authority places men over one another, as in a military structure, a business

executive hierarchy or a governmental system. This is as it should
be. Urged by the competitiveness created by the Fall, and faced with
the rebelliousness and ruthlessness of sinful human nature, the
world could not function without the use of command structure and
executive decision.'[13]

The church is different. Our Lord created the church as a family,
with brothers and sisters united by their common bond led by those
who serve from the bottom of the structure rather than the top.
'Whoever wants to become great among you must be your servant,
and whoever wants to be first must be your slave' (Matt. 20:26-27).
If the command structure of the world is a pyramid, with the boss at
the top, that of the church is an inverted pyramid, with the elders at
the bottom as their servants. Christians lead by loving example,
through consultation and by using gentle persuasion. The biblical
leader puts on the boxing gloves of tough love only when gentler
methods fail.

Unfortunately, as Stedman continues, the church has virtually
ignored the teaching of Christ and 'changed the names of executives
from kings, generals, captains, presidents, governors, secretaries,
heads and chiefs to popes, patriarchs, bishops, stewards, deacons,
pastors and elders, and gone merrily on its way, lording it over the
brethren and thus destroying the model of servanthood which our
Lord intended'.[14] (I hope it is clear by this point that I am not denying
the need for leadership but decrying some of the unbiblical trap-
pings and methods of leadership.)

Rather than search the boardrooms of modern mega-churches
for patterns of leadership, we need to return to the New Testament.
Many dynamic churches are really the spiritual empires of godly,
but benevolent dictators. One of the largest churches in my city is
run very efficiently from the top down without any membership
meetings whatever! The pattern seems to work for them. But surely
they are an exception.

In the vast majority of cases, it would seem wiser to focus on the
pooling of gifts among a plurality of leaders rather than on the search
for a super-pastor. As more believers exercise their gifts there is
more chance for the church to become a caring community. Remember Megan with her depression? A strong dominant leader, even if
he knew she had a problem, could hardly spare much time for her
pastoral care. But a congregation permeated by a sense of shepherding concern in which many believers share ministry responsibilities
could.

Conclusion

Our study of the parameters of New Testament church organization and leadership has led us to isolate some interesting contrasts
to modern practice. We noted that New Testament church leaders
were responsible for equipping believers for ministry, teaching the
whole counsel of God, giving general direction to the church and
shepherding.

Church leaders were variously called 'elders', 'shepherds',
'pastors', 'overseers' or 'bishops'. The terms, while used interchangeably, are not synonymous. The term 'elder' highlights their
maturity and responsibility, while the terms 'pastor' and 'overseer'
reflect the gifts of shepherding and leadership. To these two gifts
may be added the essential gift of teaching as well as those of
preaching and evangelism.

Since church leadership involves a cluster of gifts, practical
wisdom and biblical precedent should encourage us to share leadership. Shared leadership, however, must not be allowed to stifle
vision and direction. In every local church there needs to be a James,
first among equals, who is given honour and the scope to steer the
fellowship. Leadership, of course, presupposes a pastoral concern
for the flock. This pastoral gift — shepherding — is the subject of
the next chapter.

13.
The gift of shepherding

The Bible class on spiritual gifts is about to begin. Ann and Megan look over their notes from last Sunday. Ron and Mike Sherwin are in animated discussion. 'I've been a deacon for five years but I never realized that pastor doesn't mean pastor,' comments Mike.

'I think I know what you mean,' replies Ron. 'How do we sort out the pastoral role when church leaders, according to the New Testament, can be elders, overseers, teachers, shepherds or equippers? It blows my mind!'

'No wonder the pastor has circles under his eyes with us expecting him to wear all those hats!' Mike exclaims. He continues, 'I'm beginning to see what he's been driving at with all those studies on the body, the priesthood of all believers and the church as a caring community. In fact, I think I'm able to grapple with some disloyal thoughts I've suppressed.'

'Disloyal! What do you mean?' Ron queries.

'Well, don't get me wrong,' Mike mumbles, 'but sometimes I've wondered if I don't have more of a shepherding heart than the pastor.'

'Mike, you're off your head!' Ron replies, a little louder than he had planned. 'You should have been there when the pastor visited me in hospital. Tears came to his eyes as he prayed and read with me.'

'No, no, I don't mean he doesn't have a caring heart,' Mike interjects, 'but sometimes I've wondered why he stays in the study so much, why he's not visiting more. You remember what a visitor our former pastor was. I've got a full-time job but I'm always on the phone or talking to people or visiting... Now I realize that I'm expecting him to be like me. My own burden for hurting people has made me expect him to feel like I do. Perhaps that's my gift. I've got it all wrong.'

Is Mike right? To find out we need to define more carefully the pastoral gift. How does it differ from teaching, equipping and leading? Is this gift restricted to church leaders? These are some of the questions we need to consider next.

The Greek word

As mentioned in the last chapter, the word *poimen* is translated 'pastor' only once in the New Testament. The word, which denotes a shepherd, is much more commonly used for Christ. In John 10 he is the Good Shepherd who calls his sheep by name, who goes ahead of them so they can follow him and, most particularly, he is the one who gives his life for them. Once his sheep receive eternal life, he protects them so they will never perish. 'No one can snatch them out of my hand.' He is also the 'Lamb of God who takes away the sin of the world'.

Many commentators have suggested that as the Shepherd, Christ demonstrates his offices of Prophet, Priest and King. As Prophet he teaches us all truth. As Priest he gives his life in atonement for us and continues to intercede on our behalf. As King he rules over us as a benevolent and protective monarch who provides for our every need and protects us from all danger. Christ is the prototype of the new covenant shepherd.

Caring for the flock

While the New Testament uses the word 'shepherd' sparingly as a title for pastors/elders, nevertheless the concept commonly arises when church leadership is discussed. Paul exhorted the Ephesian elders to 'Keep watch over yourselves and all the flock of which the Holy Spirit has made you overseers. Be shepherds of the church of God' (Acts 20:28). Pastoring is like shepherding a flock.

This involves protecting the flock from danger. 'Wolves will come in among you and will not spare the flock... Be on your guard!' (Acts 20:29,31). Wolf-like false teachers and divisive leaders insinuate themselves into the midst of believers to cull out a flock of their own. True shepherds constantly watch for signs of error or division in the immature and unstable in order to 'help the weak' (Acts 20:35).

Christians, like infants, can be 'tossed back and forth by the waves, and blown here and there by the cunning and craftiness of men in their deceitful scheming'. The prevalence of threats to the health of the body necessitates the constant vigilance of those with shepherding gifts (Eph. 4:11-14).

In that poignant episode when Christ asked Peter about his love, our Lord instructed him to 'Take care of my sheep' (John 21:16). Years later in his first general epistle he echoed what he had learned by saying, 'Be shepherds of God's flock that is under your care, serving as overseers...' (1 Peter 5:2). Oversight of a flock involves a shepherd's care and concern.

The Shepherd Psalm portrays the dimensions of that care. The Lord, as our Shepherd, is the supreme example of pastoral care as he remains ever on the watch for the needs of his people. These needs include food — 'green pastures'; refreshment — 'quiet waters'; direction — 'paths of righteousness'; protection from danger and the fear of death — 'through the valley of the shadow of death'; or companionship — 'for you are with me'. Discouragement, sadness or general malaise may move him to come and 'restore my soul'. The protection, provision, guidance and companionship of the divine Shepherd exemplify genuine pastoral care (Ps. 23).

The Good Shepherd of John 10 protects the flock from outside attack and also provides nourishment, 'that they may have life, and have it to the full' (John 10:10).

A general practitioner

A picture emerges, to change the imagery, of the shepherd as a GP — a general practitioner. A church with people specializing in various ministries according to their gifts also needs some believers with a more general ministry of concern, that is, shepherding.

In past decades the trend in medicine has been towards developing highly trained specialists. Now dermatologists, neurologists and obstetricians thump and probe. Some of us, nostalgically, remember the family doctor who not only delivered us but gave us our childhood injections. He kept up with our health all through childhood and adolescence. He listened to our complaints, dispensed medicine and gave sage advice on proper health.

I remember a general practitioner from my childhood. He set my broken arm and bandaged my bleeding head where I had gashed it by falling off my dad's bench. He even took out my inflamed tonsils on the kitchen table! Family doctors are GPs. Fortunately, GPs are staging a comeback.

Those with a pastoral role are, in a sense, the congregation's GPs. They read congregational symptoms and prescribe necessary medicine. Like GPs, they keep watch for worldliness, viruses that attack from without. They deal with tumours and inflammations that attack the body from within. They prescribe a balanced mixture of healthy exercise, good diet and necessary rest. On occasion they call in a specialist.

The Holy Spirit gifts biblical shepherds to watch out for the general spiritual health of the flock. Of course, shepherds usually combine other skills, such as encouragement or teaching, with pastoral giftedness. Indeed, the linkage of teacher with pastor in Ephesians chapter 4 underlines the necessity of church leaders having both the gift of pastoral care and the gift of teaching. Most pastoral care will involve scriptural edification. Nevertheless, as gifts, teaching and shepherding are distinct.

Definition of the gift

The gift of shepherding is a spiritual endowment that involves a sensitivity to the health and hurts of other believers as well as the ability to come alongside with healing and help. The shepherd diagnoses and treats spiritual maladies as well as promoting spiritual health in the body of Christ.

The gift of shepherding particularly involves the diagnosis, prescription and treatment of spiritual maladies with a view to maintaining the body of Christ in good health. Consider first, the role of diagnosis in shepherding.

I. Pastoral diagnosis

Accurate diagnosis requires three things: an understanding of good health, a sensitivity to symptoms of sickness and an acquaintance with the patient.

Ephesians 4 defines good spiritual health in terms of doctrinal stability in the face of false teaching, love that fosters unity and gift exercise in which all members participate in body life. To these must be added a developing knowledge of Christ leading to practical godliness. Healthy growth will combine knowledge, love, ministry and godly character reflecting developing Christlikeness.

The person with the shepherding gift views the church with these biblical perspectives in mind. The Bible remains the main diagnostic tool, for 'The Word of God is living and active. Sharper than any double-edged sword, it penetrates even to dividing soul and spirit, joints and marrow; it judges the thoughts and attitudes of the heart' (Heb. 4:12). Bereft of this diagnostic tool, secular psychiatrists rely on scores of contradictory theories to explain soul-sickness. They fall short in their attempts to heal. Drugs are often over-prescribed. Fortunately, the shepherd has the Word that he can use like a stethoscope to monitor the hidden thoughts and attitudes of hurting people.

As a spiritual diagnostician, the shepherd 'watches for souls, as one that must give account' (Heb. 12:17). Charles Bridges describes the shepherd's diagnostic work well. 'He "watches for souls", lest a root of bitterness should spring up to the trouble and defilement of the church — lest unchristian tempers and practices should mar the profession of Christ — lest a lukewarm spirit should paralyse exertion, or a spirit of contention hinder Christian love. The indolent are slumbering — the self-dependent are falling back — the zealous are under the influence of spiritual pride — the earnest are becoming self-righteous — the regular, formal. Then there is the enquirer, asking for direction — the tempted and perplexed, looking for support — the afflicted, longing for the cheering consolation of the Gospel — the convinced sinner, from the slight healing of his wound, settling in a delusive peace...'[1]

Shepherds watch for symptoms of spiritual need. Young people need guidance in making choices for life. The sick need encouragement and prayer. Depressed souls need hope and companionship.

Other needs may not be so obvious: subtle pride in a teacher, lifeless formalism covered up by lusty singing, self-righteousness in zealous youth or apathy among the middle-aged. Certain needs arise as a natural result of healthy growth or common trials, while others arise more as the pathological symptoms of deeply rooted problems.

The example of the apostles

Peter was a shepherd. When he sensed discouragement spreading among believers due to suffering, he wrote his first epistle to prescribe hope. Under his incisive scrutiny other problems surfaced as well. 'Rid yourselves of all malice and all deceit, hypocrisy, envy and slander of every kind' (1 Peter 2:1). Concerned lest these infections stunt growth, he prescribes the spiritual milk of the Word (2:2). Then too, he warned about 'sinful desires, which war against your soul' (2:11).

Peter detected a spirit of self-centred independence that afflicted relationships between husbands and wives, parents and children, slaves and masters by injecting stress and competition (1 Peter 2:13 - 3:7) This virus in turn produces in some the throb of bitterness and in others the nausea of fear (3:14). Sensing spiritual passivity, he counselled a regimen of healthy exercise manifest in service (4:9-11). Throughout the epistle repeated references to the suffering Saviour, the presence of God and the need to glorify him are designed to offset the inflammation of pride (5:3,5-6). Detecting the debilitating presence of anxiety, Peter prescribed a medicine so generally useful that it has the status of a wonder drug: 'Cast all your anxiety on him because he cares for you' (5:7). The Good Shepherd had taught Peter well!

Paul, too, manifested a shepherd's concern. His first epistle to the Corinthians diagnoses their manifold illnesses and prescribes Spirit-taught remedies. He exposes the danger of competition that leaves a trail of fractured relationships (chapters 1-4). He cries out for amputation of the gangrene of immorality in chapter 5. Diagnosis and treatment continue throughout the epistle.

John includes two chapters of diagnosis in his Revelation (ch. 2-3). Five of the seven churches show signs of spiritual ill-health. In Ephesus the problem is lack of love, in Pergamum tolerance of false teaching and in Thyatira toleration of a false prophetess and her error. Hesitant obedience had debilitated Sardis. Lukewarm devotion sent Laodicea to the emergency room. Only Smyrna and Philadelphia manifested signs of glowing health — two out of seven!

The need today

Are conditions better today? No. In my experience, we desperately need diagnosis! A diagnostic ministry, uncovering as it does the sins of the saints, may be decried as negative. But we must remember that positive treatment cannot be applied without negative diagnosis. God save us from shepherds who never apply the X-ray of the Word to our manifold depravity! Sometimes we need radical surgery.

Growth in Christ requires careful evaluation. Unlike our physical well-being, spiritual growth does not proceed unconsciously. As he probes his own soul for symptoms of spiritual infection, the psalmist consciously prays, 'Search me, O God, and know my heart; test me… See if there is any offensive way in me' (Ps. 139:23,24). Maturity in Christ denotes an ability to diagnose our own ills. Unfortunately, even when we know better, the subtle depravity of our deceitful hearts often short-circuits our own attempts at self-examination. No wonder we need the ministry of spiritual GPs throughout our lives, even though healthy diagnosis must begin in our own hearts.

The prevalence and subtlety of temptation render a ministry of mutual care indispensable. We no sooner become familiar with one form of temptation than the enemy changes his tactics. Alone, we stand vulnerable and inexperienced. Paul exhorts the Galatians to 'Watch yourself, or you also may be tempted. Carry each other's burdens' (Gal. 6:1-2). In other words, we are not only to be careful ourselves, but we should watch out for temptations which creep up on other believers. 'Let him who thinks he stands take heed lest he fall.' In this sense we all need to exercise a pastoral ministry towards one another.

Eternal vigilance is the price of harmony and resultant growth in the flock of God. Of course, a shepherd cannot be vigilant without knowing his flock. That will require visiting them in their homes.

Paul reminds the Ephesians elders, 'I … have taught you publicly and from house to house' (Acts 20:20).

The importance of visitation

Someone has wisely said, 'A home-going pastor makes a church-going people.' Without visiting people in their homes or where they work we cannot really get to know them. Bridges quotes an old theologian as saying that the church leader has 'three books to study — the Bible, himself and the people'.[2] The importance of Bible study has already been emphasized. Self-understanding is foundational for our own growth and essential as a basis for understanding others. Personal acquaintance with other believers, of course, cannot be obtained in the brief time we have after church services. That time is hardly long enough to get to know their names!

For this reason home visitation has always been an integral part of church ministry. Ignatius knew every individual in his flock. Cyprian and Gregory wrote about the importance of visitation. Of Calvin we read that he 'lays down the Scriptural obligation to this work, and reports the fruitful harvests reaped at Geneva, when the ministers and elders went from house to house, and dealt closely and individually with the consciences of people.'[3] (By the way, we should note that Calvin assumes that this ministry will be carried on by a plurality of shepherds.) Richard Baxter's strategy of visiting every house in Kidderminster transformed that town.

The pressure of work combines with natural reticence to keep pastors too much in their studies and too little in people's homes. It has ever been thus. Dr Doddridge, commenting on this tendency, resolved to adopt a pattern of visitation: 'I have many cares and troubles: may God forgive me, that I am so apt to forget those of the Pastoral office! I now resolve,

1. To take a more particular account of the souls committed to my care.
2. To visit, as soon as possible, the whole congregation, to learn more particularly the circumstances of them, their children, and servants.
3. Will make as exact a list as I can of those that I have

reason to believe are unconverted, awakened, converted, fit
for communion, or already in it.

4. When I hear anything particular, relating to the religious
state of my people, I will visit them, and talk with them.

5. I will especially be careful to visit the sick. I will begin
immediately with inspection over those under my own roof,
that I may with the greater freedom urge other families to the
like care. O my soul! thy account is great...'[4]

Charles Bridges, in his classic work, *The Christian Ministry,*
from which I have culled most of the above quotations, points out
that some matters of application are so private that they require a
personal visit. He goes on to admit that visitation lacks the
excitement of preaching but genuine preaching requires it. The
preacher should develop a warm personal relationship with his
people, showing himself 'equally the friend, the father, the Pastor
of all'.[5]

These pastors of another time reflect, of course, a view of
pastoral ministry that developed during the course of history. We
would be wise to learn what we can from them without completely
adopting their methodology. Few pastors can combine exegetical
excellence in preaching with intense visitation. The appointment of
the first deacons arose because the apostles deemed it unwise to
dilute their prayer and preaching ministries. Instead, they appointed
helpers (see Acts 6:1-7).

Dr J. R. Boyd, with scores of years in pastoral ministry behind
him, reiterates the necessity of pastoral visitation while recommending a better way. He says, 'A properly planned and promoted
programme for developing and devoting Christian visitors is undoubtedly the most challenging and biblical role of pastoral responsibility. No other area of opportunity in a pastor's life affords so
much variation for extending or broadening the indirect influence of
his ministry. First of all, his pulpit performance cannot be properly
personal and practical if he just shuts himself in with books and
avoids getting a reliable, general knowledge of the hearts and homes
to which he is supposed to speak for the all-knowing God...
[However] the pastor who does visitation himself but does not take
and train others to minister in one-to-one ongoing counselling or
spiritual cultivation, pruning or burden-bearing, is missing at least
two-thirds of his calling. Every new member should be matched

with the helper/s who will be God's sanctifying means of making him/her a fruit-bearing branch of the Divine Vine.'[6]

Dr Boyd makes an important point. The task of shepherding each individual in the flock is far beyond the capacity of one man. Senior pastors must labour to train others to help with visitation. Without a core of good visitors a preacher may either rob his sermons of the careful preparation they need, or rob distressed people of the urgent help they need.

Christians, then, who manifest a shepherd's heart will strive to acquaint themselves with other believers in the setting of their own homes. Deeper acquaintance with people, in turn, provides the raw data necessary for diagnosis of spiritual health. Diagnosis becomes one of the main concerns of the shepherd. But diagnosis leads the shepherd irresistibly towards prescription and treatment.

II. Pastoral prescription

Diagnosis is the precursor of prescription. No mere exposer of hurts, the shepherd longs to pour on the balm of Gilead. For what good is it to lament about the 'hurt of my people' and provide no cure? And what good is it to cry, 'Peace, peace when there is no peace,' or, like some pill-pusher, scatter platitudes: 'Read your Bible and pray more, then you'll be all right'? Those with the shepherd's heart know that specific problems require specific prescriptions. Then, too, being a general practitioner and not a specialist, he may need to call in other help. As someone has said, 'The shepherd doesn't grow the grass; he just leads the sheep to where it can be found.'

The pastor teaching Megan's class on spiritual gifts is concerned. Megan had been cheerful, even vivacious, for the first few weeks. Recently she rarely responds in class. In spite of an obvious effort to appear cheerful, her face shows strain and melancholy. Her pastor, being a true shepherd, engages her in conversation after class. 'How are things at home, Megan?' he asks.

'Fine,' she replies. 'Jerry got a promotion with a substantial rise. Now we can afford to replace our old banger of a car. John and Debbie are doing well in school.'

'That's good to hear, Megan,' replies the pastor as he ponders what direction to pursue in tracing her problem. 'We're having a group over after church for lunch. Can you and the family come?'

'Oh, we'd love to, but Jerry is worn out from overtime and needs a long Sunday afternoon nap,' Megan answers.

'We'll have you over another time,' the pastor replies as he moves off to ask one of the deaconesses to take Megan out for coffee this week. The pastor wisely refers her to a woman with real sensitivity and love. Diagnosis of the heart-need of a woman like Megan could be beyond his male experience and take more time than he has. The degree of acquaintance required to come to an understanding of her need might also strain the boundaries of pastoral propriety.

Over coffee, the deaconess starts to diagnose the problem. A shepherdess herself, she soon begins to apply the balm of fellowship and Scripture. This highlights two crucial needs that exist in our churches in the area of shepherding: the importance of more than one person being involved in shepherding and the need for both men and women. Who but a woman can really understand the heart of another woman?

Responsibility for spiritual health does not rest upon the over-burdened shoulders of pastors alone. Believers are personally responsible to God to maintain their own spiritual health. 'Each one should carry his own load' (Gal. 6:5). In the final analysis, no one can be helped who is not willing, by God's grace, to help himself. In a recent counselling course I attended, two different lecturers pounded home the lesson: 'You are not personally responsible for the cure of souls!' None of us can bear such a heavy load of false guilt. Nevertheless, we must try to help.

Our own fallibility, the complexity of human ills and the need for the involvement of men and women should spur us to enlist a team of shepherds. One man cannot adequately shepherd a flock. It is like having a single cable, however strong, thrown out to rescue storm-blown souls when there needs to be a whole safety-net of concern under every congregation. With such a safety-net in place those who fall are caught before they are utterly cast down. Such a network of concern can be made up of men and women with shepherding gifts sharing with each other in confidential and concerned prayer for the flock.

Many churches, our own included, have profited immensely from dividing their congregations into shepherding groups with gifted men and women responsible for each group. Sharing concerns with others in a network of care immensely improves both diagnosis and treatment. But what more can we say about treatment?

Prescriptions for the ills of the soul have occupied volumes from the earliest days of the church. In our day the greatly expanded counselling field occupies what used to be called 'the cure of souls'. Much helpful material is being written. Part of the reason for the growth of biblical counselling can be found in the dearth of networks of care and concern in our churches. Larry Crabb in his books, of which *Understanding People* is an example, laments this lack of pastoral care.[7] His thesis, and that of many biblical counsellors, asserts that the church, through a ministry of enlightened lay encouragers, can do more than all the psychiatrists spawned since Freud. I concur.

This is not to undermine the need for professional medical treatment. Clinical depression, schizophrenia and related neuroses call for expertise far beyond that of even carefully trained pastors. Church care-givers, however, should be well informed about these extreme neuroses. They must also be ready to provide the huge amounts of reassurance and fellowship that are needed by those undergoing rehabilitation after hospitalization. But leaving aside extreme emotional disturbances, caring Christians, if they develop an ability to carefully diagnose and treat spiritual ills, can work wonders in the context of local church life.

With scores of books in the field of counselling filling the shelves, there is no need for me to reproduce the prescriptions of such a host of gifted men, but I want to make a few general comments.

Balanced care

The caring shepherd must take care that his own personality and experiences assist rather than distort the help he seeks to offer others. We tend to prescribe what has worked for us. Our experience in small groups might lead us to prescribe them as a kind of panacea for all ills. Our personality may be so sunny that we avoid rebuke and apply encouragement indiscriminately. Contrariwise, we might overuse rebuke or exhortation. Extensive doctrinal study might reflect a scholarly shepherd, while more simplistic deeper-life prescriptions might be the stock-in-trade of the experientially oriented. Tarrying in prayer, rigid discipline or practising praise may, in their place, be appropriate but no one aspect of care will heal all ills.

The convolutions of the human sin problem are too twisted to yield to anything but a selective and holistic approach. The shepherd needs a recognition of his or her own particular hang-ups and a healthy scepticism towards simplistic answers.

Consider the Ephesian church. As time passed the needs of the Ephesian believers changed. When Paul met their elders on his way back to Jerusalem he warned them about the virus of heresy that would spread among them (Acts 20:29-31). Later, when he wrote to them from prison, he prescribed a hefty dose of teaching about the nature of the church. Still later, John wrote to them in his Revelation. Although orthodox, hard-working and persevering, in John's day they had become cold and loveless. They needed rebuke accompanied by a challenge to repent (Rev. 2:1-7). One church needed three differing treatments.

The shepherd must carefully select the proper medicine from his scriptural store. Paul reminded Timothy that Scripture 'is useful for teaching, rebuking, correcting and training in righteousness, so that the man of God may be thoroughly equipped for every good work' (2 Tim. 3:16-17). The uninformed or imbalanced need teaching. The disobedient need a stern rebuke. Those going the wrong way need correction. Those suffering from lack of skill in righteousness need practical training from one who manifests these skills. Besides these prescriptions, the need for church discipline in cases of apostasy might be added. The prescription will vary widely.

To my mind the shepherd's prescription will fall roughly under the following headings:

1. Teaching to dispel spiritual ignorance, imbalance or heresy, as well as teaching about why we act and feel the way we do;

2. Encouragement to lift fainting spirits;

3. Rebuke to challenge disobedience and rebellion;

4. Training to mobilize the passive, unskilled or self-centred;

5. Counsel to give wisdom to the perplexed;

6. Fellowship to hearten the lonely and mellow the independent;

7. Discipline to save those who reject correction.

Other prescriptions could be added. I can do no more than treat the subject in a cursory manner. Let's take a few examples of how to express shepherding concern.

Teaching

Victor, a new Christian, voraciously reads material on end-time themes. A Jehovah's Witness feeds this hunger through a weekly Bible study in his home. Victor plies the pastor with questions every Sunday on future things.

Victor needs teaching. Paul exhorted Timothy to make preaching and teaching his main ministry. 'Preach the Word' because, 'in season and out of season,' it is the main medicine needed to 'correct, rebuke and encourage — with great patience and careful instruction' (2 Tim. 4:2). Teaching undergirds all other soul treatment.

Dr Martyn Lloyd-Jones discovered that many spiritual ills in his flock were cured simply through the preaching of the Word. I have found the same. The Word, however, can be presented in different packages. People are diverse. Some develop under intense exposition, others through personal study, still others in small group Bible studies, while many find a steady diet of solid teaching in an adult Bible Class just what their hearts need. Let us not demand that all needs be met in the same way by a single prescription.

Paul's methods were varied. He sought to be 'all things to all men so that by all possible means [he] might save some'. The healing ministry of our Master, who seldom treated two different people in the same way, was also characterized by astonishing variety. Since none of us exhibits the range of abilities of the Master, we would do well to involve others in the care of souls. In the case of Victor, a deacon in the church enlisted Gary, a young man of Victor's age, to befriend and disciple him.

Training

Agnes has scarcely missed a service for thirty years. Although her children are married and lead responsible lives, she continually worries about them. She also worries about having cancer. She obviously needs a shepherd's care. But what treatment should be given?

Like many, Agnes knows she ought not to worry. That knowledge has not helped her to stop, though. Equipping saints for joyful Christian living is one of the greatest needs in the church. Believers need to be told not only not to worry, not only to be joyful, but how to bring that about. They need to learn how to dispel anxiety, how to witness, how to pray, how to conduct personal devotions, how to study the Word and how to train their children, for example. The healthy disciple masters a complex of self-help skills.

Many Christians know a lot about the Bible but remain vague about how to put it into practice. Skill in applying truth, like digestion in the body, breaks down the biblical facts and applies them to the point of need. Maturity radiates from the life of a Christian who can take the raw materials of preaching and personal devotions and put them to work calming worry, quelling fear or healing bitterness. Without this ability Christians become dependent on professionals to help them in every crisis.

When the pastor became aware of Agnes' chronic worry, he employed the method Paul recommends in Titus 2:3-4. He assigned an older lady, a reformed worrier herself, to get to know her. As they shared their worries and the promises of Scripture over a period of six months the wrinkles of worry began to ease on Agnes' face.

Rebuke

Janice, one of the most popular leaders in the young people's group, presents another shepherding concern. Although she knows it is wrong, she has begun to go out with a non-Christian. What can be done?

Scripture shows how to pass out the bitter-tasting medicine of rebuke. Paul suggested to Titus that in dealing with the 'lazy gluttons' of Crete he 'rebuke them sharply'(Titus 1:12-13). Jesus rebuked Peter severely when Peter urged him to avoid the cross. When they met after his resurrection, Jesus treated Peter more gently. He knew that Peter still grieved over his denial at the trial. How we prescribe rebuke will vary.

In Janice's case, someone needs first to approach her gently. If she rejects a kind approach sterner measures may be necessary. Her spiritual growth from this point on is dependent upon some caring soul confronting her with her disobedience to Scripture and challenging her to break off with the non-Christian. At times there is no other way than confrontation.

Encouragement

Consider three people showing signs of a different malady. Sam phones dejectedly from the hospital. After three operations his faith shows signs of strain. Then there is Pastor Maxwell who, after ten years in a country church with little visible growth, seriously considers abandoning the ministry. Thirdly there is Rita. Everyone but Rita recognizes her skill with beginners in Sunday School. But one Sunday she returns home discouraged and writes out her resignation. Sam, Pastor Maxwell and Rita need one of the spiritual wonder drugs — encouragement. God ensured it would be in abundant supply by appointing one whole group of gifted believers to concentrate on encouragement. We will look more closely at this great boon in chapter 16.

Discipline

Occasionally serious problems force those with the shepherd's heart to adopt severe measures. Where a believer refuses to repent in spite of repeated counsel and exhortation, church discipline must be instituted. Church discipline aims both to protect the body of Christ from infection and to impress the unrepentant with the gravity of their offence, in hopes that they may bow in contrition.

Paul commanded, 'Expel the wicked man from among you' (1 Cor. 5:13). This stern discipline had a salutary effect, for in the next epistle Paul encourages them to receive the man back into fellowship. Church discipline always aims at producing reformation. Where discipline becomes necessary, reformation is impossible without it. Writing to Timothy, Paul mentions 'Hymenæus and Alexander, whom I have handed over to Satan to be taught not to blaspheme' (1 Tim 1:20). Church discipline serves as a warning to the rest of the church to avoid evil. Of course, it must be entered into with careful attention to the procedures laid down by our Lord (see Matt. 18:15-20). But even when necessary, it was one of the most painful duties I performed at Long Branch during my tenure as pastor.

Church discipline and its acceptance by sister churches have, unfortunately, become almost as rare as the whooping crane. How dishonouring it is to Christ when one church excommunicates an unrepentant Christian while another welcomes him! Enquiry from previous churches ought to be a standard practice before accepting anyone for church membership. Without sister churches standing together the discipline exercised in one may be rendered useless by another, thus destroying any hopes of the process leading to real reformation of the rebellious believer.

In summary, those with shepherding gifts prayerfully reach out to diagnose the spiritual temperature of believers around them. When they sense a need they apply the appropriate scriptural remedy. As a last resort shepherding souls refer irreconcilable problems to the church leadership for more intense effort and possible discipline. When severe discipline is the only recourse, the shepherd's heart bleeds.

III. Discerning the pastoral gift

You may have the shepherding gift. To find out, consider four qualities that characterize this spiritual boon. Firstly, good shepherds are *well trained in the Scriptures*. Secondly, concern leads those with shepherding gifts to feel *a sense of personal responsibility* for others. Thirdly, shepherds develop *an ability to diagnose spiritual health*. Fourthly, concern leads to *prescription and treatment*. Until the sheep are contentedly grazing in green pastures by still waters, the true shepherd knows no peace.

Only one person was ever a perfect model of the shepherd: Jesus Christ, the Good Shepherd. In the rest of us, shepherding skills may be present on a scale from poorly developed to highly skilled. In some the gift is latent, discernible only by a vague concern for others coupled with a desire to help. Its development will depend on the degree to which self-sacrificing concern overcomes our innate selfishness. Too often, like the priest and the Levite in the parable of the Good Samaritan, we tend to avoid getting involved in the lives of those in trouble — we pass by on the other side.

All of us should, in some degree, cultivate a shepherding concern. Of course, church leaders must have this gift. Peter states, 'To the elders among you, I appeal as a fellow elder ... Be shepherds of God's flock that is under your care...' (1 Peter 5:1,2).

As time passed, church leaders in many contexts came to be called pastors, which, in biblical terms, means 'shepherd'. Usage, however, has modified the meaning of the word. Today the term 'pastor' denotes more than shepherding care. It usually identifies the administrative head of a church. Besides pastoral care, his duties include preaching, teaching and giving direction. Because of this confusion I am using the term 'shepherding' to denote the gift and the term 'pastor' to denote the position. In biblical terms, however, the two are synonymous.

It is not uncommon for a pastor to have superb gifts of administration or preaching but to manifest weakness in shepherding. If a pastor, recognizing his own weakness, mobilizes a network of shepherds to watch over the sheep, real harm may be avoided. Arguably, the senior pastor should demonstrate good shepherding, since it is a gift required of all church leaders.

The responsibility of all believers

The gift, however, is not confined to church leaders. Scripture dictates that all believers accept responsibility for mutual care: 'Brothers ... carry each other's burdens' (Gal. 6:1,2).

As Paul so forcefully describes in his imagery of the body in Ephesians 4, every believer draws strength from Christ in order to contribute to the growth of others. God designed the body of Christ to be a network of love and care! Christian love, by its very nature, is a shepherding love. (No wonder teaching on *agape* love can be found in close proximity to each of the gift passages.) When such love speaks, it speaks as a shepherd, speaking 'only what is helpful for building others up according to their needs, that it may benefit those who listen' (Eph. 4:29).

The growing Christian is a caring Christian. The Holy Spirit nurtures caring and concern until it grows into shepherding skill. Of course, the Spirit, at his own discretion, may direct your love towards other avenues of service. But whether or not you have, or ever will have, the shepherding gift, you, along with every balanced Christian, will want to grow in your ability to care for other believers.

The general command of Christ to love one another finds its specialization in the shepherding gift. And as we noted in chapter 6, one of the best ways to discover our gifts is to get busy obeying the general commands of Christ. Do you care for others? Are you concerned for new Christians? Do you bleed for disciples who go astray? Do you long to help the troubled find peace? Are you a mother who watches over your children or a father who trains your family in God's truth? Then you may have the beginnings of this gift. If you don't feel these concerns, you need to ask the Spirit to magnify your love for others.

Women and the gift of shepherding

Women often make good shepherds. The motherly instinct naturally prepares women for a ministry of caring. The older women spoken of in Titus and the deaconesses mentioned in the epistles demonstrate that there was a place in the early church for women with pastoral skills. Priscilla's gift in diagnosing Apollos' imbalance led, fortunately, to the correction of his teaching (Acts 18:24-26). Paul commends her and her husband Aquila, whose name follows that of his wife, for their role in his own life. Phoebe is commended to the Roman church because 'She has been a great help to many people, including me.' (Her help, of course, could have been in the nature of hospitality.) Many women were involved in ministry in the early church. Overall leadership, no doubt, remained in the hands of men. The shepherding gift must be distinguished from the gift of administration.

To shut half the human race out of a ministry for which they are eminently suited is to do great disservice to the body! William McRae, himself of Brethren background, joins together the two gifts of pastoring and teaching as a necessary duo. He writes, 'This gift is distributed to women as well as men. Before you close your mind to the possibility consider it for a moment. Why not? The only restriction placed upon Christian women is the exercise of their gifts — where and when they are to be used... Surely this would not preclude a woman possessing the gift of pastor-teacher.'[8] Of course not! What confuses the issue for us is the historical baggage we have attached to the term 'pastor'. Get rid of the leadership connotation and the problem of women ministering in a shepherding capacity disappears because shepherding is a caring function more than a leadership function.

The church as a network of concern

Who has the shepherding gift? Church leaders must have it. Many women demonstrate it. Every Christian should manifest some measure of a shepherd's concern for others. In our church we adopted the motto, 'Each one reach one,' to encourage believers both to evangelize and care for one another. At Long Branch we repeatedly stressed that, as a body, the church is a network of care and concern.

Where are you on the scale of caring, which extends from the concern every Christian is to demonstrate to the more specialized shepherding care exercised by trained pastors or counsellors?

Ann leaves the Bible class on spiritual gifts in deep thought. 'I've been neglecting those shut-ins who keep coming to my mind — making excuses about being too busy. I reckon they need encouragement.'

Ron is heartened. He is beginning to realize that he may have some administrative gifts. But pastoral gifts? 'Maybe that's why my heart goes out to those kids in the boy's club,' he ruminates. 'Anyway, I need to think a little less about work and accomplishment and more about people and their hurts,' he concludes as he leaves the class.

Mike, as always, leaves the class quickly and makes a beeline for the foyer. Joining the crowd for the eleven o'clock worship service he immediately spots Chris, a young fellow who has been out of work, and who has been high on Mike's prayer list. 'Chris, I've been thinking about you,' Mike begins. 'I'm praying that you'll get that job. How did the week go?'

Before and after every service Mike can be seen moving from person to person. Every Sunday, he tries to contact his flock. He finds out their sorrows and joys. He laughs with them. He prays for them. People know he cares. They come to him. They phone him up. They ask him for advice. Mike has the pastoral gift. Oh, he is not an ordained pastor, nor has he had any formal Bible College training, but the Holy Spirit has gifted him with both concern and shepherding ability. The pastor glances over at Mike from where he is shaking hands in the foyer and offers a prayer of praise to God. 'Would that we had a dozen more shepherds like Mike,' he mumbles under his breath.

That is precisely the problem in most of our evangelical churches. We need more shepherds. The senior pastor in our modern system of church organization can never carry the whole burden of caring. The same is true in medicine. General practitioners depend on a host of other care-givers to undergird their practice. The health-care system extends to include social workers, counsellors, the judicial system, schools and colleges. There are labs to run tests, emergency crews to respond in a crisis, hospitals for serious illness and convalescent homes for recuperation. The doctor has nurses, specialists and technicians at his beck and call. The enormous pharmaceutical industry develops and manufactures the medicines he prescribes.

Are the needs of the body of Christ any less diverse and crucial? No, the hosts of spiritual wickedness that are arrayed against the church compound the problem. It is absolute folly to expect a church to be healthy while resting all the responsibility for its health on the shoulders of one man. The Master never intended it to be so. He gave gifts in order that the diverse needs in his church might be met in the context of a vibrant caring community.

Areas for development

We must recapture that pattern. Our studies in the last two chapters indicate the need for continued development in the following areas.

A change in attitudes

First, there needs to be a revolution of changed attitudes in the church. All of us, as believers, need to adopt the biblical pattern of the church as a body, an interconnected network of caring people. We need to banish once and for all the idea that we are care-receivers sitting under the ministry of one professional care-giver, the pastor.

More openness

Secondly, we need a revised attitude of openness. Since all of us are sinners in the process of sanctification we all have problems, hurts and blind-spots. Usually we don't admit this. We often come to church with a shell of piety, hiding our own struggles. But growth in Christ is tougher when we hide our struggles behind a façade of maturity. New Christians coming into the assembly are puzzled. We are too good to be true. They become discouraged by our implied perfection.

Honesty demands openness and vulnerability. Honesty expedites spiritual growth. John notes in his epistle, 'If we claim to be [or give the impression of being] without sin, we deceive ourselves and the truth is not in us' (1 John 1:8). The Bible never portrays its heroes larger than life. You can imagine how hard pastoral diagnosis is where Christians hide symptoms and needs behind an elaborate façade of clichés. Now, I am not talking about immodest or unwise sharing. Some things are private and should never be shared except with God. Some things should only be shared between husbands and wives. But to share our struggles at work, our puzzlement in seeking guidance, our difficulty in carving out time for prayer, or our fears and worries, is not to be too vulnerable; it is to be normal.

I used to think that, as a pastor, I needed to project an image of 'having it all together', of 'being a mature growing Christian who is always faithful in devotions and witnessing'. When I began to mention in a careful way some of my own struggles and failures a strange thing happened. Instead of people being put off, they came to me after the service to mention how helpful the messages had been to them in their own struggles!

Transparency reduces shepherding problems. Martin Luther and Spurgeon, in common with many saints, were subject to times of deep discouragement and even depression. What an encouragement that knowledge has been to me as a minister of the gospel! But what if that had remained hidden? Generations of discouraged ministers might have thought their own depression was unique. What helps a church leader also assists a struggling saint.

Shared leadership

Thirdly, shared leadership reduces the risk of dictatorial pastorates while at the same time enriching the pastoral office. Leadership requires gifts such as administration, shepherding, preaching, teaching, evangelism and equipping — gifts that rarely all reside in any one man. By sharing the task, a group develops a fund of wisdom and expertise that expedites church growth and contributes to balance. We have already noted in the previous chapter how the benefits of shared leadership far outweigh the dangers.

For a leadership team to function smoothly, the pastor's role must be clarified. The pastor should give himself to communicating an overall vision, teaching the whole counsel of God and equipping believers for ministry.

The slow process of equipping believers to disciple others, in the long haul, reaps lasting church growth. Discipling churches become the training-ground where new soldiers are trained to man the frontiers of the kingdom, rather than congregations of passive listeners drawn by the charisma of one man. The training of soldiers, of course, requires intense shepherding.

A *pattern of shepherding*

Thus, fourthly, some shepherding pattern needs to be developed in each congregation. In our church we divided the congregation into little flocks, shepherding groups, with a church leader responsible for each group. Ten to twenty-five people became the flock of a deacon, deaconess or an elder with shepherding gifts. These shepherding-group leaders met monthly for prayer and discussion of the needs and problems of individual believers. They sought to get to know their flock by visits, telephone calls and hospitality.

Some churches break their church up into groups that meet as classes for Bible study, whether on the church premises or in members' homes. Each group then becomes both a caring, shepherding unit and a class. Class-members develop a rapport and concern for each other. In our church we call these 'encouragement groups'. No system works perfectly. Every church will need to be sensitive to the combination that works best for them.

A *speedy response to problems*

Fifthly, shepherding involves a commitment to handle problems with speed. If defective patterns of living or harmful relationships are allowed to fester the whole body can suffer. Absence from the Lord's table, gossip, temper and other obvious symptoms of sin need to be handled carefully but expeditiously. Many of our larger problems are the result of failing to deal with problems quickly. The guilty, of course, should be dealt with patiently and gently. This does take time.

Leading from the top down

Sixthly, a commitment to shepherding must be demonstrated from the top down. Pastors and church leaders need to be examples of both concern and transparency. Biblical teaching on body life, spiritual giftedness and mutual care should be accepted first by the leadership and then passed on to the whole church. An overall plan needs to be developed to guide church leaders as they slowly institute the changes necessary to call the assembly back to New Testament body life. This vision should be communicated carefully to the whole church.

Conclusion

How about you? Do you have the stirrings of shepherding concern burning within you? Do you sense needs in the church? Are danger signals flashing in your brain as you note what is happening in a family? Remember that the shepherding gift exhibits the following characteristics:

1. A desire to see the body of Christ full of loving, growing, healthy Christians.
2. A developing concern for other believers, exhibited in a sensitivity to their hurts, their triumphs and their problems.
3. A desire to draw nearer to other believers in order to understand and encourage them.
4. A developing ability to pinpoint symptoms of spiritual need.
5. A developing ability to suggest steps hurting believers may take to find healing and growth.

Return at this point to the chart explained in chapter 6 and make an evaluation. Fill in the various columns in the light of our study of this gift. When you have finished this evaluation move on to consider, in the next chapter, the cluster of gifts that encircle our need to understand the Word of God.

14.
The gifts of knowledge and wisdom

The gifts of knowledge and wisdom immediately confront us with the need for theological literacy. Unfortunately, in many Christian circles the theologian is *persona non grata*. Mental images of white-haired men consulting mouldering old tomes while they debate how many angels can dance on the head of a pin jaundice our view of theological learning.

The prevailing suspicion is so widespread that J. I. Packer piqued our interest by giving one of his books the intriguing title, *Hot Tub Religion*. Inside he further fans our curiosity by entitling his first chapter, 'Danger! Theologian At Work.'[1] Only powerful curiosity can induce many of us to tackle a serious theological work. Like those expensive photo-essays we put on our coffee tables, theological works serve too often more to beautify our bookshelves, or perhaps prop our doors open in the spring, than anything else.

Too often, our perceptions lead us to dump theology in a mental dustbin along with pioneer crafts like candle-making. We think of it as quaint, but not much use any more. How sad and dangerous! Without theological moorings we are adrift in a sea of conflicting ideas without charts or compass, and without any engine to give steerage. The gifts of knowledge and wisdom restore perspective and direction.

The class on spiritual gifts is about to begin. Ann and Megan chat over coffee. Ron and Bob share events of the past week. Three other class members, Beverley, Harry and Andy, converse near the back of the class. 'The pastor is a terrific teacher,' enthuses Beverley as she rummages in her handbag for a pen.

'He's OK,' Harry responds. 'But being a teacher myself, I wonder how he'll distinguish Christian teaching from secular school teaching.'

'He's not a bad teacher,' Andy replies, 'but I wish he was a little more practical. I'm having trouble seeing how all this applies.'

'Not practical enough! Hey, Andy, he sometimes seems too practical,' says Harry, frowning. 'He is a good teacher, but I wish he was more doctrinal. We need more meat!'

Like Beverley, Harry and Andy, we look for different things in a Bible teacher. Interestingly enough, our taste in teachers may reflect our view of theology and our preference for either knowledge or wisdom, or a mixture of both. Harry seems to have the gift of knowledge, while Andy shows signs of the gift of wisdom. Both are essential to the health of the church, and both — as we shall see in the next chapter — are related to the gift of teaching. As an initial guide for our study in this chapter let me lay down a couple of definitions.

Defining the gifts

The *gift of knowledge* is that Spirit-endowed ability to search and systematize the Scriptures into a progression of logical categories.

The *gift of wisdom* is the spiritual ability to apply comprehensive knowledge of the Scriptures to issues of practical living and problem-solving while ensuring that God receives due priority.

From beginning to end, the Bible emphasizes the pivotal place God gives to wisdom and knowledge. But before we can treasure their role in the church, we need to understand the importance of Christian scholarship.

I. The importance of Christian scholarship

While we pay universal homage to the Bible we often fail to understand its teachings properly and apply them to daily living. Even in the United States, where church attendance remains high and 95% of people are said to believe in God, biblical literacy has plummeted while social evils such as divorce, alcoholism, homosexuality, violence and drug abuse have soared.

Why is evangelical faith so shallow? A partial answer can be found in recent history. Under the onslaught of scholastic liberalism, many churches retreated from Christian scholarship. Instead of contending with the dragons of humanism and impaling them on their own dead-end presuppositions, Christians in great numbers left the field of scholarship to retreat into their own bastions of 'simple faith'. (I do not decry true faith, but rather simplistic belief in shibboleths that do not reflect the whole counsel of God.) They overlooked the Lord's directive to 'contend for the faith that was once for all entrusted to the saints'.

Fortunately B. B. Warfield and a few others stood their ground to defend doctrines under attack, such as the deity of Christ, the authority of Scripture and the necessity of atonement. Their lonely voices failed to galvanize the church at large. Many retreated into fundamentalist ghettos. So quickly did believers abandon scholarship in the early years of this century that Gresham Machen, among those who carried on the fight, had to write a booklet entitled *The Importance of Christian Scholarship* to call Christians back to the field of battle.

The importance of scholarship had not been challenged on such a widespread scale since the Reformation. Warfield and Machen, followed in later years by men such as Cornelius Van Til and Francis Schaeffer, fought hard to press the truth home to liberal hearts. Unfortunately, we have not yet recovered a sense of the crucial importance of scholarship. Machen's booklet has long been out of print.

True, we have never had so many Christian radio and TV programmes nor so many books. Yet never have I seen so few Christians interested in turning off 'the box' to read serious books. Experiential and light devotional books capture a large Christian market. Too few Christians read biblical material that grapples with modern thought and lifestyle trends.

The fact that the rise of cults corresponds so closely with this decline in evangelical scholarship suggests a direct connection. No sooner were the catechism-taught congregations of our remote past decimated, than cults such as the Jehovah's Witnesses and Mormons sprang up.

For several centuries the strong doctrinal preaching of men like Martin Luther, John Calvin, Jonathan Edwards and George Whitefield had turned men's attention to a holy God. Serious theological decline can be traced back to Whitefield's contemporary and understudy, John Wesley. Wesley broke with Whitefield's biblically rooted view of God and proceeded to popularize Arminianism. Spurred on by men such as Finney, and to a lesser extent Moody, Arminianism won the day. This new emphasis served to turn men's eyes away from a sovereign God to focus on their own imagined autonomy and free will.

As an Arminian view of evangelism gained the field, the rigorous scholarship of a Calvin or an Edwards became largely extinct. As experiential preaching prevailed, scholarship declined. Topical and selective use of the Word overwhelmed the more rigorous exegesis and doctrinal preaching of the past.

Christians now pick and choose their teachers according to personal taste. Yet Scripture warns, 'For the time will come when men will not put up with sound doctrine. Instead, to suit their own desires, they will gather around them a great number of teachers to say what their itching ears want to hear. They will turn their ears away from the truth and turn aside to myths' (2 Tim. 4:3-4). The rise of the cults exactly reflects this prophecy. Unfortunately, a populist approach to doctrine furthers this decline in scholarship.

We live in an egalitarian age. Democracy is everything. The consumer is king. Reginald Bibby, in his major study about the preferences of Canadian Christians, describes the faith of evangelicals today as a kind of consumer Christianity.[2] Christians go from church to church searching for the kind of programme that suits their taste. We stray far from a broad-based evangelical ethos.

Throughout most of church history, Christians viewed theology as the queen of sciences. Great colleges and universities sprang up around theological schools. Great Christian scholars founded many of the foremost colleges of America. Christian missionaries, like William Carey, established pioneering universities in India and around the world. The Ontario educational system owes a tremendous debt to Ryerson, a Methodist lay preacher. Now, unfortunately, psychology and sociology compete for first place with theology even in many of our seminaries.

Perhaps believers, like the population at large, simply mirror the anti-intellectual age in which we live. According to Phil Donahue, a popular daytime US talk-show host, 'The worst thing to be known as is intelligent. If that happens, we're doomed. Please do not call me intelligent. Call me outrageous. I'd rather be called sleazy than identified as intelligent.'[3]

In his article, 'Keeping America Stupid,' K. L. Billingsley laments the anti-intellectualism rampant in American life where literacy is, too often, television literacy. Although media information comes highly edited and beautifully choreographed, 'In terms of useful knowledge, these shows (talk shows) constitute a kind of brain reduction surgery... How this television-based mass stupidity is to be resolved remains to be seen.'[4]

An aversion to scholarship, whether it seeps in through television or sneaks in via other media, must be resisted at all costs. Fortunately, there is still hunger for the Word of God among believers who understand scriptural injunctions. 'You will know the truth, and the truth will set you free' (John 8:32). If we are to be free, the mind matters! 'Sanctify them by the truth,' Jesus prayed. 'Your word is truth' (John 17:17). The importance of mental apprehension of God's revealed truth permeates Scripture. We find it in the Pentateuch, throughout the wisdom literature and documented by the prophets. Paul takes up the theme: 'Do not conform any longer to the pattern of this world, but be transformed by the renewing of your mind' (Rom. 12:2). Because the mind matters, doctrine matters, and because doctrine is foundational, scholarship is essential! No wonder, communication gifts such as knowledge, wisdom and teaching fulfil a crucial role in the kingdom.

II. The relationship of revelation, wisdom and teaching

All the speaking gifts in some way aim to storm the bastion of the will and capture the keep of our emotions by breaking down the mind-gate. Of twenty-three different words used to describe apostolic ministry in the book of Acts all but seven deal with the communication of truth to the mind.[5] Apostolic church-planting, prophetic preaching, evangelistic appeal, shepherding care and encouraging exhortation all, in some way or other, depend upon knowledge of the Word. Teaching, in turn, lifts truth from the pages of Holy Writ and passes it through the corridors of the mind to store it in the cupboards of our memory. Wisdom takes truth and applies it to concrete situations.

God uses the gifts of knowledge, wisdom and teaching to nourish the church. Like the digestive system, these gifts take the raw material of the Word and break it up into digestible morsels of spiritual nourishment. In the Spirit-anointed hands of those with these gifts, the profound mysteries of revelation become the milk, meat, honey and bread that feed our hungry hearts. This rich feast nourishes and enlightens our minds, producing warm and responsive hearts.

All three lists of spiritual gifts mention teaching. Wisdom and knowledge, which we shall study in this chapter, are described only in 1 Corinthians: 'To one there is given through the Spirit the message of wisdom, to another the message of knowledge by means of the same Spirit...' (1 Cor. 12:8). An allied word, 'revelation', should also be noted. 'Now, brothers, if I come to you and speak in tongues, what good will I be to you, unless I bring you some revelation or knowledge or prophecy or word of instruction?' (1 Cor. 14:6).

Revelation, knowledge and wisdom undergird teaching. Let me illustrate in a diagram the relationship these four different concepts bear to each other. Imagine a wheel. The axle upon which the wheel revolves illustrates revelation. As recorded in the Word of God, revelation is the source of whatever content the gifts of knowledge, wisdom and teaching communicate.

These gifts all revolve around revealed truth. Knowledge of that truth becomes the most basic gift, because it breaks up revelation into systematic categories. Teaching takes the truth sytematized by those with the gift of knowledge and communicates it to believers in memorable form. The spokes of the wheel illustrate teaching. On the other hand, the gift of wisdom applies truth to life in practical and problem-solving situations. Wisdom puts truth into practice where the rubber meets the road. As the next two chapters develop, I trust that this illustration will help to integrate these closely related concepts.

To begin to appreciate their distinct roles, we need to look at each of these in the context of Paul's argument in 1 Corinthians. Consider first the place of revelation.

Revelation

Texts that list spiritual gifts do not include 'revelation'. It does occur several times, however, in the context of gift abuse in 1 Corinthians: 'Now, brothers, if I come to you and speak in tongues, what good will I be to you, unless I bring you some revelation or knowledge or prophecy or word of instruction?' (1 Cor. 14:6). While this passage might indicate a relationship between revelation and spiritual gifts, it hardly goes so far as to define 'revelation' as a gift.

The word occurs again in the context of Paul's description of a service at Corinth: 'When you come together, everyone has a hymn, or a word of instruction, a revelation, a tongue or an interpretation. All of these must be done for the strengthening of the church' (1 Cor. 14:26). While instruction, tongues and interpretation are gifts in other contexts, a hymn and a revelation are not.

Some commentators, mainly of the charismatic persuasion, do view revelation itself as a spiritual gift. Most traditional interpreters do not. A study of the broader context, as reflected in the word's basic meaning and general usage, corroborates the more traditional interpretation.

The meaning of 'revelation'

The word literally means 'an uncovering'. The same word is used for the revelation of Christ at the Second Coming (1 Cor. 1:7; 1 Peter

1:7) and as a title for John's final book, the Revelation. In 2 Corinthians 12:1 it is akin to vision. Dr Luke picks this word to describe how God revealed Christ to Paul on the road to Damascus. Paul himself uses it later to describe how the mysteries of the gospel were communicated to him (Gal. 1:12,16; 2:2; Eph. 3:3).

Revelation describes the divine process God used to communicate what we could never acquire by our own reason. For example, God gave Moses the Ten Commandments by divine revelation. Down through history he gave prophets many other revelations, including the prophecies about the coming of the Messiah. In the fulness of time, he revealed the secrets of the gospel and the kingdom through his Son to the apostles and prophets. The term 'inspiration' denotes the way God superintended the communication and writing of revelation so it would be kept free from error and human adulteration.

Revelation deals with mysteries, revealed through a rare supernatural movement initiated by God. Paul explains: 'The mystery of Christ ... has now been revealed by the Spirit to God's holy apostles and prophets' (Eph. 3:4-5). Apostles and prophets, of whom Paul was one, received the gospel by revelation (Gal. 1:11-12). The teachings of the apostle Paul remained a mystery, unknown in previous ages until revealed to him (along with other apostles and prophets) by the Holy Spirit.

Revelation is complete

The Bible contains the record of everything that God chose to reveal. The Bible is complete. We have no need to beseech God for further revelation. Instead, then, of waiting for the rare and unique process whereby God inspires new revelation, we are to depend upon the Holy Spirit to illuminate already recorded revelation. If, instead of giving ourselves to study the Word, we yearn for some new revelation, our thirst for novelty will override our hunger for the Word. Such an approach is foolish. Why not thoroughly delve into what God has already revealed and wait for heaven to seek further mysteries?

God has given us a great privilege, to hold in our hands the complete revelation of his will. The early church could not do that while the process of revelation and canonization continued. In their day the Bible remained incomplete. During this period God guided

Paul to write the very Corinthian letter that we are discussing. It became part of the, as yet incomplete, corpus of God's will for your life and mine.

Consider for a moment revelation in the context of Corinthian church life. Paul wrote two epistles to this church during a period of transition. Some practices needed correction. Disorder vied with genuine freedom in their services. During the general meetings of the church different people would come forward to share either a hymn, or a word of revelation, or a teaching or the interpretation of a tongue. Since the Bible was incomplete, prophets probably received special revelations. Sometimes one speaker would, rather unceremoniously, interrupt another. A certain amount of chaos reigned, which Paul tried to regulate. Probably this practice of sharing mystical messages from God was not widespread or long-lived.

We find no evidence of the Corinthian model in any of the other epistles. It would seem that, as a rule, God gave words of revelation only in a context where the uniquely inspired apostles and prophets operated. This should not be surprising. The Corinthian letter does not describe normative church practice. Paul wrote to correct error and bring order in the midst of their chaotic practice.

Even in 1 Corinthians, Paul links revelation with the ministry of prophets: 'Two or three prophets should speak, and the others should weigh carefully what is said. And if a revelation comes to someone who is sitting down, the first speaker should stop. For you can all prophesy in turn so that everyone may be instructed and encouraged. The spirits of prophets are subject to the control of prophets' (1 Cor. 14:29-32). The text clearly shows God gave words of revelation to prophets. The eminent commentator Charles Hodge joins many others in tying revelation to prophecy: 'Revelation and prophecy belong to one... He who received revelations was a prophet...'[6]

Grosheide points out that 'It is difficult to distinguish prophesying from revelation,' and then defines revelation as 'the setting forth of a new truth.'[7] He goes on to point out that, 'Prophecy and revelation are closely connected (v. 6). Our verse implies that revelation precedes and is thereupon given utterance in prophecy.'[8]

We have already established in chapters 8 and 9 that apostles and prophets — alone — received inspired revelations. The incompleteness of Scripture rendered their ministry necessary.

With the canon complete, revelation ceased because it became unnecessary.

While I do believe that some aspects of the apostolic and prophetic gifts continue in the form of church-planting and preaching, I do not believe that God gives revelation today, any more than I believe that infallible apostles and prophets exist today. The original apostles and prophets laid a scriptural foundation that does not need to be relaid!

The place of revelation

In summary, revelation is not a spiritual gift in current use. Essential before the canon of Scripture was complete, it is no longer needed and we should seek it no more. Rather we should seek to understand the recorded revelation of God's will in his written Word, the Bible. In its written form, revelation undergirds everything that those with the gifts of knowledge, wisdom and teaching do. It becomes the axle around which all communication gifts revolve. But what about the gift of knowledge?

The word of knowledge

While the broader context of usage limits revelation to the apostolic age, that same wider context opens the door for the continuation of the gifts of knowledge and of wisdom. Many esteemed commentators disagree with this assessment, believing that these two gifts were confined to the apostolic era. Let me explain my reasons for putting forward a different view.

Does the gift continue today?

First, we note that Scripture actually refers to both knowledge and wisdom as gifts. Paul begins his Corinthian letter by commending believers there: 'You do not lack any spiritual gift.' This giftedness includes an enrichment 'in every way — in all your speaking and in all your knowledge'. They excelled in speaking gifts which, as we shall see later, depend to a great extent on the gift of knowledge (1 Cor. 1:5-7).

In the context of listing gifts, Paul writes about 'the message of knowledge' (1 Cor. 12:8). This message of knowledge is closely related to the gift of prophecy: 'If I have the gift of prophecy and can fathom all mysteries and all knowledge…' (1 Cor. 13:2). Nevertheless it is distinct from prophecy: 'Where there are prophecies, they will cease … where there is knowledge, it will pass away' (1 Cor. 13:8).

All the communication gifts are closely linked. The gift of knowledge is closely connected with prophecy, yet distinct from it. Knowledge, like other gifts that communicate understandable language, excels tongues: 'If I come to you and speak in tongues, what good will I be to you, unless I bring you some revelation or knowledge or prophecy or word of instruction?' (1 Cor. 14:6). Paul's argument in this section concerns limiting tongues in the assembly because 'No one understands … he utters mysteries with his spirit' (1 Cor. 14:2). Revelation, knowledge, prophecy and instruction (teaching), on the other hand, all relate to truth clearly understood or communicated.

No mere temporary gift, knowledge undergirds all communication of truth. In the list of gifts it is described as 'a word of knowledge'. By picking the Greek word *logos* (meaning 'word') Paul indicates that he refers to logical speech as opposed to ecstatic utterance.

To the Romans Paul writes, 'I myself am convinced … that you yourselves are full of goodness, complete in knowledge and competent to instruct one another' (Rom. 15:14). Completeness of knowledge undergirds competency to teach. Comprehensive knowledge characterized the Corinthians: 'You have been enriched … in all your knowledge' (1 Cor. 1:5).

The Corinthians' facility in knowledge, however, could not hide a glaring lack that was not found in Rome, where knowledge and practical goodness went hand in hand. Paul wrote one of his most extensive epistles to deal with the implications of this missing element in Corinth. Knowledge, never enough on its own, must be allied with practical wisdom, which they lacked. But more of the distinction between wisdom and knowledge in the next section.

A body of knowledge undergirds all the communication gifts. The church, as the pillar and ground of the truth, has been entrusted with this body of knowledge. How does one acquire this knowledge — by sudden inspiration or gradual illumination? If by inspiration, then the gift of knowledge was a sign gift restricted to the apostolic era. If the one gifted in knowledge gains that knowledge by gradual illumination of the Holy Spirit, as he reads and studies Scripture, then we can assume the gift continues today.

Knowledge is incomplete

The context indicates a progressive appropriation of knowledge. In the thirteenth chapter of 1 Corinthians Paul imagines the impossible, the ability to 'fathom all mysteries', in order to teach a lesson about the superior nature of love (1 Cor. 13:2). His expression implies a progressive search for understanding. He later states, 'We know in part,' that is, we know incompletely (1 Cor. 13:9). Until 'perfection comes' we must be satisfied with limited and developing knowledge.

Incompleteness of knowledge is also implied in his shout of praise:

> 'Oh, the depth of the riches of the wisdom and knowledge of
>   God!
>   How unsearchable his judgements,
>   and his paths beyond tracing out!
> Who has known the mind of the Lord?'
>
> (Rom. 11:33-34).

Absolute knowledge of God and wisdom about God, by definition, remain impossible of attainment. Whatever the gift of knowledge is, it will not be exhaustive knowledge. That would leave no room for growth in understanding. From the context I assume that 'the word of knowledge' describes a gift that fits one for an incomplete but above average appropriation of the corpus of revealed truth. Consider also the Greek words used.

The Greek words

One word for knowledge in Greek, *epignosis,* 'denotes exact or full knowledge, discernment, recognition' and 'a greater participation by the knower in the object known'.[9] *Epignosis* would appear to me to be the perfect word to find in the text to grant credence to the type of mystical and infallible revelation of mystery-knowledge that charismatics assume this gift represents. The actual Greek word used, however, is *gnosis*. Vine, and Robinson, whom he quotes, point out that *gnosis* is 'knowledge in the abstract ... frequently suggests inception or progress in knowledge'. *Gnosis* is 'primarily a seeking to know, an enquiry, investigation ... knowledge especially of spiritual truth'.[10]

Charles Hodge concludes that 'By knowledge is meant the intellectual apprehension or cognition of revealed truth.'[11] In referring to the first use of 'knowledge' in 1 Corinthians 1:5 he states that 'in all knowledge' means, 'in every kind and degree of religious knowledge'.[12]

Grosheide indicates that the word of knowledge in the Corinthian passage refers to 'the word that has knowledge as its contents... Knowledge implies, more than wisdom does, research and investigation, although knowledge too should not be taken in a purely intellectual sense,' since it is 'according to the Spirit'.[13]

Defining the gift

I would define the gift of knowledge as that Spirit-endowed and developing ability to search and systematize the content of the Scriptures into logically integrated categories.

The one with the gift of knowledge researches the content of Scripture. He studies the Scriptures themselves, as well as theological studies on the Scriptures, in order to gain a systematic understanding of the whole. Some specialize. As a result some become Old Testament scholars, students of the Gospels or Pauline exegetes. But although they demonstrate expertise in different areas, they share a theological sensitivity and skill in arranging ideas systematically.

We all know people who seem adept at ordering ideas. Their minds sort truths into categories — soteriology, pneumatology, eschatology — even if they don't use the theological terms. With a good supply of truth stored away in readily recalled categories in their memories, they quickly spot any deviation from truth in a hymn or message. They grasp ideas and concepts as easily as many of us gain weight.

Leslie Flynn defines the gift of knowledge as 'the charisma which enables the believer to search, systematize, and summarize the teachings of the Word of God'.[14] The marvellous doctrinal treatises written by the apostle Paul to his far-flung congregations disclose his possession of this gift.

The gift in church history

The gift of knowledge, fortunately, continued to be bestowed by the Spirit in the course of church history. Systematizers of doctrine, such as Augustine, joined other church fathers to defend the church from the doctrinal attacks predicted in the New Testament. The young churches desperately needed their keen minds to fend off heresy. The great creeds of the church developed during these early clashes with error.

Much later, during the Protestant Reformation, God raised up men such as Martin Luther and John Calvin to rescue the church from false doctrine. John Calvin's *Institutes* remain a monument of systematic theology. The able framers of the great Protestant confessions, such as the *Westminster Confession*, join the ranks of those with this gift.

Writers with the gift of knowledge have left us a priceless treasury. Though long dead, men like Matthew Henry, Matthew Poole, Charles Hodge, Alford and Lange still speak through commentaries which illuminate the pages of Holy Writ. The gift of knowledge shines not only in theological systematizers but in those who write works on ethics, counselling, church order, missions and history.

The need for the gift today

In a day of fast foods and consumer religion we ought to value this gift. Every age spawns its own brand of error that calls forth the research of men and women with the gift of knowledge. The information revolution flooding our lives with millions of bits of information will keep throwing up fresh challenges. To despise scholarship is to sink slowly into a slough of relativism and existentialism.

The devil, of course, keeps dressing up old heresies in the latest fashion. The New Age phenomenon, for example, is only old Eastern mysticism in modern dress. Without the scholarly works of past history, we might not recognize Satan's current attempts to counterfeit truth. Unfortunately, many of the great books of the past are unknown to our media-drugged generation. We must pray for scholars whose research can collate investigations both old and new, interpret them in the light of Scripture, apply them to modern errors and then break down the resulting evaluation into systematic bits of information that we can digest.

Do you have the gift of knowledge? Do you desire it? It is not only necessary in seminaries and Bible colleges. Every church needs those with this gift because every community shudders under the infernal attack of the deceiver. Men and women with the gift of knowledge can serve valiantly to unmask Satan's subtleties.

Knowledge of the Word, of course, remains indispensable to every Christian. As we seek to 'grow in the grace and knowledge of our Lord and Saviour Jesus Christ', all of us will be moved by the Spirit to seek knowledge (2 Peter 3:18). We gain freedom from the world, the flesh and the devil through Spirit-applied knowledge of the Word of God.

Like every spiritual gift, this gift gives specialized expression to a general command of Christ. Since we are sanctified as we appropriate the Word of God, every disciple is commanded to 'Do your best to present yourself to God as one approved, a workman who does not need to be ashamed and who correctly handles the word of truth' (2 Tim. 2:15). Our Sunday School curricula, our preaching and our Bible Study groups should all foster the pursuit of a comprehensive understanding of Scripture. As biblical literacy in a church rises, the Spirit finds more fuel to kindle the fire of revival.

Biblical literacy closely parallels true church growth. The most vigorous churches in Canada are those in the French-speaking province of Quebec. After generations of darkness, evangelism has borne fruit. Throughout the province new churches are springing up. From the earliest days of this growth, SEMBEQ has been at the centre of Fellowship Baptist ministry. SEMBEQ is the name given to the extension seminary through which new workers train. Young converts quickly enrol in serious Bible study. They prepare at home for classes held weekly in scattered churches. Training as they work, Quebec believers combine a mix of zeal and knowledge that is almost unknown elsewhere. Their commitment to serious Bible study is part of the exciting balance we find there.

A few hundred miles away in English Canada the climate is quite different. Biblical studies that require homework and entail tests are unpopular. The necessity of scholarly study into scriptural theology is largely ignored.

Speaking of theologians (those with the gift of knowledge), J. I. Packer asks, 'What use are such people? Is there a particular job that we should look to them to do for us? Yes, there is. By the lake in a resort I know stands a building grandly labelled "Environmental Control Center". It is the sewage plant, there to ensure that nothing fouls the water; its staff is comprised of water engineers and sewage specialists. Think of theologians as the church's sewage specialists. Their role is to detect and eliminate intellectual pollution, and to ensure, so far as man can, that God's life-giving truth flows pure and unpoisoned into Christian hearts.'[15]

We need the gift of knowledge. But lest we become theological junkies, impractical and withdrawn, God has balanced knowledge with wisdom. Without its counterweight our pursuit of knowledge may lead us far from life's real dilemmas into ivory tower musings.

I recently read about a couple with marital problems. When he arrived home from work, the man spent an hour or two reading Christian books. 'He succeeded in splitting fine hairs in theological disputes with friends.' But if his wife interrupted him during these sessions of study, or meditation, he 'could get snappy and peevish'.[16] The marriage was in trouble. Without the balancing gift of wisdom, or a family that keeps such a person down to earth, a theological-type can become very impractical.

Harry, mentioned at the beginning of this chapter, shows signs of possessing the gift of knowledge. In the pastor's class on spiritual gifts, he desires more depth and meat. Harry teaches history and geography in high school. No one can fault the factual basis of his teaching. He has written several scholarly papers on local history. Unfortunately, his attempts to teach in the adult Bible Class have not met with much success. Some in his class complain about masses of deadening detail, or intricate arguments about irrelevant issues. Sometimes, those with the gift of knowledge are chosen as teachers. Too often, they put their classes to sleep. Scholars don't necessarily make good teachers.

The place of knowledge

Despite its limitations, all other communication gifts depend upon the gift of knowledge. In the diagram used earlier, knowledge of the Word, like the hub of a wheel, fits snugly unto the axle of revelation. Without men and women with this gift to connect us to the mysteries of divine revelation we cannot move forward in the kingdom. But wisdom must be added to knowledge to render it relevant.

The word of wisdom

Wisdom, the one thing requested by Solomon, continues to top the church's shopping list of urgent needs. The gift passages list wisdom only once: 'To one there is given through the Spirit the message of wisdom...' (1 Cor. 12:8). Elsewhere in Scripture, wisdom is repeatedly lauded. This broader importance as a word and concept leads us to believe that it must have had a more important place in the body of Christ than would at first appear. Let us look first at Paul's general usage of 'wisdom'.

Paul's use of the word

The Corinthians, like the husband mentioned previously, possessed abundant knowledge but lacked wisdom. Paul commends them for being 'enriched in every way — in all your speaking and in all your knowledge' (1 Cor. 1:5). But there were plenty of practical problems. 'I say this to shame you. Is it possible that there is nobody among you wise enough to judge a dispute between believers?' (1 Cor. 6:5). As we read the first chapters of 1 Corinthians we discover that the Corinthians thought themselves wise, indeed wiser than the apostle. Paul spends three chapters correcting their worldly caricature of wisdom (1 Cor. 1-3; cf. 4:10).

Paul first argues that the wisdom of God, thought foolishness by the world because it promotes the cross of Christ, is true wisdom. He variously defines genuine wisdom as 'Christ crucified ... Christ the power of God and wisdom of God ... a demonstration of the Spirit's power... God's secret wisdom, a wisdom that has been hidden ... but God has revealed it to us by his Spirit' (1 Cor.1:23,24; 2:4,7,10). True 'wisdom from God — that is our righteousness, holiness, and redemption', finds its source in Jesus Christ (1 Cor. 1:30). Bankrupt of real power and out of touch with spiritual reality, the wisdom of the world is utter folly. True wisdom comes from God, has Christ as its starting-point and our redemption and transformation into holy people as its goal.

Their own worldliness, combined with a lack of discernment and immaturity, had blinded the Corinthians to God's wisdom (1:18-31; 2:6; 3:1). The rest of the book details this glaring deficiency. Divisions and boasting, immorality, disputes amongst themselves, marital questions, legalism, lack of church order, disorderly use of gifts and false ideas about the resurrection comprise the litany of their failure to exercise the gift of wisdom. Knowledge they had in plenty, but how to use that knowledge to demonstrate godly character, to solve problems and avoid dangerous bypaths proved beyond them. Wisdom, as we discover in the context of the rest of the New Testament, shines from the lives of practical and holy people.

The wise man who built on the rock

Jesus' wisdom astonished his hearers. He had illustrated wisdom's importance by saying, 'Therefore everyone who hears these words of mine and puts them into practice is like a wise man who built his house on the rock' (Matt. 7:24). Understanding and practising the words of Christ prepares one to stand against the storms of life. Failing to pay attention to his words prepares the way for a great fall. The foolish ignore his message and perish in the storms of life. This simple parable illustrates four basic characteristics of wisdom.

Wisdom, first, bears a *direct connection to Scripture*. The wise man hears and stores in his memory that which God has revealed. Wisdom flourishes in a heart well ploughed by Scripture.

Wisdom and knowledge find here their common source. No wonder they appear to overlap. In some contexts they seem almost synonymous. In the early chapters of Corinthians, for example, wisdom appears in a worldly dress. Paul argues that men thought wise by the world are actually foolish. And so we have foolish wisdom. Knowledge, on the other hand, can be very wise by giving 'the light of ... the glory of God in the face of Christ' (2 Cor. 4:6). We should take care not to make hard and fast distinctions between the two words. Their usage will be clarified by their context.

Nevertheless, with these cautions in mind, we can state unequivocally that wisdom adds another dimension to knowledge. Just as Christ marvelled at the foolishness of the lawyers and doctors of theology, so today the foolishness of some highly educated men continues to astonish. When a Doctor of Philosophy abandons his family and runs away with one of his students we still mutter, 'There is no fool like an old fool.' Farmers and office workers who daily live out the realities of a balanced budget have cause to shake their heads at economists who tell us not to worry about our national debt. Wisdom is a lot more than education and accumulated knowledge!

The enemies of Christ had marvelled at the wisdom he had

gleaned without benefit of the Pharisees' formal process of education. The apostles demonstrated the same kind of wisdom. When Peter healed the beggar at the temple's Beautiful Gate, we read of those who gathered, 'When they saw the courage of Peter and John and realized that they were unschooled, ordinary men, they were astonished and they took note that these men had been with Jesus' (Acts 4:13). True wisdom comes from, and is exemplified in Christ. Without understanding him, the most educated man in the world remains a fool.

Stephen's witness to Christ demonstrated the same kind of wisdom:'These men began to argue with Stephen, but they could not stand up against his wisdom or the Spirit by whom he spoke' (Acts 6:9-10). The seventh chapter of Acts gives powerful testimony to Stephen's broad comprehension of Scripture and the purposes of God. Wisdom is not equivalent to schooling, but it does include a comprehensive knowledge of Scripture.

Vine, quoting Lightfoot on the meaning of *sophia,* the Greek word for wisdom says, '*Sophia* is the insight into the true nature of things.'[17] Wisdom, except in Christ, is never totally comprehensive. Nevertheless, wisdom leads its possessor to a growing understanding of life on an expansive level. Like standing on a plateau and looking out over valleys and towns and roadways, wisdom gives us an overview of life.

Wisdom, however, is much more than comprehensive knowledge. The wise builder, in the parable, who took the words of Christ and 'put them into practice', illustrates a second characteristic of wisdom. Wisdom is *knowledge in action.* Jesus, in lamenting over his generation said, 'Wisdom is proved right by her actions' (Matt. 11:19). Scholars who live selfish and ungodly lives know a lot but act as if they don't. The wise person perceives the purpose of knowledge. He sets out to fulfil that purpose by doing what is right. 'Actions speak louder than words.'

Knowing the importance of both, Paul prays that the Colossians may excel in knowledge and wisdom: 'We have not stopped praying for you and asking God to fill you with the knowledge of his will through all spiritual wisdom and understanding ... in order that you may live a life worthy of the Lord ... bearing fruit in every good work' (Col. 1:9-10). Wisdom gleans from a knowledge of God's will the right path to tread. Not content with knowing what is right, we are motivated by wisdom to walk along that pathway, 'bearing fruit in every good work'. Wisdom moves us to put spiritual knowledge into practice.

No wonder we read, 'Be wise in the way you act … ' (Col. 4:5), for 'The wisdom that comes from heaven is first of all pure; then peace-loving, considerate, submissive, full of mercy, and good fruit' (James 3:17). 'Who is wise and understanding among you? Let him show it by his good life, by deeds done in the humility that comes from wisdom' (James 3:13). When trials challenge our perseverance in the Christian life and fill us with perplexity then James advises us, 'If any of you lacks wisdom, he should ask God…' (James 1:5).

Third, wisdom is *problem-solving ability*. The builder in Jesus' parable pondered how to build a house able to withstand the floods. Wisdom directed him to build, not on the easier sandy location, but on solid rock. Wisdom equips us to solve problems.

The apostles mentioned wisdom as a criterion to use in choosing men to solve the problem of the Greek widows' complaints in Acts 6. Wherever we find a knotty problem we need the gift of wisdom.

We also need wisdom to avoid dangers that may arise in the future. Foreseeing danger, the wise man in the parable built on a rock. Facing the challenge of leading Israel well, Solomon asked God for wisdom. Wisdom guides a congregation, or an individual, along pathways that circumvent danger. As their church practices demonstrated, the Corinthians were deficient here.

As well as comprehensive understanding, practical application and problem-solving ability, wisdom is also characterized by *its starting-point*. I remember my university course in land surveying. Survey distances and angles were useless without reference to established benchmarks. Occasionally one of us messed up our whole survey by using the wrong figure for a benchmark. The benchmark of all wisdom is, of course, *God himself.*

The Corinthians based many of their practices on reasoning infected by the logic and wisdom of the world at large. Truly wise behaviour, by contrast, begins with faith in God. And faith is born when we see 'Jesus Christ and him crucified' (1 Cor. 2:2). Without Christ, we cannot have the mind of God as revealed by the Spirit of God (note the complete argument in 1 Cor. 2). True wisdom has its source in 'Christ, in whom are hidden all the treasures of wisdom and knowledge' (Col. 2:3). True wisdom goes back to the right benchmark — what God has revealed in Christ.

To fail to begin problem-solving in the right place is like trying to stand up in a hundred feet of water. We know how foolish such an effort would be. You need to swim to shore before you can stand up. Similarly, in any area of life, we need first to return to God in repentance and faith before we can get a proper perspective on what to do. This tendency to always return first to God, in Christ, for illumination constitutes an important fourth aspect of wisdom.

Wisdom in Proverbs

While preparing this book I worked backwards from Corinthians and its use of wisdom through the New Testament at large, until finally I turned to Proverbs. Proverbs, a key wisdom book of the Old Testament, brims with applied knowledge. I was fascinated to find in the opening definitions of the book the same four characteristics of wisdom that I had discovered in the New Testament.

Solomon penned his book to encourage 'attaining wisdom and discipline; for understanding words of insight' (Prov. 1:2). Discipline, as a synonym for wisdom, reflects the fact that wisdom always aims at achieving the purpose of 'acquiring a disciplined and prudent life, doing what is right and just and fair' (Prov. 1:3). The rest of the book of Proverbs is full of practical advice on godly living. Wisdom, according to Proverbs, always leads to practical godliness.

Solomon also emphasizes that wisdom is based on a comprehensive knowledge and understanding of life principles as revealed by God, 'for understanding words of insight ... giving prudence to the simple, knowledge and discretion to the young' (Prov. 1:2,4). Wisdom personified states, 'I possess knowledge and discretion... Counsel and sound judgement are mine; I have understanding and power' (Prov. 8:12,14).

Thirdly, adjectives such as 'prudence' and 'discretion', used in this section of Proverbs, hint at the problem-solving and danger-avoiding quality of wisdom. The Lord gives wisdom and

'...guards the course of the just
      and protects the way of his faithful ones...
Discretion will protect you,
      and understanding will guard you.

> Wisdom will save you from the ways of wicked men
> ... also from the adulteress ...'
>
> (Prov. 2:8,11,12,16).

Wisdom prepares its possessor to avoid pitfalls and solve problems.

Finally, Proverbs emphatically declares that wisdom has a starting-point: 'The fear of the Lord is the beginning of knowledge'; 'You will understand the fear of the Lord and find the knowledge of God'; 'The fear of the Lord is the beginning of wisdom' (Prov. 1:7; 2:5; 9:10). Since wisdom directs us towards the goal of living in righteous fellowship with God, it begins by instilling in us a proper reverence for God. This reverence is not mere terror but respect coupled with 'the knowledge of God'. Jesus, in his high-priestly prayer, pointed out that 'This is eternal life that they may know you, the only true God, and Jesus Christ whom you have sent' (John 17:3).

The place of wisdom in Scripture

In a sense then, wisdom comes full circle. It rescues fallen men from their pagan gods, restores in them a reverence for the true God and leads them into the welcoming arms of God. Wisdom is God-centred from beginning to end. Wise men and women look at everything through spiritual Polaroid glasses that block out all the demonic and worldly distortions of reality that rob God of his central place in his own universe. Wisdom restores a balanced and divinely realistic perspective.

In the biblical record we find many characters blessed by wisdom. Jesus grew in wisdom. Old Testament prophets displayed unusual wisdom. Moses exhibited wisdom as he solved scores of logistical problems while he led Israel out of Egypt to the promised land. Samuel knit together a riven nation and went about judging difficult cases. Saul, on the other hand, lacked wisdom. David's wisdom shines through the Psalms he penned. Solomon's wisdom became so renowned that people came from far and near to hear him (1 Kings 3:16-28; 4:31; 10:3). Daniel and his three friends amazed the Babylonian court with their wisdom (Dan. 1:20). Job grew in wisdom in the midst of terrible suffering.

The need for wisdom today

Wisdom, as a gift, ebbs and flows. As Solomon adopted the practices of pagan kings in disobedience to God, his wisdom waned. In Ecclesiastes he laments the long road of foolishness he had trod while seeking to fill his cup with everything but a satisfying relationship with God. And as I survey the church scene today I am hard put to discover wisdom in any great supply.

It is not that common either in trained Christian workers. There are scholarly pastors who seem unable to stay out of debt. Others shock their congregations by the introduction of changes too quickly. Some fail to keep confidences. Come to think of it, wisdom is uncommon!

The rise of counselling as an adjunct to the church in many ways heralds a welcome and helpful addition. One cannot help wondering, however, after listening to scores of Christians with problems, what has happened to simple wisdom: wisdom in relating to one's loved ones; wisdom to forgive; wisdom to eat rightly; wisdom to trust Christ and not worry; wisdom to believe God's promises about guilt; wisdom to balance work and play; wisdom to avoid the seductive woman, or man; wisdom to give children loving but firm discipline; wisdom to reject TV addiction. Where has it gone?

In a chapter in which he describes servant leadership, Tim Hansel discusses the necessity of problem-solving ability: 'The core of life and, therefore, the core of Christian life is solving problems. In all my years of teaching on high school, university and seminary levels, I've been shocked at how little is understood about the problem-solving process. When I've asked students to give me an actual step-by-step plan for solving problems, I have never received a logical, cogent plan.'[18] An astounding evaluation! I hope it is exaggerated.

Has the rise of entertainment robbed us of the time necessary to devote to the development of wisdom? For wisdom cannot develop without time spent in thought and meditation. Then, too, wisdom is present 'in the multitude of counsellors', who hash out and ruminate over issues. Since we are not much given today to spiritual conversation perhaps we are not too rich in wisdom. Wisdom also develops when we face challenges head on and seek to solve the problems they present. With the specialized helping professions offering advice on everything from bunions to business, we may depend too much on others solving our problems for us. Fortunately, although uncommon, wisdom may be found among practical and godly people.

Examples of wisdom

One might say that among widely known men of our recent past A. W. Tozer displayed considerable wisdom. In his book, *The Root Of The Righteous,* the table of contents indicates a comprehensive analysis of Christian living that is rare. God, 'the Holy', always occupies centre stage. But applications range from advice on how to listen and how to accept advice, to incisive analyses of entertainment, personal devotions, commitment, contentment and even death — to name a few topics.[19]

Francis Schaeffer's grasp of the trends and dangers of our day also illustrates wisdom. His penetrating exposure of the irrational faith of our secular society has done much to encourage beleaguered saints.

Many of the insights of today's biblical counsellors reflect the gift of wisdom. Larry Crabb, for example, describes the root cause of many of our emotional problems in terms of the biblical concepts of deep heart longings, as illustrated in the hunger and thirst of Psalms and as found in Jesus' discourses. His analysis has provided a relatively simple, but not simplistic, way of understanding human problems.[20]

The clear insights on practical living that we find in Chuck Swindoll's writings also exemplify this gift. Of course, Puritan writers, such as Thomas Watson, abounded in practical wisdom. Pick up his little paperback, *All Things For Good,* or his longer series of books on the *Westminster Catechism* and prepare for a real treat. But what about wisdom on the local church level?

At the beginning of our chapter we mentioned Andy who had trouble with the pastor's class on spiritual gifts. He appreciated the pastor's teaching skills but preferred more application. He wondered whether the course on spiritual gifts was just another option for the Bible Class that would result in few things being changed. He saw lots that needed changing! Andy, not a critical person, felt somewhat ashamed at even mentioning his concerns about the pastor's teaching. He went on quickly to cover up any implied criticism with a roll call of the pastor's virtues.

A bricklayer, Andy loves books. His considerable library contains an abundance of volumes on witnessing, practical Christian living, Christians in the workplace, social issues and defence of the faith. Sometimes his suggestions in church business meetings lack theological sophistication, but they are often brilliant. The church adopted a new method of keeping up with missionary prayer requests at his suggestion. It avoided a divisive vote on church discipline after considering his suggestion of a Christ-honouring compromise. He often spots the missing ingredient when church activities are under consideration. For instance, a proposal to move the congregation and build in the suburbs stalled when Andy argued from Scripture about the need for city witness. Out of the defeat of the old proposal, new enthusiasm developed for imaginative programmes of city evangelism.

Andy possesses, in a modest but developing way, the gift of wisdom. As he walked out of class he noticed that the placement of a coat rack hindered traffic flow in the corridor. By moving it fifteen feet the problem was solved. Problems challenge Andy. More often than not his solutions help the church at large. The respect his family has for him finds its echo in a number of young couples who have benefited from his advice not only about the purchase of a house, but also about planning that gives to God the place he deserves. The nomination committee has their eyes on him for the deacon board.

Conclusion

Do you have the gift of wisdom? Perhaps you have the gift of knowledge? The gifts of knowledge or wisdom may be hidden by the presence of more visible gifts. Paul's powerful preaching and teaching ability might obscure for us his wisdom and knowledge. Wisdom and knowledge undergird many other gifts such as shepherding, preaching, evangelism and church-planting. They are basic to teaching, which we shall consider next. But before you move on to the next chapter, return again to the gift chart and fill in the columns that relate to knowledge and wisdom.

15.
The gift of teaching

While most gifts are mentioned in just one or two passages, the gift of teaching occurs in each of the three main passages relating to gifts. The only other gift emphasized as much is prophecy. Every local church, every foreign mission, indeed almost every parachurch ministry depends to a larger or smaller degree on the exercise of this gift.

Despite its importance, good teaching is uncommon. Its dearth may be partly due to our failure to relate our teaching solidly enough to the gifts of knowledge and wisdom. Without knowledge, teaching is shallow, and without wisdom, teaching is impractical.

But without teaching to give them voice, knowledge and wisdom remain largely mute. These two gifts, in themselves, do not enable a person to communicate. A scholar is not necessarily a communicator. Likewise, a wise man may not be able teach others how to live holy lives. The gift of teaching adds to knowledge and wisdom expertise in communication.

I owe much of my own Christian progress to good teachers. When I was a new Christian, Gil Dunkin patiently answered my many questions about the faith. Through his home Bible studies I grew spiritually. Later, at Bible College, Dr 'Buck' Hatch exemplified a different style of teaching. Intensely personal and life-oriented, his teaching melted our hearts and motivated us to pursue Christ. Still later in seminary, Dr Robert K. Rudolph probed every careless assumption. He inspired us to think critically in order to prepare us to clash with the humanistic presuppositions of our day. The Spirit used three very different teachers, each with his own unique style of teaching, at different times in my pilgrimage.

Good Bible teachers add both substance and spice to everything that goes on in our churches. Preaching, evangelism, shepherding and encouragement all depend to some extent on aptness to teach for their effectiveness. Since the speaking gifts overlap each other in various ways, we should not be surprised by the pervasive necessity of teaching ability.

Teaching, though, must not be thought of as an appendage to other gifts. Teaching fulfils a crucial role in its own right. Let us look at what we find about this gift in the New Testament.

I. The biblical roots of teaching

In Romans 12 Paul urges teachers to get busy teaching: 'We have different gifts ... if it is teaching, let him teach.' In Ephesians 4 he links teaching with shepherding: 'He [Christ] gave ... some to be pastors and teachers.' Teaching, in this Ephesian passage, ranks fifth among the special gifts necessary to 'prepare God's people for works of service'.

In Corinthians Paul writes, 'God has appointed first of all apostles, second prophets, third teachers ...' (1 Cor. 12:28). As the argument develops in Corinthians, Paul repeatedly urges them to realize that gifts such as teaching, which instruct the mind with intelligible words, exceed in importance gifts such as tongues, which project unintelligible speech.

Ranked next to apostleship and prophethood, and linked with shepherding, teaching fills a crucial place in the kingdom. No other gifts, with the possible exceptions of shepherding and hospitality, occupy so prominent a place in the list of essential qualifications for church leaders. 'The overseer must be ... able to teach' (1 Tim. 3:2).

It is significant that only prophecy and teaching occur in all the gift-lists, and that preaching and teaching often occur together (Rom. 12:7; Eph. 4:11; 1 Cor. 12:28). Undoubtedly, a preacher must demonstrate aptness to teach.[1]

Since Jesus Christ was called 'the Master', which means 'Teacher', it is no wonder that Christianity has always been, and always will be, a teaching faith. While on earth, Jesus went about teaching. In his final commission he said, 'Go and make disciples of all nations, baptizing ... and teaching them...' (Matt. 28:19-20). Following his lead, the disciples went everywhere teaching and preaching the gospel. Paul, although pre-eminently thought of as a shining example of the missionary evangelist, characterized his ministry as preaching and teaching publicly and from house to house (Acts 20:20). The four Gospels, the epistles — indeed all the books of the Bible, are great didactic documents.

Teaching occupies a central role in the body of Christ. Even music has teaching as one of its main purposes (Col. 3:16).

The Greek words

The words used for teaching and the teacher, in the lists of gifts, are *didasko/didaskalos*. From these we derive our English word 'didactic'. A broad concept, it denotes the giving of instruction.

A number of other Greek words also elaborate the concept of teaching. *Katecheo* means to teach, instruct or inform orally, as when Paul says, 'In the church I would rather speak five intelligible words to instruct others than ten thousand words in a tongue' (1 Cor. 14:19).

Paideuo (from which we get our English word 'pedagogy') is used several times in a general sense but refers mainly to training children and to family discipline. In some places it is translated 'discipline': 'When we are being judged by the Lord, we are being disciplined' (1 Cor 11:32). In this sense, pedagogy denotes correction with the aim of delivering us from our own childish, really Adamic, wilfulness. A *paidagogos* is 'a guide, or guardian or trainer of boys, lit., a child-leader, a tutor ... school-master... In this and allied words the idea is that of training, discipline, not of impartation of knowledge. The *paidagogos* was not the instructor of the child; he exercised a general supervision over him and was responsible for his moral and physical well-being.'[2] The word is translated 'guardians' in 1 Corinthians 4:15, where there is heavy emphasis on the responsibility the *paidagogos* has over the child.

Matheteuo, meaning to make a disciple, also indicates a process of instruction. *Mueo,* to instruct, means 'to initiate into the mysteries'. *Probibazo,* to be instructed, comes from a root meaning that gives the sense of leading forward or leading on. Thus, to instruct is to lead a person on in his or her pilgrimage. *Sumbibazo* is rendered 'instruct' in the second chapter of 1 Corinthians but denotes joining, uniting or knitting together, from which comes the idea of comparing two or more things. This concept portrays teaching as proving ideas or comparing things. A *kalodidaskalos,* in Titus 2:3, is one who teaches what is good, while a *pseudodidaskalos,* in 2 Peter 2:1, is a false teacher. In other contexts a similar word is used for a teacher of false doctrine (1 Tim. 1:3; 6:3).

What teaching implies

A broad range of communication concepts clusters around teaching. To teach is to inform, instruct, lead on, make disciples, discipline the wayward will, unite disparate concepts, prove and initiate into unknown mysteries. An examination of the context of teaching will further elaborate this general picture.

Jesus, the consummate teacher, commanded his disciples to make disciples of all nations by teaching them to 'obey everything I have commanded you' (Matt. 28:19-20).

In another context, teaching aims at preparing 'God's people for works of service so that the body of Christ may be built up' (Eph. 4:12). Its goal is always the production of godly character. After a chapter devoted to instructing Titus on how and what to teach, Paul notes that the grace of God 'teaches us to say "No" to ungodliness and worldly passions and to live self-controlled, upright and godly lives in this present age' (Titus 2:12). That means revolutionary change!

II. The goal of teaching

Specifically, Christian teaching aims at change, the transformation of redeemed sinners from the inside out. Teaching will be complete only when every believer is conformed to the image of Christ. Good teachers help us to achieve that goal by targeting change in four areas.

1. Change of mind

Teaching aims at mental transformation. Through the 'renewing of the mind', ignorance, misunderstanding and prejudice about the Scriptures are dispelled (Rom. 12:2). Biblical knowledge of the whole counsel of God replaces distorted and sinful concepts.

No wonder the first Christians 'devoted themselves to the apostles' teaching and to the fellowship...' with such zeal (Acts 2:42). Paul spent three years teaching and preaching in Ephesus 'the whole will of God' (Acts 20:27). Flynn reckons that his daily discussions in the hall of Tyrannus 'from the fifth hour to the tenth ... would total 3650 hours of teaching,' in two years alone.[3]

Jesus' three years of itinerant teaching have left us a goldmine of parables, discourses and examples. Jesus always left those he talked to with some portion of teaching which, if accepted, would produce dramatic or incremental change in their understanding. He helped the Samaritan woman at the well to admit her own sinfulness and led her to a new understanding of God's spiritual nature. At the Last Supper he taught the disciples servant-leadership through foot-washing.

That the apostles learned well is evidenced by the wealth of teaching material they left for us in the New Testament. All of it aims at delivering us from ignorance and leading us 'into the light of the knowledge of God in the face of Jesus Christ'. As already stressed in our study of the gift of knowledge, apostolic teaching was full of doctrinal content.

The first target of teaching, then, is the mind: its intellectual transformation and doctrinal education through imparting a comprehensive knowledge of Scripture. In the process, mental skills are developed and intellectual power stimulated.

2. Change of heart

Perhaps the failure of many theologians to go beyond scholarship to application has led some Christians to misunderstand doctrine as impractical and theology as unnecessary. As already noted during our study of the gift of wisdom, teaching which aims only to impart knowledge is not Christian, in the broader sense. Good teaching aims at the transformation of heart attitudes.

Always integrating doctrine and practice, the good teacher will aim to motivate pupils to live lives that are consistent with their beliefs. Here teachers encounter strong resistance which only divine dynamite can overcome.

Nicodemus came to Jesus by night. As a Jewish leader his grasp of Old Testament Scripture was impressive. But he had a problem which Jesus immediately perceived. Avoiding lengthy doctrinal discussion, Jesus declared his need of transformation from the inside out: 'You must be born again' (John 3:7). Jesus knew that evil comes 'out of the heart'. In the beatitudes and on numerous other occasions he had given extensive teaching about the heart and the need for love at the fount of our being (e.g., Matt. 5; 22:37-40). But the wellspring of Nicodemus' motivation had not yet been cleansed through the new birth.

From the Master the apostles learned that 'the pattern of sound teaching' can only be kept by a person whose heart is transformed by 'faith and love in Christ Jesus' (2 Tim. 1:13). Without trans-formed hearts people are 'always learning but never able to ac-knowledge the truth' because they are 'lovers of themselves, lovers of money, boastful, proud ... ungrateful ... without love...'

Knowing that the new birth precedes sanctification, Christian teachers pray for the Spirit to initiate the process of transformation. Once regenerate, a sinner can really begin to learn in earnest.

Even after regeneration a myriad of hindrances can choke growth. Many of these distractions can be traced to the heart, where unhealthy attitudes continue to sprout. Peter warns that evil atti-tudes, such as 'malice ... envy', can throttle the craving believers have for the pure milk of the Word that is so necessary for growth (1 Peter 2:1-2). One can scarcely find a paragraph in the New Testament without some appeal to weed out evil emotions and plant the good seed of faith, hope, joy or love.

I well remember Pastor John, one of my students on a course I taught on Ephesians in Pakistan. Since it was an extension course, with widely spaced classes, John had a considerable amount of homework to do. While studying the self-study materials one day, he became deeply convicted about his attitude towards a family in the church. Dropping his lessons, he immediately went to them to effect reconciliation. Love soon replaced suspicion and bitterness. His study had uncovered buried resentment. He knew that continued doctrinal study was pointless until he faced his sin, repented and made it right.

Biblical teaching always aims at this kind of genuine heart transformation. After we deal with harmful attitudes, we can joy-fully embrace obedience, like Pastor John. As the hymn points out, we need to 'dear desire, self-will resign', which leads naturally to the next teaching target.

3. Change of will

Jesus commissioned his disciples to disciple the nations by 'teaching them to obey everything I have commanded you' (Matt. 28:20). Christian teaching must always aim at producing obedience to the commands of Christ. Good teaching breaks down self-will and leads us into voluntary submission to Christ.

Rebellion wrecked the Garden of Eden. Rebellion repeatedly shipwrecked the nation of Israel. Even Saul, their first king, rebelled causing Samuel to cry, 'Rebellion is like the sin of divination [or witchcraft].'

A rich young ruler came to Jesus. Jesus discerned a tug of war in his heart between covetousness and an awakening concern for eternal life. Questions about obedience to the law followed. Obviously, the young man knew doctrine. An awakening affection for Christ smouldered within. Jesus must have pondered the best way to bring this young man to the door of salvation. Consequently, he appealed for his allegiance by testing his willingness to repudiate his deepest desire: 'Go, sell your possessions and give to the poor... Then come, follow me' (Matt. 19:16-22). The Master challenged him to submit his will. But he could not obey. He could not sublimate his love for wealth to a growing desire to follow the Master. So he went away sorrowful. Good teaching follows the Master's pattern by appealing to us at the point of our disobedience, by challenging us to submit our wills to him.

In Romans the inspired writer urges believers to 'Offer your bodies as living sacrifices... Be transformed ... then you will be able to test and approve what God's will is' (Rom. 12:1-2). Godly transformation is not possible without yielding unconditionally to God's will. We fear God's will. We hold on to our independence. We are wilful and disobedient. Spirit-anointed teaching challenges us at the point of our wilfulness. In Peter's words, 'You have purified yourselves by obeying the truth...' (1 Peter 1:22). Good teachers always aim to lead people into obedience.

John, the Pakistani pastor, learned because he obeyed. Scripture will become boring or unintelligible if we choose to disobey what is already clear to us. Disobedience conjures up the genie of self-deception within us to mix a potion of subtle deceit to mask our self-will. The potent drug of rebellion, in turn, clouds our understanding.

Good teaching is always practical. It aims at a change of mind, heart and will as precursors to transformed behaviour.

4. Changed behaviour

Jesus called down the seven woes of Matthew 23 upon the teachers of his day because their profession of faith belied their practice. These teachers and Pharisees 'do not practise what they preach' (v. 3). They burden men but 'are not willing to lift a finger'. They were filled with misdirected zeal. Although they emphasized minute details of the law, they 'neglected the more important matters of the law — justice, mercy and faithfulness' (v. 23). Their teaching had no impact on their own lives. 'Inside they are full of greed and self-indulgence,' the Master declared (v. 25). Their attempts to decorate their profession of piety degenerated into an emphasis on wordy prayers and pseudo-religious clothing. In reality they were frauds who used religious terminology to steal, to command honour for themselves and to control others in order to satisfy their own lust for power.

The teaching ministry of Jesus uncovered this festering cancer of hypocrisy and called for that consistency between profession and practice that must always accompany true righteousness. The Sermon on the Mount hammers home the lesson again and again: 'A good tree cannot bear bad fruit, and a bad tree cannot bear good fruit. Every tree that does not bear good fruit is cut down and thrown into the fire' (Matt. 7:18-19). Consistency of behaviour is so vital that it is either fruit or the fire. 'Not everyone who says to me, "Lord, Lord," will enter the kingdom of heaven, but only he who does the will of my Father who is in heaven' (Matt. 7:21).

Peter reminds his readers that knowledge of God leads to 'life and godliness', in which we 'escape the corruption in the world caused by evil desires' (2 Peter 1:2-4). Paul exhorted Timothy and Titus to 'teach what is in accord with sound doctrine', which meant to 'teach the older men to be temperate ... older women to be reverent in the way they live, not to be slanderers or addicted to much wine ... the young men to be self-controlled ... all men ... to live self-controlled, upright and godly lives in this present age' (Titus 2:1-12).

Biblical teaching aims at transformation of relationships. Good teachers will often teach about getting along with friends and relatives, with co-workers and employers, with politicians and neighbours. They talk a lot about love, honesty and mutual respect.

Teaching also aims at equipping believers with necessary skills. Once equipped, disciples can in turn train others in how to refute error, how to disciple new Christians, how to solve problems, how to develop spiritual gifts, etc. (Titus 1:9; 2:3,4; 2 Tim. 2:2).

Biblical teaching hones intellectual skills, purifies attitudes, strengthens godly will-power and inspires transformed behaviour. In other words, biblical teaching aims at sanctification, our trans-formation from the inside out.

The gift defined

We could define the gift of teaching as that Spirit-endowed ability to instruct others in the Word of God in such a way that God produces present and lasting changes in their understanding, atti-tude, will and behaviour.

Working for change

A good teacher is never content to lecture, to lay out ideas like sweets on a plate, letting hearers pick and choose. He prays, he prepares, he agonizes in dependence on the Spirit to produce change in his hearers. He glories in the cross of Christ, the foundation of real change (1 Cor. 2:1-2). Like Paul, he or she comes in weakness, fearing to teach without relying on 'the Spirit's power, so that your faith might not rest on men's wisdom, but on God's power' (1 Cor. 2:3-5).

Let us think for a moment about a teacher planning his lesson. The pastor of our typical church aims for four areas of change as he prepares his lesson on spiritual gifts. He wants Ron, Ann, Megan and others in his class to understand the biblical facts. Then, too, he will pray for God to change any wrong attitudes, such as com-placency, unconcern, pride, or lack of confidence. He will aim to motivate them actively to seek out opportunities to serve. Over the long haul, he will aim to see them all using their gifts in various ministries in the church.

Already, there are changes. The pastor rejoices to see Ann visiting a shut-in, Megan talking with several lonely women and Ron agreeing to let his name stand for election to a committee. Not only that, but their excitement about spiritual gifts has spread. A number from the congregation have come to the pastor asking for another class on the subject.

But if change sets the teaching agenda, how can one aim for transformation in so many areas? There always seems to be too much to do and too little time to do it.

III: The challenge of teaching

As we contemplate the challenges of our day, with its information explosion set against the backdrop of a breakdown in morality, we may be tempted to despair. In reality, however, the spiritual ignorance of our day is no greater challenge to the Spirit-led teacher than Ephesus was to the apostle Paul. He taught three years in a centre where the worship of the goddess Diana, with attendant prostitution and unspeakable ritual, prevailed. Many suffered through demon-possession. Magic and sorcery so pervaded Ephesian society that when a movement of God swept many into the kingdom they kindled a bonfire of scrolls on sorcery worth the equivalent of 50,000 daily wages.

Their prosperity as a great centre of commerce, as well as their trust in philosophy, furthered Satan's oppression of the Ephesians. Various schools of Greek philosophy vied with each other for disciples. Their philosophers justified slavery and a host of other evils. Eastern religions were beginning to attract a wide following. In their midst militant Jews maintained a strong presence.

Ephesus, in the first century, had it all. Materialism, philosophy, magic, the occult, idolatry, immorality, injustice and self-righteous Jewish monotheism all vied for the hearts and minds of the Ephesians. Our day is no worse. Paul plunged right into this cesspool of evil and began systematically to teach and preach the whole counsel of God. 'Paul entered the synagogue and spoke boldly there for three months, arguing persuasively about the kingdom of God. But some of them became obstinate... So Paul left them. He took the disciples with him and had discussions daily in the lecture hall of Tyrannus. This went on for two years...' (Acts 19:8-

10 — read the whole story and Paul's summary of his ministry in Acts 19-20).

Admittedly, miracles powerfully affirmed Paul's ministry. True, he was more than a teacher; he was an apostolic church-planter without peer. But surely, what he did so systematically in the midst of an antagonistic audience we can do with more sympathetic hearers. In most cases those in our churches, Sunday school classes, home Bible studies, families and discipleship groups are already predisposed to accept biblical teaching.

But are we doing a good job teaching? *Time* magazine in an article several years ago called the Sunday School hour (the adult Bible class) the most wasted hour of the week. I hope they were wrong. I do wonder if we have realized the critical importance of times set apart for Bible teaching.

Public education indoctrinates our children five days a week for twelve years with English, maths and history subtly laced with errors drawn from humanism, materialism, situational ethics, evolution and even Eastern mysticism. Young people may spend another four to six years in college. All of us watch TV and read newspapers and magazines. We live and work in a materialistic work environment. Occult practice, New Age mysticism, cultic error and Satan worship apply subtle pressure.

The Master calls us to stem this tide of unceasing indoctrination by teaching the whole Word of God. That means, we must instruct believers in basic Bible content, doctrine, apologetics and ethics, as well as teach courses on Christian living and witness. To accomplish this we have one hour a week! If we are fortunate, we may be able to encourage some disciples to give us four hours a week. If the task were assigned to a government agency, it would laugh itself out of existence. But we are commissioned to prepare God's people, not only to meet every problem they face on earth, but for heaven as well. 'Don't you know that the saints will judge angels?' The task is mind-boggling! And unlike public education, we have no power to compel our students to study. All who learn do so of their own free will.

Another factor sobers biblical teachers. They know that people will respond to their teaching in various ways. The parable of the soils reminds us that learning will depend upon how people listen. Some people have unresponsive hearts. Nothing the teacher can do will change that. Some listen on a superficial level. Others allow distractions to choke the Word. The teacher cannot let a personal sense of guilt for what he has no power to change discourage him from his commitment to excellence in teaching. Success, in part, rests in the sovereign hand of God and in the heart of the hearer.

But in another sense, success depends on the teacher. By that I mean that failure to learn may be due to poor teaching methods. If people do not learn then the teacher may not have taught well. With such a massive job to do and so little time to do it, teachers must hone their skills to utilize every tool in a drive for excellence. Teaching is not just telling. It involves coming to grips with the whole learning process.

IV: The process of teaching

A farmer sows seed in hope of a crop. That hope doesn't stop him from ploughing, cultivating, weeding and watering. In the same way, a teacher does everything in his power to plough, cultivate and water the hearts of his hearers through interesting, well-prepared material. He must design his lessons in such a way that interest may flare and a spark of understanding be ignited.

Principles of learning help to ignite that spark. In a book of this nature I can do no more than list some of them. These principles, in various combinations, will mark the teaching of a gifted educator. Of course, teachers vary. No two teachers will use exactly the same methods. But some mix of the following methods should mark the biblical teacher:

1. Teaching that progresses from the known to the unknown.

2. Teaching that leads students to perceive the relevance of what is taught to their own lives.

3. Teaching which recognizes the varied personality mix inherent in different people and thus uses a variety of methods.

4. Teaching which proceeds in an easily understandable and logical order.

5. Teaching which communicates material in small incremental steps, building precept upon precept.

6. Teaching which encourages student interaction and does not rely on the lecture method.

7. Teaching that is warm and personal, in which learners perceive how deeply the teacher is involved in what is being taught.

Teachers, like true Christians, are known by their fruit. The fruit of teaching is changed lives. The process that a gifted teacher will employ to elicit that change incorporates in some measure the principles we outlined. Why? Because these principles reflect the way people think and learn.

Teaching occupies a crucial place in the body of Christ. No teacher, of course, can possibly embody all the qualities of a good teacher. That distinction must be reserved for the Master. Then too, each teacher will have a distinct style that suits his or her personality and background. We must allow variety of methodology as long as the goal of teaching is met. Any one style of teaching, when over-emphasized, can lead a church into imbalance and contribute to boredom. And boredom produced by either teaching or preaching the incredible Word of God must be considered a great crime.

Fortunately, as with the other gifts, teaching is not a gift exercised in isolation. Teaching principles undergird many of the gifts. Since you or I may have another gift that requires some teaching, let us take a few moments to consider how teaching relates to other gifts.

V. Integrating teaching with other speaking gifts

As already mentioned, preaching, evangelism, shepherding, knowledge and wisdom are closely associated with the gift of teaching. Paul's inspired choice of the human body as an illustration of the church anticipates this close interrelationship. Just as in the body all systems are organically linked together in an operating unit, so all spiritual gifts work together to promote the progress of the kingdom.

The gift of missionary church-planting provides the structural system of bones and muscles undergirding the body. The gift of prophetic preaching, like the nervous system, communicates the will of Christ, the Head of the church, in powerful form. Without the evangelistic gift, illustrated by the reproductive system, the church cannot multiply. Like the circulatory system, the shepherding gift both distributes nutrients where they are most needed and protects the body from spiritual ills. The gifts of knowledge, wisdom and teaching, on the other hand, like the digestive system, break down the Word of God into a form that the body can assimilate. The whole body depends on these nutrients to thrive.

The gift of knowledge, as we have noted, is the spiritual ability to understand and systematize the content of Scripture. This gift provides the raw material the teacher will use to effect his first aim: change of mind through instruction in the textual and doctrinal content of Scripture. In order to effect intellectual change, a teacher needs a breadth of biblical knowledge. Either he must possess this gift himself, or draw material from systematizers of biblical truth who write Sunday School lessons, home Bible study outlines, commentaries, etc.

Wisdom, on the other hand, provides the raw material for change in the other three areas of teaching intent. Wisdom is the spiritual ability to take the content of Scripture and apply it to the day-to-day issues of life. The teacher needs wisdom to discern how to effect changes in both the internal attitudes and wilfulness of those in his class and in order to promote changed behaviour.

Without a thorough and organized understanding of biblical content, the teaching will be shallow or imbalanced. And without the wisdom to see how biblical doctrine intersects with life, the teacher will be theoretical and impractical.

Interestingly enough, Ralph Martin in his study of 1 Corinthians 12-15 states, 'We may distinguish ... gifts that are pedagogical, namely, utterances of wisdom and knowledge.'[4] The gifts of wisdom and knowledge serve the discipline of pedagogy; that is, teaching.

We have already considered in diagrammatic form the relationship of revelation, knowledge, wisdom and teaching. The three latter gifts revolve around the axle of revelation that is the source of all revealed truth.

The systematic organization of truth, which the gift of knowledge provides, forms the hub on which its communication is based.

Wisdom is where truth meets life. Taking the systematic concepts organized by someone with the gift of knowledge, the person

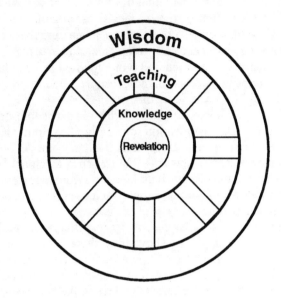

gifted in wisdom applies these ideas to practical life. He or she always asks, 'Where does this apply to my life, to our church, or to our society?' For example, the one with the gift of knowledge may organize everything he can find in Scripture about God's invisible omnipresence. But the one gifted with wisdom will not stop there but will go on to say, 'Aha, God is with me in this terrible traffic! He is also with the suffering church in China. Let's pray for the Chinese church to rejoice in the knowledge of his presence.'

Where does the gift of teaching come in? Knowledge and wisdom are not, in themselves, communication skills. Teachers are communicators. They take the basic knowledge systematized by the one, plus the suggestions by the other on how to make application to daily life, and present it in understandable form. The teacher labours so that disciples both understand the content of Scripture and are moved to change their attitudes, choices and behaviour. Good teaching becomes the catalyst that moves students to appropriate both knowledge and wisdom.

All three depend on each other. The teacher borrows content and application from those gifted in knowledge and wisdom. They in turn depend on the teacher's ability to communicate.

Because of the fundamental importance of knowledge and
wisdom at every step in the teacher's preparation and delivery,
teachers must themselves possess in some measure these two gifts.
Conversely they will need to develop great skill in using the written
resources published by men and women gifted in knowledge and
wisdom. Failing to make use of these resources dooms their students
to shallow and impractical mediocrity.

Conversely, scholars and those with biblical wisdom must avoid
occupying key teaching positions unless the Holy Spirit has specifically gifted them to teach. Unfortunately, many blunder on, operating under the misunderstanding that telling is teaching. I am sure
you have suffered under brilliant men who were inept teachers. Or
you have overheard young people lamenting their college pro-
fessors' inability to teach.

Scholarship does not necessarily imply pedagogical skill. Let me
take a simple example to show how these four — revelation,
knowledge, wisdom and teaching — are related. The example is
taken from the subject I majored in at university, forestry. Knowledge of forestry includes understanding of the various species of
trees, where they grow best, the qualities of their wood, how to
harvest them, and how to use their wood to produce newsprint,
flooring or paper towels, etc. That is knowledge. Wisdom, however,
asks moral questions about ecology and land use. Wisdom may
decree that a mountainside be left uncut or that a pulp mill should not
be situated on the banks of a trout stream. Wisdom will look far into
the future and see the ramifications to the whole society that are
inherent in the decisions loggers may take. Without revelation, of
course, ecologists and foresters have no idea that trees are a creation
of God and that he holds men responsible for the just use of all
resources.

A forester may graduate with distinction because he knows a lot
about forestry. A wise man may realize that certain logging practices will harm future generations. But it takes a teacher to be able
to communicate both knowledge about forestry and discernment
about land use to young students or the general public.

Teaching occupies a crucial place in both society and the church.
Indeed, knowledge, wisdom and teaching ability intersect crucially
with the gifts of evangelism, preaching and shepherding. Evangelism, for its effect, depends upon ability to move men and women,

through the communication of truth, to faith and repentance. (I am not discussing the crucial place of the Spirit in regeneration, but only the place of his agents.) Jesus, in the Great Commission, tied making disciples of all nations — the proper work of evangelism — with teaching them to obey all his commands (Matt. 28:19-20). The evangelist requires a thorough understanding of biblical truths such as human depravity, the incarnation, justification and redemption. Evangelism presupposes some communication skill or teaching ability in order to bring truth powerfully to bear on a sinner's heart.

The Great Commission also links missionary church-planting with teaching. Vigorous indigenous churches develop as young Christians are taught to be godly and responsible members of a local church.

Many passages link preaching and teaching. 'You know that I have not hesitated to preach anything that would be helpful to you but have taught you publicly and from house to house' (Acts 20:20). In this text, preaching seems synonymous with teaching (see also their close connection in Acts 28:31; 1 Timothy 4:11,13 and 5:17). Teaching overlaps with prophecy in several passages (1 Cor. 14:3, 29-32). Likewise, prophecy is closely related to knowledge (1 Cor. 13:2).

We have already noted in some detail, in an earlier chapter, the fundamental importance of equipping as a facet of teaching. Equipping believers to enable them to carry on the various ministries of the church remains crucial to church health. Further comments here are unnecessary.

Of all the communication gifts, teaching seems to be the most widely exercised. It undergirds other communication gifts. The gifts of knowledge and wisdom occupy a similar place. Each speaking gift depends upon the gift of knowledge to organize truth systematically and upon the gift of wisdom to focus application. In a sense, missionary church-planting, preaching, evangelism, shepherding and encouragement are only wisdom applied to different needs. All depend on teaching ability for communication effect. The diagram illustrates this integration.

If this synthesis is accurate, we can easily see why there seems to be so much overlap between these gifts. They all have one goal in common, the communication of truth. All make use, in some measure, of the process of teaching.

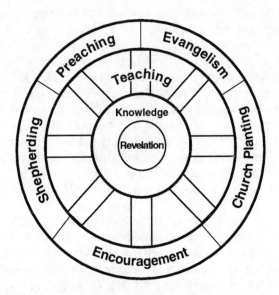

In chapter 4, we noted that spiritual gifts are not just spiritual abilities, but specific directions of ministry to which the Holy Spirit calls us. He gifts us to focus all our providentially gathered education, abilities and temperamental differences on a certain area of ministry. This becomes our main focus, although our skills could also be used in different directions.

The communication gifts target a cluster of specific needs upon which the Holy Spirit calls various believers to concentrate their energy. The evangelist concentrates on the lost. The preacher concentrates on applying the Word of God to specific situations and needs. The shepherd focuses on the health of the flock in an effort to ensure their protection from dangers of every kind. The encourager focuses on the needs believers have for encouragement or exhortation.

The teacher, on the other hand, is the generalist. He focuses on teaching the whole content of Scripture in a step-by-step process. All the others borrow from the skills of the teacher. For example, the encourager aims to produce a change of attitude. The missionary church-planter aims to see independent self-centred sinners change through Spirit-led teaching to become groups of interdependent disciples organized into local churches. The preacher seeks to move people to respond to God's will in given situations.

Since teaching is such a foundational and widespread gift, many of us need to seek it.

VI. Discovering and developing the gift of teaching

With such a dearth of good teaching around, the search is urgent. Here are some suggestions about how to go about both developing competency and testing your giftedness.

First of all, *teach yourself.* In a sense every Christian is a teacher, called of God to train him or herself for godliness. Paul reminded Timothy of the value of the training for ministry that began in his childhood and continued into young manhood. If we would teach ourselves, we, like Timothy, must systematically study Scripture so that each of us can be 'approved, a workman who does not need to be ashamed and who correctly handles the word of truth' (2 Tim. 2:15).

All Christians, including teachers, are disciples. Knowledge of Scripture undergirds all discipleship. A self-imposed regimen of biblical study is crucial. A basic library of good study and reference books can be a boon here.

To knowledge must be added wisdom, the bent to apply Scripture to the concrete situations of life. As we study, we need to keep asking ourselves, 'How does this apply to me, to my life today, to my family, to our church, to what is going on around me?' A keen sense of application is not only basic to teaching, but to our own personal growth. Begin to enlarge your library with books that apply Scripture to matters of personal discipleship, marriage, church life, social justice, etc.

While pursuing a course of personal study, notice the ways you seem to learn best. What made Scripture come alive to you? What methods of study proved cumbersome or unhelpful? Do you notice people in your own family or local church who seem to learn in different ways? These observations give you hints about how people learn. Some of the best teachers are those who taught themselves.

Second, *look for opportunities to communicate the message of the Bible to others.* Start in your own home. Set up an interesting devotional time with your family. Look for new Christians who need a caring friend to help them grow. Set up a Bible study with them. Or you may be able to take part in home Bible Studies.

Since every Christian is called to be a witness, all of us need to seek opportunities to share Christ with the lost. Pursue these. Plan how you will discuss the faith with a relative or colleague. Put yourself in your friends' shoes. Ponder how you can communicate in interesting ways. As the relationship develops aim for change in the four different areas. Teaching gifts often develop in the non-formal settings provided by personal witness, hospital visitation or simple friendship. Learning to be flexible will prepare you to deal with the unexpected that routinely crops up even in classroom settings.

Third, *seek formal teaching opportunities* as well. Offer yourself as a teacher's helper in a Sunday School class or some aspect of the youth work. Watch how the best teachers operate. Offer to give your testimony in church. Prepare your testimony so it communicates both knowledge and wisdom. Offer to present a lesson in a Sunday School class and ask for input from a teacher.

Conclusion

When we take in our hands the Word of God with the goal of teaching it to others, we never know where God will lead. Helen Keller's usefulness can be traced to a teacher. At the age of nineteen months, she was stuck deaf, dumb and mute by a virus. Silence would have surrounded her like a cocoon but for the valiant efforts of her teacher, Annie Sullivan. 'The turning point in Helen's life came when Miss Sullivan gave her one word — *water*. When Helen discovered that one word, she discovered the world.'[5]

The voyages of the imaginary Starship Enterprise are nothing compared to the voyages of discovery led by teachers. What could be more glorious than to lead a person to plumb the mysteries of the eternal God? You, like Miss Sullivan, could become the turning-point in someone's life. Who knows but that the cantankerous six-year-old you teach might not be the George Whitefield of this coming generation? Paul urged the Corinthians to desire the better gifts. To aspire to teach the Word must be one of the highest aspirations. Aim high! Shoot for the moon!

The next gift, encouragement, must also rate high in the estimation of everyone who longs for glory in the church. But before you move on to the next chapter, return to your gift-chart and fill in the columns that relate to the gift of teaching.

16.
The gift of encouragement

Encouragers are the unsung heroes that we cannot live without. Those in the spotlight of public ministry get all the glory, but in the final judgement many unknown names will emblazon the register of faith. It takes a hero not to mind playing second fiddle while he or she patiently encourages and, at times, rebukes those of us who trip over our own pretensions or keep falling headlong into the slough of despond.

We have heard of James and John, but how much have we heard of Joseph of Cyprus and Ananias of Damascus? Then besides Mary, the mother of Jesus, there were all the other Marys — Peter's mother, James' mother, Lazarus' sister Mary and, of course, we mustn't forget Martha and Salome. (Behind every great man, so the saying goes, is a great woman — an encourager.) Let's not forget Tychicus and Philemon, Phoebe, Priscilla and Aquila, Rufus and his mother, Judas and Silas, among Paul's many helpers. Heaven alone will reveal the crucial contributions these encouragers made to the establishment of the early church.

Students in the class on spiritual gifts sip coffee as they wait for the class to begin. Megan, you will remember, has been depressed. The pastor had asked a deaconess to try to discover the problem. The deaconess spotted Megan's fellow classmate Ann as a likely person to come alongside and encourage her. Ann has taken Megan out for coffee a couple of times. Already Megan looks much more cheerful. Ann asks, 'Well, Megan, how did the week go?'

'Much better,' Megan replies! 'Oh, Monday and Tuesday were disasters! No end to washing! Our dryer went on the blink and it rained for two days. Fights between the kids. But knowing you were praying for me daily helped me crawl out of depression. Jerry still comes dragging home dead tired to flop in front of the box … but knowing you went through some of the same things with your family helps to lift my spirits.'

'That's great, Megan,' Ann responds. Ann doesn't realize that she has the gift of encouragement.

'The words of that solo you sang last Sunday kept echoing in my mind all week,' Megan continues. 'I couldn't forget the chorus about the Master's presence.'

'Well, I try to pick pieces that will be a blessing,' replies Ann. 'I may have some musical talent but I still don't see what that has to do with spiritual giftedness. Music is not in any of the lists!'

Ann's musical ability surfaced early. She learned to play the piano with rare skill. Violin followed. The congregation looks forward to her solos. But what has this got to do with encouragement? And how does she represent a multitude of Christians (I'm not talking just about those with musical talents) who don't feel they have any particular gift but go around spreading sunshine? Let us find out.

I. The meaning of the word 'encouragement'

Encouragement, as a gift, is mentioned only in Paul's epistle to the Romans. 'We have different gifts… If it is encouraging, let him encourage' (Rom. 12: 6,8). The Greek verb, *parakaleo,* combines two thoughts: *para,* to the side, and *kaleo,* to call. The Greek word literally means calling someone to one's side. It suggests bringing a word of encouragement or consolation.

Striving to portray the rich application of the word *parakaleo,* the AV translators used the English words 'exhort', 'comfort' or 'console'. I have not found any example where they used the word 'encouragement'. The NIV translators, responding to modern usage, almost invariably translate *parakaleo* as 'encouragement'. The word 'exhortation' had become so laden, in English usage, with overtones of a directive from a superior that a better word was needed. The word 'encouragement' conveys more nearly the original idea of a friend who comes alongside to uplift our spirits.

Paraclete, a title given by Christ to the Holy Spirit, is a construction of the same Greek word. Translations such as 'Counsellor' (NIV), 'Helper' (NASB) or 'Comforter' (AV) reflect the differing nuances of the Spirit's ministry among us. Fortunately, Jesus promised that the Holy Spirit would 'be with you for ever' (John 14:16). In this role he is 'called to one's side, to one's aid,' with 'capability or adaptability for giving aid... In the widest sense it signifies a succourer, comforter'[1] (see also John 14:26; 15:26; 16:7).

Several other Greek words convey the concept of encouragement. *Protrepeo* means to urge someone forward, to persuade and thus to encourage. 'When Apollos wanted to go to Achaia, the brothers encouraged him' (Acts 18:27). Various forms of *paramutheo* convey the idea of coming alongside with counsel or advice, consolation or tender comfort: 'The Jews who had been with Mary in the house, comforting her...' (John 11:31). 'Encourage the timid' (1 Thess. 5:14).

Both Greek and English usages reflect a broad concept. Webster defines encouragement as 'to give courage, hope or confidence to; hearten', as well as the more demonstrative element, 'to give support to; foster; help'.[2] 'Encouragement' literally means 'putting courage into'. When we encourage, as denoted in the Greek and reflected in English, we come alongside people to pour courage into them. A study of the usage of this word in the New Testament uncovers a broad field of ministry.

Definition of the gift

We can define encouragement as: that spiritual endowment that enables some men and women to instinctively sense when others need encouragement, and that moves them to come alongside with a word of comfort, courage, hope or rebuke, all with a view to inspiring spiritual progress and health.

II. The usage of the word 'encouragement'

A survey of the use of 'encouragement' in the context of the New Testament has led me to six conclusions.

1. The proper use of Scripture

Firstly, true encouragement arises from the proper use of Scripture. 'Everything that was written in the past was written to teach us, so that through endurance and the encouragement of the Scriptures we might have hope' (Rom. 15:4). In writing to the Colossians, Paul states, 'My purpose is that they may be encouraged in heart and united in love so that they may have the full riches of complete understanding...' (Col. 2:2). Understanding depends not only upon how we relate to other believers in love, but whether or not our hearts are encouraged! No wonder Timothy was exhorted to 'Preach the Word; be prepared in season and out of season; correct, rebuke and encourage — with great patience and careful instruction' (2 Tim. 4:2).

Encouragement, like other communication gifts, excavates no new mine of ministry materials but returns again and again to the primordial bedrock to quarry from the Word the raw materials necessary for a Spirit-led ministry.

2. The source of encouragement

While believers may be agents of encouragement, true consolation comes from the triune God. The Holy Spirit is the Comforter (John 14:16). 'The church throughout Judea, Galilee and Samaria ... was strengthened and encouraged by the Holy Spirit...' (Acts 9:31). Paul prays in similar vein about the two other members of the Godhead. 'May our Lord Jesus Christ himself and God our Father, who loved us and by his grace gave us eternal encouragement and good hope, encourage your hearts and strengthen you in every good deed and word' (2 Thess. 2:16-17).

3. The responsibility of all believers

Thirdly, responsibility for encouragement rests upon the shoulders of all believers. We read, 'Encourage one another daily'; 'Let us encourage one another'; and 'Encourage the timid' (Heb. 3:13; 10:25; 1 Thess. 5:14). Since God has linked believers together in the body of Christ they must speak only 'what is helpful for building others up' (Eph. 4:29). God calls all of us to a one-to-one ministry of speaking appropriate words of reassurance to one another. Paul sent Tychicus in person to encourage the Ephesian believers (Eph. 6:22). Since Tychicus excelled at encouragement, Paul also sent him to the Colossians to 'encourage your hearts' (Col. 4:8) .

By emphasizing the personal nature of the gift, I do not discount its use in a group setting. Teachers and preachers must join hands with individual Christians in a covenant of encouragement. In Antioch we read, 'Judas and Silas, who themselves were prophets, said much to encourage and strengthen the brothers' (Acts 15:32). Paul urged Timothy to encourage as well as rebuke in his preaching (2 Tim. 4:2). Peter encouraged his readers (1 Peter 5:12).

Encouragement in general, however, is a more personal ministry than preaching. Encouragement occurs even within the confines of our own hearts. Indeed, we must not expect to leave the uplifting of our spirits to others. Our devotional study of the Word ought to encourage us (Rom. 15:4). Paul urged Timothy to give attention to his own development (1 Tim. 4:15-16; 6:11-14,20; 2 Tim. 1:14; 2:1; etc.).

None of us may blame our own downward spiral of discouragement on others. In the same epistle in which the author exhorts believers to encourage one another, he commands them to individually assume responsibility for their flagging spirits: 'You have not yet resisted to the point of shedding your blood... Therefore strengthen your feeble arms and weak knees' (Heb. 12:4,12). The Hebrews had much more cause than we for discouragement! We must not let the failure of any church to provide an ideal climate of encouragement become an excuse for our own limping spirits.

4. The right words

Encouragement also involves well-chosen words. Something so obvious needs little emphasis, and yet we often forget self-evident truths. Paul exhorts the Ephesians to replace any hurtful and unhelpful words with words that 'benefit those who listen' (Eph. 4:29). I do not deny the important place of just being with people nor the blessing of a hand on our shoulder. Nevertheless there is nothing like the power of written or spoken words of encouragement: 'A word aptly spoken is like apples of gold in settings of silver' (Prov. 25:11).

While pastor at Long Branch I was fairly sure that the church and its people appreciated my ministry. Nevertheless, from time to time I grew discouraged. Words of encouragement at such a time did wonders to improve my attitude. Someone might comment after a morning service, 'Pastor, I'm praying for you every day.' Another might come by and talk about last Sunday's message. Suddenly, a ministry that had seemed hard and fruitless became worthwhile. To prepare for those inevitable times when the spirit droops, I keep an encouragement file of notes people have written.

We all need to have appreciation put into words. Since Gary Smalley and John Trent published their book, *The Gift Of Honor,* they have been inundated with letters. Many letters tell tragic stories of bitterness and insecurity that could be traced to the failure of parents to verbalize their love and encouragement. Smalley and Trent recount meeting 'Betty' on a plane. She was returning home with her pilot's wings after graduating from a military academy. This academic and career success which should have filled her with warm feelings of accomplishment had instead saddened her. On this occasion, as always, her father had failed to express any pride in her achievements. She had waited in vain all her life for any expression of approval.[3]

5. The goal of encouragement

Encouragement largely targets the emotional life of believers. Depression and dejection, heaviness and melancholy, sadness and fear, worry and timidity, as well as coldness and malaise of heart, like killer bees, sting and paralyse our spirits. These debilitating feelings occur so widely that God designed a special spiritual gift to offset their effects.

Encouragement brings comfort and consolation in the midst of grief and trouble (2 Cor. 1:3-7). Paul sent Timothy to the Thessalonians 'to strengthen and encourage you in your faith so that no one would be unsettled by these trials' (1 Thess. 3:2-3). Trials tend to upset us. The book of Hebrews and the epistles of Peter were written, in large part, to warn believers of their effects, and thus to encourage them.

When Christians are persecuted or facing difficulties they need encouragement, lest they become timid and shy away from their responsibilities (1 Thess. 5:14; Acts 15:32). Knowing that long service can have the same effect, Paul wrote to the Galatians, 'Let us not become weary in doing good, for at the proper time we will reap a harvest if we do not give up' (Gal. 6:9).

Encouragement injects new hope and confidence in the midst of weariness and dejection, new courage in the midst of timidity and fear. Despondency can touch off a downward spiral. 'See to it, brothers, that none of you has a sinful, unbelieving heart that turns away from the living God. But encourage one another daily ... so that none of you may be hardened by sin's deceitfulness' (Heb. 3:12-13). Throughout Hebrews we are warned about slipping back. No wonder the writer exhorts us to 'consider how we may spur one another on towards love and good deeds... Encourage one another' (Heb. 10:24-25).

The goal of encouragement, then, is to modify attitudes that arrest spiritual development. Encouraged individuals and churches grow (Acts 9:31). Negative emotions weaken our resolve and arrest our growth. We read about encouragement and spiritual strength in the same breath (Acts 9:31; 15:32; 2 Thess. 2:17). Dejection erodes the desire to grow. Reassurance gets the believer back on track. No wonder Paul wrote, 'encouraging, comforting and urging you to live lives worthy of God, who calls you into his kingdom and glory' (1 Thess. 2:12).

I am not denying that great men such as Job, Jeremiah and Jesus suffered agony and pain of soul. They went, however, to the source of encouragement by taking their respective sorrows to God in prayer. In Jesus' case the angels strengthened him.

6. Encouragement includes rebuke

Encouragement, since it is always truthful, may at times seem stern. The support we find in Scripture bears no resemblance to the sentimental 'Everything will be OK — You're a wonderful fellow' type of false optimism so popular in certain quarters. Encouragement is not positive thinking. It is not giving someone a little 'pep-talk'. It is not a technique like that used by salesmen to manipulate customers into feeling good about buying their product.

Sometimes, encouragement involves the use of seemingly harsh words. In the context of outright rebellion and wilfulness, stern rebuke is necessary. Some texts closely connect encouragement with rebuke (2 Tim. 4:2). Paul reminded Titus that 'He must hold firmly to the trustworthy message ... so that he can encourage others by sound doctrine and refute those who oppose it' (Titus 1:9). Here 'exhortation', the word used in the Authorized Version, fits.

Encouragement, in these contexts, may be couched in strong language. 'Encourage and rebuke with all authority. Do not let anyone despise you' (Titus 2:15). Biblical encouragers don't shrink from exposing sin. Of course, they don't leave those they rebuke in the dust. They reach down and help them up. But without rebuking those who stray so they can face their flight from the Spirit, uplift is impossible.

I am sure that some of those I have had to rebuke over the years — fortunately not a large number — thought my words harsh. In Pakistan, as field leader, and in Toronto, as pastor, I have been compelled from time to time to reprimand believers. This is a responsibility we may try to avoid, but cannot escape.

Encouragement, as we have seen, takes a variety of forms. In most cases it aims to lift our emotions. And that bears further consideration.

III. Encouragement and our emotional life

Too often our emotions overwhelm our reason. No wonder Solomon counsels, 'Above all else, guard your heart, for it is the wellspring of life' (Prov. 4:23). As we progress in sanctification we become less and less driven by every wind of feeling and more and more led by faith in the objective Word of God. As truth renews our minds, God sets us free (John 8:32; Rom. 12:2).

Jesus pointed to the heart as the poisoned spring from which flows all kinds of evil. He warned of envy and hatred, lust and all manner of evil thoughts. Without purity of heart we shall never be able to truly follow Christ by loving the Lord with all our hearts and our neighbour as ourselves. 'All the Law and the Prophets hang on these two commandments' (Matt. 22:37-40).

We have another problem. We are poor at diagnosing the condition of our own hearts. Jeremiah warned us about our hearts' capacity for distortion and self-deceit. We need external help to cleanse the fountain! When we wallow in discouragement, timidity or doubt we are in no condition to help ourselves. We desperately need someone to come alongside and lift us up.

Hebrews was written 'so that you will not grow weary and lose heart' (Heb. 12:3). Paul sent Tychicus to the Colossians 'to encourage your hearts' (Col. 4:8). Joseph of Cyprus 'encouraged them all to remain true to the Lord with all their hearts' (Acts 11:23). Encouragement, in its various forms, aims at neutralizing negative or destructive emotions that fester in the heart. Consider the various manifestations of encouragement.

1. Comfort

The apostle Paul did not want the Thessalonian believers 'to grieve like the rest of men, who have no hope' (1 Thess. 4:13). Since bottomless sorrow can be totally debilitating, he gave extensive teaching on the hope we have in the resurrection of the dead. He concludes that section by saying, 'Therefore encourage each other with these words' (1 Thess. 4:18; see also 1 Cor. 15). The Bible was written so that 'through endurance and the encouragement of the Scriptures we might have hope' (Rom. 15:4).

Separation from friends and loved ones, brought on either by travel or problems in relationships, often produces melancholy. The Corinthians had become estranged from the apostle Paul. Sorrow filled his heart. Concerning this period, when he travelled to Macedonia, Paul wrote, 'We were harassed at every turn — conflicts on the outside, fears within. But God, who comforts the downcast, comforted us by the coming of Titus, and not only by his coming but also by the comfort you had given him. He told us about your longing for me, your deep sorrow, your ardent concern for me, so that my joy was greater than ever... By all this we are encouraged' (2 Cor. 7:5-7,13). Titus was an encourager. News of the Corinthians' renewed concern dispelled sorrow. Troubles and trials, such as the apostle met in Macedonia, often increase the risk of discouragement.

Too often we overlook how others need encouragement. Then suddenly we find ourselves in the midst of troubles and we ache for comfort. Often those who have never suffered lack empathy. It almost seems as if we must personally go through suffering before we acquire skill in giving comfort. For this reason, God uses tribulation to teach us how to comfort others. 'Praise be to the ... God of all comfort who comforts us in all our troubles, so that we can comfort those in any trouble with the comfort we ourselves have received from God' (2 Cor. 1:3-4).

No wonder people who have suffered a lot often become great encouragers. Fanny Crosby, blind since infancy, wrote more hymns than any known author. According to Ira Sankey the hymns that she wrote, including 'Blessed assurance' and 'Saved by grace', contributed more to the success of the Moody-Sankey crusades than any other purely human factor.[4]

In spite of the accident that left her paralysed, Joni Eareckson Tada has become an encouragement to many. We may never really understand exactly how Joni feels but we must try. We desperately need to learn to empathize with those who are hospitalized, struck down with cancer or suddenly out of work. All need comfort.

2. Boldness

The early church, faced by grave threats to their existence, prayed that God would give them boldness (Acts 4:29). Paul wrote to Timothy to embolden him in service. He urged Thessalonian believers to 'encourage the timid' (1 Thess. 5:14). Thirty years ago, when I was a new Christian, I was fearful of witnessing until encouraged by an older Christian to join him in passing out tracts. Eventually I became confident enough to volunteer for missionary service.

3. Inspiration to persevere

All believers must 'fight the good fight of faith', in order to persevere. The temptation to give up, which we all deal with at some time, may arise from a cooling of zeal, from unconfessed sin, from nagging doubts, or from the exhaustion of dealing with a myriad of difficulties.

Hebrews repeatedly encourages believers, who are in danger of giving up, to persevere. We are warned about having 'a sinful, unbelieving heart that turns away from the living God'. The antidote to this malaise of the spirit is to 'encourage one another daily ... so that none of you may be hardened by sin's deceitfulness' (Heb. 3:12-13). Since coldness steals over us so subtly, we must commit ourselves to watch out for signs of sin and unbelief in each other.

Hebrews describes the antidote: 'Let us not give up meeting together, as some are in the habit of doing, but let us encourage one another — and all the more as you see the Day approaching' (Heb. 10:25). Joint services for prayer, worship, teaching and fellowship build a wall of protection around us that keeps at bay the dragon of discouragement. Since we are exhorted to 'consider how we may spur one another on towards love and good deeds', the pattern should be planned and not haphazard (Heb. 10:24).

Sanctification is like swimming upstream. It takes constant effort. When discouragement sets in, we may slacken our efforts and begin to drift downstream. Carelessness leads to small sins. Small sins magnify our insensitivity to the Lord. Our hearts in turn become hardened to the things of God. Before long, fully fledged rebellion may produce unbelief. An active ministry of encouragement seeks to rescue believers from this backsliding process before carelessness leads to open sin.

4. Rebuke and rescue

When a sinner does fall, the ministry of encouragement wades into the muddy waters of rebellion with a view to rescue. In the early stages gentleness may turn the tide. Later strong rebuke may become necessary, leading ultimately to church discipline. Timothy was exhorted to 'be prepared in season and out of season; correct, rebuke and encourage — with great patience' (2 Tim. 4:2).

The ministry of encouragement cannot be divorced from rebuke and correction. Perhaps this explains why the translators of the Authorized Version used the word 'exhortation' instead of 'encouragement'. Exhortation carries more the idea of earnest urging or warning than that of comfort and encouragement. The biblical concept encompasses a whole spectrum of ideas.

The word denotes spurring believers on in their faith, whether that involves gentle comfort or stern rebuke. If backsliding is the problem, a serious warning may be more in order than words designed to lift the spirit. Although Hebrews is a book of great encouragement, nevertheless it contains more warnings than any other epistle. We read, for example, 'Do not harden your hearts.' 'You are slow to learn ... you ought to be teachers... You need milk!' 'Strengthen your feeble arms... Our God is a consuming fire' (Heb. 3:7; 5:11,12; 12:12,29).

Occasionally, after a lengthy process of trying to help problem Christians, I have finally been compelled to use hard words. Here are some examples I remember with a certain sadness:

> 'Sister, your belief that it is God's will for you to marry this man is but a deceptive expression of your own desires.'
>
> 'Brother, outbursts of anger like those you have displayed are sin. Christ declares that they violate the Ten Commandments. This sin is harming your witness and the work of the gospel here.'
>
> 'Sister, what you are telling me about "X" should be kept private and confidential unless carefully substantiated. If substantiated, you have a responsibility to first go to "X" about the matter. Have you talked this over with "X"? ... No. Then, you must refrain from this kind of sharing. It is the sin of gossip.'

Where rebuke is heeded and the Spirit grants repentance, the encourager stands ready with the balm of restoration. Jesus restored Peter. Paul restored the sorrowful Corinthians, and you and I must do the same.

Many of us have been uplifted by the writing and ministry of Gordon MacDonald, a well-known pastor in the United States. We were distressed to hear of his fall. We seem to live in a day in which Christian leaders fall like tenpins all around us. But some time after his fall, MacDonald wrote *Rebuilding Your Broken World*. It tells the heartening story of his forgiveness and restoration. He dedicated the book, 'To Gail and the "Angels" — the inner core of many who have helped me rebuild my broken world.' By this he meant his wife and 'the incredible team of godly men who long ago surrounded Gail and me and determined that here was one broken world that was going to be rebuilt'.[5] That this team was made up of encouragers, there can be little doubt.

The very fact that this book has been written is encouraging. We don't hear a lot about restoration, but, as MacDonald says so poignantly, the Bible records the stories of hundreds of men and women who fell but were restored by God. There was Abraham who lied, Jacob who deceived, Moses who murdered, David who lusted and Mary Magdalene who prostituted her body, to name but a few! The restoring power of grace tenderly offered through the hands of an encourager does more than most things to make me shout 'Hallelujah!' Where would you and I be without the restoring grace of God?

The heart is the wellspring of life. Encouragers come alongside us and strive to neutralize the harmful and destructive emotions that threaten to discourage, depress and dampen our spirits. Encouragers seek to chase away the cold storms of unbelief that rattle the windows of our faith.

Let's return to the metaphor of the body. The glandular system produces hormones to keep our body operating in balance. The attitudes of our heart — love, hatred, envy, sadness and joy — resemble the hormones that provide the motivation, or lack of it, for our Christian life. Jesus preached a sermon about these attitudes. Paul dedicated the thirteenth chapter of 1 Corinthians to the pursuit of them. And the Holy Spirit concentrates on producing in us fruitful attitudes.

Let's look at the profile of an encourager. His name was Joseph of Cyprus. Do you know him?

IV. An example of encouragement — Joseph of Cyprus

An immigrant from Cyprus, Joseph the Levite became an important figure in the infant church in Jerusalem. Joseph's spiritual gift became so evident that he came to be called Barnabas, meaning 'Son of Encouragement' (see Acts 4: 36-37). We next meet this man in Acts 9.

1. Encouraging an unusual convert

Converted on the road to Damascus, fleeing the city in a basket — Saul, the Pharisee, could hardly have been a more improbable convert. When he arrived in Jerusalem, the disciples refused to accept his profession of faith. Barnabas, however, immediately stepped in to encourage Saul. After listening to his story, 'Barnabas

took him and brought him to the apostles,' explaining to them what
had happened (Acts 9:27).

Encouragers realize that a failure to affirm new Christians can
start even the most genuine convert on a downward spiral. A
struggling alcoholic, a divorced woman, an unemployed youth, an
old reprobate — encouragers take chances with questionable people
who profess faith in Christ.

At great risk to his own reputation, Barnabas commended Saul
to the assembly. His word counted and Saul was given the right hand
of fellowship. As a direct result Saul began 'speaking boldly in the
name of the Lord. He talked and debated with the Grecian Jews, but
they tried to kill him' (Acts 9:28-29). Convinced now of his
sincerity, the Jerusalem brothers took him down to the seaport of
Cæsarea and shipped him off, for his own protection, to his home
town of Tarsus.

Encouragers watch out for new converts. When God converted
me from agnosticism at nineteen, I was completely at sea about the
Christian faith. I had been a member of a large liberal church since
childhood. Fortunately, a burly hockey player, recently converted
himself, saw my name on one of a stack of decision-cards in the
minister's office. Taking me under his wing he introduced me to his
sister, also a new Christian, and a group of believers that met in his
home for Bible study. My probing questions didn't dismay this
bunch of encouragers. Even though real faith in the total inspiration
of the Bible took time, they were patient. New converts need lots of
patience!

2. Encouraging a non-conformist church

The stoning of Stephen kindled the fires of persecution and scattered
believers to the four winds. Wherever they went they took the good
news.

In the northern town of Antioch transplanted believers shocked
the Jewish churches by the innovation of their witness. Up to this
point scattered Christians, all from a Hebrew background, had
spoken only to Jews. They believed that their message was a Jewish
gospel. In Antioch the unthinkable happened. Some converts shared
their faith with Greeks. As a result, 'A great number of people
believed and turned to the Lord' (Acts 11:21).

News from Antioch stirred up a storm of controversy in the very conservative and very Judaistic Jerusalem congregation. Church leaders expected new converts to be circumcised and continue to keep the Jewish law.

Wisely, they sent Barnabas to Antioch to assess the situation. 'When he arrived and saw the evidence of the grace of God, he was glad and encouraged them all to remain true to the Lord with all their hearts' (Acts 11:23). Although the new church failed to live up to Jewish expectations, Barnabas rejoiced in the genuine faith he found there. He knew that this new church needed both teaching and support. 'He was a good man, full of the Holy Spirit and faith,' and 'He encouraged them all.'

Those with the gift of encouragement have considerable tolerance both for new Christians and for non-traditional expressions of faith. Instead of raising the eyebrows and muttering, 'But we don't do that,' or 'We've never done that before,' they affirm those whose faith is genuine — even though, at first, it may seem strange. Encouragers have great faith in the transforming grace of God.

Churches grow in a warm climate of encouragement. In Antioch, through Barnabas' support, 'A great number of people were brought to the Lord' (Acts 11:24). A steady diet of condemnation, introspection and challenge leaves believers limp and uncertain. A pastor who knows when to pour on the balm of comfort and encouragement will do much to hearten and inspire his congregation. Too many congregations languish from a steady diet of exhortation and condemnation!

3. Encouraging an untried teacher

As Barnabas continued to preach and teach in Antioch, he began to realize that he needed help. Even though several years had elapsed, he remembered Paul, whose untapped potential had so impressed him. (Encouragers have an uncanny ability to recognize potential in people that many of us might overlook.)

Although Paul was untried as a teacher, Barnabas set off immediately for 'Tarsus to look for Saul'. Finding the famous convert, he persuaded him to return with him to Antioch where a team ministry developed. 'For a whole year Barnabas and Saul met with the church and taught great numbers of people' (Acts 11:26).

Encouragers are team-players, always seeking to involve and inspire others.

In the years that followed we notice a strange change in this team. The order in which their names appear in the record illustrates this development. At first the team is labelled 'Barnabas and Saul' (see Acts 11:26,30; 12:25; 13:2,7). But after the first stop on their first missionary journey together Paul's ministry so far eclipses that of Barnabas that we read, 'From Paphos, Paul and his companions sailed to Perga' (Acts 13:13). Subsequently we read, 'Paul and Barnabas…' (Acts 13:42,43,46; 14:1, etc.).

It would appear that Barnabas, true son of encouragement that he was, affirmed Paul's greater gifts. From this point on Paul's ministry soared. During this time he wrote his priceless epistles. Would he ever have embarked on his great journeys or written his letters without Barnabas' encouragement at this crucial juncture in his life? Encouragers of this sort do not mind playing second fiddle. Encouragement, by its very nature, is a gift that succeeds if others develop. Encouragers cannot afford to be jealous. The people to whom they minister often receive more attention than they do. Encouragers usually dwell in the shadow of great men and women.

4. Encouraging an unfaithul worker

Encouragers, however, not only fade into the background but must also handle misunderstanding. As Paul's ministry soared, a rift developed with his old team-mate over John Mark.

John Mark, a young man from the big city of Jerusalem, had returned with Barnabas and Paul after their excursion to Jerusalem. Subsequently he joined them on their first missionary journey. An alien culture and conflict with sorcery, encountered at their first stop in Cyprus, must have been too much for John. No doubt homesick for Jerusalem and his mother's home-cooking, he abandoned the missionary team and returned home. John Mark's venture into ministry ended in ignominy.

When Paul and Barnabas laid plans for a second journey, Barnabas recommended that they give John Mark another chance. But 'Paul did not think it wise to take him, because he had deserted them in Pamphylia and had not continued with them in the work' (Acts 15:38). A heated argument ensued. Barnabas defended John

Mark while Paul refused outright even to consider allowing John Mark to accompany them. As a result, 'They parted company. Barnabas took Mark and sailed for Cyprus, but Paul chose Silas and left, commended by the brothers to the grace of the Lord' (Acts 15:39-40).

This is the only time we see Barnabas in a 'sharp disagreement' (Acts 15:39). Like all of us, Barnabas had feet of clay. He could have been at fault here. Since Paul received the church's commendation while Barnabas and Mark are not mentioned in this regard, it would seem that the church sided with Paul. After all, John Mark was Barnabas' nephew. Softness for a relative could have coloured Barnabas' judgement. But I personally believe that Barnabas did what his spiritual gift impelled him to do.

Encouragers seek to restore those who fall. They don't give up easily. Barnabas had to do something for John Mark or bury his gift. Paul, on the other hand, would not tolerate failure. I wouldn't be surprised if his thorn in the flesh and the multitude of sufferings he enumerates in 2 Corinthians didn't mellow him and make him more compassionate as the years rolled by.

Whatever happened in the ensuing years, of one thing we are can be sure — John Mark was rescued. Paul in later years writes to Timothy, 'Get Mark and bring him with you, because he is helpful to me in my ministry' (2 Tim. 4:11). Barnabas, son of consolation, rescued and restored Mark to usefulness. His faith in Mark, I am sure, went a long way to encouraging this timid young man to develop his gifts.

We owe a great debt to Barnabas. The Gospel of Mark stands as an outstanding monument to his ministry of encouragement. But even more astounding, thirteen epistles and one Gospel owe their existence, in some measure at least, to a man from Cyprus, called Joseph, who came to be nicknamed Barnabas!

None of us is perfect. We all fall. And when we fall we need men and women like Barnabas who will come alongside to help us up.

V. Developing the gift of encouragement

The butcher, the baker, the candlestick-maker — everyone needs encouragement. And yet it is not all that common. Tim Hansel describes visiting a large church to listen to a Christmas presentation of a Bach oratorio. The music thrilled him. At the end he went forward to congratulate the elderly man who had conducted the entire performance as well as played the organ. Grabbing his arm he exclaimed, 'It was wonderful! It made my whole Christmas season! It was the best performance I've ever heard!'[6]

Without warning the elderly choir director began to weep. Fearing he had deeply offended him, Tim Hansel apologized profusely. He explained that he was not a member, and hadn't meant to offend him. As he sought to get away through the crowd the choir director caught his sleeve and explained: 'Son, you just caught me by surprise. You see, I've been here eighteen years and you are the first person who's ever done that.'[7] Imagine, a church with three or four thousand members and none had thought to encourage the choir director!

From that point on Tim Hansel resolved never to overlook another opportunity to offer encouragement. We need to make the same resolution. To fail is to disobey the Master.

1. Obeying the command to encourage

It seems hardly necessary to rehearse the biblical commands to encourage one another. But if we were obeying them, there would not be so many disheartened Christians around. And I have met a lot of discouraged believers — wives and husbands, Sunday School teachers, youth workers, college students, bedridden senior citizens, and not a few missionaries and pastors. Behind a brave front despondency hangs heavy in many a heart.

No wonder the Bible commands us, 'Encourage one another' (1 Thess. 4:18); 'Encourage one another daily, as long as it is called Today, so that none of you may be hardened by sin's deceitfulness' (Heb. 3:13); and 'Let us consider how we may spur one another on towards love and good deeds... Let us encourage one another' (1 Thess. 4:18; Heb. 10:24,25).

If we walk in obedience, we shall embark on a ministry of mutual encouragement, and that fosters the discovery of gifts. But how, you may ask, can we develop such a ministry? What do we actually do? First of all, we need to watch out for those needing help.

2. Sensitivity to need

Spiritual gifts, you will recall from chapter 5, focus on meeting various needs. The Holy Spirit sensitizes those with the gift of encouragement to react to the feelings and moods of others.

Many things may signal the possible presence of melancholy. Sickness, overwork, lack of fellowship, grief, failure, loss of a job, unconfessed sin and poor devotional habits are only some of the circumstances that provoke discouragement. Personality and background, as well, may affect people's ability to cope joyfully. Depression tends to be more habitual in those with an introspective, legalistic or perfectionist personality. In people with these tendencies, a deep malaise may settle on their souls.

Barnabas' example hints at the kind of people who need affirmation. New converts, such as Saul, non-traditional churches, such as that in Antioch, untried teachers, such as Saul, and unfaithful workers, like John Mark, call out the best efforts in encouragers. Encouragers, of course, don't concentrate only on the more obvious needs. Everyone needs encouragement. Those who seem the most self-reliant and persevering need encouragement lest they grow weary in well-doing. We never know when an Elijah, a David or a Jeremiah needs an uplifting word.

3. Is too much encouragement harmful?

Perhaps you think I am overdoing this encouragement bit. 'Surely we are not babysitters?' you might ask. 'When are we going to get it all together and stand on our own two feet?'

Could it be that too much encouragement would hinder the development of reliance on God? Does it pander to self-pity or cause pride? Clearly, encouragement does not mean overlooking defects or distorting the truth. Encouragement is a fruit of biblical love, love that is both honest and kind. If encouragement serves to inflate our pride or hinder the development of spiritual self-reliance, it must be wrong. Consider the issues.

The felt need many have for 'affirmation', coupled with today's fixation on 'low self-esteem', could be the fall-out of a generation brought up to believe that praise led to pride. 'Good work is its own reward,' we were taught. Many of our forefathers, Christians among them, believed in a 'pull-yourself-up-by-your-own-bootstraps' brand of self-reliance. This bred a fierce independence that no doubt won the west and contributed to the strength of Western industry. But at what cost?

Smalley and Trent in their book, *The Gift Of Honor,* tell the story of George. His parents instilled in him the belief that he would make it on his own, or not make it at all. George vividly remembers how, when he was a boy, three older toughs beat him up badly while his father watched from the front porch. When he asked his father why he hadn't come to his aid, his father replied, 'No one can fight your battles for you.'[8]

George became strong and self-reliant. Unfortunately, he never learned to reach out to others, even to his wife and children. Deep down he longed for words of acceptance and appreciation. He was hungry for love even while his tough-guy image of self-reliance held people at a distance. His marriage groaned under the strain and threatened to shatter.[9]

This kind of fierce independence fails to satisfy our deep hunger for relationship. Behind an image of self-sufficiency, independent people often hide insecurity and self-doubt. What a waste! God never made us to be independent. Otherwise why would he have created Eve? Why would he have bothered to walk with Adam and Eve in the cool of the evening?

Redemption aims to restore our broken relationships with God and with our neighbours by creating a new interdependence. The church is the context of that restoration. The image of the church as a body vividly illustrates our interdependence on each other and on Christ.

Our society elevates independence as if it were a cardinal virtue, while in reality self-centred independence is one of the premier sins of Western culture. If we could strip away the layers of pretence, we would find that many a brave front hides an empty heart, hungry for love and encouragement. It took me a long time to shake off the legacy of my own 'stiff-upper-lip, Everything is OK' childhood training.

In my younger years I quickly learned not to expect praise for schoolwork completed or work done in the garden. Striving for affirmation but never achieving the necessary perfection, my soul often got bogged down in the slough of despond. Melancholy and insecurity dogged my youth. Even after all these years, I sometimes wake up in the morning with a vague sense of doom, of failure, hanging over my sleepy soul. It comes from deep in my psyche.

Experience, first in mission administration, and then in a church pastorate, has confirmed that my case is far from unique. Until recently — now social welfare has swung to the opposite extreme — our culture indoctrinated us to avoid admission of need. As boys, we were taught that only wimps and sissies admit weakness and need comfort. No wonder most mask their neuroses and insecurities behind a stoic countenance.

In reality, everyone needs encouragement from time to time. To appreciate encouragement is not weakness. After all, the returning Master in the parables was wont to say, 'Well done.'

If we would become encouragers, we need to take a chance and assume everyone needs encouragement — they probably do! But you may ask, 'How do we actually carry on a ministry of encouragement?' Here is where we need creativity.

4. Creative encouragement

Encouragement, as we saw earlier, is a Spirit-given ability to come alongside someone with words of edification. But in order to do that, the encourager first learns to listen. Listening is the encourager's golden key. Without it, he or she will find it almost impossible to open a window of insight into a person's inner struggles. Real listening is hard work. It is rare. Paul Tournier believes that most conversations are 'dialogues of the deaf'. By that he meant that in conversation we seldom listen to what others say. Instead, while another person takes a turn at conversing, we often daydream or plan our next rejoinder.

Fredrick Faber wrote, 'Kind listening is often an act of the most delicate interior mortification.' How so? To really listen we will have to deny our own agenda and crucify our longing to get our point across in order to concentrate fully on the concerns of the other person.

Real listening takes time. Before we can really understand people, we need to develop a friendly relationship with them. That will probably mean inviting them home for lunch or taking them out for coffee. Of course, chatting after a church service is a good start.

We shall want to learn about their homes and hobbies, their work and families.

An article in *Power* magazine gives several other suggestions for the would-be Barnabas. First, it suggests we *express appreciation* to people for what they have done. Sadly, few people say thanks — even though expressions of appreciation are powerful encouragement tools.

The *Power* article suggests *praying with people* as another way of encouraging. Instead of parting with an 'I'll pray for you', we could stop and actually pray for them. Prayer encourages.

Thirdly, we should *ask for specific suggestions* on practical things we can do. It is not enough to say, 'Just give me a call if you need help.' People often interpret such an indefinite statement as a polite way of breaking off a conversation. Instead, ask what the present need actually is. Offer to bring in a casserole meal, or wash clothes, or do whatever is needed. We encourage when we show our concern by doing practical things for people. [10]

Sharing a verse that has touched our heart or talking about a book we have just read should be added to the list of ways to encourage. Sending a note in which you have written down a few thoughts or copied appropriate verses can do a lot to lift the spirits. (The encouragement file in which I drop the heartening notes people have sent me has proved to me the value of a written note.)

Fifthly, we can encourage by carefully choosing whom we *sit next to* in church. It is great to sit with friends or family, but if we all do that many lonely or discouraged people, along with a host of visitors and new Christians, will warm an isolated pew. By sitting selectively, we affirm our interest in different people.

Sixthly, many encouragers will want to *use their telephone* to spread cheer. Just before a student faces an important test, phone up with a promise of prayer. Before someone faces surgery, phone up and say, 'I am thinking of you. Our family will be praying for you tomorrow when you face surgery.' Shut-ins can be reached by phone. People overlooked at church may be rescued from feeling that no one cares by your phone call.

Finally there is *music*. Music, rightly used, can powerfully encourage the saints. Think of the choir leader who proved such a blessing to Tim Hansen, but who himself had never been encouraged.

It is no accident that the command to 'Be filled with the Spirit' immediately precedes an exhortation to sing. A ministry of musical encouragement is one evidence of that filling. 'Speak to one another with psalms, hymns and spiritual songs. Sing and make music in your heart to the Lord, always giving thanks to God the Father for everything…' (Eph. 5:18-20). Isn't it interesting that when we sing to one another we make music to the Lord as well? God rejoices when we speak to one another in song.

How many times have your spirits been raised by music? It might have been 'A mighty fortress is our God,' or 'Blessed assurance,' or 'Amazing grace,' or one of the psalms set to music. Hymns serve not only as vehicles of praise but also as channels of mutual encouragement. And no wonder!

Hymns often reflect the comfort men and women have found in trying circumstances. Many of us have heard how the author of 'It is well with my soul,' wrote the hymn on a ship in the Atlantic over the spot where his family had perished in a storm. Luther's 'A mighty fortress' resounds with the victory of the Reformation in an age 'with devils filled'. Fredrik Blom wrote, 'He the pearly gates will open,' after restoration from deep sin that sent him to prison. Our hymn-books abound in encouragement!

Ann's eyes grow moist as she ponders this fact. Ann, you will remember, is a student in the class on spiritual gifts. Up to this point she had been puzzled about her own giftedness. Skilled as a pianist, violinist and soloist, she has wondered where she fits in the ministry of the kingdom. Megan's happy face as she recounted how the solo Ann had sung the previous week kept brightening her gloomy week cast a warm glow over Ann's puzzled mind.

'I do believe God has given me the gift of encouragement,' she muses. 'I'm going to use my musical abilities to encourage and exhort.' Few of us have musical gifts to match Ann's, but we can all develop a ministry of encouragement.

Conclusion

Encouragement is an art. Be creative. Remember, your encouragement may make a great difference in the growth of another Christian. Jonathan's friendship made the difference in David's life. Nathan's harsh rebuke — in marked contrast to Jonathan's kind words — also contributed mightily to David's growth in God. Barnabas blessed both Paul and the writer of the second Gospel. You never know where your encouragement may lead. Take the plunge. Be an encourager.

In a sense encouragement is to salvation what after-sales service is to making a sale. Have you ever been frustrated in your efforts to get good service for the car or the washing machine you purchased? 'Salesmen and insurance agents always display great enthusiasm in selling their goods ... but poor after-sales service' is common.[11] Once you pay your money it is hard to find the same enthusiasm for service and repairs!

In our churches we put a lot of effort into winning lost men and women to Christ. New converts also, I trust, get considerable attention. But what about those same converts five, ten, fifteen or fifty years later? Conversion occurs in an instant; sanctification takes a lifetime. All of us need encouragement whether we are new believers or seasoned saints. Lifelong encouragement provides the spiritual 'after-sales-service' that we all need. Whether you have the gift of encouragement or not, begin your own personal encouragement ministry.

God's history — not the history we know and read in school — highlights the names of encouragers. Have you ever heard of Edward Kimble, who led Dwight L. Moody to Christ? How about Norman Harrison, through whom Theodore Epp bowed to the Saviour? Do we remember the name of William Carey's crippled sister, who held the ropes of intercession for so many years?

We don't know these people. God does. He keeps a different kind of record than we do. In that record the role of those who serve in the wings shines as brightly as those who ascend the pulpit. Probably we shall never be able to change all this but we can spread the word that the gift of encouragement and other inconspicuous gifts of the same type are as precious as gold in the presence of God.

The serving gifts, which follow, are closely linked to encouragement. Helps and hospitality, administration and leadership, faith and discernment, as well as giving and mercy, all promote encouragement. Perhaps one of these is your special spiritual gift. But before you read on, return to your gift-chart and fill in the columns that relate to the gift of encouragement itself.

Part III
The serving gifts

17.
The serving gifts: an introduction

As children we heard the story of Chicken Little, who went around crying, 'The sky is falling! The sky is falling!' If the sky is not falling, the stars certainly are. Political luminaries fall from grace as scandal dogs their steps. The gambling of baseball heroes and the abuse of steroids by Olympic athletes catch the headlines. Gossip columns probe the private lives of the royal family.

Evangelicals have felt a certain smug satisfaction about being above all that — until, in the eighties, the tabloids detailed the fall of, first, the Bakers and then Jimmy Swaggart. Of course, those of us from non-charismatic churches comforted ourselves with the thought that our theology would insulate us from similar scandals. Then some of our own heroes began to fall and some of our own pastors quietly slipped away under a cloud! Now we ask, 'Why?'

Philip Yancey puts his finger on the real issue: 'Maybe the underlying problem behind the scandals is that we have distorted the kingdom of God by training our spotlight not on the servants, but on the stars.'[1] As Christians we have too often become hero worshippers just like our contemporaries. We have our 'star preachers' and our favourite Bible teachers. Is our hero worship really that much different from what we find in the culture of the world at large?

Spectator sport promotes hero worship in athletes. The entertainment world creates its own idols — Elvis Presley, the Beatles, Arnold Swartzeneggar. The craving for entertainment demands ever more elaborate theme parks, and Disneyland-type meccas sprout like mushrooms across the Western world. No wonder, then, that a generation of spectators demands that church too, become 'user-friendly,' 'consumer-oriented'.

How dangerous! How contrary to the nature of the church. God's *ekklesia* — his called-out bride, should seek his will, not parrot the trends and whims of society at large. Worship is not a consumer product to be evaluated on the basis of its entertainment value. The kingdom of God grows through participants, not spectators; servants, not stars. Servants are the real heroes.

Who are these servant-heroes? Some famous preachers and evangelists who maintain a humble walk may be among them, but the majority come from the ranks of those unsung servants who are the church's foot-soldiers. Good Samaritans, the foot-washers, those who serve with a glass of cold water, a visit, a meal, a pair of shoes — these are the kingdom's heroes.

Throughout this book, I have sought to emphasize servanthood. In a sense all the gifts are serving gifts. 'Each one should use whatever gift he has received to serve others, faithfully administering God's grace in its various forms' (1 Peter 4:10.) If we fail to exhibit a servantlike attitude we exalt ourselves above the Paraclete who dwells within to serve as our Comforter. If we fail to embrace servanthood we make ourselves greater than Christ, who took 'the very nature of a servant' and showed us the way by taking up a basin and towel to wash the disciples' feet. Surely we cannot refuse to emulate the Spirit or the Son!

But if all the gifts are servant gifts, why classify seven as 'serving gifts'? We find support for this distinction in the very text that emphasizes universal servanthood. We read, 'Serve others... If anyone speaks, he should do it as one speaking the very words of God. If anyone serves, he should do it with the strength God provides, so that in all things God may be praised through Jesus Christ' (1 Peter 4:11-12). The distinction is a practical one. It draws attention to our need for some to concentrate on communication while others bend their energies to general works of service. One group of gifts undergirds the other. Without serving gifts, speaking gifts may seem impractical, and the church a place of hollow words. Likewise, without the speaking gifts, the serving gifts are rendered mute and the gospel loses its silver tongue. Nothing less than a balanced mobilization of all gifts edifies the body of Christ and glorifies God.

The general gifts of service are helps and hospitality, giving and mercy, faith and discernment, and administration or leadership. Each gift focuses ministry skill on a certain area of need. To some the Holy Spirit gives a willingness to help anywhere, hence the gift of general helpfulness. In others the Spirit arouses a more special-ized concern, for instance, a concern for those who suffer, as exemplified in the gift of mercy. In this way we develop gifts that fit us for our particular niche.

Everyone travels along a similar route. Even those who minister in the spotlight as preachers or pastors must go through the same process of development and discovery. If not, danger lurks. Speak-ing gifts, no less than serving gifts, develop best in the boot camp of practical service.

Kent and Barbara Hughes in a perceptive book, *Liberating Ministry From the Success Syndrome,* describe a time of discour-agement. The success they had expected in a new church did not materialize. Kent was tempted to give up the ministry. Instead, they turned to the Word to discover what God said about success. Faithfulness, prayer, godly attitudes and holy lives, they found, characterize biblical success. Too often, in our hero-worshipping age, we measure success in terms of concrete statistics such as the number of baptisms, the number of conversions, or the visible tasks accomplished or the committees formed. The Hughes rediscovered that success is simply serving, in whatever capacity, in whatever way.[2]

Kent Hughes illustrates his point from the life of Samuel Brengle, who left a fine pastorate to join William Booth's fledgling Salvation Army. General Booth accepted his services reluctantly, saying, 'You've been your own boss too long.' Nevertheless, he set Brengle to work cleaning the boots of other trainees. 'Discouraged, Brengle said to himself, "Have I followed my own fancy across the Atlantic in order to black boots?" And then, as in a vision, he saw Jesus bending over the feet of rough, unlettered fishermen. "Lord," he whispered, "you washed their feet; I will black their shoes."'[3]

When Brengle accepted polishing dirty boots as from the Master, he opened his life up to learning about true service. Subsequently he went on to become a humble disciple.

Being a servant is not easy, is it? But if we want to save our life, Jesus said, we will have to lose it. The way of service leads down to the cross of self-denial. There, below the cross, our distinctions fade. Whether we be pastor or doorkeeper, deacon or kneeling saint matters little. The servant attitude, or lack of it, crowns our work with success or failure. Jesus notes what we do but sees past the pulpit or broom to plumb the motives of our hearts. If he finds love expressed in humble and practical concern, he smiles and says, 'Well done, good and faithful servant!'

Kent and Barbara Hughes discovered that, when they purified their concept of success, ministry became a blessing instead of a burden. Service on the Master's terms is sweet indeed.

What can rival the joy of knowing that one is both pleasing God and helping to meet real need? God, who is no man's debtor, fills our cup to overflowing when we serve. Tracing spiritual hunger and thirst in the Bible, Lawrence Crabb has developed a theory to explain human unhappiness. Men and women, he believes, hunger and thirst for secure relationships and for a sense of impact on the world around them that makes them feel significant. Broken relationships shake their sense of security and churn up a cauldron of emotional misery. Futility and purposelessness likewise create a sense of emptiness. A restored relationship with God brings security, while joining with God in the work of the kingdom satisfies our desire for significance. Too often we seek happiness by amassing possessions and using people. In the resultant emptiness we wonder why we feel dissatisfied.

Concerning our need to serve God Crabb says, 'We were created to be a part of God's design. In Christ, we have been re-created to participate in the clean-up campaign... We thirst to be a part of the eternal plan, to make a lasting difference in our world. We long for impact... We long to minister to others. We feel whole and good when we do. Ministry satisfies our longing for impact [significance].'[4]

God created us to glory in service. We shall be miserable until we do. Without a servantlike attitude we shall never feel fulfilled and significant. Futility and emptiness will gnaw at our innards. Finding a sense of fulfilment is, of course, not the reason why we want to serve Christ, but it is a wonderful benefit which God, in grace, throws in as a gentle reward.

We have come full circle. Spiritual gifts develop in a climate of unselfish service. But spiritual gifts, unconsciously, serve us too! They provide just what we ourselves need most. They satisfy the longings of our hearts for impact and significance. The way up to joy and gladness leads down through the valley of servanthood. 'Whoever wants to find his life must lose it.'

It is not hard to see why many Christians are miserable. Their lack of commitment to selfless service feeds their misery.

There is no other way
To be happy in Jesus,
But to trust and obey.

I know you will want to get down out of the spectator stands into the field of Christian service. Learning to be helpful is a good place to start!

18.
Helps and hospitality

While machismo marks leaders in the world at large, humility and gentleness grace those who lead the King's battalions. The pictures of a host of believers who love humble service hang in heaven's hall of heroes. Some become well known as great servant-leaders. Others serve in anonymity. My wife, Mary Helen, expects two pictures to be in that heroic gallery.

Thirty years have not dimmed Mary Helen's appreciation for two women who demonstrated happy servanthood during one of her hardest weeks. Exhausted from labour and recovery, she had just returned to our tiny one-room apartment with Stephen, our first child. I was doing an assignment in a church in Michigan, USA as part of my missionary training. Far from family and friends, financially broke and stretched in the daily round of church duties, we didn't know how we would be able to cope.

God sent two women with the gift of helpfulness. Every day Carolyn Philippe, a busy working mother, came in, gathered up whatever clothes needed washing and took them away. Next day, back they came, clean and pressed. Every evening Lois Stout brought in a delicious meal for our supper. The practical help of these two women saw us through a very difficult ten days.

They not only exhibited the gift of helpfulness. Both served the Lord in a variety of capacities. One worked in the church office and conducted Bible studies. The other kept busy in youth work and Sunday School. As the years passed, their giftedness developed in additional directions. The Holy Spirit often develops our specific giftedness by leading us through a growth process that begins with being generally available.

Helpfulness and hospitality, and other gifts that follow, are not much in the limelight. They are often overlooked. To counter this attitude Paul writes, 'You are the body of Christ, and each one of you is a part of it' (1 Cor. 12:27). 'And if the ear should say, "Because I am not an eye, I do not belong to the body," it would not for that reason cease to be part of the body. If the whole body were an eye, where would the sense of hearing be? ... On the contrary, those parts of the body that seem to be weaker are indispensable, and the parts that we think are less honourable we treat with special honour' (1 Cor. 12:16-17,22-23).

In God's scale of values, position means nothing, while faithfulness in fulfilling our task, whatever it is, means everything. If we fail to appreciate that, gifts that carry no official position in the church lose their importance. We dare not allow that to happen. These gifts are indispensable, as Mary Helen and I discovered through two women with the gift of helpfulness.

I. The gift of helpfulness

Of the general gift of helpfulness Paul commands, 'If it is serving let him serve' (Rom. 12:7). This gift, variously called 'helps', or 'service', or 'ministry', occupies a crucial place in the first list of spiritual gifts. It often becomes the seedbed in which other gifts grow. Unfortunately, too many believers who have been entrusted by the Spirit with this gift fail, to use Paul's terminology, to 'think of [themselves] with sober judgement'. If they did, they would not underestimate their value in the kingdom.

Some years ago a pastor came up to me after a message I had given on the gift of helpfulness at a Bible conference. He said, 'I have a man just like you described in my congregation, but he thinks of himself as a failure because he can't teach or preach.' I learned that the rest of the congregation valued his helpfulness so much that they wondered what they would do if he ever moved. He showed uncanny ability in many directions. If drywall needed to be nailed up to prepare a new room he proved his skill. If the grass needed to be cut or the church to be painted he rose to the occasion. Needs that no one else noticed around the building caught his attention. He kept busy taking care of odds and ends, and yet he sorrowed that he had no gift!

Actually God had obviously entrusted this man with the gift of helpfulness. The rest of the church thanked God for him! This jack-of-all-trades freed up the church leaders so they could get on with other affairs. What do the Scriptures tell us about this boon of the Spirit?

1. The biblical roots

The Greek word

In Romans, Paul calls this gift *diakonia*. Vine mentions dozens of derivatives of this useful Greek word — servant, attendant, minister and deacon.[1]

Vine lists the following uses for *diakonia*:

Firstly, it can describe general service, such as domestic duty (Luke 10:40).

Secondly, and more frequently, it is used of 'religious and spiritual ministration'. In this latter sense, spiritual service, it may refer to:

apostolic ministry(Acts 6:4; Rom. 11:13);

the service of believers to one another. An abundance of references illustrate this usage and highlights the variety of applications of this gift;

the ministry of the Holy Spirit in the gospel (2 Cor. 3:8);

the ministry of angels to the heirs of salvation (Heb. 1:14);

the work of the gospel in general (2 Cor. 3:9);

the general ministry of a servant of the Lord in preaching and teaching (Acts 20:24).

A calling shared by angels, the Holy Spirit, apostles and preachers of the gospel is not a ministry to despise! These applications of *diakonia* demonstrate that all ministry is service. Let us look a little deeper.

Commands to serve one another

Jesus commanded his disciples to serve one another. He used the
incident in which the mother of James and John sought a high
position for her sons to teach servanthood. In effect, he said, 'Forget
about seeking a position, seek to serve one another' (Matt. 20:26-
28). Not content to encourage a kind of grudging service, he told
them, 'Whoever wants to be first must be your slave' (v. 27). What
a high standard of obligation!

Taking up the slave-metaphor, Paul commands the Galatians to
repudiate selfishness and 'serve one another in love' (Gal. 5:13).
'Serve', as used here, describes the work of a slave. How incredibly
difficult it must have been for freedom-loving Greeks or Hebrews
to accept slavelike service as a Christian norm! In their day slaves
were treated like property, to be used at will. In our age of vaunted
independence, this kind of service grates against our sensibilities.

Husbands and wives, as well as parents and children, are commanded to prepare for harmonious relationships by adopting a
submissive attitude: 'Submit to one another out of reverence for
Christ' (Eph. 5:21). Submission, far from being a duty imposed
solely on the underdog or the powerless, denotes an approach
chosen by those who love as Christ commands.

A sense of mutual respect produces concern. Concern in turn
moves us to respond to others with practical love. Practical love
leads us to serve one another in selfless ways. Although such service
is not the grudging service of slaves under duress, nevertheless it
manifests a slavelike attention to the needs of others. Thus, true
submission — true servanthood, undergirds all Christian relationships (see Eph. 5; 6).

Wherever we find sincere disciples of Christ, we ought to find an
atmosphere where service is second nature. In the fertile soil of
servanthood all the gifts sprout and grow. The first gift to lift its head
in the springtime of our love for Christ and his people will be a gift
that expresses our general availability and desire to be helpful. This
is the gift of helpfulness.

A response to need

Consider several examples where a sensitivity to need provokes a
serving response. In the foot-washing episode, Jesus had revealed

himself as the model servant. Moved by the shocking failure of the disciples to provide a commonly bestowed courtesy in the hot and dusty climate of Palestine, Jesus had gone around the circle washing the disciples' dirty feet.

Many different kinds of practical need catch the attention of people with a servant spirit. Sometimes they help people find the necessities of life (Matt. 25:44). Peter's mother rose from a bed of fever to care for her guests (Mark 1:31). Martha had served Jesus and the disciples on many occasions (Luke 10:38-40). The epistles of Paul join Acts in recording the response of Greek churches to famine among the saints at Jerusalem (Acts 11:29; 2 Cor. 8:4; 9:1,12). Mary Magdalene, Salome and another Mary had served the Master. 'In Galilee these women had followed him and cared for his needs' (Mark 15:41). In Acts 6, seven men were chosen to ensure that the Grecian widows were not neglected in the daily distribution of food.

To these examples of response to specific needs we may add a number of more indefinite texts. Without specifying exactly what he did, Paul commends Mark for being 'helpful to me in my ministry' (2 Tim. 4:11). Paul wrote to Timothy of Onesiphorus's usefulness: 'You know very well in how many ways he helped me in Ephesus' (2 Tim. 1:18).

Ephesians 4, using the same Greek word, states that the purpose of apostles, prophets, evangelists and pastor-teachers is 'to prepare God's people for works of service, so that the body of Christ may be built up...' Similarly, 1 Corinthians mentions 'different kinds of service' (1 Cor. 12:5). It would appear that God consecrates some believers to be generally helpful.

Clearly, the gift of helps — service — is meant to demonstrate Christ's teaching on servanthood. For while God commands every Christian to serve others, the dimensions of each person's service will vary considerably. The main examples cited — serving meals, waiting on tables, washing feet and taking relief money to the stricken — all relate to very practical things, such as food and finances. Others, such as John Mark and Onesiphorus, are commended for undefined and general helpfulness.

The gift defined

The gift of helps is a Spirit-produced helpfulness characterized by the readiness to serve wherever there is a need, the ability to notice things that need to be done, the training or talents to meet practical needs and a humble attitude of happy servanthood.

This gift resides in those men and women who instinctively volunteer to care for practical needs. Helpful people notice things that many of us overlook and without much ado they pitch in and get to work.

Both Peter Wagner[2] and Leslie Flynn[3] believe that this gift frees others with more specialized gifts to do their work with greater freedom and efficiency. Good secretaries, for example, greatly multiply the ministries of others. The helpful man, in the example quoted earlier, liberated his pastor to get on with sermon preparation and visitation.

This gift should not be confused with artificial busyness. Guilt induced by avoiding evangelism may motivate some to offer to paint the church, or do whatever needs to be done, in order to mask their own disobedience in other areas.

One problem remains: what shall we call this gift? To call it the gift of 'service' seems too formal and indefinite. The gift of 'ministry', while accurate biblically, might be misunderstood in the modern context in which ministry usually means a call to full- time service such as that of the pastorate. If we label it the gift of 'helps', we conform to a fairly broad usage derived from the Authorized Version. The context where this term occurs in the AV, in my opinion, however, refers to the gift of mercy and not the gift of service (1 Cor. 12:28). I will explain my reasons for saying this in a later chapter. Besides, the term 'helps' fails to fit modern language usage.

I prefer 'helpfulness'. Helpfulness denotes both availability and practical ability of a very broad and unspecified nature. Helpfulness fits, whether it refers to helping with the affairs of life, such as food preparation or finance, building maintenance or grass-cutting, or with the affairs of the spirit that require counsel or encouragement.

The gift of general helpfulness, under the Holy Spirit's tutelage, feeds a steady stream of gifted men and women into a host of other ministries. Peter's statement, 'Each one should use whatever gift he has received to serve others,' is a broad-based call to service. The verse that follows this statement of Peter focuses that call in two specialized directions: speaking on the one hand, and varieties of service, on the other (1 Peter 4:10-11). In the early church those who cheerfully made themselves useful often went on to develop more specialized ministries. The office of the diaconate, for example, was an outgrowth of helpfulness to widows.

The office of deacon

The same Greek root from which we derive the word for this gift, *diaconos,* provides us with the English word 'deacon', a transliteration of the Greek. Deacons were originally men noted for their helpfulness. Since practical problems repeatedly surfaced, the early church soon recognized the need to assign men and women to stand by for service wherever it might develop. These people soon began to be called deacons and deaconesses because they served as general need-meeters. Once their effectiveness was demonstrated those with these labels began naturally to take care of the practical matters of the church.

As time passed, the label 'deacon' came to represent an office in the church. Of course, as history developed still further, the office of deacon and deaconess came to encompass much more than general helpfulness. They often became noted for their spiritual leadership as well. Today their role varies from church to church.

Whatever the present definition of the office, its historical development illustrates in macrocosm what often happens to individual believers who exhibit a servant spirit. General helpfulness may turn out to be just the first step onto an upward-moving escalator. Available people like Stephen may develop into teachers or evangelists or pastors.

2. Biblical illustrations

The church in Jerusalem was aglow in the wash of Pentecost. In spite of the sobering deaths, under apostolic discipline, of Ananias and Sapphira, the congregation grew apace. Then a crisis developed which only those with the gift of helpfulness could solve. We have already studied this incident in other chapters, so we can move through its current application to helpfulness rather quickly.

A pressing need

In Acts chapter 6 we read that 'The Grecian Jews among them complained ... because their widows were being overlooked in the daily distribution of food' (Acts 6:1). This oversight endangered the unity of the infant church. Even more dangerous, the crisis threatened to bog the apostles down in controversy, thus siphoning away all their energies from preaching and prayer. Such a curtailment would stunt the church's growth and leave them open to false teachers. With the apostles called away from prayer, the danger of satanic attack would be multiplied. The very life and health of the early church depended upon solving a very practical problem.

Too often churches founder on rocks such as these. Churches split over disagreements about issues as mundane as the colour of paint, the kind of pews or who controls the musical ministry. Members commonly leave churches if they feel neglected by the nomination committee or the pastor. Practical problems must be solved if a church is to prosper.

A practical proposal

Sensing trouble, the Twelve suggested choosing men to care for food distribution (Acts 6:2-4). The apostles realized that choosing men to 'wait on tables' would stave off dissension and free them to continue their work.

The seven chosen were to be as spiritually qualified as any others — 'full of the Spirit and wisdom'. Those chosen for practical jobs need the Holy Spirit just as much as any teacher or preacher. These were not lesser men chosen for a lesser job.

Nevertheless, the task was mundane — distributing food to widows. It was a practical down-to-earth kind of job. The seven accepted the assignment eagerly. Their availability demonstrates the gift of helpfulness. No task is too lowly and no need unimportant for those with this gift.

The gift of helpfulness has many faces. The secretary, the accountant, the stewards, the caretaker, nursery workers and the ladies in the kitchen all manifest practical helpfulness. Without men and women who paint walls and empty waste bins, make coffee and clean windows, run off bulletins and distribute leaflets, make posters and run the library, straighten the hymn-books and count up the offering, take flowers to shut-ins and cut their grass, our churches would be in bad shape. Unfortunately, most of these men and women probably never realize their importance.

A powerful effect

Stephen and Philip, Procurus and Nicanor, Timon and Parmenas joined Nicolas from Antioch to wait on tables. Their hard work forestalled division in the church, healed bitter feelings and met the real need the widows had for food.

Some of these men are never heard of again. But their helpfulness profoundly affected the development of the early church. Instead of internal squabbles, we read, 'The word of God spread. The number of disciples in Jerusalem increased rapidly, and a large number of priests became obedient to the faith' (Acts 6:7).

Believers who volunteer for practical tasks free others to fulfil their spiritual potential. In this case the apostles were able to give attention to the ministry of the Word and prayer with the result that many were converted, including a number from the previously resistant priestly class. Practical helpfulness unleashes spiritual effectiveness in others because it liberates them from tasks that may distract them from their ministries.

Charles H. Spurgeon, commenting about those with the gift of helpfulness wrote, 'It strikes me that they were not persons who had any official standing, but that they were only moved by the natural impulse and the divine life within them to do anything and every-thing which would assist either teacher, pastor, or deacon, in the work of the Lord. They were the sort of brethren who are useful anywhere, who can always stop a gap, and who are only too glad when they find that they can make themselves serviceable to the church of God in any capacity whatever.'[4]

Exactly! The practical availability of men and women with the gift of helpfulness greases the wheels of church progress.

A second effect of this gift underlies the story recorded in Acts 6. Two of the early church's most effective witnesses got some of their most important training by waiting on tables. Stephen's witness became so powerful that the Jews stoned him to death. In the persecution that arose on his death, Philip, another of the waiters, planted the church in Samaria (Acts 7; 8).

One shudders to think of what might have happened if these two had not been willing to wait on tables. How many great preachers, evangelists, teachers and pastors have been marred or lost to the church because they sought the limelight but shunned servanthood! The availability that characterizes the gift of helpfulness is a prerequisite for other ministries as well! Indeed, servanthood requires one to be available for any job.

The development of a ministry

Acts 6 does not accord these seven men the title of deacon. Church history, however, does. Necessity being the mother of invention, early Christians chose people to meet widely recognized needs. In this way concrete needs created church offices. Paul's letters to Timothy and Titus make clear that by the time these epistles were written, the office of deacon had already become established.

How did the office evolve? As already noted, *diakonos* means simply a servant — one who serves. Deacons were probably those whose exemplary helpfulness led to official recognition on a congregational level (1 Tim. 3:8-13). Most commentators interpret their ministry as a management of the practical affairs of the church. A person's standing (his office, in New Testament terms) depended upon both the demonstration of his character and his ability or giftedness (1 Tim 3:10).

Further biblical examples of helpfulness

Phoebe, 'servant of the church in Cenchrea,' is another example. The Greek word used here for servant — *diakonon* — may either indicate that she was a deaconess or that she was noted for her helpfulness: 'She has been a great help to many people' (Rom. 16:1-2).

In Achaia, Stephanas and his whole household demonstrated helpfulness: 'They have devoted themselves to the service of the saints.' Paul urged the Corinthians to receive with devotion the delegation led by Stephanas 'because they have supplied what was lacking from you [finance]. For they refreshed my spirit and yours also' (1 Cor. 16:15-18). Stephanas and his household were available to meet whatever need Paul might have.

If we have the gift of helpfulness we shall roll up our sleeves and get busy doing whatever needs to be done. If we hold back, the following poem might capture our future regret:

You asked my help;
I turned away.
I thought there'd be

Another day,
When, not so busy,
I'd be free
To do the things
Required of me.
The days have passed,
I know not where.
With idle hands,
And time to spare,
Lost is the opportunity
To do the things
You ask of me.[5]

3. How do we become helpful people?

Virginia Evansen gives several secrets about lending a helping
hand. Rather than saying, 'Let me know if there's something I can
do to help,' we should look around for things to do. She mentions an
elderly man who had suffered a concussion. He was unable to feed
his pigs. 'His neighbour ... arranged for the animals to be fed
morning and evening. Then she went to the hospital to assure her
friend that he need not worry about his pigs.'[6] Now that's practical
help!

Secondly, Mrs Evansen counsels us to look beyond the immediate to foresee future needs. When someone is involved in an accident
or goes through a traumatic experience, people often respond
quickly but forget that help may be needed later on. The only source
of heat for the man mentioned above was his wood-burning stove.
Every year he cut his own wood. Anticipating this need, the kindly
neighbour ordered in a load of wood.

Thirdly, we should learn to listen between the lines. Mrs Evansen
continues: 'Another secret is to listen for an indirect appeal for
assistance. All too often the words, "I'll be all right; I can manage,"
can mean, "I sure could use some help, but I don't want to impose
on you."'[7] Ask people questions to find out what help they really
need.

Fourthly, demonstrate sincerity by doing more than voicing a
general concern. Offer concrete help. 'Let me fix your fridge.' 'I'll
cut the church grass every other week.'

Being ready to help wherever we see a practical need develops a spirit of helpfulness. And those with the gift of helpfulness, as much or more than those in high profile positions, are the 'big wheels' on which the church moves forward. Hospitality, of course, is a special kind of helpfulness.

II. The gift of hospitality

It was 1961. Mary Helen and I were newly married and somewhat apprehensive as we drove into the car park of a church in Pontiac, Michigan, to begin six months of practical missionary training. What would we find in this unknown church in a strange city? We found warm hospitality.

Believers opened their arms and took us in. Mrs Souslin gave us accommodation. Money was tight. Our training programme only allowed us a few dollars a week for living expenses. Like any faith missionary, we didn't mention needs. But somehow people knew. Every other week Mr and Mrs Remley would alternate with Mrs Walker to have us for Sunday dinner. It was the best meal of the week! And every week Mrs Remley would send over some freshly baked bread. I can almost smell it now! Young couples in the church invited us to their homes as well. Then, too, every week after Bible club we went home with one of the club members to a delicious meal in her parents' home.

I shudder as I wonder what might have happened as we adjusted to each other that first year of our marriage, if Sunnyvale Chapel had not been warm and hospitable. They helped us through those adjustments, rejoiced with us at the birth of our first child and pitched in to help us prepare for missionary service.

Those who opened their homes in Pontiac began to understand what made us tick. They began to pray — and they kept on praying throughout our years in Pakistan. They wrote us letters. They also supported our ministry.

When people open their doors, they open their hearts. An open heart, in turn, melts reserve and makes people feel accepted enough to share some of their concerns. Shared burdens alert those with spiritual gifts to bring their expertise to bear. Hospitality not only encourages people to be open about their needs; it also sets the stage to meet them.

While not actually included in the lists of gifts, nevertheless, hospitality is commanded in close proximity to two lists. In the passage in Romans, Paul follows the tabulation of spiritual gifts with a general exhortation to 'be devoted to one another in brotherly love' (Rom. 12:10). The most specific example he gives to illustrate how to do that is: 'Share with God's people who are in need. Practise hospitality' (Rom. 12:13).

The last passage in the New Testament to discuss the gifts also commands hospitality. Notice the flow of Peter's argument: 'Love each other deeply, because love covers over a multitude of sins. Offer hospitality to one another without grumbling. Each one should use whatever gift he has received to serve others, faithfully administering God's grace in its various forms' (1 Peter 4:8-10). The context leads inevitably to the conclusion that hospitality is a gift of the Spirit.

The meaning of the word

The Greek word, *philoxenia,* literally means 'love of strangers'.[8] A compound of two words, *philos,* denoting love, and *xenos,* a stranger, hospitality describes the grace of opening our homes to those we do not know.

Biblical usage distinguishes hospitality from entertainment. Entertaining friends and relatives must be encouraged. Hospitality, however, differs from entertainment. When we entertain friends for a meal, we often receive something in return. We may either be invited back to their home or we may simply be warmed by their friendship. Entertaining relatives, in most contexts, comes as a duty more than a grace.

Hospitality, by contrast, refers to the opening of one's home to offer needed food, friendship or accommodation to those we may not even know and from whom we may never receive a return invitation. Hospitality expresses self-giving love that often requires a sacrifice of time or money and may entail wear and tear on our furnishings.

The English word 'hospitality' has a similar derivation. Coming from the Latin, *hospes,* the English word illustrates how time blurs original meanings. In the fifth century hotels and shelters for travellers were almost non-existent. Homes had been centres of hospitality from time immemorial. Religious leaders, concerned about the difficulties faced by travellers, established hospices for their shelter. Over the passage of time the needs of the sick and suffering pre-empted their use by regular travellers. By this time the lure of profit had led many to establish inns and hotels. Hospices developed into hospitals. What had originally served as a hostel for all became a hostel for the sick and suffering. The etymology of the word 'hospitality', however, shows that its original intent was to express love for travelling strangers.

The gift defined

The gift of hospitality is that Spirit-produced commitment of home and resources to provide a warm and loving atmosphere of acceptance in which all kinds of people are made to feel at home.

What do the Scriptures teach us about hospitality?

1. A general command

When they exhorted early Christians to 'practise hospitality', Peter and Paul were echoing the teaching of Christ. Early in his ministry, the Master sent his disciples out two by two to heal and preach good news. Hospitality was so commonly practised that he commanded them: 'Whatever town or village you enter, search for some worthy person there and stay at his house until you leave' (Matt. 10:11). Expecting that their needs would be met by their hosts, they were to travel without extra clothes, money or even spare sandals. Their reception would be gauged both by how people listened to their message and by the hospitality they received. Lack of a good reception meant that 'It will be more bearable for Sodom and Gomorrah on the day of judgement than for that town.' Jesus expected his missionary disciples to look for and receive hospitality.

In the Day of Judgement genuine faith will be discerned by seeing that 'I was hungry and you gave me something to eat, I was thirsty and you gave me something to drink, I was a stranger and you invited me in' (Matt. 25:35). Jesus declared that he, himself, is represented, metaphorically, in those who need hospitality and receive it. Without realizing it, those who offer food and shelter entertain the Master. In the same way, Abraham unwittingly entertained an angel.

During a banquet in the home of a prominent Pharisee, Jesus taught: 'When you give a luncheon or dinner, do not invite your friends, your brothers or relatives, or your rich neighbours; if you do, they may invite you back and so you will be repaid. But when you give a banquet, invite the poor, the crippled, the lame, the blind, and you will be blessed. Although they cannot repay you, you will be repaid at the resurrection of the righteous' (Luke 14:12-14). The hospitality which God rewards is not the entertainment of our friends and relatives but the opening of our home to those who may never invite us to theirs.

Hospitality ranks high on the list of qualities essential in church leaders. Both Titus and Timothy were reminded that elders 'must be hospitable' (1 Tim. 3:2; Titus 1:8).

Actually God commands all believers to exercise hospitality. It constitutes one of the external signs of internal godliness. Widows were not to be helped if they had themselves failed to show hospitality (1 Tim. 5:10).

In spite of an abundance of biblical exhortation, hospitality is somewhat rare in Western society. Fortunately many parts of the world still regard this social grace as a cardinal virtue.

Pakistanis, like others in developing countries, shake their heads in disbelief at our failure to develop what, to them, expresses most powerfully our common humanity. As Western missionaries serving in Pakistan, we were often amazed at the hospitality offered us on the edge of the desert. People might live in mud huts, but they would seat visiting guests on a string bed spread with the best linen and placed under the shade of a tree. They would prepare tea or offer a cold drink. Dinner would be cooked.

In that society, guests and their care take precedence over most other duties. Even fierce tribesmen of the frontier suspend their feuds to offer hospitality to travellers. In the light of our Western weakness in offering the time-honoured conventions of hospitality we need seriously to question our vaunted superiority. Is technological advancement more important than basic social conventions that promote human interaction? Or does our frantic busyness mask our social decline? (This is not to say that Easterners do not err in other areas, or that there are not some Asians who take shameful advantage of the conventions of hospitality.)

We might think that the decline of hospitality in the West is justified by the improvement of roads, speed of travel, availability of restaurants and the proliferation of rented accommodation for the overnight traveller. Not so.

2. A universal need

People, the world over, need hospitality as never before. No doubt, the traveller's need for overnight accommodation has eased. In the days of the New Testament there were no motels. Without homes in which to stay, Peter's itinerant ministry would have been impossible. He received his vision of the lowered sheet that catapulted the Jewish church into cross-cultural missions while staying in Joppa at the home of Simon the tanner. On that occasion, a delegation from Cornelius arrived at Simon's door seeking Peter (Acts 9:32,43; 10:1-23). Since hospitality was a common courtesy, 'Peter invited the men into the house to be his guests,' even though it was not his house! (Acts 10:23). Later on, in Cæsarea after the outpouring of the Spirit, Cornelius 'asked Peter to stay with them for a few days' (Acts 10:48).

Examples of hospitality abound in the New Testament. Throughout their missionary journeys, Barnabas and Paul enjoyed hospitality wherever they went. Lydia, a very successful merchant of purple cloth, demonstrated the genuine nature of her new faith by saying, 'If you consider me a believer in the Lord, come and stay at my house' (Acts 16:15). Phoebe was noted for being hospitable in Cenchrea. When she set out for Rome, Paul wrote to the church there to receive her warmly (Rom. 16:1-2).

In apostolic times, with no church buildings, homes served as meeting-places for worship as well as havens for weary travellers. After Pentecost the believers made use of the temple area as long as possible, but soon they began to '[break] bread in their homes and ate together with glad and sincere hearts' (Acts 2:46). The home became a place of worship, fellowship and prayer. After release from prison by an angel of the Lord, Peter knew exactly where to find the believers gathered in prayer. He went to the home of 'Mary the mother of John, also called Mark' (Acts 12:12). Another church met in the home of Priscilla and Aquila (Rom. 16:5).

The need for encouragement and friendship

While church activities commonly centre on church buildings today, nevertheless, hospitality remains as crucial as ever. In a technological age our need for encouragement, understanding and friendship has not lessened — rather it has increased. Divorce leaves behind many lonely and hurting people. Broken homes and abusive parents produce damaged children and angry young people.

In a recent course on pastoral counselling that I attended, both a clinical psychologist and a full-time pastoral counsellor warned about how the breakdown of the home is producing multitudes of disturbed young people who desperately need love and counsel. Their number will create a deepening social crisis in the years ahead. Thoughtful social commentators rightly point out that a 'high-tech' society must compensate by becoming 'high-touch', that is, caring and relational. Technology and materialism, as well as broken relationships, leave a great ache in the human psyche that only warm and meaningful relationships can assuage. Hospitable Christians need to open their homes as never before.

Christian hospitality can offer a warm atmosphere of acceptance for both hurting Christians and enquiring non-Christians alike. Non-Christians often open up to the gospel in such a climate. Knowing Christian counsellors admit that coffee-cup counselling and small group Bible studies very often achieve a considerably higher success rate than formal office counselling.[9] Where hospitality abounds the body of Christ functions as it should.

Immigrants and overseas students

Hospitality meets other needs as well. Think of the influx of immigrants to our shores, the desperate need of refugees and the bewilderment of foreign students as they enrol in our universities. Benjamin Davadason came to Canada a number of years ago as a refugee from war-torn Sri Lanka. He now works as an evangelist among Tamil immigrants and refugees in Toronto. When he arrived he wandered from church to church seeking a spiritual home. Finally a pastor invited him for dinner. The only offer of hospitality this needy refugee family found led them to a church home.

Benji's ministry in that church became so appreciated that, when their pastor accepted another call, the congregation unanimously urged him to become their pastor. While he declined to do more than preach from time to time, he has gone on to found an effective outreach to immigrants in Toronto. The church benefited from their hospitality and a suffering couple fleeing persecution found a home. What opportunities we miss and what misunderstandings we generate when we do not offer hospitality!

Today we face an opportunity unparalleled in history. Representatives from all nations have arrived in our universities. Open to our friendship, as they might never have been in their own countries, they long for a little hospitality. Students from unreachable countries like Iran, Saudi Arabia and Libya walk our streets. Unfortunately, few have found hospitality.

There are notable exceptions. Kobad Arjani represents hundreds of others who came as strangers to our shores but through hospitality became our brothers and sisters. Kobad, a Zoroastrian from East Africa, was predisposed against Christianity. But as a student in an exchange programme, he felt that he should learn everything he could about American life. When he was unable to get into his university residence, a Christian lady met him, showed him the sights of Denver and invited him to attend a church service. As time passed, other contacts aroused his interest in Jesus. Finally in an Inter-Varsity camp in California, he was converted to Christ. Hospitality literally brought him to the kingdom.[10]

The needs of the inner city

Consider the importance of hospitality in our cities. In many parts of the world, churches are leaving the cities to erect new buildings in the suburbs. In many cases these inner-city church buildings are either torn down or used for other purposes. However, once they are gone, it becomes almost impossible for churches to acquire city land again. Skyrocketing prices make a future return to the city prohibitive. Who, then, will reach the people of the inner city? It would seem wise to resist the impulse to move to the suburbs by maintaining and expanding our witness in the city. True, many city people come from ethnic backgrounds that are hard to reach. But with vision and sacrifice we can turn the tide. To succeed, many believers will have to resist the impulse to move to the suburbs and instead maintain their homes as centres of warmth and witness in the city.

The Fleischmann Memorial Baptist Church in inner-city Philadelphia exemplifies innovative hospitality. Pastor James Correnti
challenged church members to move back into the city from the
suburbs. Bruce and Amy Clutcher, among others, did choose to
relocate there. 'Bruce, a hospital pharmacist, and Amy, a nursing
supervisor, together produce enough income to live in one of
Philadelphia's more affluent suburbs. Prior to their wedding they
searched for a home in a suburban area.' Instead, their commitment
to Christ led them to locate in the inner city, near the church. At
Fleischmann Memorial a number of families such as the Clutchers
can now become involved on a neighbourhood level. A commitment to hospitality can even guide us in our choice of where to live
and what kind of house to buy![11]

Christian workers

To all those who need hospitality we could add Christian workers.
Don't forget to invite the pastor and his family over occasionally.
The stress of his job is reduced when he knows you appreciate him
enough to open your home. When missionaries return home on
furlough, after years of offering hospitality, they themselves need its
ministry. Sometimes they return home with no place to live, no car
to get around with, no blankets to put on their beds — perhaps no
bed! Many thoughtful churches provide furlough housing for their
missionaries.

New Christians, visitors, refugees, immigrants and missionaries
— everyone needs hospitality. Lonely singles, devastated divor-
cees, hurting young people, widows and widowers, non-Christian
neighbours all join the multitude who need believers to exercise this
gift. While the command comes to all of us, nevertheless the Holy
Spirit sets some aside to focus in this area.

3. A special gift

During the ministry of the Master, Peter's home was a centre of
hospitality. After Pentecost, however, Peter became a mighty
preacher and travelling apostle. This apostolic ministry would have
been impossible if Peter had continued to concentrate on hospitality

rather than become the beneficiary of its warmth. He had already proved his willingness to consecrate his home for the Master's use. Afterwards he had other tasks to accomplish for the King. Hospitality cannot become the main ministry of everyone. Some, like Simon the tanner and Lydia the seller of purple, have to be raised up in each local church to exercise this gift.

No wonder Peter, immediately after exhorting believers to 'offer hospitality to one another', comments, 'Each one should use whatever gift he has received to serve others, faithfully administering God's grace in its various forms' (1 Peter 4:9,10). As we saw in chapter 1, there are distinctions between the gifts. There is variety in the body. We cannot expect a man such as the pastor, who labours in the Word and in visitation, to also excel in hospitality. As the two examples below will show, many do excel but it is too much to expect of all. In each church there needs to be some who will focus on this gift. If we all try to do a little in this area and a few of us concentrate our main efforts on hospitality, the whole church will benefit.

At Long Branch Baptist Church we established what we called 'soup-and-sandwich Sunday'. Once a month members bring sandwiches, a group of the ladies prepare soup and a dessert and everyone in the morning service is invited to stay for a simple fellowship meal. We intended to convey that we are a hospitable church, and to encourage Christians to become more hospitable in their own homes. It became very popular.

Conducting home Bible studies is another way to encourage hospitality and discover those with these gifts. Some excel in their ability to exude warmth and acceptance. The Bible studies in their homes usually become the most popular. Success indicates giftedness.

Every church has those who are naturally hospitable. A steady stream of new Christians, visitors and hurting people pass through their doors. Some serve by inviting people out to a local restaurant for Sunday dinner.

Radical hospitality

Ruth and David Rupprecht, a pastoral couple, represent scores of Christians who have embraced what they call in their book 'radical hospitality'. For ten years they have opened their home to people with mixed-up lives. The difficulties involved have sorely tried Ruth, but the joy of seeing God heal hurting people has made it all worthwhile.

The day when a troubled woman, Virginia, and her young son Bobby, moved into their home in Hackettstown, New Jersey, Ruth went to her husband and said, 'David, pray with me. I can't take it. We already have a full house with our own two children and Sheree [another guest]. Why doesn't someone else help her?' With their arms around each other they prayed in the garage, and God answered in the days ahead.[12] Few of us know much about hospitality like that!

Fortunately, some do. Some take in orphans. Others welcome unmarried mothers. Some run shelters for the homeless. What city could do without its rescue missions? Joyce-Marie Clark and her husband, a pastor, have used a spare room in Illinois for years to help recovered alcoholics, abused women and their children and young people fleeing the drug scene.[13]

Radical hospitality doesn't come easily. Ruth and David Rupprecht stress the importance of a close tie with a neighbourhood church and the support of its members and leaders. They see it as a 'comprehensive ministry, involving all of the families of the church, the body of Christ, in helping one another'. By this they do not mean that all should be personally involved in helping recovered alcoholics, unmarried mothers, abused teenagers or divorced women — very difficult and demanding examples of radical hospitality. Instead they talk of creating a climate of concern that spreads throughout a church, so that three or four families can carry on a radical ministry without feeling they are out on a limb alone.[14]

Those with the gift of hospitality usually exercise their gift in more common ways. They may chat over a cup of coffee. They may befriend students far from home. They may open their doors for Sunday dinner. As their guests become better known to them their names recur more frequently in their prayer life and opportunities for witness develop.

Many will be surprised when the Master commends them on the Day of Judgement for inviting him into their home. According to his parable that is what hospitable people do — they open their doors to Christ. But perhaps you are worried. You may think that hospitality is not your cup of tea. Don't write it off so easily. Let us look together at some common problems that scare people away from a ministry of hospitality.

4. Some common problems

The belief that 'My home is my castle,' is firmly rooted in our Western social consciousness. Democratic movements through the centuries have entrenched in our legal codes our right to privacy and freedom from unlawful search. We have progressed a long way from serfdom to achieve the right to 'life, liberty and the pursuit of happiness'. Independence carried too far, however, would destroy not only fellowship but hospitality.

When we yield to Christ as Lord, we yield home and hearth as well as heart. We soon come to realize that we are stewards, not owners, of all we have. However, even when Christ calls us to yield unconditionally, he understands our need for privacy and quiet and the importance of having a place to bring up our children. He is not calling us to destroy our family life.

Abuse

Abuse of hopitality presents another problem. This concern, recognized in the parables of hospitality in the Gospels, has always been with us. Some take advantage of those who open their homes. The possibility of being used can't be avoided.

Mary Helen, who spent considerable time offering hospitality in Pakistan, has always threatened to write a book entitled, *They'll be so glad to see us!* It would describe Christians who travel cheap by avoiding hotels and staying with acquaintances. Breezing into mission stations, naïve travellers are sometimes oblivious of the schedules they disrupt and the strain they put on tight budgets. To avoid undue financial strain, missionaries in many parts of the world have a 'hospitality rate' which guests pay when they stay overnight.

Most social conventions about hospitality forbid such a practical solution. As a result, hospitable people inevitably suffer loss of time and money. Keeping this in mind, Christians should endeavour to be thoughtful guests.

Fears about opening up our homes

Some shrink from opening their home to strangers lest their carpet be soiled or costly china cracked. Hospitable saints, however, value people above possessions. Actually we need not worry so much. In all our years of hospitality in Pakistan, or in our more limited involvement in Toronto, personal loss has been minimal while spiritual enrichment has been maximum.

Still others avoid hospitality out of a feeling that their home is not presentable enough for guests. Others imagine they cannot afford the cost of entertainment. In the New Testament sense, hospitality is not a gift exercised by the wealthy. Its warmth is measured by the openness of our hearts and not the quality of our china, the cost of our furnishings or the richness of our fare. A cup of coffee in the kitchen or soup at the dining-room table may just as truly reflect genuine hospitality as an elaborate three-course dinner with silver and candlelight.

Learning from the Master's simple menu of bread and fish for 5000, Lora Lee Parrott urges us to overcome our fears and invite someone home. She confesses, 'When I first started my ministry of hospitality, fear was my constant kitchen companion.' Fears that the meal might not look right, of guests not coming or of them having a boring time plagued her pantry. Fear of forgetting to serve what she had prepared even dogged her footsteps. Jesus' example helped her overcome fear and really begin to enjoy hospitality.[15]

Whatever objections we advance to avoid hospitality crumble when we face the needs of lonely and hurting people. Too often the motive behind saying 'No!' to hospitality can be isolated as pure and simple selfishness. Having said that, I need to insert another caution at this point.

A word of caution

We cannot respond to every need. Each of us has to learn to say no to appeals that rely on manipulation or pressure. We have to learn to listen quietly to the voice of the Spirit directing us to concentrate where our gifts fit us for service. Often it is harder to say, 'No!' to a noisy need than to faithfully keep on doing what God wants us to do. Remember the camel who stuck his nose in the tent in an earlier chapter?

I find no basis in Scripture for the widely promoted slogan: 'I'd rather burn out than rust out.' Excessive zeal, in the long run, will prove just as harmful to the kingdom as lack of zeal. Peter exhorts his readers to faithfulness, not excess of zeal. 'If anyone serves, he should do it with the strength God provides, so that in all things God may be praised through Jesus Christ' (1 Peter 4:11). That includes hospitality.

God asks us to serve him according to our strength. Some possess greater physical stamina than others. Not all of us share Samson's physique! God understands that. What he asks is service proportionate to our strength — neither laziness nor burn-out.

I must admit, of course, that in our laid-back generation we don't have many burning out for God. There is an epidemic of lack of commitment and laziness. But lest some sensitive soul reads this section and falls under an excess of false guilt, I need to warn about the possibility of going to extremes.

All of us should try to be hospitable. Christ commands it. But the Spirit leads some into hospitality as a main ministry just as he does others into the sphere of general helpfulness.

Now, what have we discovered about these two gifts?

Summary

The gift of helpfulness resides in those men and women whom the Spirit moves to be available to meet whatever need arises. Usually those with this gift serve in spheres where their practical abilities prepare them to meet specific temporal needs such as building maintenance or finance.

In the same conference mentioned earlier, a pastor described an instance that illustrates the gift of helpfulness. His sink refused to drain. Tracing the problem outside he began to dig up the outdoor drainage pipe. While he was hard at work, a member of his congregation drove up in his truck. Without a word he got out of his truck, grabbed a shovel, jumped into the hole with the pastor and began to dig. They exchanged few words until the pipe was cleared.

The wife of the man in question had come to the pastor on several occasions to express her disappointment with her husband. He had little education and read poorly. He seldom said much in the prayer meeting or Bible study. Without condoning any of his weaknesses the pastor wisely pointed out his good qualities. Whenever there was a widow who needed wood, he would cut it and deliver it in his truck. He helped wherever he saw a need. The pastor counselled the wife to encourage and not discourage him in his helpfulness. This wife was blind to her husband's giftedness because she yearned for his prominence in other areas!

The gift of hospitality moves men and women to create a welcoming atmosphere of love and acceptance in which people feel secure enough to let down their masks and be themselves. Immigrants, refugees, new neighbours, hurting and abused women and teenagers, lonely older people, newly divorced men or women, new converts and Christian workers are some of those who need hospitality. Warm hospitality, however, accelerates the spiritual development of any Christian. Then, too, every non-Christian needs the opportunity to taste gracious Christian hospitality.

Soon after we were accepted as missionary candidates with International Christian Fellowship, now SIM International, we began to travel from church to church. Early on we were assigned to speak in an unknown church, in an unknown city, in an unknown denomination. With our two small children and our old car we set out rather fearfully for distant Chicago, renowned for its violence and gangs. Upon arrival the pastor directed us to the home of a young couple. With some trepidation we arrived on their doorstep.

Lonnie opened the door and welcomed us into her home and into her heart. As a young Christian, missionaries and church life were new to her. Her husband, Jim, was not yet converted. But both displayed the uncomplicated openness that proved so endearing in the years ahead. They soon made us feel at home. Anything they had we could use. Their generosity almost embarrassed us. Jim and Lonnie were hospitable with a simplicity and charm that won our hearts.

They opened their hearts — and everything else was thrown in. Concerned about missionary service in far-off Pakistan, both the Bones and the church loaded us down with the things we would need in the years ahead. Jim and Lonnie came to Toronto to help us pack when we were finally ready to leave for missionary service. Every time since then that we have visited Chicago, we have stayed with them.

While the first gift we noticed in them was hospitality, other spiritual gifts were soon displayed as well. Their exercise of hospitality was probably used by God to train them in other areas. We have already noted a number of cases where God uses the serving gifts as a training-ground to develop other capabilities. Humility and availability always accelerate usefulness in the kingdom.

To those who have a servant spirit the place of service matters little. An anonymous woman has captured the attitude of true service.

Lord of pots and pans and things;
Since I've no time to be
A saint by doing lovely things,
Or watching late with thee,
Or dreaming in the dawnlight,
Or storming heaven's gates,
Make me a saint by getting meals,
And washing plate.

Although I must have Martha's hands,
I have a Mary mind;
And when I black the boots and shoes,
Thy sandals, Lord, I find.
I think of how they trod the earth,
What time I scrub the floor;
Accept this meditation, Lord,
I haven't time for more.

Warm all the kitchen with thy love,
And light it with thy peace;
Forgive me all my worrying,
And make all grumbling cease.
Thou who didst love to give men food,
In room, or by the sea,
Accept this service that I do —
I do it unto thee.

Has God called you to use your gift of helpfulness or hospitality to serve him? Wonderful! Worship him and serve!

Return to your chart now and fill in the empty columns as you spend a few moments meditating on these two gifts. Next we move on to consider the gifts of giving and mercy.

19.
Giving and mercy

In Norfolk, Virginia, Charles Hassel carries on the work that his mother began in the depression of the thirties. Charles lives in a very modest retirement home. Although he is poor by the standards of many, he brings food to the hungry, clothing to the needy and donates his time to babysit for single working mothers.[1]

Even confirmed unbelievers know that the teachings of Christ extol generosity and mercy. The widow who gave her mite is renowned for her generosity while the Good Samaritan is synonymous with mercy. Consider first the gift of giving.

I. The gift of giving

Paul urges, 'If a man's gift is … contributing to the needs of others, let him give generously' (Rom. 12:6,8). Vine lists seventeen different words or combinations of words used in the Greek to translate the idea 'give'. The word used here denotes a generosity that involves a sharing of oneself.[2] True givers, in New Testament terms, open their hearts first and then their wallets.

1. A universal command

The Old Testament frequently highlights generosity. Moses wrote, 'Do not be hard-hearted or tight-fisted towards your poor brother… Give generously to him and do so without a grudging heart… There will always be poor people in the land' (Deut. 15:7,10,11).

While Israel obeyed this injunction to help the poor rather sporadically, they did respond to the building of the tabernacle with great liberality: 'Everyone who was willing and whose heart moved him came and brought an offering to the Lord for the work on the Tent of Meeting' (Exod. 35:21). They gave so generously that Moses had to call a halt to their giving: 'The people were restrained from bringing more, because what they already had was more than enough to do all the work' (Exod. 36:6-7).

Proverbs has a lot to say about generosity: 'Honour the Lord with your wealth, with the firstfruits of all your crops' (Prov. 3:9); 'Blessed is he who is kind to the needy' (Prov. 14:21). The book ends with an astounding sketch of a noble wife who, among many other godly characteristics, 'extends her hands to the needy' (Prov. 31:20).

Malachi concludes the Old Testament with a list of Israel's sins. Robbing God joins unfaithfulness, insincerity and adultery on this list. Malachi reinforces the obligation believers have to support the house of God through a system of tithing. He commands Israel to stop robbing God and to 'bring the whole tithe into the storehouse, that there may be food in my house' (Mal. 3:8,10). Hebrews reminds us that long before that Abraham had given one tenth of the spoils of his rescue operation to Melchizedek (Heb. 7:2). Since Abraham tithed before God codified the practice on Sinai, we conclude that tithing is a duty predating the Mosaic covenant.

Most Christians today regard tithing as the minimum we should give. Old Testament free-will offerings were given in excess of the tithe. And so today. But this is not the place to digress with a lengthy discussion about tithing.

While the apostles built upon Old Testament ideals of generosity, they called believers to generosity of a more spontaneous nature in line with the freedom found in the gospel: 'Each man should give what he has decided in his heart to give, not reluctantly or under compulsion, for God loves a cheerful giver' (2 Cor. 9:7).

This spontaneity led to extraordinary liberality. After Pentecost, many new believers, instead of restricting their giving to a portion of their earned income, sold their possessions in order to give 'to anyone as he had need' (Acts 2:45). A few chapters later we read, 'No one claimed that any of his possessions was his own, but they shared everything they had' (Acts 4:32). Viewed in our setting it would have been as if someone had come up to Peter and said,

'Brother, I hear you are off to Galilee. Here are the keys to my Rolls Royce. The credit cards are in the glove compartment. Have a nice trip.'

This early experiment in communal sharing may have led to extremes. Having cashed in so many assets, the Jerusalem church was not prepared for the onset of a devastating famine. This famine brought such stringency down on the Jerusalem church that appeals for help were sent out to Christians throughout the Mediterranean world. Whatever we may conclude about the social dimensions of their communal experiment in sharing, nevertheless other Christians responded liberally to their need. Even poor churches, like those in Macedonia, were eager to give. 'Out of the most severe trial, their overflowing joy and their extreme poverty welled up in rich generosity. For I testify that they gave as much as they were able, and even beyond their ability. Entirely on their own, they urgently pleaded with us for the privilege of sharing in this service to the saints' (2 Cor. 8:2-4).

By giving generously these early Christians were obeying the commands of Christ who said, 'Give, and it will be given to you' (Luke 6:38; cf. Matt. 5:42).

It is not surprising that the gift of giving flourishes in those who obey Christ's commands. It is discovered through acts of liberality. Penny-pinchers, who, like Scrooge, hoard their resources, often end up pinched themselves in either spirit or wallet — and they miss out on ministry.

On a recent holiday a friendly squirrel peeked in our window to beg for food. Every morning for a few days we rewarded his entreaty with an offering of bread. But one morning a competitor arrived and the fight began. Rather than share, both squirrels chased each other up and down the balcony. Meanwhile a bird had been watching the fray from a nearby tree. Swooping low, the bird snatched the bread and flew off to savour his conquest. Both squirrels lost. We all lose when we don't share.

2. A special gift

Twenty years of missionary experience have lined our memory-gallery with the bright pictures of men and women whose generosity overflowed in our direction. We married right after graduation from

Bible College and went on to a missionary training programme. Upon completion of that programme we became candidates for foreign service. With no salary either while we were training or during the following two years of deputation our resources were non-existent.

As deputation progressed, we worked during the week wherever we could find a job, while we held meetings at the week-ends to share our vision of Muslim evangelism. God blessed us with a second child during that period. Prayerfully, we looked to the Lord for help.

In mysterious ways, God met our critical needs through Christians who knew the grace of liberal giving. A wealthy businessman made available a small house on a corner of his beautiful property overlooking a bay. Another man, a car dealer, loaned us a station-wagon.

The pattern of amazing provision continued during the entire period of our missionary service. Of course, once we arrived in Pakistan, churches who had pledged to support the work largely underwrote our regular missionary salary. But as special needs arose, so did our memory-gallery of happy givers expand. At the beginning of every furlough, one man took me to a tailor's and bid me pick out a new suit. Another time, in a distant town where we went for further study, an unknown Christian, concerned about missions, made available part of a house for our use. That same year the owner of the local heating oil company kept our oil tank full during a cold winter. He resolutely refused payment.

I have no doubt that, scattered throughout the church, an anonymous host of men and women with the gift of giving continue to sustain the kingdom. Who are these generous people? Are they drawn from those whose disposable income leaves them with extra wealth to share?

3. Giving in the light of poverty or wealth

Barnabas exemplified both giving and encouragement. Barnabas 'sold a field he owned and brought the money and put it at the apostles' feet' (Acts 4:37). By the standards of his day, Barnabas probably would have been considered quite wealthy. Of course, God expects those with riches to exercise the gift of generosity.

Unfortunately, most who are wealthy do not respond to God's call.

Remember when a rich young man came to Jesus with the eager expectation of becoming a disciple? Covetousness quickly conquered his newly awakened interest and he went away sorrowing. Jesus explained his defection by saying, 'It is easier for a camel to go through the eye of a needle than for a rich man to enter the kingdom of God' (Matt. 19:24). Some of the disciples, including Matthew, the tax-collector, and Peter and Andrew, James and John — who owned their own fish business — knew by personal example the pull of possessions. No wonder they were astonished and cried out, 'Who then can be saved?' (Matt. 19:25). Jesus reminded them of God's ability to do the impossible by moving even rich sinners to repent, as had been the case with them.

In Old Covenant days, wealthy men, such as Abraham and David, were generous men. In New Covenant times Paul urged Timothy to command those who are rich in this world's goods to 'do good, to be rich in good deeds, and to be generous and willing to share' (1 Tim. 6:18).

The wealthy person needs to ask God, almost before enquiring about other gifts, if this gift might not be his or her area of focus. While giving is rarely the only gift such believers exhibit, there can hardly be gift development in other areas while miserliness reigns.

Since gifts develop in a climate of obedience, wealthy Christians must either consecrate their wealth to God's service or be lost to usefulness in the kingdom. It is not enough for them to be great teachers or evangelists if they hoard their riches. Disobedience here becomes the stone over which they may stumble and never recover. Paul wrote, 'Command those who are rich in this present world not to be arrogant nor to put their hope in wealth, which is so uncertain, but to put their hope in God, who richly provides us with everything for our enjoyment' (1 Tim. 6:17). Since 'The love of money is a root of all kinds of evil,' its lure must be conquered (1 Tim. 6:10).

Scripture abounds with examples of the liberality of those who were well off. A wealthy Shunammite woman shared her table with Elisha whenever he came to town. She soon built him a special room on her roof (2 Kings 4:8-10). Mary, John Mark's mother, opened her large home for church meetings (Acts 12:12). A wealthy cloth merchant named Lydia extended hospitality to Paul and Silas (Acts 16:15).

But who is wealthy today? In the eyes of much of the world, everyone in the West is wealthy, because they have disposable income that they can use not only for food and clothing but to buy homes and cars as well as to save for the future. Set off against the backdrop of history, this perception is probably accurate. The world has never witnessed a generation enjoying such widespread prosperity. Fortunately, many believers in the West accept their good fortune as a boon and use their resources to support the work of God's kingdom. More missionary support, by far, comes from the West than from anywhere else. Every middle income Western Christian should seriously consider whether or not he has the gift of giving.

On a scale never experienced before, our generation has the opportunity actually to fulfil the Great Commission. We have the resources and the technology. But with the missionary task increasing as population explodes, many organizations feel a severe financial pinch. Why? Perhaps the pursuit of a yuppie lifestyle has influenced many Western believers to back off on giving and forge ahead with consumer spending. Far too few recognize God's providence in the privilege they enjoy of being born in a Western democracy during one of the most prosperous periods of history.

Are you helping to extend the kingdom by your stewardship? Or are you using God's providentially provided wealth to fill your home with costly toys?

Are only the rich, then, called to a ministry of generosity? No! I am sure that if the truth were known the bulk of the income for churches and mission organizations could be traced to believers of modest or low income. Those who are poor in this world's goods are often the real stewardship heroes. Each testament highlights the generous poor. Elijah lived out a terrible famine in the home of the widow of Zarephath who shared her last bread with him only to find out that the jar of flour and the jug of oil never ran out (1 Kings 17:7-16).

A thousand years later, 'Jesus saw the rich putting their gifts into the temple treasury. He also saw a poor widow put in two very small copper coins. "I tell you the truth," he said, "this poor widow has put in more than all the others"' (Luke 21:1-3). This unknown widow probably exemplifies for us, more than any other, the gift of liberality.

Monetary sacrifice like hers is rare even among the poor. Many who flock to buy lottery tickets know financial stringency but lack a sense of stewardship. They dream of striking it rich. Paul warned Timothy that everyone, rich and poor, is tempted by a lust for money. 'People who want to get rich [not who are rich, but want to be] fall into temptation and a trap and into many foolish and harmful desires that plunge men into ruin and destruction' (1 Tim. 6:9).

The poor churches from Macedonia also exemplify generosity. Although no one had asked them to contribute, they begged for permission to share in the collection for the relief of the Jerusalem saints. Paul describes their giving: 'Out of the most severe trial, their overflowing joy and their extreme poverty welled up in rich generosity' (2 Cor. 8:1-5). Their example ought to pierce our comfortable suburban consciences.

Whether rich, poor or middle-class, God calls all of us to happy stewardship. In chapter 4 we talked of God's providence preparing people for Spirit-anointed ministries. If God, in his providence, has given you wealth, then you must consider whether that may not be an indication of the focus of your ministry. You may have the gift of giving.

If you eke out a living from a meagre or modest income, however, you cannot assume the Spirit will not give you this gift. A widow in each testament demonstrates how God loves to take the cruse of oil of the poor and multiply it to serve his purposes.

Definition of the gift

Whether found in the rich or poor, the gift of giving is that Spirit-endowed ability to view financial or material resources as a trust from God and to handle them according to wise principles of stewardship in order to have the wherewithal to respond to need with humility and liberality.

4. The characteristics of the generous giver

In the course of our study of the generous giver, we have already noticed considerable diversity. Nevertheless, all who have this gift share several common traits.

A sense of personal involvement

In North America, governments recognize the value of charity by allowing its deduction, up to a point, from income subject to tax. Generosity has become institutionalized. As a result many individuals and corporations toss their gifts into the uplifted collection plates of the needy more with an eye to receiving a 'tax-deductible receipt', or getting their names on the plaque of a new building, than to meeting real need. Nothing could be more inimical to genuine generosity.

Those with the gift of giving feel a kinship with those they help. Vine describes the word used in Romans for the gift of giving, as giving that is sharing oneself.[3] The same word occurs in Thessalonians: 'We loved you so much that we were delighted to share with you not only the gospel of God but our lives as well, because you had become so dear to us' (1 Thess. 2:8). Biblical giving grows out of involvement in the lives and concerns of others.

Note that the NIV translates the word as 'sharing'. When people share their resources, they do so because they have first opened their hearts. A sense of kinship with a needy person stimulates a practical response.

No explanation seems adequate to explain the widow's gift in the temple, unless we conjecture that she felt so deeply the presence of God that she shared with him her all. While many rich people went by who, with scarcely a thought, tossed in gold or silver coins, she lovingly placed two tiny copper coins in the receptacle. The tiny gift was lavish, because it came from her heart.

Almost invariably, we have found, those who supported us through twenty years of missionary service were the ones who were most interested in us as people. Those who got to know us, who loved us and who prayed for us were often the ones who regularly sent a cheque to mission headquarters so that our living expenses in Pakistan might be underwritten. In this vein, the wealthy couple who provided housing for us as new candidates continued to keep in touch with us for twenty years.

Churches with a biblical sense of mission want to be involved in the life of their missionaries, not just to write cheques. Out of this emphasis on personal concern for individual missionaries, the rather successful North American personal support system has developed. Monetary help often follows, rather than precedes, interest in a person.

A caution concerning secrecy in giving, which I will discuss more fully later, needs to be mentioned here. Some generous givers, to avoid the taint of praise for what they do, maintain a distance from those they help. While their aversion to praise is laudable, other means can be sought which will honour privacy and yet encourage sensitive involvement.

A sensitivity to the material needs of others

Spiritual gifts focus on meeting various felt needs; givers develop a sensitivity to material needs.

In defining the operation of this gift Paul describes it as 'contributing to the needs of others' (Rom. 12:8). Later he writes, 'Share with God's people who are in need' (Rom. 12:13). People with this gift develop an ability, almost like radar, to spot physical need. All of us ought to be sensitive. 'If anyone has material possessions and sees his brother in need but has no pity on him, how can the love of God be in him?' (1 John 3:17). God even commands the converted thief to get a job so he will have the means to share with those in need (Eph. 4:28).

We often overlook material needs. After hearing about a brother in real privation, we may say, 'I never knew. Why didn't he say something?' But pride keeps most people from mentioning their stringency. Even in obviously distressed countries like Somalia or Bangladesh, few like to become dependent on what society, rather disdainfully, calls 'charity'. When people do broadcast their needs, too often we suspect their motives.

No, we cannot wait for people to put their needs into words. Someone has accurately written, 'He who gives when he is asked has waited too long.' The truly generous person develops an acute sensitivity that operates without any verbal clues being dropped.

Missionary service afforded us a ringside seat from which to watch the amazing way God works through sensitive people. Serving ten thousand miles away from our supporters created a time-lag between facing a specific need and news about it reaching supporters. Yet again and again, people sensitive to the Lord in prayer were moved to take steps perhaps a month, sometimes months, before our actual need arose! A cheque was sent in, or a parcel posted, which arrived just in time to solve our practical problem.

People who desire to develop the gift of giving need to become unusually sensitive to the promptings of the Spirit in prayer. Prayer is crucial to the exercise of many gifts, but especially here.

Of course, sensitivity creates a dilemma: 'Who needs help the most? How can we respond to so many needs?' Biblical givers make careful discriminations. And although they can never meet all needs, they usually have more resources available to share, not because they are richer, but more responsible in their use.

An acute sense of personal accountability

Givers take seriously the efficient management of material resources. Jesus introduced many stories of stewardship, such as the parable of the talents (Matt. 25:14-30). Gifted givers know that the Master will call them to account for the property and possessions he has entrusted to them. They want to be able to say, 'Master, you entrusted me with five talents. See, I have gained five more' (Matt. 25:20). Like the good servants in the parable, they put his money to work.

Local churches, as regional expressions of the kingdom, become the centres from which spiritual givers reach out to the needy. In Old Testament days, giving was centred on the temple, from whose treasury the priests were paid. In the New Testament, the pattern continues. After Pentecost, the care of God's people became a crucial expression of Christian stewardship (Acts 2:44-45; 4:32-37). Even among the Gentiles, Paul exhorted, 'Now about the collection for God's people. Do what I told the Galatian churches to do. On the first day of every week, each one of you should set aside a sum of money in keeping with his income, saving it up...' (1 Cor. 16:1-2). With responsibility shared among spiritually minded elders (or deacons), local churches can become the most discriminating distributors of money. Then, too, a local church can ensure privacy of donation.

Since many dimensions of the kingdom and its extension exceed the boundaries of the local church we cannot demand that all money be given to it. Local churches, unless repeatedly refreshed by the Spirit's global vision, tend to become myopic. When a church betrays its worldwide mandate by squandering God's resources in its own aggrandizement, then sensitive givers may legitimately seek more direct ways to give. Nevertheless, many of the financial scandals involving Christian organizations that have been aired by the media would have been avoided if most giving had been directed through financially accountable local church boards.

Paul's mention of a weekly offering reminds us that stewardship of resources can never be a hit-or-miss affair. The one with the gift of giving gives regularly. His generosity is not the response of his emotions to heart-rending need. Careful, long-term, thoughtful stewardship occupies his or her attention.

One of our friends was supported to a large extent from the farming revenues of his close relatives. His brothers and father covenanted together to use profits from their farms to support his missionary service. This is responsible stewardship.

A few years ago I had the opportunity to speak at a conference on the shore of a beautiful lake in upstate New York. The site had been purchased through a gift from R. G. LeTourneau. LeTourneau, designer and manufacturer of massive earth-moving machinery, is famous for more than his machines.

Early in his career, LeTourneau went into partnership with God. Flynn quotes him as saying, 'Because I believe that God wants business men as well as preachers to be his servants, I believe that a factory can be dedicated to His service as well as a church.' In 1935 he assigned 90% of the company's profits to the non-profit LeTourneau Foundation to be used for the cause of Christ. In the first fifteen years almost five million dollars were ploughed into Christian work.[4]

Generosity

Concerning this spiritual gift Paul wrote, 'If it is contributing to the need of others, let him give generously' (Rom. 12:8). The AV translates this word 'simplicity'. Vine states that it 'denotes simplicity, sincerity, unaffectedness'.[5] The root comes from a word that means 'single'.

Generous giving, in this sense, refers to giving without a hidden agenda. It is not generosity hiding a desire to manipulate or control others, nor money used to acquire prestige. Those to whom the Spirit entrusts this gift give for the love of it, without thought of reward or thanks, without any motive whatever but to help those who need monetary help.

The widow who came to the temple and put in two small coins gave in this way. Since the act, as far as she knew, was anonymous there was no hidden desire to impress. Her act, too, was liberal in its extent. It was a sacrifice of all she had.

The proportion of their income which liberal givers share astounds most of us. The widow gave everything. The Macedonians gave out of extreme poverty, 'beyond their ability' (2 Cor. 8:3). Early Christians like Barnabas sold valuable property and gave it to the apostles to distribute at their discretion. The widow of Zarephath gave Elijah her last flour and oil. LeTourneau gave 90% of his company's profits. Stanley Tam, a businessman in Lima, Ohio, made God his senior partner and gave first 51%, then 60% and finally 100% of his company's profits.[6]

These contemporary and biblical examples illustrate a largeness of heart combined with a wonderfully cheerful spirit. All of us should aspire to such a spirit. 'Whoever sows sparingly will also reap sparingly, and whoever sows generously will also reap generously. Each man should give what he has decided in his heart to give, not reluctantly or under compulsion, for God loves a cheerful giver' (2 Cor. 9:6-7). Freedom and joy are the heritage of those who give without being constrained by personal reluctance or external influence.

A sense of privacy

Most great givers give anonymously. Jesus said, 'When you give to the needy, do not announce it with trumpets, as the hypocrites do in the synagogues and on the streets, to be honoured by men. I tell you the truth, they have received their reward in full. But when you give to the needy, do not let your left hand know what your right hand is doing, so that your giving may be in secret' (Matt. 6:2-4).

Secret giving — what a blow this strikes to the heart of too much benevolence! Money is power and men often spread their largesse around with the expectation of something in return — influence, prestige, recognition, a place on the board. Too often men and women are chosen for positions of responsibility in church organizations, not because of merit, but because of their wealth or prestige.

Those who use their wealth in this way know nothing of the gift of giving.

Fortunately, most of our churches use an envelope system that grants anonymity. Numbered envelopes have been assigned to different people. In this way, only the person who can connect a number with a name knows who gives and how much they give. Pastors and board members have no right to review this privileged information. Equality ought to characterize our churches. After all, only Christ can read the motives behind our donations to discern whether three dollars, given by one person, has more value than three thousand, by another.

Sometimes, of course, we cannot remain anonymous. If a needy person has an immediate need that we can fulfil, we cannot wait to send help indirectly. And in our era when commerce depends on the system of payment by cheque, we can't avoid signing our names! Then, too, as earlier emphasized, the desire to give often grows out of personal involvement. When we are deeply involved in the lives of others it is hard to disguise our giving. But we can try to give as anonymously as possible.

We must admit that, carnally, we like recognition. We want to be thanked for what we do. The gifted giver conquers this desire, in order to give freely, liberally and joyfully. Givers need to ask God for massive doses of humility to conquer their natural inclination to seek praise.

Could it be that you have the gift of giving? Has God given you wealth, which you need to use in his kingdom? Or has he given you ability to use what little you have in creative ways to extend the widow's cruse of oil in your church or your organization? Do you have ability with figures, with investments, with property or with business that can be used to fund that last push of the kingdom that will usher in the return of Christ? Do you just love to give, or do you want to learn how to give? Whatever our present state of giftedness, we all need to pray for a sensitivity to needs. Mercy, our next gift, develops sensitivity in another area.

II. The gift of mercy

'For years, Lori hated herself and even God for making her the way she was.' In primary school and throughout her high school years

Lori stood out as heavyset, big boned and taller than other girls. Although a Christian, anger over her appearance churned within her. Her appearance reduced her chance of getting dates.

Then during a field trip to a local hospital her view of herself, and of God, changed. The class listened as a nurse explained equipment used in one of the rooms. Suddenly a young woman with a spinal cord injury fell off her exercise machine to the floor. The woman cried out in pain. Without a second thought, Lori moved in to help. Lifting her gently, she put her carefully in her wheelchair. Although this would normally have been a job for two nurses, Lori's build enabled her to lift the woman with ease.

The experience changed her life. She went on to take occupational therapy. Upon graduation she joined the staff of a large hospital. In the process of discovering the capacity to help injured children and adults, she came to terms with herself as God had made her. Seven years later she said, 'For years I looked at the way God made me as a curse, not a blessing. But that day at the hospital, I learned that He could use me just the way He made me! That young woman needed my strong arms. That afternoon, for the first time in my life I was able to thank God for who I was and even for making me big.'[7]

Lori discovered the gift of mercy. In the process she also acquired a sense of personal acceptance and significance. Could Lori's gift be yours as well? Paul reminds us, 'We have different gifts, according to the grace given us... If it is showing mercy, let him do it cheerfully' (Rom. 12:6,8).

The Greek words

Eleos, mercy, 'is the outward manifestation of pity; it assumes need on the part of him who receives it, and resources adequate to meet the need on the part of him who shows it'.[8] Mercy, then, recognizes a need, feels compassion and gathers the resources necessary to alleviate the need. Sometimes a need is met by a visit or a kind word, but at other times a hospital visit or the offer of a job may be required.

When we demonstrate mercy we reflect an essential attribute of God. Berkhof describes the mercy of God as that attribute which leads him to feel pity even for those bearing the just consequences of their sins. 'It may be defined as the goodness or love of God shown to those who are in misery or distress, irrespective of their deserts.'[9]

Mercy refers to the compassionate response men make to those who are in distress, whether or not they deserve help. God is merciful to sinners. Men and women, too, need to be merciful even to the most undeserving.

Using another Greek word, Paul describes those with the gift of mercy as 'those able to help others' (1 Cor. 12:28). Some commentators believe this refers to the gift of helpfulness. A study of the Greek word, however, aligns it more with the gift of mercy. Vine defines the word used here, *antilepsis* or *antilempsis,* as 'a laying hold of, an exchange ... to take, lay hold of, so as to support; ... then, a help ... rendering assistance, perhaps especially of help ministered to the weak and needy'.[10]

Hort defines this gift as 'anything that would be done for poor or weak or outcast brethren'.[11]

Both Vine and Hort, whom he quotes, describe the gift alluded to in 1 Corinthians as a ministration to weak, needy or outcast brethren, which would align it with the gift of mercy. In this sense, mercy leads to rendering assistance to people by supporting them or helping them up. The description certainly fits Lori whom we mentioned earlier.

From the earliest days of the Christian faith, mercy has been a characteristic of the church. The earliest churches took in widows and orphans. They ministered in the Roman Empire in times of plague when others fled the scene. From that day to this orphanages, hospitals, nursing homes, rescue missions and a host of other institutions have reflected a laudable sense of compassion.

1. Mercy — a universal command

References to mercy are scattered throughout the Scriptures. Exhortations are rooted in descriptions of the nature of God himself: 'Be merciful just as your Father is merciful' (Luke 6:36). In spite of repeated offences against his holy law, in spite of rebellion and idolatry, Israel remained the object of God's mercy.

'They wasted away in their sin.
But he took note of their distress

> when he heard their cry;
> ... out of his great love he relented.
> He caused them to be pitied ...'

(Ps. 106:43-46).

'For the Lord your God is a merciful God'

(Deut. 4:31) .

No wonder the prophets cry out,

> 'He has showed you, O man, what is good.
> And what does the Lord require of you?
> To act justly and to love mercy
> and to walk humbly with your God'

(Micah 6:8).

God expects his people to show mercy in all their dealings with each other and with foreigners. 'When an alien lives with you in your land, do not ill-treat him. The alien living with you must be treated as one of your native-born. Love him as yourself, for you were aliens in Egypt' (Lev. 19:33-34).

Jesus continues the theme: 'Blessed are the merciful, for they will be shown mercy' (Matt. 5:7). He used parables to engrave the necessity of mercy firmly on our minds. The servant forgiven a great debt ends up suffering eternal anguish because he, in turn, failed to show mercy to one of his lesser creditors (Matt. 18:21-35). A priest and a Levite pass by a fellow countryman stripped of his clothes and lying half dead from his wounds. 'But a Samaritan ... took pity on him. He went to him and bandaged his wounds, pouring on oil and wine' (Luke 10:33-34). The despised Samaritan, demonstrating mercy, took practical steps to assist the wounded man.

In the judgement parable about the sheep and the goats, Jesus teaches that compassion demonstrated by practical mercy is one of the main criteria God will use in judging the reality of our faith in Christ. The sheep chosen to stand on the King's right hand represent those men and women who respond to the hungry, the thirsty, the stranger, the poorly clothed, the sick and the imprisoned. A merciful response denotes genuine discipleship (see Matt. 25:31-46). Whatever our gifts and abilities, we must never use them as a pretext to neglect the simple directives of the Saviour. For 'Whatever you did for one of the least of these brothers of mine, you did for me' (Matt. 25:40).

Nevertheless, the church of Christ functions best when believers specialize in the areas of their giftedness. Lori found her niche in hospital ministry. Others, too, will find mercy to be their specific area of giftedness.

Definition of mercy

We could define the gift of mercy as that Spirit-induced compassion for those in misery or distress that overflows in an abundance of cheerful and practical help for those who are poor, sick, lonely, bereft or unfortunate.

2. The special gift of mercy

Some people seem to naturally combine empathy with the practical ability to jump in and lift up those who are in distress and misery. I must admit that such an ability doesn't come easily to me. I try my hardest to heed the Master's injunctions about mercy. I have worked in a rescue mission, helped in flood relief and stood up with persecuted Pakistani tenant farmers. As a pastor, I have visited hospitals, sought to comfort the bereaved and tried to help the unemployed. But somehow physical infirmity makes me feel inadequate. Now, if I see someone with a flat tyre I know what to do. But my wife, who is a nurse and radiates calm competency in a medical emergency, wonders sometimes at my fumbling approach to sickness.

On the other hand, some believers who do not know a concordance from a commentary seem to know instinctively what to do in these cases. I will continue to try to be merciful in every way I can, but I am thankful that others, much more competent than I, can get involved here.

The believers in Joppa praised God for Tabitha, called Dorcas. When she became ill and died the disciples sent for Peter. When he arrived, 'All the widows stood around him, crying and showing him the robes and other clothing that Dorcas had made while she was still with them' (see Acts 9:36-43). Dorcas undoubtedly had the gift of mercy. She 'was always doing good and helping the poor'.

Believers like Dorcas feel special compassion for the unfortunate. Then, depending on their area of competence, they get on with whatever is needed. Dorcas spent her time sewing all kinds of clothing for those in poverty and those bereft of husbands to support them. Mercy almost exclusively focuses on obvious physical distress.

The Christian church has always led the way in founding ministries of mercy. William Carey sought to save widows from being burned alive on their husbands' funeral pyres in India. Mary Slessor rescued twins destined to be buried alive in Africa. William Wilberforce poured his whole parliamentary career into outlawing slavery in the British Empire. William Booth founded the Salvation Army to reach the down and out. Amy Carmichael saved Indian girls sold into a life of temple prostitution. Scarcely a city in the Western world does not have its rescue mission with a long history of taking in and feeding the unfortunate.

Is a ministry of mercy, in this day of government social programmes, really necessary? After all, governments sponsor hospitals, subsidize welfare programmes and organize a host of helping agencies too numerous to mention.

Despite the intrusion of governments everywhere, the need for ministries of mercy remains as crucial as ever before. Indeed that need seems to be increasing with shocking speed. Without leaving our own shores to pursue a ministry of mercy in Somalia or Haiti, a believer may spend his or her life with the unfortunate and never be out of work. Children's aid societies plead for foster-parents. With the sky-rocketing cost of medical services, hospitals will have to depend more and more on voluntary help both for on-site and out-patient care. Soup-kitchens would fold up without volunteers. Abused women and children need shelters. Unmarried mothers need support. Divorced and destitute women need help. Drug addicts and alcoholics need rehabilitation. Convicts need half-way houses. Shut-ins need warm meals. Our burgeoning population of senior citizens need visitation and housing. Sufferers from AIDS need compassion.

The needs overseas have never been greater. Famine seems to never stop stalking Africa. Millions of refugees seek shelter. Typhoons and earthquakes leave devastation. Civil wars rend many countries apart and leave misery in their wake. The falling Iron Curtain has opened our eyes to a whole new gamut of misery previously hidden behind the hammer and sickle. Our world cries out for mercy!

Today, we live in a world unable to find the solutions to its problems through political process. It is a day of enormous Christian opportunity. Every church needs a cadre of believers who manifest the compassion of Dorcas. What might the characteristics of such believers be?

3. The characteristics of mercy as a gift

James defined true religion in terms of moral purity and practical mercy. In those days of gruelling labour and widespread disease, two acts of practical mercy went to the heart of social need: 'to look after orphans and widows in their distress' (James 1:27). Many men died early, leaving their widows to carry on without support. Many women perished in childbirth, leaving their children orphans.

If he had written today, James might just as well have defined pure Christian benevolence as caring for abused children or tending drug addicts in withdrawal. Three main characteristics distinguish those with the gift of mercy. The first is compassion.

Compassion

Compassion arrested the journey of a Samaritan man and moved him to stop and help the wounded Jew who had fallen among thieves because 'He took pity on him' (Luke 10:33).

Pity, as used of the Samaritan, literally means to be 'moved in one's inwards, to be moved with compassion, to yearn with compassion'.[12] The word captures the mood of Christ towards the multitudes (Matt. 9:36). The father in the parable of the prodigal son felt the same kind pity. Some consider the verb to have been coined during the sufferings of the Jewish Dispersion.[13]

The word *'sumpatheo'* carries the connotation of suffering along with another.[14] Compassion, in this sense, carries the idea that one feels deep sympathy to the point of almost sharing the pain, the hurt, the anguish, the humiliation of another. Just as the two sides of a tuning fork resonate due to sympathetic vibrations, so the distress of others moves those with the gift of mercy to sympathize. Florence Nightingale felt so deeply the distress of men dying on a distant

European battlefield that she circumvented the conventions of her day to reach out to them in compassion.

Unfortunately, the daily catalogue of disasters and human anguish that flashes briefly on our television screens tends to anaesthetize us. We may, half facetiously, excuse a lack of involvement in acts of mercy by mumbling to ourselves, 'Didn't Jesus remind his disciples that there would always be poverty? It's no use getting fired up about what won't go away, no matter what we do.'

True, as long as societies continue to be peopled by fallen human beings, injustice will produce suffering. We shall not eradicate human suffering until Christ returns in glory. However, we can make an enormous difference. Think of what aroused Christians have accomplished. In India it is now against the law to burn widows. Twins are not buried alive in Africa. Slavery is a dim memory. Workhouses, too, are as extinct as the unicorn. Debt is not now the basis for banishment to the colonies! No, the inevitability of suffering is no cause for complacency.

Of course, some may choose apathy, out of a distorted trust in the work ethic. When things are going well, we argue with ourselves that we deserve what we get — that prosperity inevitably follows hard work. And since God does, on a law-of-average basis, materially bless hard-working people above others, such a view contains an element of truth. But what of the widow in the temple at the time of Christ? What of her kin who suffer in cities around the world through no fault of their own? Ascribing our personal prosperity solely to our own hard work is blindness of a particularly arrogant kind. Such self-satisfaction ignores the unusual post-war period in which we live, the lessons of history and the presence of suffering in churches around the world.

Suffering can rarely be attributed directly to sin or laziness. David, the sweet psalmist of Israel, pondered on the prosperity of the wicked. Contrary to what some modern proponents of the health-and-wealth gospel declare, God taught David that there is no hard and fast connection between material blessing and holiness.

Should such thinking colour our reactions to people in distress we shall find ourselves sitting in judgement upon them, a seat reserved for God alone. Under the hot sun of our own misinformed pride, compassion will wither and die.

If we have thus far avoided poverty and distress we should count ourselves fortunate. For good fortune is exactly what it is. Success and ease are not distributed according to worth in our fallen world. Farmers in El Salvador did not ask for a civil war, nor blacks in Africa ask to be enslaved.

Perhaps our prosperity has stunted our sympathy. God often develops sympathy and compassion in his children by directing them through trials. 'The Father of compassion ... comforts us in all our troubles, so that we can comfort those in any trouble with the comfort we ourselves have received from God' (2 Cor. 1:3-4). Often those who feel so deeply with others in distress can sympathize because of empathy wrung out of their own painful experiences. Charles Colson, convicted Watergate conspirator, has demonstrated forcefully there is nothing like having been in jail to arouse sympathy for prisoners. But that is a high, and unnecessary, price to pay for compassion.

Cheerfulness

Scripture directs those who exercise the gift of mercy to 'do it cheerfully' (Rom. 12:8). The Greek word, *hilarotes*, is the word that is used in 2 Corinthians 9:7 to describe the cheerful giver. In an effort to counteract the gloomy way some give, some commentators have called for hilarious giving, since 'hilarious' is the English transliteration of the word. According to Vine, it 'signifies that readiness of mind, that joyousness, which is prompt to do anything'.[15]

Cheerfulness characterizes the person who eagerly serves by responding promptly to distress. A gloomy appearance may indicate a grudging attitude. When we are not happy about what we do, it usually shows on our faces. Since those in pain or distress are often already severely tempted to gloom and melancholy, a cheerful countenance on the part of those who help them is highly valued. Help offered out of a grudging sense of duty may do more harm than good.

Some erstwhile helpers seek to empathize by going into great detail about their own past operations, their own aches and pains. Before long, instead of a 'lifting up to the downcast', a pity-party develops. Merciful saints avoid spreading gloom, realizing that 'A cheerful heart is good medicine, but a crushed spirit dries up the bones' (Prov. 17:22).

Hendriksen suggests that when we visit a hospital or a shut-in 'a brief, cheering visit by a wise and sympathetic fellow-member, who is willing to help in every possible way, is certainly of far more benefit than the almost endless recital of all the horrendous details of the operation recently performed'[16]

Joyce Sanford felt constrained to visit old Mr Bittner early one day in December 1982. Never one to talk much, he seemed to keep his mouth permanently twisted in a sarcastic, hopeless expression. Joyce knew how complaining, self-pitying or pessimistic attitudes harmed the patients among whom she worked in the nursing home. As she sought to minister faithfully for Christ, Joyce had seen a number of attitudes soften. She wanted to be Mr Bittner's friend. 'He would brush me off with a grunt or dismissing wave when I tried to find some common ground with him,' she wrote.

On this particular day Joyce felt constrained to go early to give him his bath. Much to her surprise, the extra time she had with him led him to open up. His disappointments came pouring out. After listening, she shared how much Jesus loved disappointed and sinful people. To her surprise he began to cry and soon came to put his faith in a forgiving Saviour. 'Half an hour later, Mr Bittner suffered congestive heart failure.' God used the prompt and cheerful ministry of this woman with the gift of mercy to prepare the way for entrance into heaven![17]

In stories which illustrate mercy, we see not only a cheerful spirit, but a commitment to offer practical help. The need to give him a bath led Joyce Sanford to Mr Bittner's room that day.

Practical help

In the face of distress, the merciful feel constrained to do something practical. When the Good Samaritan saw the man lying by the road, he staunched the flow of blood with bandages after pouring on oil to promote healing and wine to disinfect. He interrupted his journey to take the injured man to an inn where he paid for his follow-up care (Luke 10:25-35). The sacrifice of time and money counts little to those motivated by compassion for the unfortunate.

The noble wife of Proverbs 31 exemplifies practical mercy as well. Her industry and skill provide food and clothing for her family but she also 'opens her arms to the poor and extends her hands to the needy' (Prov. 31:20).

A desire to meet physical need has always moved Christians to action. For years C. H. Spurgeon and his wife helped a widow through the profits they gleaned from the sale of eggs. Love for Christ and compassion for a population without medical care moved Dr V. Olsen to establish a hospital in a needy part of Bangladesh. Compassion moved the founders of the Blind Mission to reach out to help blind people around the world.

Practical mercy can take as many forms as compassionate imagination can conceive. A mechanic, moved by concern for poor and uneducated young men in Bangladesh, began a small mechanics' school in Dacca. Doug and Margaret Bastian decided to establish a hostel so that the children of itinerant tribal Marvaris in Pakistan could get education. Many of these boys will probably become leaders in the growing Marvari church.

Two cautions need to be mentioned here lest we get the wrong idea about mercy. First, the gift of mercy is mainly directed towards meeting external physical needs. Practical mercy, such as that of Mother Theresa on the streets of Calcutta, captures the imagination of even the most hardened atheists. But if we are not careful, we shall forget that the greatest act of mercy, the death of Christ for our sins, was aimed at spiritual, not physical rescue. The most widespread and the most eternally dangerous condition on earth is not poverty or sickness but sin. In this sense evangelism, which aims to rescue lost men and women from eternal doom, is the most merciful ministry of all.

We must never allow a valid appreciation for practical acts of mercy to obscure our view of the primacy of evangelism and missions. Practical deeds of compassion should naturally flow from the reality of our Christian walk and some believers with the gift of mercy will be called by the Holy Spirit to concentrate on ministries of practical mercy. But the Great Commission calls us to go into all the world with the gospel. It does not specifically call us to go into all the world to heal and educate. These later ministries must be adjuncts to, and the fruits of, the fundamental ministry of extending the kingdom.

A second concern relates to the number of illustrations I have used about acts of mercy beyond our shores. Need seems so glaring and obvious in places like Somalia and India. But in reality the needs surround us. Exhausted single parents need encouragement. Senior citizens need visits and care. In New Zealand a woman struggling through a long period of debilitating illness could find no place in which to recuperate quietly. On her feet again, she established Te

Waiora, a centre sixty kilometres from Christchurch, to which men and women could go to find quietness and loving support in times of pain and perplexity.

Refusing to leave the inner city, Fleischmann Memorial Baptist Church in Philadelphia opened 'Reborn Thrift Shop'. Geared to meet the practical needs of people in a poor neighbourhood, the thrift store 'offers second-hand and donated new clothing and household items for resale'.[18]

While I have distinguished in this book the work of mercy from the work of evangelism, the two are closely linked. The love of Christ that constrains us to seek lost sinners also constrains us to help those in distress. Bear Valley Baptist Church has demonstrated that astonishing church growth can be the result of targeting need. From unpretentious facilities seating 275, the 1,000 members of this church in Denver fan out in a bewildering array of ministries including work with street people, refugees, artists, international students, mothers of preschool children, ex-convicts and delinquent girls. From a small beginning the church grew mightily.[19] Love expressed in both evangelism and mercy may be the real secret of genuine church growth.

Conclusion

The Spirit expects you and me to demonstrate mercy. Mercy, of course, costs money. The Good Samaritan paid out cash for the care of the wounded Jew. The gifts of giving and mercy complement each other. Spirit-filled givers view their resources as a stewardship from God. Through careful handling they stand ready to rise to any real need with a response of unbridled generosity. Have you been moved by the Spirit in either of these directions? Look around you in your church and community. What needs particularly move you to action? If either financial need or human distress repeatedly arrest your attention, God may be preparing you for an enlarged ministry in one or both areas.

Of course, selfishness will stifle gift development. Lloyd Ogilvie, in a recent television broadcast, expressed his appreciation for receiving so much mail. He was saddened, however, to note that 99% of his correspondents talked about their own needs. He lamented that the tragedy of American Christianity is that Christians have turned what was intended as equipment for ministry (prayer, for example) into a means of personal comfort. Christians rip New Testament promises, such as, 'Whatever you ask I will do,' out of context and make them serve narcissistic desires. He explained that this promise of answered prayer is a promise for the road, a promise for missionary ministry. God promises to help us so we can join with him in ministry to a suffering world.[20]

Return to your chart on the gifts. Fill in the columns related to the gifts of giving and mercy. Then, move on to a consideration of visionary faith and discernment that helps to avoid danger.

20.
Faith and discernment

Faith and discernment, on the surface, hardly seem to qualify as gifts. But without their presence, any church is in danger of either getting stuck in a rut or falling in a ditch. Faith calls us out of the ruts of lazy complacency or empty tradition to move mountains for God. Discernment keeps us from falling in a ditch dug by error. Let's look first at the ruts.

An endless round of activities and meetings within the four walls of our church buildings may develop a fortress complex that, in reality, is nothing but a deep rut. Time and repetition forge traditions disguised as orthodoxy. Scripturally based patterns of worship become mixed willy nilly with cultural forms frozen from the fifties, or even the nineteenth century.

Howard Snyder, in his stimulating book, *The Problem Of Wineskins,* argues that human nature leads us to pass up the freshness of the gospel to settle for controlled and predictable patterns. He begins by shocking us: 'It is hard to escape the conclusion that today one of the greatest roadblocks to the gospel of Jesus Christ is the institutional church.'[1] The church plods along in a deep rut.

Fortunately, the sovereign God repeatedly calls his people to renewal through men of faith. Martin Luther, mourning over religious abuses all around him, heard God's call and stepped out in faith to call the dead church to rise in newness of reformation vigour. George Whitefield shocked traditionalists by daring to preach in the unhallowed ground of open fields. Their descendants, men and women of faith, call us to step out of our stultifying ruts into a life of freedom and vision.

Immobility often hinders the progress of the kingdom. As Will Rogers said, 'Even if you are on the right track, you will get run over if you just sit there.'[2] Many of us grow uncomfortable with inaction, but we are uncertain about direction. Men and women of faith sense the leading of God and inspire us to step out of our ruts to break new ground. Thank God for the gift of faith!

I. The gift of faith

In describing spiritual gifts to the Corinthians, Paul labels one of these 'manifestations of the Spirit' as 'faith' (1 Cor. 12:7,9). Mention of faith, as a spiritual gift, occurs only in this text. In other contexts, however, we read about a kind of faith that can move mountains.

In most cases, faith is the English translation of one Greek word, *pistis,* which Vine defines as '(1) a firm conviction, producing a full acknowledgement of God's revelation or truth, (2) a personal surrender to Him, (3) a conduct inspired by such surrender.'[3]

All genuine believers must exercise some measure of faith. 'Without faith it is impossible to please God' (Heb. 11:6). Our salvation depends on faith. 'For it is by grace you have been saved, through faith — and this not from yourselves, it is the gift of God — not by works, so that no one can boast' (Eph. 2:8-9). God justifies us, delivering us from the guilt and penalty of our sin through faith received as a gift.

Disciples depend on faith for every facet of the Christian life from regeneration to glory. Every Christian needs to quench the fiery darts of the evil one by taking up 'the shield of faith' (Eph. 6:16). 'We live by faith, not by sight' (2 Cor. 5:7). Believers grow in faith (2 Thess. 1:3). Along with love and hope, faith abides (1 Cor. 13:13). Through faith we overcome the world (1 John 5:4).

Although all Christians should live by faith, God gifts some believers with unusual faith, 'faith that can move mountains' (1 Cor. 13:2). Some writers believe that all Christians should demonstrate mountain-moving faith. While I agree that all of us need to aspire to more faith than we presently possess, 1 Corinthians 12:9 indicates that some have this gift and some don't: ' ... to another faith by the same Spirit'. According to the context, every believer does not possess the gift of faith which I equate with the mountain-moving faith mentioned in chapter 13.

Jesus twice mentions faith of this calibre. Apparently his disciples needed mountain-moving faith to undergird a ministry of healing and exorcism. You may recall the incident in which they had been unable to deliver a boy suffering demon-induced seizures. When they enquired of the Master why their efforts had failed, he said, 'Because you have so little faith. I tell you the truth, if you have faith as small as a mustard seed, you can say to this mountain, "Move from here to there" and it will move. Nothing will be impossible for you' (Matt. 17:20-21). On this occasion, Jesus lamented not only their lack of faith but its widespread scarcity: 'O unbelieving and perverse generation, how long shall I stay with you?' (Matt. 17:17).

Jesus' ability to heal the sick, to cast out demons and to raise the dead had astounded the disciples. His ability to cause a fig-tree to wither had amazed them. Later they would remember Jesus' words: 'I tell you the truth, if you have faith and do not doubt, not only can you do what was done to the fig-tree, but also you can say to this mountain, "Go, throw yourself into the sea," and it will be done' (Matt. 21:21).

With some notable exceptions, the disciples' faith remained weak until Pentecost. Peter's attempt to walk on water ended when he quickly sank. But after the descent of the Holy Spirit, the apostles demonstrated remarkable faith. Three thousand responded to Peter's call for repentance. Peter and John healed a man on the steps of the temple. At a word, Ananias and Sapphira fell dead. God used Peter to raise Dorcas from the dead. The church expanded as faith soared.

After Pentecost, the apostles did go out and move mountains. The Jewish establishment ground their teeth in frustration in the face of their boldness but it could not stop them. In a few short years Jewish hopes perished in the ashes of Jerusalem. Out of the ashes a vibrant church rose like a phoenix. It spread its wings wider and wider. Even the power of Rome could not tame the soaring faith of the early Christians. Rome shrivelled and shook while simple believers went out and turned the world upside down!

Down through history God has continued to turn the world on its ears through men and women of faith. In the nineteenth century, Hudson Taylor cast his eyes longingly towards inland China. Missionaries of that era, believing that evangelizing the interior was impossible, worked along the coast. But impossibilities challenge people of Hudson Taylor's ilk. When established missionary societies wouldn't rise to his vision, he founded his own society, the

China Inland Mission. From the beginning, mountain-moving faith became the undergirding principle of its operation. They made their needs known to God alone who honoured their faith and poured out his blessing.

In the early years, Taylor badly needed co-workers. He sought eighteen in prayer. Within a year, eighteen were dedicated. Before long, by faith, a hundred workers joined him in reaching inland China. The CIM, now the Overseas Missionary Fellowship, became one of the largest missions. Scores of other missions, inspired by this so-called 'faith principle', soon sprang up. Today mission boards carrying the nickname 'faith missions' form one of the largest Protestant groups.

But is the gift of faith, in distinction from faith in general, restricted to the likes of a Peter or a Hudson Taylor in days long ago? Far from it! Every age has those with the gift of faith. John Perkins believed that the love of God could overcome racial prejudice in the strife-torn '60s. He founded Voice of Calvary in Jackson, Mississippi to serve the medical, housing and spiritual needs of Jackson's poor. For over thirty years it has been a testimony to what one man can do, given faith in God and a vision of what can be.

Faith like that inspires others to believe in the impossible. In 1988 a work crew of eighteen white, mostly upper-income professionals from the northern U.S. twin cities of Minneapolis/St Paul paid their way to Jackson because they joined John Perkins in believing God can work today. While there, they renovated a six-room house, one of fourteen similar houses Voice Of Calvary planned to renovate. A white worker in a lumber yard commended them but said, 'We don't want you gettin' no ideas it'll make a difference. Nothing will change.' No? Those workers from Minnesota chose to believe God![4]

In almost every church there are unsung men and women who inspire us to step out of the well-trodden way, which may be a rut in disguise, to pioneer new challenges.

A definition of the gift

We could define the gift of faith as an endowment of the Spirit that produces a deep dissatisfaction with present conditions, glimpses a vision of what God can do, faces seemingly insurmountable obstacles and yet feels a deep assurance that God will work.

Visionary faith grows restless with the status quo and launches out in confidence that God can overcome any obstacle.

1. Confidence in God

Hebrews 11 lists many whose lives pleased God. Why did they please him? 'Without faith it is impossible to please God, because anyone who comes to him must believe that he exists and that he rewards those who earnestly seek him' (Heb. 11:6). Abel, Enoch, Noah and Abraham, to name a few, pleased God because their lives were marked by a passionate search for God. The flame of faith, in turn, illumined their search.

Confidence in God has undergirded every man and woman of faith, from Abraham, who fathered the Hebrew nation, to Joy Ridderhof, who gave birth to Gospel Recordings. Only trust in God could inspire Abraham to leave home to journey into the unknown. Only confidence in God made him ready to sacrifice his own son. Although the patriarchs never received in their own lifetimes the land which God promised, nevertheless, they trusted him so implicitly that, like Joseph, they even made arrangements for their burial in Canaan. Like Moses, who 'persevered because he saw him who is invisible', their faith sustained them in the midst of tribulations (Heb. 11:27). This confidence in the invisible God anchored their lives.

While each of us knows that we are to 'trust in the Lord with all [our] heart' (Prov. 3:5), most of us have back-up systems in case God doesn't meet all our needs. For example, we may avoid a career move that would leave us without the security of a steady income even though we feel pulled to seek a more satisfying calling. We may overprotect our children because we cannot trust in God's ongoing care. We may move to the suburbs to improve our assets instead of toughing it out with a struggling inner-city church. We may avoid opportunities to mingle with unbelievers lest we face opportunities to witness that we are unable to handle.

Instead of confidence in God moving us continually to push back the frontiers of our experience we opt for the safe, the secure, the known, the predictable. How do I know? I have been there many, many times. Sometimes it takes divine dynamite, doesn't it, to jolt us out of our comfortable ruts?

Those with the gift of faith probably struggled, like all of us, with fears of the unknown. But confidence in God led them to shrug off acceptance of the status quo to venture forth in new directions.

George Müller was such a man. Without making any needs known, and without any resources of his own, he launched out on the promises of God to help thousands of orphans. His venture grew into care for 10,000 orphans through a programme costing five million dollars over sixty years. With only God to rely on, he built five large homes in Bristol, in the south-west of England, to house two thousand orphans at a time. Every day he depended on God to feed and clothe his orphans.

To Müller, faith was more substantial than money in the bank. He said, 'Faith is the assurance that the things which God said in His Word are true; and that God will act according to what He has said in His Word. This assurance, this reliance on God's Word, this confidence, is Faith.'[5]

In those with the gift of faith, this calm assurance overrides doubt and anxiety. Of course, every believer aspires to absolute confidence in the trustworthiness of scriptural promises manifest in a daily trust in the Lord. But too often we choose the easy way.

While faith calls us to step out in absolute confidence in the risen Christ, sometimes that kind of faith seems unattainable. When we wrestle with our own doubts, it is comforting to know that the giants of faith were made of the same stuff as you and me. The gift of faith doesn't come full-blown. Often necessity, and even failures of faith, contribute to its development. Abraham doubted God's ability to provide a son in his old age. At first Moses protested vigorously about his unsuitability to lead Israel from Egypt. Spiritual gifts, like tender plants, need to be nurtured if they are to grow. No one should expect to have faith like a George Müller or a Mary Slessor overnight — but all of us should be disturbed by the conditions we see around us.

2. Dissatisfaction with present situations

Spiritual discontent moves sensitive souls to trust God for something better. Noah, 'a righteous man, blameless among the people of his time ... walked with God'. All around him, 'The earth was corrupt in God's sight and full of violence' (Gen. 6:9,11). The social evil in the midst of which he lived must have vexed his sensitive soul. He must have longed for justice. When God warned him of impending judgement and commanded him to build an enormous ark, Noah 'did all that the Lord commanded him' (Gen. 7:5; cf. 6:22; 7:9,16). His wholehearted obedience to this astounding command demonstrates the reality of his unusual faith. 'By faith Noah ... built an ark' (Heb. 11:7).

The author of Hebrews traces a common attitude in those he catalogues. He says, 'They admitted that they were aliens and strangers on earth. People who say such things show that they are looking for a country of their own ... a better country — a heavenly one' (Heb. 11:13-16). Men and women of faith recognize in the world around them the marks of depravity and impermanence. They long for something better, both in heaven itself, and in that preview of heaven, the kingdom of God. Targeting sin as the main despoiler, they fix their eyes on Jesus while they struggle with evil, resisting it even to the point of shedding their own blood (Heb. 12:2,4).

Mountain-moving faith is dissatisfied with the ruts in which we grind along our predictable way. It encourages the belief that revolutionary change is not only possible, but must be attempted. The thought of sitting back in a comfortable pew alarms those with the gift of faith.

Many of our churches — I can think of no kinder way to say it — are in a rut. Oh yes, many stalwart saints face shrinking attendance and dying witness with a grim determination to hang on. But perseverance and faithfulness, while laudable, are not the need of the hour. We need discontent! Look around! Hurting men and women, today's lost generation, eddy around these bastions of faded vision with scarcely a glance at what are, in their view, irrelevant and rusty relics of the past.

Fortunately, you and I know a few men and women of faith who refuse to die a slow death with a shrinking church. They will not give up. They demonstrate tenacity and creativity as they seek to call these bastions of musty history to a vigorous new outreach to the people of today. Not content with the status quo, they pray, they read, they go out into the highways and byways trying new ways of reaching yuppies and single mums, teenagers and senior citizens. I take my hat off to these heroes of faith, who often stand alone in the midst of a sea of complacency, a tide of backward-looking nostalgia, crying out against the slow demise of our evangelical witness!

Yes, there has scarcely ever been a day when we have so desperately needed men and women of faith to raise a hue and cry against the downgrade in our country and city churches. Some have been notably successful.

A man rose to preach to a rather large congregation. Many yawned as he announced that he had three points. For his first point he noted that nearly two billion people are starving. Since the congregation had heard this many times, they reacted with indifference. But when he went on without elaboration to his second point people began to sit up.

He paused before announcing his second point: 'My second point is that most of you don't give a damn!'

Tim Hansel describes the scene; 'He paused again, as gasps and rumblings flowed across the congregation, and then said: "And my third point is that the real tragedy among Christians today is that many of you are now more concerned that I said 'damn' than you are that I said that two billion people are starving to death." Then he sat down.'[6]

According to Tim Hansel, the sermon took only one minute but was one of the most powerful he had heard. Sadly, we have to admit that the tragic apathy highlighted by the speaker too often marks our walk with Christ. Those with the gift of faith hate apathy as much as they hate doubt.

Throughout my life I have personally had to struggle to avoid apathy. Fortunately God has repeatedly put me into situations where I needed to trust him. At Columbia Bible College, where I took my first Bible training, we were urged to live a life of daily faith. One year, as Christmas approached, I knew that I needed to get home for the holidays. Except for my mother, my family expressed extreme scepticism about my new faith. But I had no money and was a thousand miles away from Toronto. The Lord convinced me that I should go home and challenged me to trust him to get me there. But how? Why not settle down for the holidays in the hall of residence and use the meal ticket I already had? Why? Because my infant faith told me that the easiest way is seldom the way of faith.

3. Insurmountable problems

Those with the gift of faith tackle seemingly insurmountable problems with a confidence that God will work out a solution. If I had possessed the gift of faith while in Bible College the minor problem of getting home for the holidays would not have worried me. I must confess, though, that I was somewhat worried as I set out to hitch-hike home. I knew that, with only a short break over Christmas, I couldn't expect to hitch-hike to Toronto and back in time for college. A thousand miles and an empty wallet, to my mind, meant — impossible! I shall return to this story later.

Visionaries thrive on the impossible. Noah built an enormous boat to ride out a rainstorm even though he had never seen rain. Abraham willingly offered up Isaac, his only son, to God, knowing God could do the impossible (Heb. 11:19). After learning to trust God, Moses smote the Red Sea, confident that God could do the incredible. Joshua faced the impossible task of breaking down the walls of Jericho. Nehemiah lived with the hopeless job of rebuilding the walls of Jerusalem.

Unused as most of us are to living by faith, the solutions proposed by those with the gift of faith often seem outrageous. In the nineteenth century, Adoniram Judson's friends thought him reckless to turn down a fashionable church for a fever-infested Burmese jungle. But in spite of failing to baptize one convert in six years, he continued to preach the gospel. The resistance of Buddhists, far from discouraging him, challenged him to trust the Lord more.

The difficulties that most Christians cautiously avoid, those with the gift of faith embrace with verve. They realize, as Samuel Johnson has said, 'Nothing will ever be attempted if all possible objections must first be overcome.'[7] Men and women of faith view difficulties as doorways of opportunity.

Too often we settle for whatever is convenient and end up satisfied by trivial banalities. We plan our lives to avoid the unpredictable. The government jumps in, too, with safety nets from the cradle to the grave. But where there is no risk, there is no progress.

Tim Hansel maintains that 'Risk is at the very core of the Christian life.'[8] Tozer reminds us that 'The faith of Paul and Luther was a revolutionizing thing. It upset the whole life of the individual and made him into another person altogether.'[9] He laments the replacement of venturesome faith by sickening passivity. Those with the gift of faith sing joyfully,

Faith, mighty faith, the promise sees,
And looks to God alone,

Laughs at impossibilities,
And cries, 'It shall be done!'

Opportunities disguised as impossibilities capture the vision of those with the gift of faith.

4. Vision

Vision propels men and women of faith above mountainous problems to soar in the stratosphere of their imagination. They know that God loves to turn problems into runways from which to launch believers on new flights of exploration for the kingdom. As someone has said, 'God's best gifts are not in things but in opportunities.' And opportunity knocks, not when things are easy, but in the midst of vexations.

Faith opens the door for believers to wander in their imaginations through God's workshop where solutions are forged, instead of stumbling along in pessimistic gloom. 'Faith is being sure of what we hope for and certain of what we do not see. This is what the ancients were commended for' (Heb. 11:1-2). Vision is sanctified imagination. Noah could scarcely imagine a flood. But his assurance that this improbable judgement would come was so strong that fear spurred him on to build an ark to provide safety for his family and the animals (Heb. 11:7). A vision of what would be inspired Noah to heroic effort.

Abraham, too, went forth without knowing exactly where he was going. Vision of a promised land populated by an, as yet, unborn nation spurred him on.

William Carey challenged a group of ministers in Nottingham in these now famous words: 'Expect great things from God; attempt great things for God,' a motto that has inspired thousands since.

Adoniram Judson laboured for six years without a convert. After his fifth year he was asked about prospects. He replied in what has become a rallying cry of those with vision: 'The future is as bright as the promises of God.'

Without leaders who possess the farsightedness that vision produces we may shrink from untried paths to sink into comfortable ruts. If the Great Commission is to be obeyed we need vision. If our cities are to be evangelized we need vision. Yet vision seems rare. Someone has said,

So few men venture out beyond the blazed trail,
That he who has the courage to go past this sign
Cannot in his mission fail.
He will have left at least some mark behind
To guide some other brave exploring mind.

Müller, Taylor, Carey and Judson have left their mark. But we
need men and women like them in each of our churches to jolt us out
of apathy. Personally, I have always been challenged by men and
women of vision. When, as a young Christian, I set out from
Columbia for Toronto without a dollar in my pocket, dimly believing I would make it, it was hardly vision, but it was a start.

5. Checking vision for legitimacy

We have all known those who claim infallibility for their own
presumption. You and I may have been tempted ourselves to set off
on a wild-goose chase, foolish enough to think that we were sent by
God, when it was really our own imagination. In the late '80s TV
healer Oral Roberts claimed that God had inspired him to stay up in
his prayer tower until viewers sent in millions in donations. He
might have really believed what he claimed, that if the money didn't
come in he would die, but I don't believe the message came from
God. His claim of receiving a word from God is a clear example of
self-deception. Scripture records no precedent of God holding any
man hostage until believers cough up a ransom!

Faith always rests on clear biblical promise or precedent (Rom.
10:17). Noah believed there would be a flood because God had said
so. Abraham set out from Ur of the Chaldees because God had
directed him. Along the way he received assurance from God that
a son would be born and from that son a nation would be conceived.
Moses, too, excelled in faith because he had something solid to base
that faith on, the clear directives of God.

Those with the gift of faith continually check the direction in
which their faith would lead them with what they know of God and
his promises. They flee anything inconsistent with the God they
serve. For example, they know that God, who created the universe
and owns the cattle on a thousand hills, is not one to condone
begging for money. They also realize that God has not promised
freedom from troubles or persecution. From the biblical precedent

of Paul suffering from a thorn in the flesh, they conclude that freedom from physical suffering is not promised by God. Hence extreme difficulties do not dull their vision.

Then too, biblical visionaries ought to seek counsel. The exercise of the gifts of wisdom and of discernment in the local church is meant to confirm or refine the vision of those with the gift of faith. In some cases, however, men and women of vision have presented bold ideas that frightened less venturesome members of the body. If a congregation rejects a genuine vision of a man of faith, the visionary may have to move out in faith anyway. But let him first have patience with God's people and seek to explain his vision in a biblical manner. William Carey's vision for evangelism in India met with a distinctly chilly reception, as did Taylor's burden for inland China. Sadly, the church has often been tardy in verifying the vision of men of faith.

Flynn remarks that 'Müller always first satisfied himself that he was doing God's will before he started a project. Then, resting on the promises of the Bible, he came boldly to the throne in prayer, pleading his case argumentatively, giving reasons why God should answer. No delay discouraged him. Once he was persuaded that a thing was right, he went on praying for it till the answer came.'[10]

The person with this gift will be able to give, like Müller, clear scriptural reasons for his vision. The gift of faith is no fuzzy impression or brilliant idea. It must coincide with the will of God.

Thirty years ago, as I set out for Toronto, I had gone over in my mind the biblical rationale for my trip. God wanted me to honour my parents who were sceptical about my new faith. Although I was broke, God was not. He had promised to supply my need, especially since I was preparing for missionary service. I had worked when I could, but as a Canadian citizen, I could not take a part-time job in the U.S.A. Going home seemed to be consistent with what I knew about God and his promises.

But as our next section indicates, the gift of faith is more than guidance about the will of God.

6. A sense of certainty about the future

The Scriptures inform us that 'Faith is being sure of what we hope for and certain of what we do not see' (Heb. 11:1). Even as he lifted the knife to slay Isaac, Abraham was sure that God would restore his son. Noah, likewise, laboured to build a boat for a flood he knew would come. Joshua believed the walls of Jericho would crumble.

Few of us would claim to have faith like that of Noah or Joshua, but we do believe in what we have never seen. Although we have never gazed upon God with our own eyes yet we believe in his existence. 'Anyone who comes to him must believe that he exists' (Heb. 11:6). Without faith we cannot approach God in prayer. Without faith we can neither be saved nor enjoy assurance of salvation. Faith of this calibre, far from being mystical, is rooted in the explicit statements of the written Word of God.

The faith demonstrated by God's visionaries, however, goes beyond the explicit statements of Scripture. Men and women of faith express certainty concerning matters not explicitly mentioned in Scripture. They trust God for buildings to be built, funds to come in, workers to be raised up, missionaries to be supported, orphans to be fed, homeless to be housed, declining churches to be renewed and street kids to be reached. While the Scriptures cover these matters in general terms, it does take venturesome faith to apply them to concrete situations today.

In spite of six years without a convert, Adoniram Judson remained confident that God would raise up a church in Burma. The first Sunday of every month he celebrated the Lord's Supper with his wife, believing that they were the seed of a future church in Burma. Years later the churches he founded had 50,000 converts!

Concerning his vision of 100 new missionaries, Hudson Taylor said, 'If you showed me a photograph of the whole 100 taken in China, I could not be more sure than I am now.'[11] His new mission carefully chose 102 from among the more than 600 who volunteered that year and sent them on their way by 29 December.

The example of men like Judson and Taylor, and women like Amy Carmichael and Mary Slessor, have encouraged many others to trust God explicitly. Of course, in these stalwarts, the gift of faith could not be separated from a life of prayer. James reminds us, 'The prayer of a righteous man is powerful and effective. Elijah was a man just like us. He prayed earnestly that it would not rain, and it did not rain on the land for three and a half years. Again he prayed, and the heavens gave rain...' (James 5:17-18). Like Elijah everyone is made of the same frail stuff. Prayer is not the recourse of strong self-

confident men and women, but the inspiration of those who know
they have a great God.

As Hallesby points out, 'The essence of faith is to come to God...
To pray is nothing more involved than to let Jesus into our needs.'
Men and women of faith learn to bring their needs quickly to the only
one who can meet them. They are people just like you and me, but
they have learned to accept their own helplessness and look to God.
'Listen, my friend! Your helplessness is your best prayer.'[12]

George Müller, understanding his inability to supply the needs
of multiplied hundreds of orphans, prayed. He would keep praying
until the answer came. The record of those prayers and their answers
covered three thousand pages. He recorded some 50,000 answers![13]

Vision leads those with the gift of faith to seek the face of God.
In the place of prayer, the Holy Spirit produces within them a deep
conviction that their vision will become a reality.

But what of you and me? Every Christian should aspire to
mountain-moving faith. In each of our lives, and in each of our
churches, situations arise, from time to time, that require this kind
of faith. At such a juncture a failure to trust God dooms us to
stagnation.

Personally, I don't believe a qualitative difference separates the
faith every Christian is called to exercise from mountain-moving
faith. Perhaps the difference is more quantitative. Probably God
chooses some to concentrate their energies on inspiring others to
step out into the unknown. It could be that obedient saints experience some measure of this gift from time to time. For example, I
must say that I am unsure as to whether I personally have potential
to stir up the gift of faith or not. Several deacons during a recent
pastorate have indicated in the affirmative. At any rate I have had
some challenging experiences in which I was compelled to trust
God in unusual ways.

I have already referred more than once to the time when I headed
home for Christmas with an empty pocket. I began to hitch-hike.
First I got a ride in a pick-up truck, only to find myself dropped off
on the wrong road. Rather upset at this inauspicious beginning to my
venture of faith, I waited for another ride. Next a man picked me up
who was only going a short way. He enquired about my destination
and studies. When I mentioned my studies at Bible College he
became thoughtful, and suggested I come to his house. Puzzled, I
agreed.

In the driveway stood a low-slung Corvette sports car, the envy of any young man. Ducking inside the house, the man bid me wait a moment. When he came back out he told me that he had phoned his insurance agent. He wanted me to drive the Corvette to Buffalo, not far from Toronto. Along with the address in Buffalo, where I was to deliver the car, he gave me more than enough money for petrol. Heads turned as I cruised northward in somewhat of a daze!

Arriving in Buffalo, I found there was enough money left to buy a bus ticket to Toronto. It was evening and the last bus had left. As I settled down on a bench in the terminal for a long, restless night, a man next to me struck up a conversation. I soon discovered that he was a fellow believer. He insisted I stay with him overnight. A soft bed to sleep on and a hearty breakfast in the morning sent me on my way rejoicing in the wonder of God's omnipotence. I discovered that Christmas that God could be trusted to help me to do what was right, and sometimes he would throw in a sports car just for the fun of it!

Every Christian should experience some measure of venturesome faith. I have to keep reminding myself to trust God; probably you do too. As we push against the confining limits of our uncertainties we may discover the Spirit developing within us mountain-moving faith. Such a discovery could open the door to opportunities for service. We may be used of God to inspire and motivate others. Each local church needs believers with this gift to help us out of our ruts — just as each church needs those with the gift of discernment.

II. The gift of discernment

A Christian woman married to a non-Christian came to me one day in a state of some agitation. Another couple, long-time friends and professing Christians, were breaking off all fellowship with them on the advice of their pastor. The Christian woman who came to me traced the cause of this breach to a friendship both couples had maintained for some time with a third couple who were somewhat influenced by a cult. The pastor had urged them to break off all social fellowship with anyone having even a distant connection with cultic belief. Was the pastor right to enforce what has been called 'second-degree separation'? Such a scenario calls for careful discernment.

Of course, many professing Christians settle questions like this with ease. Quoting Jesus' dictum that we must not judge lest we be judged, they blithely refuse to make any kind of evaluation. 'Love your enemies,' in their minds, decrees tolerance at all times of everyone. In some circles tolerance is elevated above truth. Strangely enough, such people exhibit tolerance of anyone except fundamentalists — whom they consign to oblivion for the sin of intolerance! In their view, intolerance is the unpardonable sin!

Scripture — and common sense — however, requires us to separate truth from error. Jesus, not Buddha or Krishna, is 'the way and the truth and the life' (John 14:6). Early Christians were often called people of 'the way'. That path is the straight and narrow way of Jesus. If the gift of faith keeps us from being stuck in ruts as we walk in the way, the gift of discernment keeps us from falling headlong into the ditch of error. As we walk in the way of truth, the subtle forces of relativism would woo us into a quagmire of pietism or New Age pantheism, into Unitarianism or pragmatism, into legalism or licentiousness, into existentialism or mysticism. We need discernment!

Every arena of human activity cries out for those with discernment. Sprinkled throughout our congregations are those who seem to be on astonishingly intimate terms with the Almighty. 'God told me to marry Sally,' one declares. (Sally, of course is either an unbeliever or a young divorcee with two children.) Another informs the deacon board, 'I know it's God's will for me to go to Bongo Bongo as a missionary.' (The deacons roll their eyes and wonder how much a long stretch of unemployment has contributed to this decision.) 'God led me directly to this car! It was a miracle,' enthuses a third. (Friends, eyeing the red Mercedes convertible, wonder if it was leading or lust.) You get the picture.

Each of us must be able to distinguish the voice of God from the whispers of our own desires. What do the Scriptures teach about discernment?

1. Discernment and judgement

The Scriptures present us with a paradox. On the one hand, Jesus severely warns us against judging one another: 'Do not judge, or you too will be judged... Why do you look at the speck of sawdust in your brother's eye and pay no attention to the plank in your own eye?' (Matt. 7:1,3). On other occasions, Christ himself pointed out faults in quite strong language: 'Hypocrites! You know how to interpret the appearance of the earth and the sky. How is it that you don't know how to interpret this present time? Why don't you judge for yourselves what is right?' (Luke 12:56-57).

How do we know when to judge and when not to? Part of the problem can be traced to terminology. Both terms come from the same Greek root that means 'to separate, select or choose'. *Krino*, used in the reference from Matthew 7 quoted above, carries the connotation of separating, so as 'to judge, pronounce judgement'. On the other hand, *diakrino,* used in the first part of the reference from Luke, denotes 'discriminate, discern, and hence to decide, to judge'.[14] In the latter case the NIV translators used the English word 'interpret', meaning to make a careful discrimination.

Balance is continually at a premium in the Christian life. Jesus was supremely balanced. On the one hand, he could exhort us not to condemn our brothers by judging them from the lofty heights of our own pride while on the other he expected us to be discriminating.

How foolish to seat ourselves on a lofty judgement seat when we have faults the size of a plank in our eye while others have only a speck of sawdust in theirs! We are not called to a ministry of judgement because, first of all, judgement belongs to God, and secondly, when we judge, we set ourselves up as better than others. If the great apostle could say, 'I am the chief of sinners,' surely we need to readily admit our share of humanity's common depravity.

On the other hand, we do need to be able to discriminate between true and false beliefs, and between good and evil practices. If the interpretation of weather can save us the grief of being unprepared for tornadoes and frost, surely the interpretation of human teaching and behaviour can save us from personal turmoil and congregational grief. Discernment is not condemnation.

2. Discernment and maturity

According to the author of Hebrews, failure to develop discernment dooms us to spiritual babyhood. Like babies who live on milk, naïve Christians, unacquainted with 'teaching on righteousness', toddle around in spiritual infancy. 'Solid food is for the mature, who by

constant use have trained themselves to distinguish good from evil'
(Heb. 5:13-14). If we fail to distinguish good from evil, we shall
remain infants, because we shall constantly make bad choices.
Unless we discern where a choice is likely to lead us, we may end
up going astray. As discernment develops, through practice in
making the right choices, our ability to recognize and flee temptation produces strength of character. Discernment and maturity are
two sides of the same coin.

Christians ought to emulate the Bereans. Paul and Silas had fled
to Berea after persecution in Thessalonica. Fortunately, on arrival,
they found that 'The Bereans were of more noble character than the
Thessalonians, for they received the message with great eagerness
and examined the Scriptures every day to see if what Paul said was
true' (Acts 17:11).

The Bereans used the Scriptures as a yardstick to measure
everything the missionaries taught. Attention to the Word, as it is
preached, accompanied by personal and corporate study, equips a
believer with the biblical data necessary to discern good and evil.
The discerning find here the commands of God, in terms of prohibitions and exhortations, as well as the principles and examples
which enable them to develop a sense of truth and error, of right and
wrong.

Discernment is not intuition. Biblical discernment rests on the
firm base of objective revelation. Specific principles, commands
and precedents direct the discerning in their examination of any
situation. While vague feelings of uneasiness may unconsciously
stem from a mature believer's almost instinctive sense of right and
wrong, nevertheless the discerning will always test their intuition by
Scripture. Subjective feelings cannot be trusted.

Conscientious believers use their knowledge of biblical principle and precedent as the basis upon which to make assessments
and choices. Good choices, in turn, develop character. As character
matures, discernment grows.

Unfortunately immaturity in Christians is common. Individual
believers are not always fully to blame for such a state. Some groups,
by their heavy-handed legalism, hinder character development. In
the mistaken belief that where the Scriptures are silent on current
issues definitive rules need to be supplied, some well-meaning
Christians set out to build a massive superstructure of prohibitions.
Rules are laid down for everything from the length of dresses to the

style of hair. And, since the necessity of making difficult choices and exercising careful discernment is bypassed, many believers respond to such a procedure with relief. Legalism saves a lot of hard thinking and study.

Sadly, these well-meaning brothers miss the purpose of God and stifle the process of sanctification. Maturity can only develop in a climate where believers have freedom to make personal choices. As part of his work of restoring in us the image of God, the Holy Spirit encourages us to develop the ability to discern clearly and choose decisively. As sinners we were in bondage to the influence of the world, the flesh and the devil. Our decisions, in the main, were motivated by our desires rather than by clear and logical thought based on moral principles. Redeemed by the power of God, we are freed to make good choices.

Strong decision-making ability, however, takes time to develop. When we were children, we reacted to specific prohibitions and exhortations. Rules are fine for children. But our children develop best when we gradually free them to make their own choices based on the principles we have inculcated. In a similar way, mature Christians must be free to ponder how Scripture applies in their day-to-day lives. Choices have to be made. No wonder Paul, in his concern for believers to grow strong in Christ, laid such an emphasis on liberty under the law of love.

Since God works all things for our sanctification, he has as much purpose in the silences of Scripture as in the declarations. In areas in which the Scriptures are silent, God expects us to bring to bear general scriptural principles and precedents to make consistent decisions about right and wrong. God did not redeem us to make us puppets, but to set us free.

Like adventurers exploring new territory with only a compass and the stars overhead to guide them, we face our daily challenges with the Scriptures to direct us. Practice in developing discernment undergirds us. But if we developed in a church where we were spoon-fed, we will find decision-making agonizing and we may often stumble badly. Indeed, we may never know the thrill of discovery that God grants to those who boldly strike out with the compass of the Word in their hands!

Elizabeth Elliot addresses the issue in an article entitled 'Maturity, The Power To Discern'. 'God has deliberately left us in a quandary about many things. Why did he not summarize all the rules in one book, and all the basic doctrines in another? ... He wants us to reach maturity. He has so arranged things that if we are to go on beyond the "milk diet" we shall be forced to think.'[15] The gift of discernment develops where believers creatively grapple with questions of right and wrong.

3. The gift of discernment defined

Discernment is that Spirit-endowed ability to discriminate between truth and error in teaching, and between good and evil in behaviour. In some cases, it involves recognizing demonic influence in individuals or groups.

As we have already established, the mention of a gift such as discernment in a list of assorted gifts indicates that some, but not all, Christians may receive it. 'To one there is given through the Spirit the message of wisdom ... to another distinguishing between spirits' (1 Cor. 12:4,8,10).

Discernment between spirits

Distinguishing between spirits is the gift being considered at this point. The Greek word used here, *diakrisis,* means to make a 'distinguishing, a clear discrimination, discerning ... in 1 Cor. 12:10, of discerning spirits, judging by evidence whether they are evil or of God'.[16]

The Holy Spirit endows some believers with the ability to weigh the evidence of ear and eye in order to come to a clear decision about the influence behind a given idea or person — is it from God or the devil? Discernment prepares a person to read, behind subtleties of phraseology, the real intention of the speaker or writer. The discerner sees through the disguise of one who comes under the influence of Satan but appears as 'an angel of light'.

The qualifying phrase, 'between spirits', limits the field of operation of this gift. It would seem to indicate that it refers, not to discernment in general, as we have been discussing it, but to one facet of discernment, the ability to discern between good and evil spirits.

What is meant? Does this refer to distinguishing demonic spirits from angelic spirits? Many of our charismatic brethren would opt for this interpretation. As a number of examples that I will introduce later in this chapter show, the ability to sense the presence of demon possession is only one facet of this gift. The apostles quickly sensed demon activity. In Pakistan, we have had reason to appreciate this aspect of the gift.

One day we were called to a village to help a girl from a family to whom we had given extensive teaching. The girl shook and trembled. She seemed to be in an extremely advanced state of mental breakdown. The pastor present at that time diagnosed her condition as demon possession. A group of national believers, led by this pastor, laid hands on her and sought to exorcize the demons.

As new missionaries, we had little experience with demon possession. We talked to her mother and father and then sought to comfort her. Somehow we sensed that the problem was not demonic, but emotional or physical. I tried to question the national pastor carefully concerning his diagnosis. But we did not feel we could interfere. We sought the Lord in prayer.

Before long Pastor Hidayat strode into the compound. Hearing about the problem he had come as soon as possible. After a few minutes, Hidayat declared, 'This is not demon possession. The girl is sick.' We quickly arranged for her to travel to the nearest mission hospital. It turned out that her problem was physical, St Vitus's Dance. She made a full recovery.

Pastor Hidayat, in this and other cases, evidenced the gift of discerning the presence or absence of demonic spirits. Sometimes he was wrong. More often he was correct. No one today possesses apostolic infallibility, but thank God for the gift! Demonic activity increasingly manifests itself in our so-called developed countries. But is the gift of discernment confined to discerning the presence of evil spirits?

While writing to the Corinthians about the orderly use of gifts, Paul counsels the church in Corinth about prophecy: 'Two or three prophets should speak, and the others should weigh carefully what is said... Prophesy in turn so that everyone may be instructed and encouraged. The spirits of the prophets are subject to the control of prophets' (1 Cor. 14:29,31-32).

The phrase translated in the NIV 'weigh carefully what is said' is the same word translated elsewhere 'discern'. New Testament prophecy, as established in chapter 10, was akin to present-day preaching. (The infallible prophets of the Bible are distinguished from the fallible preachers of our day by their inspiration.) This passage in 1 Corinthians indicates that while one prophet instructed a congregation, the other prophets present were to discern whether his message was consistent with divine revelation. Awareness of this continuing process of evaluation would have moved prophets to take great care that their preaching was accurate. Apparently, prophets exercised the gift of discernment in two directions: first to discern the accuracy of their own teaching, and secondly to evaluate that of others.

The spirits spoken of in the context of these verses were not angelic or demonic spirits as such. The text refers to the general influence under which prophets spoke. Since God revealed his will through prophets 'as they were moved by the Holy Spirit', their utterances were to be carefully weighed. Prophets present in a congregation might ask themselves as they listened to a message, 'Is this message consistent with what the Holy Spirit has already taught? Is it accurate? Is it balanced? Is it personal opinion? Does anything ring false?'

John broadens the application: 'Dear friends, do not believe every spirit, but test the spirits to see whether they are from God, because many false prophets have gone out into the world' (1 John 4:1). By testing the spirits, John means us to discern both the hidden motivation of the prophet and the influence behind the messages which preachers and teachers bring.

In the following verses John gives a litmus test to use in discerning the origin of a prophet's message. Should the speaker acknowledge 'that Jesus Christ has come in the flesh', it can be assumed that he is speaking under the influence of the Spirit of God (1 John 4:2). Should his teaching, however, detract from the person of Christ, it can be assumed that he speaks under the influence of the 'spirit of the antichrist' (1 John 4:3). John, in his epistle, and others, in their writings, amplify this basic test to include a check on behaviour as well as doctrine.

Those with the gift of discernment evaluate both messenger and message. They distinguish between teaching which accurately reflects God's revelation and that which shows the influence of the devil. They also discern insincerity.

Failure to discern accompanies failure to submit to the Spirit. 'The man without the Spirit does not accept the things that come from the Spirit of God... He cannot understand them, because they are spiritually discerned. The spiritual man makes judgements about all things ... we have the mind of Christ' (1 Cor. 2:14-16). Paul then goes on, in this passage, to lament the Corinthians' failure to rise above worldliness by discerning how to deal with one another.

Biblical examples of discernment

Jesus manifested marvellous insight. He could deal tenderly with rapacious tax collectors, like Zacchæus, and immoral women, like the one caught in adultery. Nicodemus, the Pharisee, came by night and was received kindly. Most Pharisees, Sadducees and scribes, however, smarted under the lash of his tongue. 'Woe to you, teachers of the law and Pharisees, you hypocrites! (Matt. 23:13). 'Everything they do is done for men to see' (Matt. 23:5). How could he know their hearts? How could he be so judgemental?

As the Judge of all the earth, Jesus had the right to judge. As the eternal Son of God, he had the ability to read men's hearts. This is not, however, all the story. While on earth Jesus voluntarily surrendered the independent exercise of his divine attributes in order to identify fully with our humanity (see Phil. 2). It didn't take omniscience to read the Pharisees. Their hypocrisy was well documented. But until he spoke out, no one had the courage to expose their sin.

Most probably, discerning men were not surprised by Jesus' revelation of Pharisaic duplicity. Of course, only Christ could speak in terms of absolute certainty. Nevertheless, astute men and women realize that the profession of many is a sham. Words and actions, like the labels on a medicine bottle, identify the contents within. Those gifted with discernment are able to read the external signs and sense duplicity. Church committees, who examine people for baptism and membership, desperately need men and women of discernment who can read beneath a person's verbal profession.

Peter discerned evil motivation behind Ananias and Sapphira's offering. Barnabas had just sold a field and brought the proceeds to the apostles. Before long Ananias came with some money from the sale of his property. Sapphira and he had decided to retain part of the money, and put the rest in the offering. There was nothing wrong with that. But when he brought his gift, he gave the impression that, like Barnabas, his offering was a complete sacrifice.

Peter immediately perceived their deceit. Confronting each separately, he asked, 'How is it that Satan has so filled your heart that you have lied to the Holy Spirit?' Each in turn fell dead at the apostle's feet. Having enquired about the exact details of the sale, Peter had sensed their duplicity and realized that they had listened to the temptation of the devil (Acts 5:1-11).

A similar situation faced Peter in Samaria when Simon, the sorcerer, professed faith and was baptized. Before long Simon offered money to acquire the apostle's amazing power. Instead of granting his request, Peter called him to repent: 'I see that you are full of bitterness and captive to sin' (Acts 8:23). Discernment uncovered Simon's greed.

No one, as the apostle Peter found out, stands on a pedestal above evaluation. Paul had to rebuke Peter to his face for prejudice towards Gentile believers (Gal. 2:11-21). Priscilla and Aquila took the mighty preacher Apollos aside to correct his teaching (Acts 18:24-26). Happy is the pastor who has discerning believers who are not afraid lovingly to correct a mistake he might have made, which brings us to discernment in the local assembly.

Discernment and the local church

Peter minces no words: 'There were also false prophets among the people, just as there will be false teachers among you. They will secretly introduce destructive heresies, even denying the sovereign Lord who bought them... Many will follow their shameful ways... These teachers will exploit you with stories they have made up' (2 Peter 2:1-3). Clearly we must be aware that Satan has sown the seeds of moral and doctrinal evil in every church. Even now, new heresies and deceptions germinate in the midst of our most devout assemblies.

If church life in the first century depended so desperately on discerning men and women, how much more do we need the gift today! False teachers who infiltrate churches may be extremely difficult to recognize. Some come disguised as fine, upstanding Christians. Some are naïvely unaware of the havoc they threaten.

Perceptive church leaders work hard to head off false teaching. Danger comes in various guises. Disunity is one. How many church splits could have been avoided if a divisive spirit, such as Paul found in Corinth, had been dealt with in time? Cliques fracture too many churches. One group may push its view of eschatology. Another may coalesce around dissatisfaction with the pastor. Others may find common cause in complaints that the church is not doing enough about social issues like abortion. Still others may gravitate together because of unhappiness over innovations in worship.

Distinct emphases such as concern for a deeper life, inner healing, sovereign grace, or even a desire for revival can spawn cliques. Leaders are tempted to promote their own following. At other times, fearing a loss of control, some leaders discourage even legitimate small groups meeting for Bible study. Discernment is needed to distinguish healthy groupings, such as that which Jesus formed with his disciples, from unhealthy and divisive cliques. Discerning men and women head off disunity by channelling diverse emphases into a harmonious balance that reflects biblical parameters.

Obviously, preachers must have this gift. They need it to discern the times in which they live and the teaching of other preachers. But without discerning their own hearts how can they know whether or not their message is motivated by holy love? Base emotions such as pride or bitterness, frustration or anger, fear or jealousy could jeopardize their ministries.

A caution is in order at this point. No believer today can claim infallible ability to discern the intent of someone else's heart. The apostles were inspired in an infallible sense. I have repeatedly noted the damage caused by those who advance their opinion as if it were the voice of God. In certain circles some even categorically state, for example, that a certain person is demon-possessed, a claim too often proved to be questionable and hurtful. (Satanic oppression and demonic influence are qualitatively distinct from demon possession.) In other circumstances churches or individual Christians have been carelessly labelled 'liberal' or 'ecumenical' or 'Arminian', without real basis in fact.

Pride goes before a fall, no less in those with spiritual gifts than in others. Without extreme care the gift of discernment can lead to pride, carelessness and overconfidence. No wonder multiple leadership, which promotes mutual consultation, is to be preferred over individuals who make pronouncements. Proverbs repeatedly warns, 'Plans fail for lack of counsel, but with many advisers they succeed' (Prov. 15:22). We need wisdom as well as discernment.

Discernment and wisdom

How do we distinguish discernment from wisdom? No doubt they overlap. The gift of wisdom, however, is more a spiritual ability to advise on direction — what to do in given situations — than an evaluation of people or institutions already in motion. Discernment operates in the area of assessing people or organizations in action. Discernment asks, 'Are they teaching truth or error? Are they practising good or evil?' Wisdom, on the other hand, operates more at the crossroads where people or organizations seek direction. It asks, 'Which way should we go?' 'What is God's will in this situation?' 'How should we apply Scripture to this situation?'

Discernment analyses the present and past, while wisdom charts the future. Wisdom is more positive, while discernment is more negative. As shown in the famous case in which Solomon discerned which of two prostitutes was the real mother of a child, wisdom and discernment overlap. Perhaps wisdom represents a broader, more all-encompassing ability and discernment a specific application. We must allow for some flexibility where Scripture withholds clear discriminations.

Without a squad of those with the gift of discernment standing guard, the kingdom is at risk. We dare not leave any loophole unguarded. What can we do to ensure that men and women receive training to stand guard duty on the ramparts of the kingdom?

III. The development of discernment

In the introduction to his book *The Root of the Righteous,* A. W. Tozer comes directly to the point: 'Much that passes for Christianity today is the brief bright effort of the severed branch to bring forth its fruit in its season. But the deep laws of life are against it. Preoccupation with appearances and a corresponding neglect of the out-of-sight root of the true spiritual life are prophetic signs which go unheeded. Immediate "results" are all that matter, quick proofs of present success without a thought of next week or next year. Religious pragmatism is running wild among the orthodox. Truth is whatever works. If it gets results it is good.'[17]

Since A. W. Tozer demonstrates the gift of discernment, I shall be quoting him several times in this section. The passage just quoted, written forty years ago, could have been penned today. He foresaw the danger of seemingly innocent trends that were to lay waste the churches. He concludes the above article by saying, 'The masses are always wrong. In every generation the number of the righteous is small. Be sure you are among them.'[18]

Are we among those who can distinguish worldly weeds from the root of the righteous? We cannot afford to spend our energies growing weeds while the root of truth shrivels. Whether you and I have this gift or not, we need to develop discernment both for our own sake and for the sake of the church. Scripture lays out a series of parameters to use in exercizing discernment.

1. Biblical standards for discernment

Discernment is not intuition or instinct, but the incisive application of biblical principles to concrete situations. Discerning men and women train themselves to view situations by comparison with three kinds of biblical material:

1. Doctrine — theological truth;
2. Morality — practical holiness;
3. Balance — the right combination of truth and practice.

Discernment, then, requires first the assessment of doctrinal fidelity.

Assessing doctrinal fidelity

John writes, 'Test the spirits ... many false prophets have gone out into the world' (1 John 4:1). John specifically warns believers to shun any teacher who does not acknowledge the deity and incarnation of Christ.

Those with the gift of knowledge have prepared a host of doctrinal summaries for our use at this point. Berkhof's *Systematic Theology,* for example, defines for us, in scriptural terms, the deity, humanity, personality, incarnation, atonement, death and resurrection of Christ. It also lists a multitude of heresies that have denied Christ.

We would do well to purchase some key books that analyse non-Christian thought in the light of the Bible. Discerning believers, depending on their area of responsibility, need some awareness of how dualism, deism, pantheism, agnosticism, atheism and Unitarianism attack the nature and reality of the triune God. New Age and oriental cults reflect Buddhist and Hindu ideas about God, man and reality itself. Mormonism, Jehovah's Witnesses, Spiritism and a host of other cults distort the revelation of Jesus Christ the Lord. Heresies also distort the truth that salvation is by grace alone. Satan has been so busy down through history in spawning error that we need all the help we can get to unmask him.

The tragic fallout of doctrinal laxity is evident in liberal institutions and denominations throughout the Western world. Many of the great denominations that sprang to life in revival fire carry on empty rituals. When converted as a young person of nineteen, I returned with awakened zeal to the church in which I had been brought up. An older Christian asked me to join him in teaching Sunday School. All went well until the minister called us in and requested that we either cease disturbing the children with teaching about the necessity of the new birth, or leave. Sadly, we had to leave. That church remains a fashionable landmark but its lamp grows steadily dimmer.

Discernment covers a broad field. So subtle and hard-working is the evil one in manufacturing error that the church should encourage the development of specialists in specific areas such as the cults, non-Christian religions, modern life, politics, business ethics, etc. The main focus of the gift, however, remains the discerning of the reliability of teachers and preachers within the visible church.

Like the Bereans, those with the gift of discernment search both the Scriptures and the books of dependable systematizers to establish a grid of truth that they can use to evaluate new ideas and teachings.

Assessing moral practice

The apostle John, in his first epistle, warns against moral evil: 'Dear children, do not let anyone lead you astray. He who does what is right is righteous... He who does what is sinful is of the devil... This is how we know who the children of God are... Anyone who does not do what is right is not a child of God' (1 John 3:7-10).

Love is the hallmark of genuine faith. It produces a cluster of fruits: joy, patience, gentleness and self-control, to name several. While true believers are not perfect, else they would not need to confess their sins, yet they do keep aspiring to walk holy lives. They do seek to love as they have been loved. These aspirations energize spiritual growth and fuel an abhorrence of evil that inspires increasing holiness.

Holiness is both the presence of godly love and the absence of moral evil. Paul identifies moral evil as (to give only a few examples) immorality, idolatry, witchcraft, hatred, jealousy and drunkenness (Gal. 5:19-23). Other contexts decry bitterness, gossip, anger and a refusal to forgive. Real believers hate and flee these things, because the Spirit within them enables them to discern between good and evil.

On the need for practical godliness, Tozer writes, 'There is an evil which I have seen under the sun and which in its effect upon the Christian religion may be more destructive than Communism, Romanism and Liberalism combined. It is the glaring disparity between theology and practice among professing Christians... So wide is the gulf that separates theory from practice in the church that an enquiring stranger who chances upon both would scarcely dream that there was any relation between them.'[19]

What a terrible anomaly — that multitudes profess faith in creeds and doctrines while failing to evidence their belief in their daily lives! Balance is a third consideration.

Assessing balance

A truth held in extreme becomes error. Discerning believers look for a balance between doctrinal accuracy and holy living. Beliefs undergird practice. Godly behaviour reinforces truth.

Truth needs to be held in balance. Believers need not only love for Christ, but also a love for the Father and the Spirit — a triune faith. Both Old and New Testaments need to capture the attention. Faith and works need demonstration in daily life. Believers must steer a course between legalism and loose and licentious freedom. Teachers need to emphasize all doctrines: depravity as well as redemption; sovereignty as well as human responsibility; the body of Christ as well as the individual liberty; evangelism as well as eschatology.

Tozer exposes an imbalanced emphasis on doctrine to the detriment of practice. He says, 'Many of us Christians have become extremely skilful in arranging our lives so as to admit the truth of Christianity without being embarrassed by its implications. We arrange things so that we get along well enough without divine aid, while at the same time ostensibly seeking it... The man of pseudo-faith will fight for his verbal creed but refuse flatly to allow himself to get into a predicament where his future must depend upon that creed being true.'[20]

God calls us to encourage a balanced emphasis on both doctrine and practice. We shall next consider how discernment operates.

2. The practice of discernment

Up to this point we have mainly been emphasizing the need for us to discern heresy and imbalance in others. In reality, discernment begins with an examination of our own hearts.

Examining ourselves

David wisely prayed,

> 'Search me, O God and know my heart;
>   test me and know my anxious thoughts.
> See if there is any offensive way in me,
>   and lead me in the way everlasting'
>
> (Ps. 139:23-24).

If we follow David's pattern we shall soon unearth our own depravity. Depravity spawns a multitude of distortions. Our own particular brand of imbalance has a lot to do with our temperament. Consider some examples of various temperaments.

Some of us tend towards always finding fault, while others lean towards tolerating anything. Which propensity is ours? Discernment guides us carefully between these twin abysses.

Gloom and doom dog the footsteps of the hypercritical person. I know from painful experience how distorted a picture the built-in radar of the negative person can bring. I grew up, it seems, naturally gifted at finding fault in others. The Spirit has often wrestled me to the ground over this issue!

On the other hand tolerance, just as surely as criticism, short-circuits discernment. Some people trust everyone. They see life through rose-coloured glasses. They abhor pointing out either doctrinal error or practical transgressions. Sometimes positive thinkers of this variety actually believe that by emphasizing the positive and ignoring the negative, reality itself can really be altered.

People with discernment recognize that tolerance can positively encourage evil and error, while hypercriticism can discourage people from taking the high road to godly growth.

Self-assessment involves coming to grips with our own temperament, checking our profession of faith and evaluating our grasp on doctrinal and ethical issues.

Assessing others

While most of us shrink from evaluating others, from time to time we are thrust into situations where we must make discriminations. The command to restore a fallen brother caught in sin, which we find in Galatians chapter 6, presupposes a clear perception of the sin involved. Then, too, encouraging discouraged believers, as urged in Hebrews, assumes we shall approach a discouraged brother with discernment (Heb. 10:25).

Nomination committees must make character and gift assessments, before recommending nominees. Pulpit committees, church boards and preachers — along with leaders of all kinds — must demonstrate insight. Mothers and fathers need it to assess their own children. To fail here is to abdicate our God-given responsibility!

Perhaps I can demonstrate the process of discernment best by means of an imaginary, but true-to-life, scenario. Trish has been a follower of Christ for ten years while her husband Bert made a profession of faith only a year ago. Every afternoon Trish settles down to watch soap operas on TV for several hours. Bert plays cards with the boys at work during the lunch-hour. He buys lottery tickets and continues to smoke and drink.

Their friends, Steve and Pat, are both unsaved. Steve's quick temper has repeatedly got him into trouble with his wife, Pat. Several times he has left her for other women. Pat is a very critical person. Being a Mormon she will not drink or smoke.

The church officers need discernment as they consider Trish for a position as a Sunday School teacher and as they evaluate Bert for membership. As a Christian wife, Trish needs discernment to know how to handle Bert and his habits. Both Bert and Trish need acumen about how to handle their friendship with Steve and Pat since he obviously lives an immoral life and she belongs to a cult.

'Where do they stand?' is probably the first question to ask. Two are professing Christians and two are not. We should expect considerably more of Trish, as a professed Christian of long standing, than we do of Bert who seems to be a babe in Christ. Bert's position inside or outside of Christ needs to be evaluated by looking for evidence of a changed life. Since Steve and Pat are completely outside of Christ, any relationship with them will remain on a somewhat superficial level. However, Christians are not forbidden friendship with unbelievers as long as that friendship does not compromise Christian ideals and is pursued with the goal of winning the lost to Christ. Pat's Mormon connection complicates the issue.

The spiritual position a person occupies bears heavily on how a church should act towards him or her. The gift of discernment helps to identify where people are. Christ's treatment of people was dependent on his assessment of where they stood. He treated the Pharisees and the woman caught in adultery, Nicodemus and Peter quite differently in different circumstances. Following his example, we need to discern where people are in their eternal pilgrimage.

We can ask ourselves some of the following questions. These are only intended as suggestions; the list is not exhaustive.

1. Has the person professed faith in Christ?

2. If the person is a professing Christian, does he or she show credible evidence of conversion?

3. Is the person a new believer or a mature saint? Discerning Christians understand that new believers and immature Christians must be dealt with patiently.

4. Is the person a long-time believer who shows little current evidence of growth in grace? In Hebrews those who 'are slow to learn' are censured for failing to come to grips with the 'elementary truths of God's Word'.

5. Does this person believe or practise anything clearly contrary to Scripture — or are his beliefs or practices merely matters of sincere difference of opinion in areas where God grants Christians liberty?

6. Is the person being considered for a teaching or leadership position? Individual eccentricities of belief and practice that can be tolerated when held by a new Christian or a weak older Christian may have to be censured when a person is given a position of responsibility. (Consider the matter of circumcision in diverse passages in Acts and Gal. 5:2,6.)

7. Is this person causing others to stumble by his or her actions — even in an area of Christian liberty?

We have pursued a tortuous path in seeking to discover the parameters of discernment. The paucity of discernment necessitated the exercise. May God preserve us from becoming, on the one hand, hysterical witch-hunters — professional critics, and, on the other hand, from being too tolerant. The pattern of the Bereans, who searched the Scriptures daily, ought to be our pattern. Loyalty to our church and its leadership does not sentence us to naïvety!

The need is desperate. Why else would we read that since the fall of Jimmy Swaggart and Jim Bakker, Robert Schuller has become the top-rated religious broadcaster in the United States?[21] Yet Schuller is the one who writes, 'The most serious sin is the one that causes me to say, "I am unworthy" ... For once a person believes he is an "unworthy sinner", it is doubtful if he can really honestly accept the saving grace God offers in Jesus Christ.'[22] Schuller is ignoring the importance of conviction of sin in the process of conversion! How can such a distortion of the faith be so popular among professing North American Christians? How can so-called Christian bookshops carry his positivist non-gospel? Discernment is needed.

What about A. W. Tozer himself? Must we read the writings of even this master communicator with discernment? What do you think about the following quotation? 'The converted man is both reformed and regenerated. And unless the sinner is willing to reform his way of living he will never know the inward experience of regeneration... The promise of pardon and cleansing is always associated in Scriptures with the command to repent... What does this teach but radical reformation of life before there can be any expectation of pardon?'[23] Ponder the quotation and then see if you agree with my comments in the notes.

Discernment is both a mark of Christian maturity and a spiritual gift. All believers must strive to develop the ability to discern good and evil, truth and error. As we grow in Christ, the Holy Spirit may sovereignly choose to set us apart for more specialized tasks in areas where we care for souls or watch over the state of the church. What we should do if we discern error or evil is a subject that has already been covered in the chapters on shepherding and encouragement.

Conclusion

Every believer and every church needs both faith and discernment.
Faith rises to the fore when we face insurmountable problems in the
process of seeking to rise above the status quo; it is confidence in
God, a biblically qualified vision of what can be and the certainty
that the vision will become reality.

Oswald Chambers writes, 'Faith is the heroic effort of your life.
You fling yourself in reckless confidence on God. God has ventured
all in Jesus Christ to save us. Now He wants us to venture our all in
abandoned confidence in Him... Jesus Christ demands that you risk
everything you hold by common sense and leap into what He says...
Christ demands of the man who trusts Him the same reckless spirit
... that is daring enough to step out of the crowd and bank his faith
on the character of God.'[24]

I love Chambers' appeal to the heroic! But even as one side of me
says, 'Yes!' to his call to heroic faith, the other side cautions me to
be discerning. Discernment whispers to my heart, 'Heroic, daring,
venturesome — watch out! Reckless abandonment of common
sense contradicts the book of Proverbs! A clarion call to heedless
abandonment could lead to all manner of excesses.' I am sure you
know of zealous young men and women who have taken words such
as these as the basis of commitment to a missionary cause or full-
time ministry without training, without gifting and without involvement in the local church. Discernment cautions us to check out the
vision of men of faith, without dampening their enthusiasm. Of
course, it calls us just as surely to decry the sluggish devotion of
spectator Christians.

Faith and discernment, we need them both! Do you have either
one — or both? Before going on to consider a gift that ties all the
others together into a co-ordinated purpose, return to the chart and
fill in the columns that relate to the gifts of faith and discernment.

21.
Administration and leadership

We all owe an enormous debt to godly leaders. Where would Israel have been without Moses? Or Deborah? Or David? And yet few gifts are as shunned or as coveted as their gift.

Leadership inspires a strange paradox. On the one hand, some with administrative ability flee leadership either for fear of being thought 'bossy', or because they worry about the stress of responsibility. Perhaps they have experienced some of the loneliness and misunderstanding that seem inevitable with leadership. No wonder, then, that many who could serve Christ by leading his people to press back the frontiers of the kingdom shy away from responsibility as if it were the plague. These refugees from responsibility are not alone. Long ago Moses tried to avoid leadership. Jeremiah did as well.

On the other hand, attracted by the prestige of position, some seek to lead who lack the necessary management skills. Nomination committees routinely require the wisdom of Solomon to fend off unqualified volunteers for prestigious positions. Bible colleges and seminaries commonly deal with young people more eager to train for leadership than for servanthood.

What a paradox! Some with the gifts flee responsibility; others desire position yet lack the skills. No wonder we suffer such a shortage of spiritual leadership. Administration must join gifts such as knowledge, wisdom and discernment on the list of scarce endowments.

John Stott comments on the broader perspectives of this phenomenon: 'There is a serious dearth of leaders in the contemporary world... People feel confused, bewildered, alienated... We seem to be like "sheep without a shepherd", while our leaders often appear to be "blind leaders of the blind".'[1]

An abundance of problems cry out for leadership. Stott mentions human rights' violations, increasing violence, environmental and energy problems, along with the tragic economic inequities between countries. He lists moral problems such as the breakdown of the family, the deterioration of sexual ethics, the scandal of abortion and the spread of greed. Technical know-how, which could help to find solutions, abounds as never before. But where are the leaders with the will to lead us away from the disasters ahead?

Personally, I believe there is no lack of administrative skill in our world. Highly motivated leaders stumble over each other in business and politics. Multi-millionnaires are common. Corporations and industries daily solve monumental problems with verve. Entrepreneurs compete fiercely for new inventions, new products and new markets. No, the vacuum of moral leadership cannot be blamed on either a lack of ability or a scarcity of resources.

Nevertheless, we lack volunteers willing to bend their abilities to the solution of our moral and ethical problems. These concerns call for a servant-leader demonstrating a qualitatively different kind of leadership style from that to which the world aspires.

Brochures advertising leadership seminars routinely show up in my mail. These seminars open to sell-out crowds because they give aspiring executives what they want. A sentence in one brochure sums up what administration means in the world in which we live. The seminar was designed to help participants 'project the personal power that makes others support your goals'.[2] Another brochure, just to hand, appeals for leaders to take 'assertiveness training'.

Worldly leaders want to learn how to motivate others to help them achieve their own selfish goals. Selfishness, power and manipulation of others characterize administrative skill, as our fallen world conceives it. Of course, managers are taught to mask manipulation by projecting a sociability, charm and apparent concern for others. A close friend of mine, not a Christian, once expressed it succinctly: 'Christian ethics, "Do unto others as you would have them do unto you," works. I find that when I treat my secretary kindly, I get more work out of her.' Secular leaders don't hesitate to use Christian values if they will further their own personal goals.

Biblical leadership, while it shares many common principles of planning and goal-setting with leadership in general, could hardly be more different. Leaders who follow Christ lead by serving. Their goals centre on glorifying God. Fortunately, because of common grace at work in our world, we can find examples of good leadership even in those who do not personally acknowledge Christ.

Lena Kuchler Silberman showed incredible leadership after the horrors of the Second World War. Gathering together 100 Jewish children, made orphans by the camps, she set out for Palestine. Overcoming all obstacles, she led these children to sanctuary.

Mother Theresa, however much we may disagree with her theology, earns our admiration. From the starting-point of her outrage over conditions in Calcutta, she has put together a world-wide organization aimed at alleviating suffering in scores of locations around the world. She manifests amazing leadership.

Unfortunately, too few are upset by injustice or ecological danger. A leader in the scientific community, seen on television recently, lamented the lack of outrage expressed at the destruction of forests, the increase in air-borne pollution and the holes in the ozone layer. No, the world has leaders, but few concentrate their efforts on solving problems that do not contribute to their own hidden agenda. By contrast, biblical leadership bends all efforts to the concerns of God.

I. The biblical roots of Christian leadership

The apostle to the Gentiles twice mentions leadership as a gift. 'We have different gifts... If it is leadership, let him govern diligently' (Rom. 12:6,8). In 1 Corinthians Paul writes about 'those with gifts of administration' (1 Cor. 12:28). Few gifts are listed twice.

Although the priority given to leadership in our churches, as well as these two references to it, indicates its importance, I have purposely dealt with it last. But since, as Jesus said, 'The first shall be last and the last first,' those who have learned servant leadership from the Master will not mind. Leadership is a serving gift.

The Greek words

The Greek word used in Romans, *proistemi,* means, 'to stand before,' hence, 'to lead, attend to (indicating care and diligence)'.[3]

Leaders stand before a group charged by God with the responsibility of caring for them through diligently attending to their needs and directing their progress. It is important to note that leaders do not stand above others to dominate or boss them about, but before them to lead the way.

A second Greek word, *kubernesis,* occurs in the Corinthian list. Translated 'governments' by the AV and 'administration' by the NIV, the word comes from a root meaning 'to guide'.[4] It denotes 'steering, pilotage' and thus 'metaphorically ... governings, said of those who act as guides in a local church'.[5] In this sense the leader, like the captain or pilot of a ship, guides others through dangerous waters to a safe harbour.

Paul's choice of these two words, from among many available to him, underscores the qualitative difference which Jesus declared must exist between Christian and worldly leaders. Paul could have chosen words more freighted with power, authority and domination, such as those from which our English words 'despot' or 'hegemony' originate, or terms used by the Romans to describe their absolute power. Instead, he chose milder words that highlight a leader's responsibility more than his authority. (I am not denying the realities of spiritual authority.) The gift of leadership, in this sense, would indicate a call to go before a group of people to steer them in a productive direction or to guide them safely through treacherous problems to a safe haven.

One gift or two?

Another question arises at this point: are administration and leadership one gift or two? Peter Wagner, Earl Radmacher and others distinguish the two. According to their interpretation, administration is an ability to assess situations and formulate plans for action. They define leadership, on the other hand, as 'the God-given executive ability to stand before people and to inspire followers by leading them aggressively but with care'.[6]

These commentators make an important distinction. For any organization to move ahead, two things are required: firstly, skill in assessing the current situation in order to formulate a plan, and secondly, the ability to inspire and lead others in the accomplishment of that plan. In modern usage the former skills are often termed administrative, while the latter are commonly defined as leadership.

The Greek words, however, do not lend themselves to such a modern distinction. Both words lean more towards the concept of one who leads rather than those to whom a leader delegates responsibility to administer a plan. For this reason, I am happier to go with those commentators, such as Flynn and McRae, who include administrative skills under the general umbrella of leadership.[7]

To distinguish too radically between different facets of leadership would serve to obscure the similarity of function that exists between a father leading his family and a director leading a mission of a thousand members. Such a division would also serve to break up the leadership development process guided by the Spirit. The Holy Spirit superintends the change that occurs when an individual, saved out of depravity, begins to organize the chaos of his broken life. The Spirit may subsequently develop that same person into a leader able to deal with disorganization on a broad scale. Let me explain my meaning.

Organizing our personal lives

Like other gifts, we first meet administration in the context of commitment to the commands of Christ. As soon as God rescues us from the pit of our own bondage to the world, the flesh and the devil, he calls us to walk the path of sanctification. But our past memories and guilt, our present appetites and temptations and the siren call of friends and society all place obstacles in the way of our progress. Somehow we must circumvent them to reorganize our lives so that devotion to the Lord and his will replaces the old tyranny.

The biblical exhortations to discipline our lives, in order to pursue godliness, are but disguised commands to administer our lives. 'Like a city whose walls are broken down is a man who lacks self-control' (Prov. 25:28). Solomon compares personal self-control with the running of a city. When the administration of a city deteriorates, as is currently happening all over the world, its defences against crime, drugs and violence break down. The search for new leadership begins. The AV translates the last phrase in this verse, 'he that hath no rule over his own spirit'. Proverbs calls us to rule our spirits just as we should rule our cities, or face anarchy. Self-control denotes that we are being administered or led by our renewed will.

In redemption, God rescues us from the chaos produced by our own bondage to sin. He teaches us how to take charge of our lives in order to overcome evil and produce something good. Sanctification is another word for Spirit-led personal administration.

This administrative challenge is not new. God originally instructed Adam, in the cultural commission, to subdue and rule the earth. This will be fulfilled when, 'At the name of Jesus every knee [shall] bow, in heaven and on earth and under the earth' (Phil. 2:10). The kingdom, in its fullest form, will usher in everlasting order. But till then, we face chaos, anarchy and evil. No wonder God calls each of us to leadership!

When we take charge over our own chaotic lives, we gain the practice we need to learn how to administer other responsibilities. Thus, fathers and mothers are called to administer their homes. When they prove successful here, they qualify to help in leading committees, Sunday Schools or home Bible studies. Elders and deacons qualify for leadership if they have already demonstrated this gift in a home setting. Of elders, Paul writes, 'He must manage his own family well ... (If anyone does not know how to manage his own family, how can he take care of God's church?)' (1 Tim. 3:5). A similar qualification relates to deacons (1 Tim. 3:12). The family provides a training-ground where leadership skills should develop.

No redeemed sinner can please God who fails to help organize the disorganization around him. Sometimes the organization may be as simple as planting a garden and keeping it free of weeds. It might be maintaining a house free of dust and dirt. Sometimes it will be joining others to oppose ecological destruction. For those with families, it certainly means organizing family life to glorify God. Each of us must organize his or her life to dispel evil and anarchy.

Whether we lead in the microcosm of directing our own spirits or in the macrocosm of administering a mission organization with a budget of fifteen million dollars, we follow similar principles.

Church leaders

God calls elders to a responsibility between these two extremes. The same Greek word, *proistemi,* used in Romans for the gift of leadership, describes one of the main functions of church elders. Paul reminds Timothy to see that 'the elders who direct the affairs of the church well' receive honour and support, especially if that work involves teaching and preaching (1 Tim. 5:17). Likewise, Paul exhorts the Thessalonians to respect their eldership, those 'who are over you in the Lord' (1 Thess. 5:12).

Church leaders were called overseers as well as elders. 'Bishop', the transliteration through Latin for the Greek word *'episkopos'*, literally means 'an overseer'. 'Overseer' is derived from two words meaning 'over', and 'to look or watch'. Clearly, God has made elders responsible to watch over the flock.[8] Christian leadership, in this sense, reflects genuine concern for others.

Hebrews uses another word, *hegeomai,* for church leaders: 'Remember your leaders... Obey your leaders and submit to their authority... Greet all your leaders, and all God's people' (Heb. 13:7,17,24). Since we have already established that local church leaders are called 'elders', we may conclude that this verse refers to them. *'Hegeomai'* means 'to lead, rule or guide'. Leaders wield authority. They, in turn, must give an account for their use of that authority to Christ from whom it was delegated.

Administrative skills develop as we wrestle with confusion. Of course, some choose inaction and sink deeper into chaos. Others, influenced by the world, turn their developing administrative skills to organize and empower evil. Many hone their skills to seek personal goals. But most believers do grow in administrative skill. They learn to rule their spirits and consequently graduate to wider responsibilities in the kingdom.

Leadership is needed everywhere. Building maintenance requires organization. The missions' committee calls for vision and direction. Ladies with the gift of leadership must head up the Ladies' Fellowship. Some become deaconesses. Others direct sections of the Sunday School or outreach to single mothers. A few men become elders or pastors. Without the exercise of administration, the thrust of almost every other gift in the body of Christ is weakened.

Dr William McRae once taught a series on spiritual gifts. Through the series a certain woman concluded that her gift was administration. As a result of this knowledge, she volunteered to accept total responsibility for registrations and accommodations during a retreat the church was planning. A large retreat, such as the one in question, entails a great amount of time spent in organizing people and handling money. Although a young married woman new to such ventures, she handled the task beautifully. All were pleased.[9]

The church always benefits when we find our niche and get on with the job. And while the office of eldership is restricted to men, a host of other administrative positions ought to be open to women.

The gift defined

Whether manifest in men or women, we can define leadership as follows: leadership (administration) is a Spirit-endowed ability to serve the Lord and his people by taking a vision of what should be, evaluating the present situation, planning what to do, motivating, organizing and directing until a plan is brought to completion.

II. The characteristics of biblical leadership

To modify slightly one of Shakespeare's famous sayings, some leaders are born to greatness while others have it thrust upon them.[10] Moses, so reluctant to accept leadership, became one of the greatest leaders the world has ever seen. Though reticent, like Jeremiah, he was 'set apart' before he was born (Jer. 1:5).

For the purposes of illustration, we could turn to Joseph or Gideon, David or Paul, or even the Master himself. Consider instead Nehemiah, who rose out of obscurity to lead Israel in rebuilding the wall around Jerusalem. Nehemiah illustrates eight steps that competent administrators take. Those with leadership responsibility who skip any of these steps, show either that their grasp of biblical leadership is rudimentary, or that they do not have the gift.

Leadership begins, as in Nehemiah's case, in that wellspring of personality, the human heart.

Preparation

Good leaders are not galvanized into action by an idea suddenly flashing into their minds. They realize that success depends upon careful preparation. Administrators go through several steps in their own minds before they communicate anything to others. In Christian ministry, this process begins with self-examination.

1. Purify motivation

'Why do I want to do this?' must be one of the earliest questions a leader asks himself. As cupbearer to the king of a vast empire, Nehemiah was responsible to ensure that no poison compromised the safety of the king's table. He held a position of trust and power. The importance of his role can be gauged by the letters of authority later issued to him under the king's seal. By the king's order, soldiers guarded his caravan and letters of introduction gained him grants of money and timber. As a man of wealth and power, Nehemiah had every reason to be content with his position at the king's side.

Nehemiah's thoughts, however, turned frequently to Jerusalem. He sought news from every returning traveller. They told him that 'Those who survived the exile and are back in the province are in great trouble and disgrace' (Neh. 1:3). Concern for their pitiful condition, coupled with the distressing news that the wall of the city was broken down and the gates burnt, set Nehemiah to weeping.

The first chapter, indeed the entire book, mirrors the heart of a man burdened for his people and his God. We read, 'When I heard these things, I sat down and wept. For some days I mourned and fasted and prayed before the God of heaven' (Neh. 1:4). Nehemiah's response reflects the purity of his desire to please God and help his people.

Nehemiah did naturally what every Christian must do. He chose to sidestep security and contentment out of concern for others. Compassion overcame self-interest. This is rare in the exalted towers of power and influence. Few things gratify the fallen heart like the elixir of power. The seminar brochure previously quoted talked of projecting 'person power'.[11] Another brochure, in the most prominent place on the front page, promises 'unlimited power'.[12]

Jesus warned his leaders-in-training to avoid lusting after either control or the pagan 'bottom line'. Land, food, fancy clothes, money —'the pagans run after all these things' (Matt. 6:32). Worldly leadership manipulates people to achieve personal, usually materialistic, goals. The career brochure already mentioned promised training in how to 'project personal power that makes others support your goals'.[13]

Since leaders can be tempted to use their position to manipulate people with a view to enhancing salary or benefits, every Christian leader needs to ask himself repeatedly, 'Why do I want to do this?'

Because of this danger, men could not be considered for office in New Testament churches who had shown evidence of covetousness. One writer on spiritual gifts warns about administrators 'using people to accomplish personal ambitions. When administrators have people, money or materials at their disposal to accomplish a group "goal", it is all too easy to divert these resources to accomplish personal goals or ambitions.'[14]

Christians are also tempted to abuse authority to acquire prestige. The Master warned about the Pharisees who used their positions of power to enhance their image. He said, 'They have received their reward in full' (Matt. 6:16). The bows and salutations in the marketplaces, the best seats at feasts — these the Pharisees had already received. They should not have expected more.

Pride is the great enemy here. The would-be leader needs to kneel often and ask God to ruthlessly expose pride and help him follow the model of Moses, the meekest man on earth.

Of course, a servant attitude short-circuits pride, selfishness and lust for power. We have already discussed Jesus' teaching on servant leadership at considerable length in earlier sections of the book. God calls leaders to serve, never to dominate or manipulate (see Mark 10:42-45).

The stringent spiritual qualifications laid down for eldership are meant to guard against the choice of unworthy men. Elders, as recorded in Timothy and Titus, must be blameless in their community, be faithful in marriage and live balanced and self-controlled lives free of addiction, anger and covetousness. They should be hospitable and holy. They must prove themselves over a considerable span of time, ensuring that those will be selected who have gifts to lead and who can handle the authority and stress of leadership (1 Tim. 3:1-7; Titus 1:6-9).

Biblical leaders prepare by ensuring that their motives are pure. Pure motivation alone, however, cannot guarantee good leadership.

2. Clarify vision

For centuries Jewish expectations focused on the prosperity of Jerusalem. In the agony of the Babylonian captivity, a vision of restoration and their return from exile kept hope alive.

But the bad news from Jerusalem moved Nehemiah to fast and pray (Neh. 1:4). As he prayed, Nehemiah mourned for the sins of his nation. He pleaded with God to remember his promise to Moses to gather his sorrowing people back to Jerusalem (Neh. 1:5-11). Then he requested, 'Give your servant success today by granting him favour in the presence of this man' (Neh. 1:11). A scripturally rooted vision of a restored city compelled Nehemiah to do what he feared to do, confront the king.

Genuine Christian leaders share a common vision of God being glorified through the extension of his kingdom as the church obeys the Great Commission. They see with John the fruition of this vision: 'I looked and there before me was a great multitude that no one could count, from every nation, tribe, people and language, standing before the throne and in front of the Lamb... They cried out...

> "Salvation belongs to our God,
>   who sits on the throne,
>   and to the Lamb"'

(Rev. 7:9-10).

Ronald Knox of Oxford wrote, 'Men will not live without vision; that moral we do well, to carry away with us from contemplating, in so many strange forms, the record of visionaries. If we are content with the humdrum, the second-best, the hand-over-hand, it will not be forgiven us.'[15]

To be visionary does not mean to be impractical. A vision is, in reality, a long-range goal containing a whole hierarchy of practical objectives. Nehemiah, for example, knew that his first task was to fast and pray. In prayer he realized that a trip to Jerusalem would be necessary. But before he could do that he had to seek the agreement of his master, the king. Nehemiah began to formulate a list of intermediate goals.

As believers, we operate under a vision of redeemed representatives from every tongue and tribe and nation, some day standing before God in joyful worship. Under this general umbrella vision we need to set out intermediate objectives leading up to that final goal. These sub-goals, or intermediate objectives, become the raw material out of which more restricted visions are formed.

For example, a deacon, with a vision of extending the kingdom, ponders the needs of his community. He realizes that Christ would have his church reach his locality for Christ. He sees in his mind's

eye lost men and women coming to Christ, as the church reaches out
into the neighbourhood. He sees the need for a building as the church
grows. Next, he realizes the need for prayer meetings and discipleship groups. Thinking back, step by step, from the broader vision,
he begins to work out a plan. He shares his dream of what he believes
the church can become in fifteen years. Where there is no vision
people do perish, because zeal to extend the kingdom smoulders and
then dies.

To John Perkins, the conditions of his black brothers and sisters
in the fifties must have seemed like that of the exiles in Nehemiah's
day. As mentioned in an earlier chapter, a vision of racial harmony
moved John Perkins to establish Voice of Calvary in Jackson,
Mississippi. A vision of Christ's concern for the medical, housing
and spiritual needs of people of all races has fired Voice of Calvary
for almost thirty years.[16] Vision leads to thought.

3. Evaluate the situation

Visionary leaders are not enthusiasts who react viscerally and go off
wildly in many directions. Their eyes are on heaven, but their feet
are solidly on terra firma. As they prepare for action, they go about
gathering facts. Evaluation of the exact dimensions of a project,
analysis of difficulties and anticipation of possible problems all
occupy their attention.

Nehemiah grappled with the problem of restoring Jerusalem.
First, he gathered all the facts about the actual situation by questioning Jews who returned from Jerusalem. The temple and walls were
in a shambles. The gates were burned. The people struggled to
survive. And their enemies mocked them. What to do?

Biblical leaders pray, both before any action is taken, and
throughout any project. Nehemiah spent days of intensive prayer,
reviewing the promises of God, talking to God about the misery of
his people and asking God to prosper his plans. Nehemiah realized
that his master, the king, might refuse to grant him leave. He knew
that only God could touch the king's heart. But even before he went
into the king's presence, he had rather carefully prepared a shopping
list. He was ready when the king asked what he needed: 'May I have
letters to the governors ... safe-conduct ... a letter to Asaph, keeper
of the king's forest, so he will give me timber to make beams for the
gates of the citadel by the temple and for the city wall and for the

residence I will occupy?' (Neh. 2:7-8). The king not only granted Nehemiah's requests but insisted that a troop of cavalry accompany him for protection.

Upon arrival in Jerusalem, Nehemiah continued to take stock. Without telling anyone what he purposed to do, he set out 'during the night with a few men...' to inspect the walls (Neh. 2:12). Assessment precedes action.

Before they commence work, leaders ponder how to move ahead. They list what is needed and who needs to help. Facts inform vision. 'Suppose one of you wants to build a tower. Will he not first sit down and estimate the cost to see if he has enough money to complete it? For if he lays the foundation and is not able to finish it, everyone who sees it will ridicule him, saying, "This fellow began to build and was not able to finish"' (Luke 14:28-30). Jesus underscores the necessity of foresight.

Whether a person exercises the gift of leadership in an area of large or small responsibility, the principles remain the same. A father and mother sit down and assess what their family needs financially, socially and spiritually, before formulating a plan for the development of their children. A Sunday School teacher considers the ages and needs of pupils, the teaching resources available, whether pupils are converted or not, the teaching environment and the length of her term before drafting an effective teaching programme. A deaconess ponders the women assigned to her care, her own training in biblical skills and her weekly schedule as she considers how to inspire women to follow Christ. Good administrators instinctively 'look before they leap'.

4. Formulate a plan

Planning follows assessment. Nehemiah had clarified his first goal. He foresaw that the pagan peoples around would oppose any attempt to restore Jerusalem as a centre of Jewish national life. A wall, for protection, must come first. But he knew that without authority from the king he could not proceed, and without timber there would be no gates. Next, he would need labour to construct the walls. Besides all this, it would be wise to set a deadline for completion of the task. His initial plan had been formulated in prayer before he even went to the king. As soon as he arrived in Jerusalem, he refined that plan by visiting the site and locating the gates.

Apparently, after three days in Jerusalem, he was ready to go. Nehemiah teaches us not to overplan. Sometimes we tend to spend so much time drawing up detailed plans that they never evolve beyond the dream-stage. There comes a time, better sooner than later, when vision and holy daring lead the godly leader to step out to share his vision with others. Usually, enough time will be spent in protracted committee meetings, after communicating the vision, to allow time for further planning. I do not mean that a leader presents his vision prematurely. No, as soon as he has discerned that his own motivation is pure, that his vision is consistent with the will of God, that he has all the facts necessary and a rough outline plan of what to do, he should go ahead. Refinements can be worked on as the process continues.

Planning skill is a remarkable gift. I stand amazed at the ability some have to plan monthly women's meetings or a retreat for senior citizens. They seem to have the ability to look at the spiritual needs people have, assess what resources are available to meet those needs, anticipate problems that may crop up and put it all down on a calendar half a year ahead of time. That takes planning!

Unfortunately, other believers just let things happen. Perhaps they have the mistaken belief that a casual approach shows their dependence on the Holy Spirit. God, however, is a God who plans. Anyone who has studied natural science must believe in the marvellous intricacy of God's design. Every phase of our redemption depends on the plan of salvation.

To avoid chaos we need to plan our lives. Parents face planning challenges as they try to balance the calendars of four or five members going in a dozen different directions with the need to have family devotions. That takes leadership! Working singles need to plan how to balance a full-time job, household chores, recreation, spiritual development and outreach for the kingdom. Even children need to be taught how to plan their lives so play-time doesn't swallow up study-time.

God gifts some men and women with exceptional planning ability. Ralph Winter, a teacher in a seminary in Guatemala, pondered a problem. How could the seminary fulfil its vision of training leaders to reach Guatemala when their graduates kept being deflected away from outreach in the countryside where most of the people lived? The seminary staff tried to solve the problem by moving the school to the country on the thesis that graduates would stay in the country. Unfortunately, graduates still left for better positions in the city. What should they do?

Ralph Winter and his colleagues developed a plan. Since part of the problem could be traced to the youth and immaturity of some seminary trainees, why not choose more mature students? They began to think in terms of reaching lay leaders already involved in local church ministries. But how could leaders such as these, obviously chosen of God, be trained? These men worked to support their families. They could not travel to the seminary. They did not have much time to study. And their level of education varied widely. What could be done?

What was done became Theological Education by Extension (TEE), one of the most innovative and effective modern ideas to come out of missionary work. Teachers would travel to the students! Self-teaching materials would be prepared to guide them in home study. They would only be required to study a few courses at a time. TEE was born! It worked. Lay leaders were motivated and faithful. They could immediately practise what they learned, so the learning process was enhanced. And they stayed in their churches and developed their gifts.

Today hundreds of thousands of students study by extension all over the world. Ralph Winter has gone on to pioneer other innovative ideas as well. Like other gifted Christian leaders, he has a penchant for planning.

Presentation

Up to this point our discussion has involved what takes place, mainly in the mind and heart of the leader. Administration involves considerable thought and personal reflection. But a time comes when leaders must present their ideas to the group of which they are an integral part. They need to share both their vision and their plan.

5. Motivation

The great rock on which much inspired planning shatters is the rock of public opinion. No matter how wonderful a vision and its subsequent plan may be, without the wholehearted support of a working team, it remains a dream. Somehow, the leader must communicate his vision so that others become as excited about it as he. That means motivation.

Nehemiah presented his thoughts to the disheartened group of Israelites in Jerusalem. He called together officials, priests, nobles and anyone else whom he would need for the task. He realized that without their hearty endorsement, his plan was impossible. They would provide the labour and supervision!

What did Nehemiah say? First he made clear what they all knew: 'You see the trouble we are in: Jerusalem lies in ruins, and its gates have been burned with fire' (Neh. 2:17). He pointed out what a disgrace it was in the eyes of the nations around for God's chosen people to be in such miserable circumstances.

Then he suggested a solution: 'Come, let us rebuild the wall of Jerusalem, and we will no longer be in disgrace' (Neh. 2:17). They all wanted exactly what he suggested. All could see clearly that it was both for their own benefit and that of their witness to the nations. He avoids saying, 'I have a plan,' or 'I want you to build Jerusalem.' He identifies with their longings by saying, 'Come, let us rebuild the wall.'

Nehemiah went on to share what God had done: 'I also told them about the gracious hand of my God upon me and what the king had said to me' (Neh. 2:18). His testimony of God's care, as well as reference to the king's help, encouraged all to believe the project possible. He carefully marshalled all the positive motivation he could, without relying on manipulation through asserting his authority or inducing guilt.

Motivation dissipates like the morning mist at the first sign of problems if leaders do not act decisively. In Nehemiah's case, no sooner had they agreed to rebuild the wall, than they were opposed by Sanballat and his henchmen. Sanballat's ominous ridicule could have been disastrous to morale. But Nehemiah dealt decisively with him (Neh. 2:19-20).

Biblical leaders, however, do not boss others around. They know that success comes through team effort. Team effort follows acceptance of a shared goal. Communicating a vision in such a way that others embrace it as their own may take considerable time. Highly charged leaders often become impatient here. Studies of worker dissatisfaction show that poor communication from the management is often the main cause. Leaders need to communicate clearly, sincerely and without condescension. Leaders should be open to the give and take of sessions in which they answer questions directed to them. This openness clarifies and solidifies a sense of group vision.

Fortunately, Scripture has given us ample precedent for the sharing of major problems with a whole church. The apostles asked the entire Jerusalem assembly to choose seven men to solve the problem of serving widows in Acts 6:2-3. The council of Jerusalem included widespread representation (Acts 15). While democratic procedures slow up action, they aid motivation through encouraging participation.

Engstrom and Mackensie, in their book on management, point out that 'One of the least recognized but most important principles in motivation is that of "participation in decision-making".'[17] Nehemiah delayed action until the group themselves said to him, 'Let us start rebuilding' (Neh. 2:18). Team consensus becomes a dynamic force for progress.

Engstrom and Mackensie highlight another truism about motivation: 'Virtually all consultants in the personnel field relate a manager's success as a leader and a motivator to his sincerity in demonstrating his concern for his subordinates.'[18]

A climate of trust and respect, built up over a period of time, reduces greatly the resistance a leader will find to a shared vision. If in the past, a leader has been manipulative or self-centred, his credibility will be low. The leader must take great care to ensure that his motives are pure and his vision Christ-exalting before he comes before others.

The responsibility leaders receive from God is so sacred that they must treat the people of God with great respect. Some motivate God's people by guilt. They project their plan as if it was revealed on Sinai, with the implication that failing to participate would be failing God. Guilt is a poor motivator. Grudging participants do not become hard-working team members.

Nor can an appeal to one's own position and authority motivate any except those in the kindergarten. 'I'm the pastor. God has called me to begin this work. If you don't get behind me you will be fighting God!' Or, 'I'm a deacon, and I say we need a church extension!' Appealing for action on the basis of one's position yields dismal results.

Biblical leaders try to motivate by appealing on the basis of spiritual principles. Love for Christ, compassion for the homeless, concern for our neighbourhood, desire to obey a command of the Lord, love for other believers and a desire to join hands with them in a united task — appeals such as these truly move us. With few exceptions, God's people need to be free to respond personally to any task they are asked to join. There is no substitute for a willing worker. God's people cannot be driven, they must be loved and led by those who pitch in beside them in the work.

Winston Churchill's ability to motivate the British people during the dark days of World War II is legendary. He pulled no punches, warning members in the House of Commons that he had 'nothing to offer but blood, toil, tears and sweat', with 'many long months of struggle and suffering'.[19] In spite of horrendous difficulties, the British people reacted with enthusiasm to his famous speeches. Churchill galvanized a nation, partly because all recognized the sincerity of his loathing for Nazism and saw him participate with them in the daily round of air-raids and shortages.

Churchill, no doubt, loved his country. It is not hard to motivate others if love motivates us — love for Christ, love for the lost, love for the team we are a part of. Then, when others willingly offer to get involved, the work of the leader begins in earnest.

6. Organize the task

With the people behind him, Nehemiah began to organize. Ammonites, Horonites and Arabs, who had poured into the area when Israel was led into captivity, stepped up their fierce opposition. Sanballat, Tobiah and Geshem ridiculed Nehemiah's plan and even accused him of rebellion. Nehemiah knew that danger lay in delay. But how could they tackle the enormous task of rebuilding the wall and putting up the gates? Where to start?

Often the simplest organization works best. In the third chapter we read of Nehemiah's brilliantly simple organization. He divided the whole wall into small sections. Each gate also became a work station. Then he broke the people up into work parties that reflected their natural affinities. Relatives worked with relatives. Priests worked together. Men from the same town laboured side by side. We even read, 'Between the room above the corner and the Sheep Gate the goldsmiths and merchants made repairs' (Neh. 3:32). Where possible, people worked on that portion of the wall near their own house: 'Benjamin and Hasshub made repairs in front of their house... Azariah ... made repairs beside his house' (Neh. 3:23).

Nehemiah exhibits amazing skill in organizing the people on the basis of existing structures — relatives, town loyalties, guilds and neighbours. Labouring with those you already know in front of your own house can be powerfully motivating! By breaking the gargantuan task into small units that a group could tackle, the exiles could conceive of their challenge in manageable terms.

The task was urgent and the organization simple. Almost everyone took part. Priests left their sacred duties. Goldsmiths endangered their hands, which were skilled in crafting silver and golden filigree, by heaving stones and carrying materials. Even rulers of provincial government rolled up their sleeves (Neh. 3:14-18). Servants dedicated to the temple turned their untrained hands to the wall. Both men and women helped (Neh. 3:12). Those few who did not pull their weight were censured. 'The next section was repaired by the men of Tekoa, but their nobles would not put their shoulders to the work under their supervisors' (Neh. 3:5).

The mention of supervisors reminds us that Nehemiah organized the work in such a way that a network of men were appointed to supervise the work, section by section. Without oversight to co-ordinate the disparate parts of a task, enthusiasm and hard work go for nought.

The enormous challenges we face, as Christians, are not impossible. They are unorganized tasks awaiting leadership. Reach Toronto for Christ! Reach Russia for Christ! Reach the world by the year 2000! God promises to enable us to do the impossible. But the main obstacle continues to be our unwillingness to unite for an organized team effort. Too many Christians shun organization as if it would sting like a scorpion. Perhaps, instead of looking for those gifted by the Holy Spirit with administrative ability, we expect the Spirit to do all the hard preparatory work.

Of course, the old proverb, 'Once bitten twice shy,' may hold true here. Many have been discouraged by unworthy leaders who could organize but not display servanthood. But we must not let the abuse of some deter us from the crucial necessity of organization.

The most hopeless situation becomes possible when organized. Letellier is a small prairie town south of Winnipeg in Manitoba. A tragic accident left Joel Barnabe, aged four, without the ability to walk, talk or even eat. Pulled unconscious from an icy pond, Joel was brought back to life, but suffered severe brain damage. Although not paralysed, he had lost all speech and all control of his limbs. Rejecting the easy route of committing him to an institution, his parents sought expert help. Finding a group working with the neurologically disabled, they learned that an extremely long and tedious process was necessary. Through intense and regular stimulation the unused part of the brain might be reprogrammed to take over functions lost in the accident.

As soon as word of the need spread, a team of voluntary helpers was organized. At least fifty volunteers a week were needed. They came to the Barnabes' home in teams of five to gently massage his limbs, shine lights in his eyes, lead Joel through precisely timed exercises and help in the home. For over a year this continued. At the last count, 130 volunteers from a town of only 200 — farmers, friends, relatives, managers, shopkeepers and schoolgirls — joined hands in a heroic effort to restore movement to Joel.[20]

Behind the whole story is an outpouring of compassion and empathy rarely seen. The tragedy itself and the friendly relationships of a small town provided the motivation behind this heart-warming story. But without careful organization this outpouring of unusual neighbourliness would have been impossible. Michelle Cadieux, long-time friend of the Barnabes, served as co-ordinator of the volunteers.

If a prairie town of 200 can mobilize 130 volunteers to help a stricken boy, what exploits could the church militant accomplish? Too often, like Joel's immobile body, the body of believers remains passive and uninvolved in the extension of the kingdom. We need to call every believer to use his or her gift to massage the degenerated limbs of our outreach and ministry. Without their involvement the body of Christ remains inert and ingrown.

We shall need organizers. Unfortunately, too few believers seem either trained in organization or desirous of learning this skill. Fortunately there are some. I remember Gary with affection. The member of a board on which I served, he could take any task that needed to be done and organize it. It might be a fellowship time for 200 or a conference over a weekend. We would ask Gary to take charge. Immediately he would begin to write down things to be done and possible people to contact. Ideas on programmes would spill forth. Before long, whatever programme we assigned him would be organized. With the task broken down into different responsibilities, volunteers would be working each on their segment. Gary was a gem, and Spirit-led.

Action

Perhaps, you are thinking, 'No wonder so few want to be involved in administration. It takes so long to do anything!' Sometimes, it may seem as if all the planning and organizing is an excuse to avoid action! But soon vision and organization give place to action.

7. Action

Nehemiah continues with the exciting story: 'We rebuilt the wall till all of it reached half its height, for the people worked with all their heart' (Neh. 4:6). Nehemiah continued to show good leadership by directing the whole work through a network of supervisors. A man who devises a brilliant plan but doesn't remain to see that plan to completion fails as a leader. As situations change, he must continually improvise and modify the agreed plan. Nehemiah had to make sure that resources, such as timber, were allocated as needed, that morale remained high as weariness set in and that unforeseen problems were tackled as they arose.

Nehemiah dealt skilfully with a host of problems that would have discouraged a less determined man. Sanballat and his cronies ridiculed the work in an effort to dishearten the workers. Nehemiah went to prayer: 'Hear us, O our God, for we are despised. Turn their insults back on their own heads' (Neh. 4:4). Working with all their heart, the people closed the gaps in the wall and rebuilt it to half its height. But now Sanballat grew angry and plotted a violent attack on the workers.

Nehemiah called the people to prayer and 'posted a guard day and night to meet this threat'. Like Cromwell, who urged his men to trust God and keep their powder dry, Nehemiah prepared for attack.

Nevertheless, discouragement began to spread in the camp. Days of labour had sapped the strength of the workers and rubble from the wall obstructed their progress. Their enemies spread among them fear of attack in the middle of the night: 'Then the Jews who lived near them [their enemies] came and told us ten

times over, "Wherever you turn, they will attack us'" (Neh. 4:12).
The work was threatened by a crisis in morale fostered by pessimists
in their midst.

Nehemiah first toured the site and then gathered the people
together. Encouraging them not to be afraid, he reminded them of
the greatness of their God and urged them to 'fight for your brothers,
your sons and your daughters, your wives and your homes' (Neh.
4:14). Then he proceeded to modify his organization. He divided the
people into two groups, half to continue the work on the wall, and
half to stand guard in full armour. He posted officers all around the
wall behind the workers and guards. He stationed special guards
behind low or exposed portions of the wall. Everyone, including
workmen, wore their swords at all times. Since the wall was so long
and they were 'widely separated from each other along the wall',
Nehemiah kept in constant touch through a trumpeter by his side
(Neh. 4:18-20). Wherever an attack appeared they planned to sound
the trumpet, calling for help. He repeatedly reminded them that 'Our
God will fight for us!' (Neh. 4:20). Days were stretched from dawn
to starlight to press on with the work. At night guards kept watch.
The work progressed until a new crisis arose.

Chapter 5 records a sordid tale of exploitation. Evidently, prof-
iteers from among their own people had taken advantage of previous
famines and this new crisis to line their own pockets. Finally the
people could take it no longer. They cried out to Nehemiah, 'We are
mortgaging our fields, our vineyards and our homes to get grain'
(Neh. 5:3). Priests, nobles and officials were chief among those
implicated in this terrible business. They had even demanded that
children be enslaved as collateral for loans.

Nehemiah was angry. In one sense, internal problems such as
these threaten more seriously the progress of God's work than
attacks from without. Nehemiah confronted the perpetrators and
demanded an end to their actions in the name of God and brotherly
love. Shamefacedly, they promised to restore all that had been
confiscated as surety for debt. He required a public oath from them
to seal their promise to cease profiteering. Perhaps his own example
shamed the perpetrators and inspired the victims. When he was
appointed as their governor, he had refused to accept a salary from
public tax. He had supported himself, and others, from his own
pocket.

Christian leaders like Nehemiah work hard. While Nehemiah did not personally labour with his hands on the wall, as we learn from the text, he worked harder than any. So ceaseless was he in his direction of the work that he slept in his clothes. Too often, Christians who have not themselves been in positions of responsibility fail to appreciate the long hours, the hard work, the agonizing thought that goes into leadership. Leadership is hard work. Accept it, and don't shy away from this crucial calling if you show signs of administrative skill. And encourage other leaders. Those who lead committees, activities or organizations need to know from time to time that they are appreciated.

Christian leaders, nevertheless, need thick skins. They are bound to be misunderstood. If you have the gift of administration, realize that the 'buck has to stop' somewhere, and where it stops there will be heat. Expect it. Commit it to the Lord in prayer. Many believers who do not understand leadership think that leaders enjoy bossing others around. They fail to understand the stress and pressure which Paul so graphically describes in his second letter to the Corinthians: 'I face daily the pressure of my concern for all the churches' (2 Cor. 11:28).

One of the most important of leadership skills is the ability to delegate responsibility to others. Few realize so clearly the need for team effort as the good leader. For this reason they keep a sharp eye open for potential abilities in others. God often uses them to encourage reticent saints to step into positions where dormant gifts burst into flower.

Leaders have to lead. Someone has to take charge and graciously direct a group to pursue a course of action. Sometimes, our firmly held belief in our equality before the cross makes Christians suspicious of authority. Knowing this, Christian leaders must move with humility, patience and great gentleness. But in the final analysis they must stand up and exercise their gift by directing the work of God. When inaction would be sin, the leader must take action. Just as it would be failure for a teacher to shun teaching, in the same way it is a failure for a leader to fail to take charge. Those gifted to lead must lead, or live disappointed and unproductive lives.

8. Complete the task

Nehemiah completed the task: 'So the wall was completed ... in fifty-two days' (Neh. 6:15). Good leaders not only plan, but complete what they plan. Nehemiah exemplifies the hard-working perseverance of biblical leadership.

Not only completion but continuity marks good administration. Far from taking his ease after this victory, Nehemiah continued to deal with other problems as they arose. He formulated policy about when to open and when to close the gates. He chose his brother to administer Jerusalem, not because he was a relative, but 'because he was a man of integrity and feared God more than most men do' (Neh. 7:2). He tackled the matter of genealogy, so important in Israel. Then, he gathered all the people together and encouraged Ezra to teach the law. When all began weeping as they saw their sins in the light of God's law, Nehemiah reminded them that it was a day of victory, not sorrow. Encouraged, they proclaimed a great and joyful festival with feasting and teaching for seven days. Two weeks later they proclaimed a fast and laid out the steps leading to national reformation. Nehemiah led the people through a period of testing and trial, to a time of joy and reformation. Renewal came. A good leader perseveres as long as needs exist.

No wonder Paul adds to his exhortation about leaders the words, 'Let him govern diligently' (Rom. 12:8). The gift of administration/ leadership, more than almost any other, requires diligence. Should a leader err by laziness or carelessness, all those who look to him for leadership will suffer. Should the administrator fail to bring a project to completion, his team will become disillusioned through seeing their efforts come to nought. Leaders like Thomas Edison, the inventor, know that inspired leadership is 'one per cent inspiration and ninety-nine per cent perspiration'.

Few have demonstrated perseverance in leadership more thoroughly than William Wilberforce. Driven by an antipathy towards slavery, he worked to secure freedom. In 1787 he first presented a motion to the House of Commons about the slave trade. John Stott describes his career and comments that he 'was not a very prepossessing man. He was little and ugly, with poor eyesight and an upturned nose.'[21]

In the years that followed, this small man became a giant in the cause of emancipation. In order to abolish trade in slaves both at home and throughout the empire, Wilberforce introduced bills in the Commons in 1789, 1791, 1792, 1794, 1796, 1798 and 1799. All failed. Finally a bill was passed in 1806 to prohibit the use of British ships in the trade of slaves. In 1807 another bill abolished the trade itself. Eighteen years had elapsed but the battle was not yet complete.

The previously mentioned bills had abolished the trade but not ended slavery itself or emancipated those already in bonds. He formed the Anti-Slavery Society in 1823 to pursue the fight. But in 1825 he was forced to resign as a member of Parliament due to ill-health. From the outside he continued the struggle, sending a message to his society: 'Our motto must continue to be persever-ance. And ultimately I trust the Almighty will crown our efforts with success.' Finally, three days before he died, both Houses of Parlia-ment passed the Abolition of Slavery Bill. The year was 1833. It marked forty-five years of struggle for African slaves. Wilberforce is a shining example of the perseverance of a Christian leader troubled by great injustice.[22]

Conclusion

We have seen reflected in Nehemiah some of the main characteris-tics of a leader. Biblical leaders walk humbly with God because they prepare themselves before they enter into an administrative chal-lenge. First they check the purity of their motivation; then they proceed to clarify their vision by making sure it conforms to God's overall will, and evaluate the nature of the task and its problems, before formulating a proposed plan to complete the task assigned. After considerable preparatory work, they present the challenge to the Lord's people with a view to, first, motivating those involved and then to organizing a work team. When organization is complete, the biblical leader will initiate the project and proceed to direct the various aspects of the work by means of supervision, delegation and problem-solving. Finally, the work is brought to completion.

Leaders are needed everywhere. John Stott comments, 'God has a leadership role of some degree and kind for each of us. We need, then, to seek his will with all our hearts, to cry to him to give us a vision of what he is calling us to do with our lives, and to pray for grace to be faithful (not necessarily successful) in obedience to the heavenly vision.'[23]

Almost everything we do requires some administration. Con-sider, for example, the leadership parents need to exhibit in their family. Gary Smalley, in a book he wrote jointly with John Trent,

describes life in his family. His younger son, Michael, seems prone
to accidents. Being stung by hornets, nearly drowning in a neighbour's pool, various falls, a car accident, bruises — Michael has
experienced them all. What should a mother and father do to make
such painful experiences meaningful? Gary Smalley suggests that
parents use these opportunities to prepare their children for life by
teaching them the value of trouble. He suggests that children can
learn empathy, humility, endurance and how to help others through
thinking about their own trials.[24]

But for parents to be ready to use whatever comes into their
child's life, they need to be organized. Chaos usually descends
during a family crisis. Christian parents who exercise leadership
learn to direct chaos and shape it into productive channels. They
have already thought through what they want to teach and how to
respond gently and positively. They will have studied parenting in
the Word and in good books. Good leaders learn how to use crises
constructively.

Take a few moments to ponder the course of your life. Where
does God want you to exercise leadership? Has the Holy Spirit been
gifting you in this area? Before I conclude this book with several
suggestions about implementing a process of gift development in
your own life and that of your church, return to the chart and fill in
the columns under leadership.

Conclusion:
Developing a personal and congregational gift strategy

For the past few years Toronto has been justly proud of the prowess of the Toronto Blue Jays baseball team. Last year they concluded a great season by winning the world series. Not only that but the Skydome, the Toronto sports facility where the Jays play, set a new league record in attendance with over four million spectators going through the turnstiles.

Toronto has Blue Jay fever whenever the team has a chance at the pennant. Indeed, having a Canadian team so successful in an American sport captures the imagination of the country. People as far away as Alberta cheer, 'Go Jays, go!' Baseball is a powerful spectator sport!

But behind that success in drawing spectators is success on a team level. The Jays, while they do have a number of really good players, are outstanding as a team. A co-ordination of good coaching, pitching, fielding and running makes the Jays a winner.

Healthy churches manifest a team spirit. I seem to run into this concept wherever I turn. Speakers and books talk about body life, the priesthood of all believers, participation, the motivation of volunteers and the mobilization of human resources. A new emphasis on meta-churches is replacing the stress on mega-churches. It seeks to foster the need to involve all God's people in the work of ministry. I even find missions talking about the need. At a three-day conference on the re-entry of retired missionaries into Western church life, the speaker stressed the importance of knowing one's gifts. He lamented the lack of a theology of spiritual gifts. This book is an attempt to inspire the development of just such a theology.

What a strange paradox! We have a highly developed theology of redemption and of sanctification. We study pastoral theology, the doctrine of the church and of missions. But in spite of the fact that spiritual gift exercise is crucial to sanctification, essential for healthy church growth and critical in foreign missions, we have failed to develop a theology of gifts. How can we minister effectually without it? How can we edify one another in our local churches or plant self-propagating churches in alien cultures without a carefully developed strategy of gift discovery and development? Without it, ministry will be hit and miss. Unless we want to doom our churches to remain largely congregations of spectators, we must resurrect the biblical material on spiritual giftedness and strategies until it is at the heart of church life and worship.

Most of us learned about spiritual gifts almost by accident. Bill Hybels, pastor of Willowcreek Community Church, describes a common experience. His family went to a church with a high commitment to theology and the catechism. 'Growing up, I had no desire to be a preacher... But in my late teenage years, I found myself in the Chicago area. The youth pastor of the church I was attending had left, and I was asked to give some leadership to the young people... What actually happened was that I discovered I had spiritual gifts of preaching and teaching and at the time I'd never heard of spiritual gifts!'[1]

Bill Hybels' experience has been duplicated many times. Fortunately, since the Holy Spirit superintends the church, he ensures that essential gifts are discovered and developed in spite of our disregard for the powerful ministry-tools he has crafted. The Spirit's overruling providence, however, is no excuse for us to neglect developing a conscious pattern for the discovery and development of gifts.

Bill Hybels went on to plant a thriving church in suburban Chicago. One of their key innovations has been the development of the sophisticated gift discovery and development materials entitled *Networking*. In the forward of this manual, Hybels writes, 'We discovered years ago that believers flourish in their service to Christ when they are serving in the area of their giftedness and in conjunction with who God made them to be. The Networking materials grew out of our desire to be able to help believers discover their spiritual gifts and then determine where to use them in our body. The results of Networking have been astonishing. Imagine having hundreds of fresh servants entering the work force of the church, confident of their giftedness and eager to invest them in service for God's glory... It is happening!'[2] Increased participation in ministry is exactly what we need today.

Peter Drucker has been called 'the father of modern management'. Few realize that this writer of twenty-two books, including *The Effective Executive,* has worked for thirty-five years for non-profit organizations as well as businesses. In an interview in *Leadership,* he demonstrates an incisive understanding of the mission of the church that he describes as: 'To change the parishioner's values — into God's values ... to bring the gospel to all of mankind.'[3]

In Drucker's view, pastors and church leaders must ask a key question: 'What can I do in this organization that nobody else can do?' Several other questions emerge from that: 'What did the good Lord ordain me for? Drucker is asking the very questions we have been addressing in this book on gifts. He continues in the interview to discuss giftedness. 'The mistake that really kills the church is when the pastor ... "labours to be effective where he is not gifted". As a result he spends inordinate amounts of time on these things, does them poorly and slights the things he is good at, and thus does them poorly too. Within a few years, you have an ungodly mess on your hands.'[4]

I. Gift development in the congregation

1. Evaluate people

Drucker goes on to urge church leaders to evaluate the people involved in ministry. He advises the making of lists of people and their strengths along with the key jobs that need to be done in a church. 'After you've evaluated strengths and key activities, then you begin matching them up, making sure each key activity is covered, and you're beginning to build an effective team.'[5]

Let me echo Drucker's suggestions. Since spiritual gift exercise is a group activity, ideally gift development should begin at the level of the church officers. They should hammer out a strategy that fits their particular church. Such a strategy will, probably, include a sermon series on the nature of the church as a body and the rôle of spiritual gifts in its edification and outreach. An array of good books and resources on gifts ought to be purchased and promoted.

While basic teaching on the subject is being presented, church leaders need to be sure they have identified their own gifts. This is not as easy as it seems. I would suggest that a series of studies be arranged at the beginning of meetings of church officers, or in a retreat setting, to lead the pastor and church leaders, with their wives, to identify their own and each other's gifts. The more input we can have on any one person from his or her spouse, other deacons and church leaders, the more accurately we can identify gifts. Once identified, responsibilities need to be shifted around to reflect gifts more accurately. The church officers need to realize that believers, including their pastor, should be freed to concentrate where they have the most skill.

2. Identify jobs

Another step to take involves identifying all the jobs that need to be done. Every church needs Sunday School teachers, organists or pianists, those who run the catering, stewards, treasurers, visitors, caretakers and a hundred and one other jobs. When we identify the tasks that need to be done, we can then look around for someone who can do them. When we fit gifted people to appropriate tasks we promote a sense of joy and fulfilment that further encourages participation. Conversely square pegs in round holes mean unhappy and frustrated people (Willowcreek Community Church has done admirable work in developing a list of church tasks).

. When we identify all the jobs that need to be done, we can take concrete steps to match people and ministries. Churches should pick their most discerning people to form a resource committee. That committee should then be commissioned to search for gifted people to fill vacancies. Matching human resources with glaring needs fulfils a crucial church need.

3. Give teaching on gifts

After the church leadership have progressed in their own understanding of gifts and begun to develop a gift strategy, then more extensive teaching on gifts can be given. This could take place in adult Bible class or during home Bible studies. Whatever setting is chosen, adequate time ought to be given for interaction with the goal of enabling participants to identify their gifts, in a general way at least, before the study concludes. By the end of the course, the teacher ought to have a general idea about participants' areas of giftedness. For example, he might write, 'Ann's main gift seems to be encouragement both through her music and through one-to-one relationships. She also seems to be developing latent gifts of shepherding and evangelism.' This preliminary gift evaluation data ought to be forwarded to the church leadership team responsible for people resource development where a record of the whole membership can gradually be formulated. A year or so after introducing the subject, the church might plan a spring or autumn gifts festival. This could take the form of a day-long or weekend retreat in a country setting. A workbook could be prepared with space for each participant to pursue a gift discovery process adapted from the chart used with this book. The workbook could include basic definitions, space for notes from the messages and workshops and space for the comments of friends, the pastor or other church leaders.

The retreat should aim to capture the interest of the whole church by careful promotion and by providing a parallel programme for children so that adults can be involved in the main sessions. The retreat should be designed to give both an overview of gifts and a series of workshops on three or four key gifts. Workshops could contain a basic segment of teaching which includes reference to specific service roles in the church that need volunteers. Teaching could be augmented by role-play to demonstrate the gift in use, a workbook exercise to do on the gift and concluding time of questions and answers. During the retreat, opportunity should be given for friends to evaluate each other in terms of gifts and abilities. The pastor should be available to conduct informal interviews designed to help those seeking to discover their gifts.

Once a gift development strategy is in place, teaching on gifts will become an important part of orienting new members. Each new member should be led through a process of gift discovery. As soon as practicable, new members ought to be involved in simple ministries that test their gifts and give them a sense of identification with their new church home.

II. What the individual can do

Should gift discovery and development not be high on the agenda of your local church, you need not despair, Since you have stayed with me to this point, I am sure you have already made great strides in discovering your own gifts. You can continue to develop them on an individual basis.

We have progressed through a number of gift discovery steps. They are tabulated on the chart you have been filling in as you progressed through the book. Before you leave these pages, seek to conserve the knowledge you have gleaned. Review the definitions of the various gifts. (A summary is included in Appendix I.) Remind yourself about the various components that determine the gift discovery process: *a balanced view of the Holy Spirit* that produces a sense of both awe and adequacy, *submission to the lordship of Jesus Christ* and openness to servanthood as he exemplified it, an *inventory* of your providentially developed skills, interests, hobbies, training etc., a *burden* for specific needs, *effectiveness* in certain areas of service and a greater *sense of satisfaction* in some ministries than others and a tabulation of *the evaluation of mature Christian friends*.

Take out your completed chart and review your findings. Circle what seem to be your top three gifts. All of us have a gift-mix; different gifts come to the fore in the face of different needs. Ask yourself a series of penetrating questions such as those which follow: Are you using your main gifts? If not, is it because you are legitimately helping to meet a special need present in your church at this time? If you are not ministering in an area of your main giftedness, why are you holding back? Could it be lack of opportunity or fear of failure?

Ponder the ministries with which you are now involved. Is it time for a change of task? Is it time to hone your ministry skills? Where do you sense the most personal satisfaction or find the most response? Do you have unfulfilled ministry dreams? Could you volunteer for an area of service that would be more in line with your gifts? Do you need training in order to become effective in a new ministry, or more effective where you presently serve?

Whatever you discover about yourself, be assured that the Lord is concerned as much with you and your spiritual development as with the work you do in the church. Why not set down a concrete plan of what you will do in the years ahead to grow not only in grace, but in gracious ministry? Such a plan may include courses you want to take, seminars you should attend, training needed, books to read, service opportunities to explore, or areas of weak obedience that need to be corrected. May God fill you with his joy as you pursue the path of gift discovery.

If I can be of help to you, or if you have corrections, or suggestions or disagreements with the material in this book, don't hesitate to write me care of the publisher.

Creating a harmonious unit

Perhaps you have enjoyed, as I have, the experience of witnessing a symphony concert. I'm always awe-struck by the harmonious music that emanates from such diverse instruments. Violins and drums, cymbals and tubas, clarinets and cellos all combine under the conductor's baton to weave together from disparate notes a harmonious mingling of sound that may move us to tears.

Each of us is unique and God wants something different from each of us, something that is distinctly our own. But when he has his way in our churches, our disparate temperaments and contrasting gifts are woven by his hand into an almighty symphony of praise. May the years that follow witness a mighty revival of joyful participation in ministry inspired by the rediscovery of spiritual gifts.

Appendix I:
A brief description of spiritual gifts

Gifts can be divided into *speaking* gifts, *serving* gifts and *sign* gifts. Definitions for the sign gifts have not been included at this point. See chapter 4.

I. Speaking gifts

Speaking gifts comprise those endowments of the Spirit primarily involved in the communication of biblical truth.

Apostleship, although extinct as an office, continues in the special ability of those who do church-planting. We cannot call anyone today an apostle. But pioneer missionaries who seek to establish new churches in unreached areas reflect, in some measure, the original apostolic gift.

Prophecy, also extinct as an office, continues, however, in prophetic preachers, those who bring God's Word to bear on a specific situation with power and relevance. It may include instruction, encouragement, exhortation and comfort.

Evangelism is that Spirit-produced concern for lost men and women that moves the gifted person towards outreach wherever that may lead. This concern is combined with the spiritual ability to so proclaim the gospel, either in personal or corporate witness, that lost men and women respond in faith and repentance. The evangelist is a soul-winner.

Shepherding ability resides in those, whether they be lay or full-time ministers, who watch over the flock to ensure they receive wholesome spiritual nourishment. Those with the shepherding gift manifest a spiritual sensitivity that leads them to draw near to others to understand their concerns and needs, to protect them from danger and to suggest steps to take to develop vigorous spiritual health. Shepherds serve as spiritual GPs gifted in the diagnosis, prescription and treatment of spiritual ills.

Teaching aims at lasting spiritual change from the inside out. It is the spiritual ability to communicate biblical truth in such a way that believers demonstrate present and lasting changes in understanding, attitudes, decision-making and behaviour. The Spirit uses teaching to transform believers into obedient disciples of Christ.

Those gifted with *knowledge* are able to search out, organize and summarize the content of the Bible into a series of systematic and logical categories without necessarily being able to communicate that knowledge.

Wisdom, as a spiritual gift, involves the application of a comprehensive and balanced understanding of the Scriptures to practical issues. It takes biblical knowledge and applies it to solve moral and practical problems while ensuring that God receives due priority in everything that occurs.

Those gifted in *encouragement* (exhortation) exhibit unusual sensitivity to the emotional needs of others. They come alongside people because they want to understand them and help them grow in godliness and personal fulfilment. The encourager seeks to apply comfort, inspiration, encouragement, exhortation, restoration or rebuke, depending upon the need he or she senses at the time.

II. Serving gifts

Serving gifts demonstrate a propensity to serve humbly and happily. They endow believers with the spiritual ability to demonstrate Christian love in practical ways.

Helpfulness is the general spiritual gift of those who are especially sensitive to, and quick to reach out to meet practical needs, whatever they may be. It involves the talent or training to do practical things like painting, finance, cooking — or a host of other things. It may be just as surely manifest in a general spirit of humble and happy helpfulness.

Those with the gift of *hospitality* generously use their home and possessions to provide a warm atmosphere of openness and acceptance conducive to making strangers, new Christians, immigrants — indeed all kinds of people — feel at home.

Giving is that Spirit-produced ability to view finances and material resources as a stewardship — a trust from God to be used wisely, generously, cheerfully and systematically in the furtherance of God's purposes on an individual, local or world-wide scale.

The gift of *mercy* is that Spirit-produced compassion for those in misery or distress that overflows in an abundance of cheerful and practical help for those who are poor, sick, lonely, bereft or unfortunate. Those with this gift manifest abundant empathy.

Administration or *leadership* is a Spirit-produced ability to serve the Lord and his people by taking a vision of what should be, breaking it down into goals and objectives, evaluating present conditions, planning what to do, motivating others to take part, and organizing and directing the resultant work until the plan is brought to completion.

Those with the gift of *faith*, mountain-moving faith, feel a deep dissatisfaction with present conditions, glimpse a vision of what God can do, face seemingly insurmountable obstacles and yet perceive that God will overcome the impossible.

The gift of *discernment* is that spiritual ability to discriminate between truth and error in teaching, between good and evil in conduct and between genuine and hypocritical expressions of the Christian faith. It sometimes involves recognizing demonic influence in individuals or groups.

Appendix II: Gift evaluation chart

Gifts / Speaking gifts	1. Providential preparation A. Skills, exp., hobbies, educ.	B ministry experience	2. Sensed needs and burdens	3. Area of effectiveness	4. Sense of fulfilment, enjoyment	5. Counsel of others	6. Degree of present obedience	Notes
Missions (Church-planting)								
Preaching								
Evangelism							'You are my witnesses'	
Shepherding							'Bear one another's burdens'	
Knowledge							'Know the truth'	
Wisdom							'Walk in wisdom'	
Teaching							'Teaching them'	
Encouragement							'Encourage one another'	

Gift evaluation chart

Gifts Serving gifts	1. Providential preparation A. Skills, exp., hobbies, educ.	B ministry experience	2. Sensed needs and burdens	3. Area of effectiveness	4. Sense of fulfilment, enjoyment	5. Counsel of others	6. Degree of present obedience	Notes
Helps							'Care for one another'	
Hospitality							'Be hospitable'	
Giving							'Give liberally'	
Mercy							'Be merciful'	
Faith							'… only believe'	
Discernment							'Test all things'	
Leadership (Administration)							'Rule your spirit'	

Bibliography

Books on the Greek text

Henry Alford, *The Greek Testament*, vol. II, Chicago: Moody Press, 1958.
Joseph Henry Thayer, *Greek-English Lexicon of the New Testament*, New York: American Book Company, undated but corrected edition of Harper & Brothers, 1886.
Vine, *An Expository Dictionary of New Testament Words*, Lynchburg, Virginia: The Old Time Gospel Hour edition, undated.
Kenneth S. Wuest, *Untranslatable Riches from the Greek New Testament*, Grand Rapids: Eerdmans, 1952.

Commentaries

F. Keil and F. Delitzsch, *Commentary of the Old Testament in Ten Volumes*, vol. 2 of the Pentateuch, Grand Rapids: William B. Eerdmans, 1981.
W. Grosheide, *Commentary on the First Epistle to the Corinthians*, Edinburgh: Marshall, Morgan & Scott Ltd, 1954.
William Hendriksen, *New Testament Commentary — Ephesians*, Grand Rapids: Baker, 1967.
Charles Hodge, *The First Epistle to the Corinthians*, London: Banner of Truth Trust, 1959.
Kling, *The First Epistle of Paul to the Corinthians*, vol. X, *Lange's Commentary on the Holy Scriptures*, Grand Rapids: Zondervan, 1969.
John Peter Lange, *The Gospel of Matthew*, Grand Rapids: Zondervan Publishing House, 1960, vol. 1 of the New Testament.
Ralph Martin, *The Spirit of the Congregation — Studies in 1 Corinthians 12-15*, Grand Rapids: William B. Eerdmans, 1984.

Robertson C. McQuilkin, *Studying our Lord's Parables for Yourself,* Columbia: Columbia Bible College, 1933.
Campbell Morgan, *The Parables and Metaphors of our Lord,* London: Marshall, Morgan & Scott Ltd.
Matthew Poole, *A Commentary on the Holy Bible,* London: Banner of Truth Trust, vol. III.
Matthew Henry, *Commentary on the Whole Bible,* Revell, undated.

Books about spiritual gifts

Books quoted

Privately circulated paper, Institute of Basic Youth Conflicts, *Additional Insights on Understanding Spiritual Gifts,* 1981.
Ronald E. Baxter, *Gifts of the Spirit,* Grand Rapids: Kregel Publications, 1983.
Bruce L. Bugbee with Bill Hybels & Don Cousin, *Networking, Leader's Guide,* Pasadena: Charles E. Fuller Institute, 1989.
Leslie B. Flynn, *Nineteen Gifts of the Spirit,* Wheaton: Victor Books, 1981.
E. O'Day, *Discovering Your Spiritual Gifts,* Downers Grove, Illinois: Inter-Varsity Press.
William McRae, *Dynamics of Spiritual Gifts,* Grand Rapids: Zondervan, 1976.

Other books on gifts

Oswald Sanders, *The Holy Spirit and His Gifts,* Grand Rapids: Zondervan Publishing House, 1979.
Merrill F. Unger, *The Baptism & Gifts of the Holy Spirit,* Chicago: Moody Press, 1978.
Peter Wagner, *Your Spiritual Gifts Can Help Your Church Grow,* Glendale, Calif.: Regal Books, 1979.

General books quoted

E. H. Andrews, *The Promise of the Spirit,* Welwyn: Evangelical Press, 1982 (now published as *The Spirit has Come*).
Harry Blamires, *The Christian Mind,* Ann Arbor, Michigan: Servant Books, 1978.
Richard Nelson Bolles, *The 1991 What Color Is Your Parachute?,* Berkeley: Ten Speed Press, 1991.

Charles Bridges, *The Christian Ministry,* London: The Banner of Truth Trust, 1967.

John A. Broadus, *On the Preparation and Delivery of Sermons,* New York: Harper, many editions, this edition 1943.

Oswald Chambers, *My Utmost For His Highest,* New York: Dodd, Mead and Co., 1935.

Lawrence J. Crabb, Jr, *Understanding People,* Grand Rapids: Zondervan, 1987.

Ted W. Engstrom & R. Alec MacKenzie, *Managing Your Time,* Grand Rapids: Zondervan, 1967.

Richard J. Foster, *Celebration of Discipline,* San Francisco: Harper & Row, 1978.

Michael Green, *I Believe in the Holy Spirit,* London: Hodder and Stoughton, 1975.

Sidney Greidanus, *The Modern Preacher and the Ancient Text,* Grand Rapids: Eerdmans, 1988.

David B. Guralnik, Gen. Ed., *Webster's New World Dictionary,* New York: Avenel Books, 1978.

O. Hallesby, *Prayer,* Minneapolis: Augsburg, 1931.

Tim Hansel, *Holy Sweat,* Waco, Texas: Word Books, 1987.

Alex Rattray Hay, *The New Testament Order for Church and Missionary,* Buenos Aires, Argentina: New Testament Missionary Union, 1947.

Michael Scott Horton, ed., *Power Religion,* Chicago: Moody Press, 1992.

Kent and Barbara Hughes, *Liberating Ministry from the Success Syndrome,* Wheaton: Tyndale, 1987.

Roy Joslin, *Urban Harvest,* Welwyn: Evangelical Press, 1982.

Monsignor Ronald Knox, *Enthusiasm,* Oxford University Press, 1950.

Samuel Logan Jr, ed., *The Preacher and Preaching,* Phillipsburg, N. J.: Presbyterian and Reformed/Welwyn: Evangelical Press, 1986.

John E. MacArthur, *The Charismatics,* Grand Rapids: Zondervan, 1978.

Gail MacDonald, *High Call, High Privilege,* Wheaton: Tyndale House.

Gordon MacDonald, *Rebuilding Your Broken World,* Nashville: Oliver-Nelson Books, 1988.

Kenneth W. Osbeck, *101 More Human Stories,* Grand Rapids: Kregel Publications, 1985.

J. I. Packer, *Keeping in Step with the Spirit,* Old Tappan, N. J.: Fleming H. Revell, 1984.

J. I. Packer, *Hot Tub Religion,* Wheaton: Tyndale Publishers Inc., 1987.

J. I. Packer, 'Why preach?' *The Preacher and Preaching,* Samuel T. Logan, ed., Phillipsburg, N. J.: Presbyterian and Reformed /Welwyn: Evangelical Press, 1986.

Earl D. Radmacher, *Spiritual Gift Inventory, An Explanatory and Developmental Outline,* Portland: Western Conservative Baptist Seminary, no date.

Haddon Robinson, *Biblical Preaching*, Grand Rapids: Baker, 1980 (8th printing, May 1983).

E. Sangster, *The Craft of Sermon Construction and Illustration,* Grand Rapids: Baker, reprint 1984.

William Shakespeare, *Twelfth Night,* II. iv. 158.

Robert Schuller, *Self-Esteem: the New Reformation,* Waco, Texas: Word, 1982.

Gary Smalley & John Trent, *The Gift of Honor,* Nashville, Tennessee: Thomas Nelson, 1987.

George Smeaton, *The Doctrine of the Holy Spirit*, Edinburgh: The Banner of Truth Trust, Reprint, 1980.

Howard Snyder, *The Problem of Wineskins,* Downer's Grove, Ill.: Inter-Varsity Press, 1975.

John Stott, *A Call to Christian Leadership,* Marshall, Morgan & Scott, 1984, booklet.

Charles Swindoll, *The Seasons of Life*, Portland: Multnomah Press, 1983.

Frank R. Tillapaugh, *Unleashing the Church*, Ventura, California: Regal Books, 1982.

A. W. Tozer, *The Root of the Righteous*, Harrisburg, Pa: Christian Publications, 1955.

John Wimber with Kevin Springer, *Power Evangelism*, also *Power Healing*, London: Hodder and Stoughton, 1985 & 1986 resp.

The Westminster Confession, chap. V.

Eric Wright, *Tell the World*, Welwyn: Evangelical Press, 1981.

Periodical sources

Joseph C. Aldrich, 'Lifestyle Evangelism', *Christianity Today*, 7 January 1983.

Kobad Arjani, 'Decision for Eternity', *HIS*, December 1961, pp.22-3.

L. Billingsley, 'Keeping America Stupid', *World*, 18 February 1989, p.16.

Dr J. R. Boyd, *Alumni Association Newsletter of Toronto Baptist Seminary*, January 1989.

Raymond Carlson, 'The Role of the Prophet Today', *The Pentecostal Testimony,* March 1991, p.22.

Anthony Coppin, 'Life in the Spirit', *Reformation Today,* No. 97, May/June 1987, p.22.

Elizabeth Davey, 'Does Your Pastor Need Your Ministry?', Miscellaneous article.

James Davey, 'How to Discover Your Spiritual Gift', *Christianity Today,* 9 May 1975, p.138.

Peter Drucker, an interview, 'Managing to Minister', *Leadership*, Spring 1989, (vol. X, No. 2), p.15.

Marilyn Dunlop, 'Genes Can "See" Child's Future', *Toronto Star,* 2 May 1987.

Elizabeth Elliot, 'Maturity, the Power to Discern', *Brigade Leader*, undated, p.15.

'Stressing the Right Vocation', *Eternity,* April 1985, p.16.

Virginia Evansen, 'Five Secrets of Lending a Helping Hand', magazine clipping of unknown source.

Christopher Rule, 'George Fox and Early Quakerism', *Reformation Today*, No. 95, p.15.

Peter Carlyle-Gordge, 'Boy's Plight is Town's Mission of Love', *Toronto Star*, 3 January 1987, A1, A8.

Norman L. Geisler, 'Excuses Why I didn't Witness', *Canadian Challenge,* Summer 1986, pp.5-6.

Wayne A. Grudem, 'What Should be the Relationship Between Prophet and Pastor?, *Equipping*, Fall 1989, p.8.

Chua Wee Hian, 'After the Sale is Over', *Eternity,* September 1968.

Bill Hybels (interview with three other preachers), 'The Pulpit's Personal Side, A Leadership Forum', *Leadership;* Spring 1990 (vol. XI, No. 2), p.19.

Ethel Marr, 'Is there a Camel in your Tent?', *Eternity*, January 1977, p.40.

Michael G. Maudlin, 'Seers in the Heartland', *Christianity Today*, 14 January 1991, p.18.

Paul Mickey with William Proctor, 'Too Busy for Sex', *Marriage Partnership,* Winter 1989, p.106.

Lyle L. Mook, 'You can be a Barnabas', *Power for Living,* Wheaton, Ill., 1983.

Elizabeth O'Connor, 'Releasing Angels: Uncovering Our Gifts', *Partnership,* September/October 1986, p.27.

Lora Lee Parrott, 'Learning Hospitality from the Master', *Sunday To Sunday*, Winter 1989, p.20.

Jill Pinch, 'That's not my Job', *Team Horizons,* January/February 1987, p.6.

John Prin, 'The Rehabbing of 807 Pascagoula,' *Christianity Today*, 18 November 1988, pp.12-13.

Charles C. Ryrie, 'Receiving the Spirit's Gifts, *Eternity*, February 1975, p.19.

Joyce Sanford, as told to Majorie Zimmerman, 'The Closest of All', *Power For Living*, 1 December 1985, pp.4-5.

Dennis M. Schultz, 'Fleischmann Memorial Baptist Church — Ministering in the Inner-City', reprint, *Baptist Herald,* June 1982.

Interview by Lois Sibley, 'The Joys and Risks of Radical Hospitality', *Eternity*, October 1983.

Tim Stafford, 'Evangelism: The New Wave is a Tidal Wave', *Christianity Today*, 18 May 1984, p.43.

John Wimber, 'Introducing Prophetic Ministry', *Equipping*, Fall 1989, pp.4-6.
Ray Wiseman, 'Square Pegs', *The Christian Perspective*, October 1989, p.2.
Philip Yancey, 'Low Pay, Long Hours, No Applause', *Christianity Today*, 18 November 1988, p.80.

Other media sources

Brochure, Career Track Seminars, January/February 1988 Schedule.
Brochure of MICA Management Centre Seminar, received 30 October 1987.
N.B.C. Evening News, 17 March 1989.
Radio Programme, Canadian Broadcasting Corporation, Toronto, 29 May 1987.
Lloyd J. Ogilvie, TV programme #1109R, *Let God Love You,* Los Angeles, 8 April 1989.

Poetry

Anonymous poem, *LeTourneau Christian Camp newsletter.*

References

Chapter 1 — Spiritual gifts: variety, sovereignty, unity
1. Gary Smalley and John Trent, *The Gift of Honor,* Thomas Nelson, 1987, p.77.
2. Leslie B. Flynn, *Nineteen Gifts of the Spirit,* Victor Books, 1981, p.9.
3. Charles Hodge, *The First Epistle to the Corinthians,* Banner of Truth Trust, 1959, p.242.
4. Henry Alford, *The Greek Testament,* vol. II, Moody Press, 1958, p.577.
5. F. W. Grosheide, *Commentary on the First Epistle to the Corinthians,* Marshall, Morgan & Scott, Ltd, 1954, p.283.
6. C. F. Kling, *The First Epistle of Paul to the Corinthians,* vol. X, *Lange's Commentary on the Holy Scriptures,* Zondervan, 1969, p.249.

Chapter 2 — The Holy Spirit: awe and adequacy
1. E. H. Andrews, *The Promise of the Spirit,* Evangelical Press, 1982, pp.118-19.
2. Richard Nelson Bolles, *The 1991 What Color Is Your Parachute?* Ten Speed Press, 1991, p.393f.

Chapter 3 — The Son of God: source and goal of gifts
1. *Westminster Confession of Faith,* II, 3.
2. J. I. Packer, *Keeping in Step with the Spirit,* Fleming H. Revell, 1964, p.64.
3. *Ibid.,* pp.65-6.
4. Kenneth S. Wuest, *Untranslatable Riches from the Greek New Testament,* Eerdmans, 1952, pp.101-2.
5. Michael Green, *I Believe in the Holy Spirit,* Hodder & Stoughton, 1975, pp.52-3.
6. *Ibid.,* pp.55-6.

Chapter 4 — Spiritual gifts and charismatic experience
1. See John Wimber with Kevin Springer, *Power Evangelism,* Hodder and Stoughton, 1985 also *Power Healing,* Hodder and Stoughton, 1986.
2. John E. MacArthur, *The Charismatics,* Zondervan, 1978, pp.143-9.

Chapter 5 — Gifts and talents

1. Elizabeth O'Connor, 'Releasing Angels: Uncovering Our Gifts,' *Partnership*, Sept-Oct. 1986, p.27.

2. *Ibid.*

3. Ronald Baxter, *Gifts of the Spirit*, Kregel Publications, 1983, p.39.

4. 'We recognize that there are men who are naturally gifted, or talented; who by birth have a higher intelligence quotient and abilities, which put them head and shoulders above other men. But when we speak of the gifts of the Spirit, we are not speaking about the native talents with which certain individuals have been endowed by natural birth. We are speaking of supernatural endowment' (*Ibid.*, p.40).

5. *Ibid.*, p.38.

6. *Ibid.*, p.40.

7. 'That a certain amount of natural "capacity" must be there before God can give the gift of teaching, for example' (*Ibid.*, p.41).

8. *Westminster Confession*, V.1.

9. *Ibid.*

10. C. F. Keil and F. Delitzsch, *Commentary of the Old Testament in Ten Volumes*, vol. 2 of the Pentateuch, Eerdmans, 1981, p.217.

11. G. Campbell Morgan, *The Parables and Metaphors of our Lord*, Marshall, Morgan & Scott Ltd, p.138.

12. *Ibid.*

13. Matthew Poole, *A Commentary on the Holy Bible*, Banner of Truth Trust, vol. III, pp.118-19.

14. *Ibid.*

15. 'That every man had a natural endowment, a sacred trust, and mission to fulfil in this world' (John Peter Lange, *The Gospel of Matthew*, Zondervan, 1960, vol. 1 of the New Testament, p.443).

16. 'When the Divine Providence has made a difference in men's ability, as to mind, body, estate, relation, and interest, divine grace dispenses spiritual gifts accordingly, but still the ability itself is from him... All are not alike for they had not all alike abilities and opportunities' (Matthew Henry, *Commentary on the Whole Bible*, Revel, vol. V, p.313).

17. 'The talents represent not the special abilities of the servants of Christ, but the capital He gives them to work with, that is, the opportunities for service, together with all their gifts, material, mental and spiritual... He gives opportunities and equipment in accordance with ability' (Robertson C. McQuilkin, *Studying our Lord's Parables for Yourself*, Columbia Bible College, 1933, p.36).

18. 'Through the Old Testament, oil is ever the symbol of the Holy Spirit. Whether in the lamp burning in the Holy Place, or whether in the symbolism of such a one as Zechariah; whether in all those anointings of the ancient ritual, the oil was always typical of the Spirit and of power... The great word is "Watch". The interpretation of the watching is having oil supplied. In the supply of the Spirit of God, and the life yielded to that Spirit, and dominated by that Spirit, there is always the oil that provides the light' (Morgan, *Parables and Metaphors*, p.134).

19. J. I. Packer, *Keep in Step with the Spirit*, Fleming H. Revell Co., 1984, pp.84-5.

Chapter 6 — Spiritual gifts and response to need

1. Cited from an article in the *Ontario Bible College Recorder* by Elizabeth Davey, date unknown, p.8.
2. Cited in Richard J. Foster, *Celebration of Discipline,* Harper & Row, 1978, p.110.
3. Quoted in Tim Hansel, *Holy Sweat,* Word Books, 1987, p.81.
4. Frank R. Tillapaugh, *Unleashing the Church,* Regal Books, 1982.

Chapter 7 — Steps to gift discovery

1. Howard Snyder, *The Problem of Wineskins,* Inter-Varsity Press (US), 1975, p.138.
2. Quoted in Charles Swindoll, *The Seasons of Life,* p 312.
3. James Davey, 'How to Discover your Spiritual Gift,' *Christianity Today,* 9 May 1975, p.138.
4. *Ibid.*
5. Gail MacDonald, *High Call, High Privilege,* Tyndale House, p.79.
6. Snyder, *Problem of Wineskins,* p.137.
7. From Elizabeth O'Connor's book, *Eighth Day of Creation,* quoted in Snyder, *Problem of Wineskins,* p.137.
8. Charles C. Ryrie, 'Receiving the Spirit's Gifts,' *Eternity,* February 1975, p.19.
9. MacDonald, *High Call, High Privilege,* p 79.
10. Ethel Marr, 'Is there a Camel in your Tent?' *Eternity,* January 1977, p.40.
11. *Ibid.,* pp.40-43.
12. *Ibid.,* p.41.
13. Davey, 'How to Discover your Spiritual Gift,' p.10.
14. *Ibid.*
15. *Ibid.*
16. *Ibid.*
17. J. E. O'Day, *Discovering Your Spiritual Gifts,* Inter-Varsity Press (US), 1985, pp.13-14.
18. MacDonald, *High Call, High Privilege,* p.80.
19. *Ibid.*
20. Davey, 'How to Discover your Spiritual Gift,' p.10.
21. Ray Wiseman, 'Square Pegs,' *The Christian Perspective,* October 1989, p.2.

Chapter 8 —The speaking gifts — an introduction

1. J. E. O'Day, *Discovering Your Spiritual Gifts,* pp.9,10.
2. Packer, *Keep in Step with the Spirit,* p.83.
3. Eric Wright, *Tell the World,* Evangelical Press, 1981, p 141.

Chapter 9 — The apostolic gift

1. Cited in *End-Time Evangel,* vol. XX, No 1, Sept. 1979.
2. Baxter, *Gifts of the Spirit,* p.96.
3. William McRae, *Dynamics of Spiritual Gifts,* Zondervan, 1976, p.56.

4. Flynn, *Nineteen Gifts of the Spirit*, p.39.
5. *Ibid.*, p.46.
6. Baxter, *Gifts of the Spirit*, p.89.
7. Flynn, *Nineteen Gifts of the Spirit*, p.43.
8. *Ibid.*, p.42.
9. E. H. Andrews, *Promise of the Spirit*, Evangelical Press, 1982, p.210.
10. Flynn, *Nineteen Gifts of the Spirit*, p.44.
11. Thayer, *Greek-English Lexicon of the New Testament*, American Book Co. edition of Harper & Bros, 1889, p.68.

Chapter 10 — The prophetic gift
1. Marilyn Dunlop, article in *Toronto Star*, 2 May 1987.
2. Radio programme, Canadian Broadcasting Corporation, Toronto, 29 May 1987.
3. Packer, *Keep In Step With The Spirit*, p.215.
4. George Fox, 'Christ is come to teach his people himself.' Christopher Rule writes that 'Fox sometimes seemed to think himself infallible... He advised a woman not to tell Parliament that the King would be restored, but seemed to have accepted it as true prophecy. He also said he had premonitions of Cromwell's death and the fire of London, but his Journal was written years later. Hindsight can change the perspective...'(George Fox and Early Quakerism, article in *Reformation Today*, No. 95, p.15).
5. Cited by Flynn, *Nineteen Gifts of the Spirit*, p.53.
6. Cited by Baxter, *Gifts of the Spirit*, p.99.
7. Packer, *Keep in Step with the Spirit*, p.217.
8. Anthony Coppin, article in *Reformation Today*, No. 97, May/June 1987, p.22.
9. Andrews, *Promise of the Spirit*, p.215.
10. L. Gaussen, *The Inspiration of the Holy Scriptures*, Moody Press (reprint of a classic). Brian H. Edwards, *Nothing But The Truth*, Evangelical Press, 2nd edition 1993.
11. George Smeaton, *The Doctrine of the Holy Spirit*, Banner of Truth Trust, reprint 1980, p.152.
12. G. Raymond Carlson, 'The Role of the Prophet Today,' article in *The Pentecostal Testimony*, March 1991, p.22.
13. Michael G. Maudlin, 'Seers in the Heartland', article in *Christianity Today*, 14 January 1991, p.18.
14. John Wimber, 'Introducing Prophetic Ministry,' article in *Equipping*, Fall 1989, pp.4-6.
15. Maudlin, 'Seers in the Heartland', p.20.
16. *Ibid.*
17. Wayne A. Grudem, 'What Should be the Relationship Between Prophet and Pastor?' article in *Equipping*, Fall 1989, p.8
18. Carlson, 'The Role of the Prophet Today,' pp.23-4.
19. Flynn, *Nineteen Gifts of the Spirit*, p.53.
20. *Ibid.*, p.52.
21. Packer, *Keep in Step with the Spirit*, p.217.

22. J. I. Packer, T*he Preacher and Preaching,* Samuel T. Logan, Presbyterian and Reformed, 1986, p.21.

23. Books on preaching:

W. E. Sangster, *The Craft of Sermon Construction and Illustration,* Baker (reprint), 1984.

John A Broadus, *On the Preparation and Delivery of Sermons,* Harper (my copy is dated 1943).

Haddon Robinson, *Biblical Preaching,* Baker, 1980.

D. Martyn Lloyd-Jones, *Preaching and Preachers,* Zondervan, 1971.

Samuel Logan Jr, ed., *The Preacher and Preaching,* Evangelical Press/Presbyterian and Reformed, 1986.

Sidney Greidanus, *The Modern Preacher and the Ancient Text,* Eerdmans, 1988.

24. Packer, in *The Preacher and Preaching,* pp.8-13.

Chapter 11 — The gift of evangelism

1. Davey, *How to Discover your Spiritual Gifts,* p.9.

2. Flynn, *Nineteen Gifts of the Spirit,* p.61.

3. Wright, *Tell the World,* p.141ff.

4. Cited by Joslin, *Urban Harvest,* Evangelical Press, 1982, p.97.

5. Quoted on the back cover of Tillapaugh, *Unleashing the Church..*

6. Tim Stafford, 'Evangelism: The New Wave Is a Tidal Wave', *Christianity Today,* 18 May 1984, p.43.

7. *Ibid,* p.63.

8. Cited in *Canadian Monthly of OM,* October 1986.

9. Joseph C. Aldrich, 'Lifestyle Evangelism,' *Christianity Today,* 7 January, 1983.

10. Alex Rattray Hay, *The New Testament Order for Church and Missionary,* New Testament Missionary Union, 1947, p.226.

11. *Ibid,* p.227.

12. Cited by Joslin, *Urban Harvest,* p.118.

13. William Hendriksen, *New Testament Commentary — Ephesians,* Baker, pp.196-7.

14. Cited in Flynn, *Nineteen Gifts of the Spirit,* p.59.

15. Norman L. Geisler, 'Excuses Why I didn't Witness,' *Canadian Challenge,* Summer 1986, pp.5-6.

Chapter 12 — The office of the pastor

1. Hodge, *1 Corinthians,* pp.226-7.

2. Hay, *NT Order for Church and Missionary,* p.235.

3. *Ibid.*

4. W. E. Vine, *An Expository Dictionary of New Testament Words,* The Old Time Gospel Hour edition, undated, p.351.

5. Ray C. Stedman, *Body Life,* Regal Books, 1979, pp.78-9.

6. Hay, *NT order for Church and Missionary,* p.248ff.

7. Stedman, *Body Life,* p.82.

8. Elizabeth Davey, 'Does Your Pastor Need Your Ministry?', Miscellaneous article.
9. Snyder, *Problem of Wineskins*, pp.81-2.
10. Stedman, *Body Life*, pp.85-6.
11. Hendriksen, *Ephesians*, p.189.
12. Tillapaugh, *Unleashing the Church*, p.107.
13. Stedman, *Body Life*, pp.79-80.
14. *Ibid.*

Chapter 13 — The gift of shepherding
1. Charles Bridges, *The Christian Ministry*, Banner of Truth Trust, 1967, p.350, footnote.
2. *Ibid.*
3. *Ibid.*, p.348.
4. *Ibid.*, p.349.
5. *Ibid.*, various quotes from pp.350-60.
6. Dr. J. R. Boyd, *Alumni Association Newsletter of Toronto Baptist Seminary*, January 1989.
7. Lawrence J. Crabb, Jr, *Understanding People*, Zondervan, 1987.
8. McRae, *Dynamics of Spiritual Gifts*, p.63.

Chapter 14 —The gifts of knowledge and wisdom
1. J. I. Packer, *Hot Tub Religion*, Tyndale Publishers Inc., 1987.
2. Reginald W. Bibby, *Fragmented Gods*, Irwin Publishing, 1987.
3. K. L. Billingsley, 'Keeping America Stupid,' article in *World*, 18 February 1989, p.16.
4. *Ibid.*
5. Wright, *Tell the World*, p.141ff.
6. Hodge, *1 Corinthians*, p.282.
7. Grosheide, *1 Corinthians*, pp.320, 336.
8. *Ibid.*, p.338.
9. Vine, *Expository Dictionary*, p.631.
10. *Ibid.*, pp.628,629,631.
11. Hodge, *1 Corinthians*, p.267.
12. *Ibid.*, p.7.
13. Grosheide, *1 Corinthians*, pp.285-6.
14. Flynn, *Nineteen Gifts of the Spirit*, p.90.
15. Packer, *Hot Tub Religion*, pp.12-13.
16. Paul Mickey with William Proctor, 'Too Busy for Sex,' *Marriage Partnership*, Winter 1989, p.106.
17. Vine, *Expository Dictionary*, p.1233.
18. Hansel, *Holy Sweat*, p.165.
19. A. W. Tozer, *The Root of the Righteous*, Christian Publications, 1955.
20. Crabb, *Understanding People*.

Chapter 15 — The gift of teaching
1. See also Acts 20:20; 1 Cor. 14:6; Matt. 28:20; 1 Tim. 4:6,11; 2 Tim. 4:2; Titus 2:1-15.
2. All material on Greek words in this section from Vine, *Expository Dictionary*, p.595.
3. Flynn, *Nineteen Gifts of the Spirit*, p.91.
4. Ralph Martin, *The Spirit and the Congregation — Studies in 1 Corinthians 12-15*, William B. Eerdmans, 1984, p.12.
5. Hansel, *Holy Sweat*, p.27.

Chapter 16 — The gift of encouragement
1. Vine, *Expository Dictionary*, p.200.
2. *Webster's New World Dictionary*, Avenel Books, 1978, p.248.
3. Smalley & Trent, *The Gift of Honor*, pp.11-12.
4. Kenneth W. Osbeck, *101 More Human Stories*, Kregel Publications, 1985, p.237.
5. Gordon MacDonald, *Rebuilding Your Broken World*, Oliver-Nelson Books, 1988, pp.v, ix.
6. Hansel, *Holy Sweat*, pp.178-9.
7. *Ibid.*
8. Smalley & Trent, *Gift of Honor*, pp.93-4.
9. *Ibid.*
10. Some of the ideas in this section are adapted from Lyle L. Mook, 'You can be a Barnabas,' *Power for Living*, Wheaton, Ill., p.8.
11. Chua Wee Hian, 'After the Sale is Over,' *Eternity*, Sept. 1968.

Chapter 17 — The serving gifts: an introduction
1. Philip Yancey, 'Low Pay, Long Hours, No Applause', *Christianity Today*, 18 November 1988, p.80.
2. Kent and Barbara Hughes, *Liberating Ministry from the Success Syndrome*, Tyndale, 1987.
3. *Ibid.*, p.45.
4. Lawrence J. Crabb, Jr, *Understanding People*, Zondervan, 1987, p.110.

Chapter 18 — Helps and hospitality
1. Vine, *Expository Dictionary*, p.746.
2. 'The gift of helps is the special ability that God gives to some members of the Body of Christ to invest the talents they have in the life and ministry of other members of the Body, thus enabling the person helped to increase the effectiveness of his or her spiritual gifts' (Wagner, *Your Spiritual Gifts Can Help Your Church Grow*, Regal Books, 1979, p.224).
3. 'The gift of helps is the Spirit-given ability to serve the church in any supporting role, usually temporal, though sometimes spiritual ... lending a hand wherever it will release workers in their spiritual ministries...' (Flynn, *Nineteen Gifts of the Spirit*, p.101).

4. Cited in Baxter, *Gifts of the Spirit,* p.220.

5. Anonymous poem, *LeTourneau Christian Camp Newsletter.*

6. Virginia Evansen, 'Five Secrets of Lending a Helping Hand,' magazine clipping of unknown source.

7. *Ibid.*

8. Vine, *Expository Dictionary,* p.565.

9. Personal class note, Reformed Theological Seminary from the class of Dr Richard Lewis and Rev. Robert Stuart. Dr Lewis further commented that, in his belief, 55% of all mental problems would be resolved if the church would do its job. They both believe that 75% of problems are relational in nature. By correcting relationships or providing a warm atmosphere of support healing is promoted.

10. Kobad Arjani, 'Decision for Eternity,' *HIS,* December 1961, pp.22-3.

11. Dennis M. Schultz, 'Fleischmann Memorial Baptist Church — Ministering in the Inner-city,' reprint, B*aptist Herald,* June 1982.

12. Interview by Lois Sibley, 'The Joys and Risks of Radical Hospitality,' *Eternity,* October 1983, p.70.

13. *Ibid.*

14. *Ibid.*

15. Lora Lee Parrott, 'Learning Hospitality from the Master,' *Sunday To Sunday,* Winter 1989, p.20.

Chapter 19 — Giving and mercy

1. *N.B.C. Evening News,* 17 March 1989.

2. Vine, *Expository Dictionary,* pp.478-80.

3. *Ibid.,* p.479.

4. Flynn, *Nineteen Gifts of the Spirit,* p.120.

5. Vine, *Expository Dictionary,* p.663

6. Flynn, *Nineteen Gifts of the Spirit,* p.121

7. Smalley & Trent, *Gift of Honor,* pp.67-8.

8. Vine, *Expository Dictionary,* pp.732-3.

9. Berkhof, *Systematic Theology,* p.72.

10. Vine, *Expository Dictionary,* p.543.

11. Cited in Vine, *Expository Dictionary,* p.544.

12. Vine, *Expository Dictionary,* p.210.

13. *Ibid.*

14. *Ibid.*

15. *Ibid.,* p.176.

16. *Ibid.*

17. Joyce Sanford, as told to Marjorie Zimmerman in an article, 'The Closest of All,' found in *Power For Living,* 1 December 1985, pp.4-5.

18. Dennis M. Schultz (Article reprint).

19. Tillapaugh, *Unleashing the Church,* pp.5,8.

20. Lloyd J. Ogilvie, TV programme, *Let God Love You,* Los Angeles, 8 April 1989.

Chapter 20 — Faith and discernment
1. Snyder, *Problem of Wineskins,* p.21.
2. Cited by Hansel, *Holy Sweat,* p.69.
3. Vine, *Expository Dictionary,* p.401.
4. John Prin, 'The Rehabbing of 807 Pascagoula,' *Christianity Today,* 18 November 1988, pp.12-13.
5. Cited by McRae, *Dynamics of Spiritual Gifts,* p.67.
6. Hansel, *Holy Sweat,* pp.40-41.
7. *Ibid.,* p.69.
8. *Ibid.,* p.72.
9. Tozer, *Root of the Righteous,* p.46.
10. Flynn, *Nineteen Gifts of the Spirit,* p.142
11. *Ibid.*
12. O. Hallesby, *Prayer,* Augsburg, 1931, pp.29, 12, 17.
13. Flynn, *Nineteen Gifts of the Spirit,* p.142.
14. Vine, *Expository Dictionary,* pp.307, 610-11.
15. Elizabeth Elliot, 'Maturity, the Power to Discern,' *Brigade Leader,* undated, p.15.
16. Vine, *Expository Dictionary,* p.307.
17. Tozer, *Root of the Righteous,* pp.8-9.
18. *Ibid.*
19. *Ibid.,* p.51.
20. *Ibid.,* p.49.
21. *World,* 18 March1989, p.11.
22. Robert Schuller, *Self-Esteem: the New Reformation,* Word, 1982, p.98.
23. Tozer, *Root of the Righteous,* pp.42-5. I believe he is right to emphasize the need for repentance. It has been widely ignored. He is right in saying that a desire to repudiate evil must characterize anyone who is truly converted. To call, however, for reformation before regeneration subtly opens the door to salvation by works. Justification is by grace alone. Regeneration is a free gift of God which produces in us the desire to turn from evil. We cannot produce that desire nor can we reform ourselves without the new birth. This quote seems to be a momentary lapse in Tozer's generally stimulating writing.
24. Oswald Chambers, *My Utmost For His Highest,* Dodd, Mead and Co., 1935, p.151.

Chapter 21 — Administration and leadership
1. John Stott, *A Call to Christian Leadership,* Marshall, Morgan & Scott, 1984, booklet, pp.7-8.
2. Brochure, CareerTrack Seminars, Jan./Feb. 1988 schedule.
3. Vine, *Expository Dictionary,* p.979.
4. *Ibid.,* p.498.
5. *Ibid.,* p.979.

6. Earl D. Radmacher, *Spiritual Gift Inventory, An Explanatory and Developmental Outline,* Western Conservative Baptist Seminary, no date.

7. Flynn, *Nineteen Gifts of the Spirit,* p.127; McRae, *Dynamics of Spiritual Gifts,* p.52.

8. Vine, *Expository Dictionary,*p.120.

9. McRae, *Dynamics of Spiritual Gifts,* pp.52-3.

10. William Shakespeare, *Twelfth Night,* II. iv. 158.

11. Brochure of CareerTrack Seminars.

12. Brochure of MICA Management Centre Seminar, received 30 October 1987.

13. *Ibid.*

14. Privately circulated paper, *Additional Insights on Understanding Spiritual Gifts,* Institute of Basic Youth Conflicts, 1981.

15. Ronald Knox, *Enthusiasm,* Oxford University Press, 1950, p.591, cited in Stott, *Call to Christian Leadership,* p.9.

16. Prin, 'Rehabbing of 807 Pascagoula', pp.12-13

17. Ted W. Engstrom & R. Alec MacKenzie, *Managing Your Time,* Zondervan, 1967, p.139.

18. *Ibid.,* p.137.

19. Cited by Stott, *Call to Christian Leadership,*p.15.

20. Peter Carlyle-Gordge, 'Boy's Plight is Town's Mission of Love', *Toronto Star,* 3 January 1987.

21. Stott, *Call to Christian Leadership,* pp.18-20.

22. *Ibid.*

23. *Ibid.,* p.27.

24. Smalley & Trent, *Gift of Honor,* pp.49-74.

Conclusion

1. Bill Hybels (interview with three other preachers), 'The Pulpit's Personal Side, A Leadership Forum', *Leadership,* Spring 1990, vol. XI, no. 2, p.19.

2. Bruce L. Bugbee with Bill Hybels & Don Cousin, *Networking,* Leader's Guide, Charles E. Fuller Institute, 1989, iii (An assortment of material, including tapes and study guides for individuals and churches, is available. While I disagree over their inclusion of some of the charismatic gifts, nevertheless their material can be very helpful, especially for a church setting up a gift development process.)

3. Peter Drucker, interview, 'Managing to Minister', *Leadership,* Spring 1989, vol. X, No. 2, p.15.

4. *Ibid.,* pp.18-19.

5. *Ibid.,* p.20.

Index

(Authors and books are not listed below. See Bibliography, pp. 440-45, or References, pp.446-55)